Pittsburgh Series in Labor History

PITTSBURGH SERIES IN LABOR HISTORY

WOMEN AND THE TRADES

PITTSBURGH, 1907–1908

By

ELIZABETH BEARDSLEY BUTLER

With a new introduction by
Maurine Weiner Greenwald

UNIVERSITY OF PITTSBURGH PRESS

Library of Congress Cataloging in Publication Data

Butler, Elizabeth Beardsley.
  Women and the trades.

  (Pittsburgh series in labor history)
  Originally published in 1909.
  Bibliography: p. 419
  Includes index.
    1. Women—Employment—Pennsylvania—Pittsburgh.   2.   Labor and
laboring classes—Pennsylvania—Pittsburgh.   3. Pittsburgh (Pa.)—Industries.
I. Greenwald, Maurine Weiner, 1944-   . II. Title. III. Series.
HD6096.P57B9   1984   331.4'09748'86   84-5175
ISBN 0-8229-5901-1

CONTENTS

WOMEN AT WORK
THROUGH THE EYES OF
ELIZABETH BEARDSLEY BUTLER
AND LEWIS WICKES HINE

Maurine Weiner Greenwald

I
THE PITTSBURGH SURVEY:
SNAPSHOTS OF INDUSTRIAL LIFE

First Prince, then Pauper;
overwork, then underwork;
high wages, no wages;
millionaire, immigrant;
militant unions, masterful employers;
marvelous business organization,
amazing disorganization.
Such are the contrasts of "Pittsburgh
the Powerful," the "Workshop of the World!" [1]

WOMEN AND THE TRADES is the masterwork of a master
craftswoman in the field of social investigation. Originally published in 1909, *Women and the Trades* was one of the six volumes
of the pathbreaking Pittsburgh Survey, the first attempt in the
United States to study life and labor in one industrial city in a
comprehensive and systematic manner. A small group of local
business, professional, and welfare leaders joined with the Charities
Publication Committee of New York to launch and design the
study. The Pittsburgh Survey brought together statisticians, social
workers, engineers, lawyers, physicians, economists, labor investigators, and city planners to examine the quality of life in a repre-

sentative modern industrial community. Between 1909 and 1914, four major books and two anthologies of articles published by the newly established Russell Sage Foundation, examined workers, working conditions, housing, civic organizations, economic and social problems, and health care in Pittsburgh and nearby Homestead. The four book-length studies are now classics in the genre of social investigation. Elizabeth Beardsley Butler's examination of Pittsburgh wage-earning women complements John Fitch's *The Steelworkers*, the Survey volume on skilled male wage earners; Margaret Byington's *Homestead: Households of a Mill Town*, the investigation of family budgets and domestic management; and Crystal Eastman's *Work-Accidents and the Law*, a study of the causes and consequences of industrial accidents. Collectively, the Survey volumes document far more than the situation in Pittsburgh, which the authors regarded as but a case study in a widespread system of human waste and misery caused by labor exploitation and perpetuated by governmental and civic disorganization.[2]

The Survey was launched at a time when native-born Americans were publicly agitated about the influx of millions of immigrants from southern and eastern Europe into American cities. The descendants of the "old" immigrants from northern and western Europe looked askance at the "new" immigrants, who spoke foreign tongues, wore unusual clothing, practiced non-Protestant religions, and adhered to strange ethnic customs. Even worse, in the minds of many native-born Americans the newcomers were responsible for the many ills plaguing American cities. Urban poverty, crime, disease, crowding, and decay, natives asserted, derived from the hordes of recently arrived foreigners. The Survey investigators shared the concern of their day about the ability of the United States to survive so fundamental and extensive a transformation of population.

DOCUMENTARY SUPPORT FOR INDUSTRIAL REFORM

The Survey researchers viewed Pittsburgh as a microcosm of American urban life under industrial capitalism.[3] While corporate leaders in the steel industry grew wealthy from their productive, sprawling riverside plants, the majority of Pittsburgh workers, mostly from southern and eastern Europe, worked excessively long hours for wages below the cost of decently feeding, clothing, and housing their families. Frequent work accidents, poor health, and long workweeks complicated family life. Municipal services, plentiful among the middle and upper classes, did not provide for the needs of the majority of the population. The school systems, funded by property taxes, were best in the richer neighborhoods and understaffed and ill-equipped in the poorer communities. Hospital and other medical facilities existed for those who could pay for the services. Typhoid fever, endemic among the poor, was a major health hazard that went unchecked by local government, which provided grossly inadequate sanitation systems in poor neighborhoods.[4]

Women and the Trades underscored the thrust of these general findings in the Survey. Butler skillfully documented the virtual absence of occupational mobility among wage-earning women in early twentieth-century Pittsburgh. After ten months of rigorous research, she concluded that the fruits of economic growth in the early twentieth century were unequally distributed among wage earners on the basis of gender, skill, and ethnicity. None of the women depicted in Butler's book are shown as reaping material benefits from the startling success of American business and industry. All of the Survey researchers concluded from the disparities of status and need that the government had an obligation to protect the health and welfare of the people with state and federal legislation.

The Pittsburgh Survey had a mixed effect upon the course of American social reform. Its importance lies more in the persuasive example of its scholarly methods and observations than in explicit solutions to American social problems. Unlike previous investigations, this study was broadly conceived and executed, encompassing civic, social, and industrial concerns. As historian Roy Lubove has noted, the Survey's innovative method "achieved . . . an impressive synthesis between the statistical, empirical perspective of the census report, and the vivid personalized touch of the journalist."[5] Lubove's characterization of the Survey as a whole applies equally well to Elizabeth Beardsley Butler's particular contribution to the project. *Women and the Trades* was the first general survey of wage-earning women in an American city and a model combination of facts, figures, and description that, according to Paul Kellogg, the Survey's editor, had "a certain epic quality."[6] Butler's expertly designed framework for the study of labor conditions set the standard for future investigations. For every workplace, the author assessed not only wages and hours but also the work environment, production processes, technological innovations, work pace, job training and mobility, co-worker relations, labor-management relations, and unionization.

The Survey's impact on reform directly in Pittsburgh was quite modest. According to one historian the massive social investigation resulted in only two concrete reforms. The United States Steel Corporation destroyed or repaired dilapidated housing for one hundred families, which had been singled out for criticism in the Survey. And Crystal Eastman's study of more than one thousand industrial accidents helped to advance the movement for workmen's compensation laws.[7] Other tangible results included an increased number of sanitary inspectors, a comprehensive housing census, a typhoid fever commission, and a civic-improvement commission to study city planning, sanitation, housing construction, industrial accidents, and other urban problems.[8] Beyond that, the Survey did gain a large audience inside and outside Pittsburgh. It especially received attention from sociologists, economists, and social workers, who frequently consulted the six volumes for research designs, methods, and findings. The thousands of pages of research about labor exploitation contained an arsenal of ammunition for social reform. Like other progressive-era studies, this one could educate public opinion but could not bring its reform agenda fully to fruition.[9]

BUTLER AND HER GENERATION OF URBAN REFORMERS

In marked contrast to the prominent place that the Pittsburgh Survey has achieved in the history of American social investigation, Elizabeth Beardsley Butler has almost disappeared from the historical record. Unlike her famous peers in social reform—Florence Kelley, Grace Abbott, Josephine and Pauline Goldmark, Crystal Eastman, and Julia Lathrop—whose biographies and achievements have been recorded for posterity, Butler has received little attention in historical scholarship, and then only in connection with the Pittsburgh Survey.[10] Scant information about her life survives. She left no personal papers, nor does her name appear in any of the standard or new biographical reference sources. She was one of the many foot soldiers in the war against industrial exploitation. Her two books and numerous articles are her sole legacy.[11] An obituary in the *Survey* takes sad notice of her youth and impressive accomplishments at the time of her death in 1911 at the age of twenty-six.[12]

It is possible to discuss Butler's life and work in the context of her generation of female social reformers. First and foremost, she was a pioneer in social investigation, a new social science that, unlike the male-dominated professions of law, medicine, science, and engineering, welcomed women and gave them an opportunity to be socially useful.[13] Butler was a member of the second generation of college women in the United States, and as such she embarked on her undergraduate studies at a time when feminist academics were waging a successful battle to open graduate education to women in the United States and abroad.[14]

As with many of her peers, Butler's undergraduate education ably prepared her for her chosen career. She spent her first two years at the Packer Collegiate Institute, switched to Adelphi College for her third year, and graduated from Barnard College. During her senior year she pursued a course of study that familiarized her with liberal, socialist, and communist theories of social change, political and social ethics, and the principles of sociology. After she graduated from college in 1905, Butler accepted executive positions with the Consumers' League of New Jersey and the New Jersey Child Labor Committee.[15]

Founded in 1899 to improve the working conditions of women, the National Consumers' League soon became a formidable reform organization composed mainly of middle- and upper-class women. The league undertook industrial investigations and promoted the passage of maximum-hours and minimum-wage laws for women. In its consumer program, the league united economic activity with moral and personal considerations. Every business transaction was regarded as part of a larger social process that could impede or

accelerate social progress. The league encouraged women to purchase only those goods made under decent working conditions. As
one of the league's hired staff, Butler associated with some of the
most important social reformers in the United States, many of
whom subsequently rose to public prominence in state or federal
positions. Perhaps even more importantly, the league formed part
of an extensive organizational network of women activists from
hundreds of social settlement houses, labor-reform organizations,
suffrage groups, and women's clubs, which collectively was instru-
mental in the passage of social-welfare legislation in the United
States in the late nineteenth and early twentieth centuries.[16]

ELIZABETH BEARDSLEY BUTLER
Survey 26 (August 19, 1911): 743.

As was common among social investigators, Butler took courses
at the New York School of Philanthropy, noted for its specialized
curriculum. Later she would become a staff member of the school's
distinguished Bureau of Social Research. She no doubt received
personal encouragement from other women social workers while
she lived at Whittier House in 1905, a social settlement in Jersey
City, and investigated working conditions in department stores and
sweatshops. Then she became the assistant secretary of the Rand

School of Social Science, which she left in 1907 to undertake the field work for *Women and the Trades*. With the completion of the Pittsburgh study, she investigated the wages and working conditions of Baltimore saleswomen, which led to a posthumously published book in 1912. Tuberculosis, a dreaded infectious disease in the early twentieth century, had ended Butler's life in the preceding year.[17] Tuberculosis was a common disease in the United States seventy-odd years ago and was especially virulent among young adult women. It is not possible to say whether Butler's survey research among the urban poor contributed to her early death, but frequent exposure to women with tuberculosis may well have put her at greater risk of dying from the disease.

Despite the brevity of her career, Butler had become an outstanding practitioner in the field of industrial studies. The Survey's editor, Paul U. Kellogg, described her as "venturesome, incisive, quick to pare away the husk of a thing and lay bare the truth back of it." During her field work for *Women and the Trades* she visited over four hundred shops and factories, charting the contours of women's employment without the aid of a census to guide her work. Butler's pioneering inquiry, according to Kellogg, "meant valor of a refined sort."

> It meant tramping up and down the crooked streets and cellar-ways of the Hill district, up the stairs of loft buildings of the "Point," along the old Allegheny City river front and out to the new industrial suburbs. It meant visits down out-of-the-way streets to girls' homes to talk with them . . . and to the glass houses to check up [on] night work. [She] mapped out her field with rare deftness and held to her working scheme with a persistence which was born of a marvelous fund of buoyant energy.[18]

Social investigation was not merely a job to Butler. She was an "interpreter of rare gifts" of the degrading industrial conditions which confronted wage earners in the United States. As a "convinced socialist" with a profound sense of "injustice at wrongs under the present economic order," she argued passionately in print and in person for a more equitable economic system.[19]

Other educated women were recruited to participate in the

Pittsburgh Survey. It would not stretch the truth to argue that women provided the impetus, financial support, and backbone for the Survey. Alice B. Montgomery, chief probation officer of the Allegheny Juvenile Court—a jurisdiction across the Allegheny River from Pittsburgh—conceived the idea for a large-scale survey of Pittsburgh after she read the study of Washington, D.C., conducted by the Charities Publication Committee of New York in 1905.[20] Margaret Olivia Slocum Sage, America's foremost female philanthropist between 1906 and 1918, established the Russell Sage Foundation in 1907 in honor of her deceased husband and subsequently provided a grant specifically for the Pittsburgh Survey. A graduate of the pioneering Troy Female Seminary, Sage believed, in the fashion of her day, that women were intellectually equal but morally superior to men. As an active reformer she campaigned for temperance, the rehabilitation of prostitutes, woman suffrage, higher education, and home and foreign missions. The largesse of her contributions to American philanthropy, in the range of eighty million dollars, approximated those of Andrew Carnegie, John D. Rockefeller, and J. P. Morgan, although she never achieved the national recognition of these men.[21] Two other women, in addition to Butler, each wrote one of the four book-length Pittsburgh Survey studies. Crystal Eastman, ardent socialist and feminist, with degrees from Vassar, Columbia University, and the New York University Law School, was responsible for *Work-Accidents and the Law*. Margaret F. Byington, graduate of Wellesley College and Columbia University, where she earned a master's degree in sociology and economics, wrote the most popular of the Survey volumes, *Homestead: Households of a Mill Town*, which sold one hundred thousand copies between 1911 and 1929.[22]

Women also contributed articles to the Survey anthologies. Each one had impeccable academic credentials, extensive experience as a leader of civic organizations, and an influential voice in social reform. Emily Wayland Dinwiddie, housing expert, and F. Elizabeth Cromwell, public-health nursing administrator and expert on tuberculosis, jointly wrote about local housing for wage earners. Lila Ver Planck North, professor of Greek at Goucher College and manager of the Consumers' League of Baltimore, examined Pittsburgh schools. Beulah Kennard, president of the

Pittsburgh Playground Association and director of the Department of Play (later physical education) in the School of Education at the University of Pittsburgh, discussed public recreation facilities for children. Frances Jenkins Olcott, organizer and chief of the Children's Department, Carnegie Library of Pittsburgh, gave an account of the public library. Florence Larrabee Lattimore, associate director of the Department of Child Helping, Russell Sage Foundation, reported on foster care institutions for children.[23] Together these women represented the breadth of interests among women reformers and the outstanding achievements of career women in the early twentieth century.

II
WOMEN AND THE TRADES:
ITS LASTING VALUE AND LIMITATIONS

Women and the Trades has earned a well-deserved place in the history of social investigation, labor, and women in the United States. No other single book of its kind documents with precision so many of the technological and organizational changes transforming the nature of wage work for women in an industrial city in the early 1900s. It also inadvertently reveals a great deal about the concerns and prejudices of middle-class female reformers in that era.

Women and the Trades examines women's employment at one moment in Pittsburgh's industrialization, but the book must be understood within the larger time frame stretching from 1865 until the United States' entry into World War I in 1917. During those fifty-two years industrial and commercial expansion fundamentally altered the American social and economic landscape and along with it the patterns of women's wage work. By 1909, when *Women and the Trades* was published, the location of women's employment had changed radically. In 1865 most women who worked for wages did so in the fields of agriculture or domestic and personal service. By the first decade of the twentieth century, most working women received their pay envelopes in factories, offices, stores, and telephone exchanges.[24]

The birth of the modern corporation marked the beginning of

important changes in the location and nature of women's paid labor. The reorganization of capital into corporations facilitated the development of large-scale manufacturing, the national distribution of goods, and the growth of a host of associated commercial enterprises. The manufacturing sector expanded and reorganized toward the turn of the century with the development of metallurgy, engineering, electrical, and chemical industries. At the same time, food processing and canning grew rapidly, as did the production of paper and cardboard boxes. The market for support services expanded in direct response to the size and complexity of industrial production. Banking, telephone systems, insurance firms, advertising companies, and mail-order houses grew rapidly. In the latter part of the nineteenth century the department store began to acquire significant segments of the retail sales market in metropolitan areas.[25] These new and expanded enterprises created thousands of jobs for women.

BUTLER'S PERCEPTIONS AND PREJUDICES

Women and the Trades is an important analysis of the scope and nature of women's new jobs. Butler's survey of women's employment in Pittsburgh and its environs challenges the historical stereotype of Pittsburgh as a male-oriented steel town. Although rolling mills and open-hearth furnaces dominated the physical landscape of the city, stretching for miles along the Monongahela River and employing fully one-third of all Pittsburgh workers in manufacturing, the city offered many other means of earning a living. Pittsburgh factories produced pickles, confectioneries, crackers and cakes, cheap cigars, workingmen's overalls, paper boxes, clothbound books, glassware, and electrical equipment. The city also played host to many offices, department stores, and telephone exchanges. The combination of manufacturing, distribution, and communication services made Pittsburgh a microcosm of national economic developments.[26]

Butler's picture of women's employment did not flatter the city, its employers, or its wage earners. From one end of Pittsburgh to another, in workplaces as different as canneries and department stores, Butler found that women's jobs were rigidly segregated, low-paying, deadend, usually seasonal, and always insecure. In telephone companies women operated the switchboards, whereas men repaired the machines. In lamp manufacturing men shaped brass and iron, but women riveted and punched holes in metal. In cracker factories men prepared the dough that women baked. In glass manufacture, men produced the glass objects that women painted and packed. Rarely did men and women perform the same work or earn the same pay.[27]

Gender segregation was only one of the many characteristics of women's work experiences. Ethnic distinctions formed powerful barriers between different groups of women. Employer and employee prejudices mutually reinforced hiring and employment patterns. Polish women dominated the female labor force in the cracker industry. In cigar factories the Hungarian, Croatian, and Polish women were barred from every process except the stripping of tobacco leaves. In the metal trades two-thirds of the women making cores and winding coils were Slavic. Jewish girls and women concentrated in the stogy (cheap cigar) and garment factories and the "cheap and hustling" shops, while American-born women could be found mostly in the "better-class" stores, telegraph and telephone exchanges, book binderies, candy factories, and millinery houses.[28]

Butler's "racial analysis of industries employing women" not only objectively reported where particular ethnic groups of women worked, but also revealed her subjective characterizations of minorities. Jews were supposedly bright, Italians socially conservative, Slavs docile and easily exploited, and native-born women of Irish and German parentage ambitious.[29] These labels were not meant as character assassinations, but they inadvertently perpetuated ethnic stereotypes at a time when native-born Americans—especially white, Anglo-Saxon Protestants—were questioning the ability of immigrants to assimilate fully into American society.

Butler found that the very nature of particular jobs separated women wage earners from one another as strongly as did ethnic boundaries. She observed that in commercial laundries an invidious hierarchy divided women workers into several distinct groups. Those women who performed the semiclerical tasks of checking clothing when it first arrived at the laundry and sorting it before

delivery were the "aristocrats of the trade." The sorters and checkers did not fraternize with other laundry workers. They traveled
to and from work by themselves. At work they ate lunch in a
different room and at a different time from other workers. "Pride
of cast," Butler noted, "confines each girl socially to the group to
which her ability has brought her. . . . Starchers are a degree
above mangle girls, ironers are a degree above starchers, but between the ironers and the checkers and sorters is a sharp barrier."[30]
Even the "aristocrats of the trade," the checkers and sorters, needed
only a common school education, accuracy, and speed, minimal
attributes that made for an enormous gulf between women in the
same workplace.

Butler's study is one of the most authoritative statements on
the specialized, monotonous, mind-numbing, and nerve-wracking
nature of women's wage work. In manufacturing women were the
machine tenders, the workers who performed one task over and
over for ten, twelve, even fourteen hours a day without a sense of
personal accomplishment or pride in their product. In canneries
women washed bottles, scrubbed floors, sorted food, bottled,
labeled, and filled jars. In the metal trades women produced small
cores, armatures, and coils. In glass factories women decorated the
edges of innumerable tumblers, each with the identical pattern. In
lamp factories they lacquered metal parts. In commercial laundries
they either sorted, starched, ironed, or packed clothing. In sweatshops they stripped or bunched tobacco or rolled cigars. In all
trades, one woman, one task. The "flushed cheeks and white lips"
of the cracker-box workers, the stoop-shouldered women in incan-
descent-lighting shops, the emotionally spent young girls in stogy
production, and the pale, anemic-looking telephone operators are a
few of the many negative images that pervade the pages of *Women
and the Trades*.[31] These images symbolized for Butler and her
generation of social reformers the human costs of an industrial
system largely built on speed and profits.

Butler's numerous factory visits acquainted her with the many
strategies that employers used to maximize profits at their employees' expense. The abusiveness of piecework payment particularly angered her. Employers often cut piecework rates whenever

women's or men's wages exceeded some privately predetermined amount. Girls who earned three cents for putting sticks into nine hundred candies per box were transferred to other work before they could acquire enough speed to earn more than seventy-five cents a day or four dollars and fifty cents a week.[32] Butler asserts that women employed in incandescent-light factories suffered a piecework rate cut every time their earnings exceeded fourteen cents an hour.[33]

In some fields of work, employers paid premiums to encourage wage earners to exceed their production goals. To take advantage of bonus payments, stogy makers drove themselves to the point of exhaustion.[34] Speed, according to Butler, was both the "talisman" which "opened the way to a higher wage rating" for a minority of female wage earners and a major contributor to women's ill health.[35]

Butler's wage data clearly confirmed women's second-class economic status. Women workers in Pittsburgh fared neither better nor worse than female wage earners in other cities. They all earned wages that fell well below the level needed for self-support. Over three-fifths of Pittsburgh working women aged fourteen to fifty earned less than seven dollars a week, one-fifth between seven and eight dollars, and the rest eight dollars and over for a six-day, often sixty-hour week. A comparison of men's and women's wages always resulted in a ratio of two to one. Unskilled men earned twelve dollars per week to women's six dollars.[36] Even when women and men performed identical tasks, men earned double the wages of women. Men who checked in clothes at commercial laundries, for example, earned seventeen dollars a week to women checkers' eight dollars. Butler concluded that employers paid women supplementary rather than living wages, assuming that their employees would "secure financial backing from outside relationships."[37] Employers gauged the situation correctly. Women often accepted lower wages precisely because they were part of a complex family economy in which everyone contributed to the welfare of the household. Women who lived independently and those who assumed the role of breadwinner in their families suffered the most from the gender-based inferior wage scale.

JOBS OMITTED FROM BUTLER'S SURVEY

Women and the Trades discusses all but two of the most important fields for women workers in early twentieth-century Pittsburgh. Domestic service and clerical work are notably absent from the Pittsburgh study because Butler was intent upon examining the work settings that she viewed as problematic—factory, sales, and telephone work. Numerically the most important field of employment for women, locally and nationally, was still private and public housekeeping. In 1910, 22,209 or 43 percent of the 51,678 women in the Pittsburgh labor force earned their livelihoods as servants, waitresses, charwomen, cleaners, porters, housekeepers, or stewardesses.[38] Butler consciously focused instead on the 25,555 women employed in the newer jobs in manufacturing, sales, and communications. It was well understood in the early twentieth century that women wage earners readily fled from the physical and social isolation, low status, and unregulated hours that characterized private housekeeping. Only personal circumstances or racial discrimination discouraged women from abandoning such work.

The federal census confirms this shift away from domestic service. In 1870, 60.7 percent of the women and girls who were engaged in nonagricultural pursuits were employed as service workers in private and public housekeeping. With each successive census, this figure dropped, so that by 1910, only 25.5 percent of working women outside agriculture were members of the servant class.[39] In addition to the new job opportunities, the simplification of housekeeping resulting from the popularity of apartment living among the middle class, the invention and mass marketing of domestic appliances, and the commercialization of laundry work and food preparation all contributed to the decline in the percentage of female servants.[40]

The other occupation that Butler omitted from her study was clerical work. Had Butler investigated the clerical occupations she would have found a shift in work processes and the organization of labor akin to what was happening in manufacturing and communications. Business consolidation and expansion after 1900 increasingly demanded larger secretarial staffs. At the same time a technological revolution in office equipment and procedures occurred.

The widening use of the typewriter, as well as addressograph, calculating, card punching, sorting, and duplicating machines dramatically transformed the speed and methods for performing office work. With the spread of public school education, especially high school training, a growing supply of persons, particularly women, became available and eligible for office employment. These developments resulted in the gradual replacement of the male all-round clerk by specialists such as executive secretaries, stenographers, typists, receptionists, bookkeepers, and office-machine operators. Between 1870 and 1910 women's percentage of all office workers in the United States jumped from 2.6 to 37.7.[41] In Pittsburgh in 1900, 7.2 percent of women workers earned their living as clerks, stenographers, and typists, but they comprised fully 22.7 percent of the city's clerical employees. By contrast, 21.7 percent of Pittsburgh's working women were employed in manufacturing, but they made up only 10.5 percent of all workers in that economic sector.[42]

In the early twentieth century few social investigators paid much attention to the clerical occupations. Offices seemed safe, secure, and civilized in comparison to home manufacturing, factories, department stores, and telephone exchanges. Women wage earners regarded secretarial work as prestigious since it required machine skills, literacy, proper etiquette and attire. Dressed in their freshly starched shirtwaist dresses, women office employees considered themselves superior to factory operatives. When Butler undertook her study, sexual harassment and the deleterious effects of gender segregation and specialized labor in clerical occupations had received little public attention. Only since the 1960s has office work come to be viewed as yet another among the myriad job ghettoes of low-paying, deadend, monotonous work for women.[43]

WOMEN WAGE EARNERS: PASSIVE OR ACTIVE?

According to Butler, the very nature of women's work experiences—the low wages, unskilled or semiskilled labor, gender segregation, and job insecurity—made women economically powerless and dependent. From this perspective the vast majority of women workers apparently responded to these conditions in accordance with the conventional stereotype of female behavior—acquiescence and docility. Butler portrayed saleswomen as ignorant of their bargaining power as a group and therefore unable to resist the "petty exactions" of their bosses.[44] Telephone operators were characterized as passively accepting the demands of a rigidly regulated work routine. Women cigarmakers in Butler's eyes were the apathetic victims of a brutal piecework production system.

It was certainly true that the majority of women workers' reactions to their paid employment infrequently took a public or clearly identifiable political expression. Working for wages for only a brief period of their lives and concentrated in seasonal industries, domestic service, offices, or stores, women wage earners often stood apart from the labor movement. Furthermore, women happened to work in the largest proportions precisely in those occupations which were weakest in labor organization even among men. In 1910 more than 56 percent of the women gainfully employed worked in the fields of trade, professional service, domestic and personal service, and clerical occupations, but in that year less than 17 percent of the male working population of the United States were employed in the same groups.[45] What is more, custom and/or legislation barred women from the two strongholds of men's trade union organization in mining and building. These factors help to explain why in 1910 only 1.5 percent of women workers were organized into formal collective-bargaining units in the United States.[46]

Part of the explanation for the portrayal of women wage earners in *Women and the Trades* as downtrodden and passive has to do with Butler's ambivalence toward the American industrial system. On the one hand, she viewed corporate capitalism as a technologically innovative system with unprecedented capacity for prosperity. On the other hand, she was convinced by her investigations of women's wage-earning at home, in factories, stores, and telephone exchanges that women workers were exploited, cheap labor driven to work at inhuman speeds under wretched conditions. She believed that night work, seasonal employment, wages far below the cost of living, and unsanitary and unsafe working conditions destroyed the fabric of family life and made women into economic pawns. To Butler and other social reformers only the state and federal governments could effectively curb the excesses of economic development.

Women wage earners did in fact suffer from industrial fatigue and poverty, but they did not always accept their exploitative wages and working conditions with apathy or acquiescence. Some of Butler's own evidence can be used to challenge her view of women as mere cogs in the industrial machine. Labor turnover was one way in which women covertly expressed their discontent with their jobs. In cracker factories where women had to stand all day on "scorching" floorboards above the intense heat of the factories' bread ovens, employers complained about the problem of retaining their female help. The same was true in commercial laundries where the danger from unprotected irons or the heat from washing machines drove women to look for less strenuous work.[47] Voluntarily leaving a job was one way that women asserted some control over their work lives.

Few women belonged to trade unions in Pittsburgh in 1910, but those who did worked in concert with their male co-workers to better their labor conditions. Butler found that of the ninety female telegraphers in the city, 42 percent joined the telegraphers' union and went on strike with men to demand equal pay for equal work, among other changes. Even though unorganized women contributed to the strike's defeat, the labor contract resulted in the abolition of wage differentials based on gender at one of the city's two telegraph companies.[48]

Recent occupational studies of women sales clerks, telephone operators, and cigarmakers have also shown that docility cannot be indiscriminately assumed for all women wage earners in the early twentieth century. One historian has found that sales clerks in large department stores developed a distinct work culture to cope with their job-related problems. From this vantage point saleswomen were independent-minded persons who vehemently disliked store policies and rules which made them feel subservient. They objected to separate employee entrances, special systems of checking employee's packages, the notion of customer infallibility—a practice that could at times impugn their own integrity—and the enforcement of a rigid dress code. On the selling floor women created "free" time to chat with one another about their personal concerns.

Of particular importance, they defined what constituted "a good day's work" by limiting the amount of their sales. The "clerking sisterhood" also celebrated their members' birthdays, engagements, marriages, and births at their places of work.[49]

Another study challenges the image of telephone operators as passively tied to their rigidly supervised switchboards. In 1912, three years after Butler completed the research for *Women and the Trades,* telephone operators began to organize for the improvement of their working conditions. In the first five years of organization thousands of telephone operators in New England and as far west as the Rocky Mountain states won an eight-hour day, two-week vacations, standardized pay scales with automatic increases, modification of their split-shift work schedules, and clearer grievance procedures. The militant actions of these women posed a formidable, though short-lived, threat to the labor policies of one of the most powerful American corporations—the American Telephone and Telegraph Company.[50]

The stogy industry, one of Butler's most prominent examples of wage exploitation and harsh working conditions, provides yet another instance of women's militancy. Several years after *Women and the Trades* was published, Pittsburgh's Hill District, then populated by Jewish immigrants and stogy sweatshops, erupted with labor activity. In 1912, two hundred Hill District cigarmakers formed the Industrial Workers of the World Local No. 101 and went on strike in July and August. They struck again in July 1913 for higher pay and improved sanitary and safety conditions. Since entire families made stogies together in the Hill District sweatshops, women participated in the union campaign both as family members and as workers in their own right. After an eighteen-week work stoppage in 1913, the cigar workers won full recognition of their union, a fifty-hour workweek, better sanitary conditions, and improved pay—advances that were maintained in some cigar factories into World War I.[51]

In light of these examples Butler's characterization of women wage earners as passive and powerless needs to be reassessed. Butler used union membership as the sole measure of women's awareness of their bargaining strength. Since few women belonged to unions, Butler understandably concluded that women workers were passive beasts of burden, unable or unwilling to do anything about their work situations. But women did actively respond to their working conditions, in ways that were not always apparent, even to the keenest of outside observers. Informal work groups went undetected by employers and reformers alike because they were based on trust and secrecy, a sort of silent sisterhood.

Women's participation in strikes for union recognition and better working conditions were more pronounced after the publication of Butler's study in 1909 than before. Between 1909 and 1922 women participated in union campaigns and work stoppages as part of a widespread labor revolt that characterized the nation's labor force. Workers' discontent grew principally in response to management's introduction of new efficiency schemes, such as premium-pay plans, time-and-motion studies, personnel record-keeping, and speed-ups. Unskilled workers from traditionally unorganized industries spontaneously struck for better conditions in workplace after workplace. Garment factories, telephone exchanges, meat-packing plants, textile mills, together employing tens of thousands of women, witnessed bitter, widespread labor-management conflicts.[52] Understandably, Butler could not foresee this explosion of labor activity. Her graphic description of dismal labor conditions, however, helps to explain why workers were so discontent.

HOME LIFE:
CHRONIC HARDSHIP AND SURVIVAL STRATEGIES

Butler's view of the impact of industrial employment on wage earners' family life would also benefit from a comparison with recent findings of social historians. Until a few years ago Butler's analysis of the fate of working-class family life under industrial capitalism was shared by most social scientists. Like other reformers of her day, Butler viewed the family as a barometer of the nation's social and industrial health. She believed that the family was the bulwark of civilization to be protected at all costs from the harmful effect of industrialization. Her model of family life was based on the middle-class ideal of father as sole breadwinner, wife as full-time homemaker, and children as carefree playmates or schoolmates. What Butler observed in the homes of Pittsburgh wage earners fell far short of that ideal. Home manufacture, child labor, and chronic poverty characterized the homes of Pittsburgh unskilled and semiskilled wage earners.

Butler criticized outwork or homework, the subcontracting of labor for domestic manufacture. Garment-making and homework were practically synonymous in the early twentieth century. Wherever the garment industry existed, homework flourished alongside factory manufacture. In Pittsburgh and elsewhere in the United States, outwork was a byproduct of difficult economic circumstances. Families undertook garment work at home when they lost their primary breadwinner as a result of desertion, irregular employment, or work accident. Steel production was a particularly hazardous occupation in the early twentieth century. Many families whose breadwinners had been either maimed or killed in the mills turned to outwork as a means of survival. Homework enabled crippled men to contribute to their families' welfare and widows to earn a wage while caring, as best they could, for their children. In communities surrounding Pittsburgh, Butler found that entire families, including small children, worked twelve or thirteen hours a day for meager piecework wages, making forty-five to fifty dozen pairs of workmen's pants per family each week.[53]

Butler was dismayed by the adverse effects that homework had on living conditions and the rearing of children. For the poorest of wage-earning families housewifery was a fiction because there was no time to clean the combined work-living quarters. From babyhood to adulthood children shouldered an unremitting responsibility to their families' economic welfare. Daughters and sons did what their parents expected: they supported themselves and their kin as soon as possible and lived at home or boarded elsewhere depending on what was considered best for the family as a whole. To Butler the industrial system was mortgaging the future of the American family.

Recently social historians have shifted their focus from the hardships of working-class family life to the survival strategies families devised for their unpredictable economic circumstances. Where Butler saw only the pathology of family life, scholars are now examining the ways that working-class families ingeniously coped with seasonal employment, work accidents, labor-management disputes, illness, economic downturns, and migration. Wage earners weathered hard times because they functioned as family members first and as individuals second. Kinship ties were essential to survival in many ways. Kin connections provided the crucial link between job seeker and job. Wage earners aided the emigration of their distant and close kin as well as members of their ethnic group by providing shelter and advice. Within the majority of working-class families wives assumed the roles of homemakers, boardinghouse keepers, or outworkers. Daughters and sons turned their pay packets over to their mothers for the payment of utility, food, or housing bills. Daughters also regularly performed domestic and childcare responsibilities from which their brothers were usually excused. Under the most dire circumstances older children assumed the lion's share of income earning. At a time when unemployment insurance and workmen's compensation were nonexistent or at best meager and a national social security system still a pipe dream, wage earners tried to protect their families from market forces and job hazards. Given the magnitude of the problems wage earners faced, they could not always successfully cope with changing circumstances. Wife and child abuse, desertion, prostitution, and alcoholism were clear signs of the limitations of families to withstand economic adversity. That wage earners survived as well as they did is what impresses many social historians.[54]

PROTECTIVE LEGISLATION:
A PROBLEMATIC REMEDY

More than any previous generation of social reformers, Butler and her peers made occupational health and safety an issue of public concern. Ironically, Butler advocated protective legislation for women even as she recounted the widespread disregard among employers for Pennsylvania laws intended to regulate working conditions. According to *Women and the Trades*, protective legislation for women existed more on the statute books than on the shopfloor. Although Pennsylvania law explicitly prohibited women from working more than sixty hours per week or ten hours per

day, commercial laundries, canning factories, and casket manufacturers, among others, set women's hours to suit their own interests. Safety devices prescribed by law, such as the skirt boards
designed to protect sewers from catching their own clothing in
the wheels of revolving shafts on commercial sewing machines,
were never installed. Cracker factories lacked fire escapes despite
the danger presented by hot ovens. Seats to ease saleswomen's
fatigue from long hours of standing were not installed in Pittsburgh department stores.[55] Collectively, these employer practices
made a sham of the law and underscored the failure of the state
to enforce its statutes.

Butler's concern for occupational health and safety extended
to matters not then covered by laws. She criticized employers for
paying no heed to gas or lacquer fumes, mica dust, or excessive
heat and steam. She took employers to task for not properly training their employees and for refusing to schedule regular rest breaks.
She blamed manufacturers for the unnecessary maiming of wage
earners. After observing the many young girls who had lost parts
of or entire fingers, Butler labeled one lamp factory a "butcher
shop" because its poorly trained foot-press operators often acci-
dentally amputated parts of their hands.[56] As Butler's choice of
words suggests, she was outraged by employers' unwillingness to
accept responsibility for workers' physical welfare.

Butler's critical assessment of protective legislation begs an
important question: If the laws were not wholly effective, why did
social reformers work so hard for their passage? To answer this
question, it is necessary to know how protective laws for women
came into being.

Efforts to protect workers through legislation originated in the
United States in the 1820s when the country's first female and male
factory workers sought hours legislation so that they could share
available work and assure themselves leisure time. State and federal
courts repeatedly struck down the hours laws on the grounds that
labor and capital bargained as equals and that labor, therefore, did
not need state protection. During the nineteenth century judges
applied the doctrine of freedom of contract uniformly to men and
women. In response to the legal battles over protective laws, the

labor movement changed its strategy in the 1880s and 1890s. Instead of lobbying for governmentally defined working conditions, unions sought collective-bargaining agreements. In effect, this meant that skilled male wage earners with bargaining power ably defined their conditions of labor through union contracts, while employers retained the upper hand in setting the terms of labor for the unorganized men and women with unskilled and semiskilled jobs.[57]

At the same time that organized labor turned away from political reforms, women's groups like the National Women's Trade Union League and the National Consumers' League placed protective legislation at the center of their political concerns. Advocates of gender-specific labor laws, like Butler, viewed women as physically, morally, and socially weak and, therefore, incapable of successfully negotiating nonexploitative terms of employment or withstanding the temptations or hazards of certain work environments. Butler and her peers argued that the states had an obligation to protect the country's future mothers. To them, more and better-enforced legislation would also help women overcome their handicaps in the marketplace.[58]

The Supreme Court accepted these arguments in the landmark Muller versus Oregon case in 1908, legitimating maximum-hours laws and indirectly setting in motion the passage of laws specifically regulating women's working conditions or prohibiting women's admittance to jobs deemed unfit for the "weaker" sex. The National Consumers' League leaders helped to prepare the brief in defense of protective legislation for women, a document that would influence the outcome of subsequent legal cases involving labor laws for women.[59]

As the mainstay of support for protective laws shifted from the trade unions to women's reform organizations, certain kinds of labor legislation became identified with the inferior position of women as wage earners. It was no accident that male adults were never covered by night-work regulations and were only rarely covered by restrictions on their weekly hours of work. Male employees regardless of their actual circumstances were viewed as capable of protecting themselves.

Regulatory and Restrictive Laws

Numerically, laws regulating women's daily or weekly work hours led the field of protective legislation for women. The greatest growth in hours legislation took place between 1900 and 1920 when 76 percent of the states passed maximum-hours laws and 60 percent adopted night-work laws. Despite the frequency of such laws, their coverage was highly selective. The new protective labor laws mostly restricted the hours of women employed by manufacturing and mercantile enterprises, commercial laundries, and telephone and telegraph companies. The fields of domestic service and agriculture, although they ranked first and second in the number of women workers, were totally passed over in such legislation and so went unregulated. Although the percentage of women covered by the hours laws increased over the course of the twentieth century, barely a majority of adult women (52 percent) were covered by maximum-hours laws in the peak year of 1960, while only 16 percent of adult females were covered by night-work laws in their peak year of 1940. More than any other group, female minors were targets of the laws. In 1960, 59 percent of female minors in the labor force were covered by maximum-hours laws and 30 percent of them were covered by night-work laws in the same peak year.[60]

Butler would have been very pleased to have learned from a study of protective legislation in the United States, issued in 1928 by the federal Women's Bureau, that the hours statutes had successfully paved the way for even shorter shifts than specified by law. Initially, violations of the laws were common since employers tended to view them as illegitimate curbs on their freedom to negotiate terms of employment directly with their workers. The persistent efforts of social reformers and trade unionists for a shorter workday, whether through legislation or collective bargaining, ultimately persuaded the business community to accept a shorter workweek. Two decades after the 1908 Supreme Court decision validating maximum-hours legislation for women wage earners, businessmen finally accepted the well-established wisdom that long workdays resulted in industrial fatigue, chronic inefficiency, and lower overall productivity. During the 1920s employers yielded to the demands of the hours legislation, and many of them even reduced the length of the workday below the prescribed legal standards.[61]

In stark contrast to the hours legislation, the results of social reformers' campaigns for minimum-wage laws for women and minors fell far short of their mark. The laws were conceived as a way to insure that unorganized, short-term workers would be paid a "living wage." By 1927, only nine states had passed minimum-wage statutes. Thirty-nine states, including most of the major industrial commonwealths, had no legal pay-minimums at all for women and children. Where fully enforced, the minimum-wage laws did relieve the wage exploitation of female workers, but most state laws did not have adequate enforcement provisions so that statutes were observed more in the breach than the promise.[62] Further weakening the laws' effectiveness was the 1923 United States Supreme Court ruling in Adkins versus Children's Hospital in which the court undercut the very legitimacy of the minimum-wage statutes. In Adkins the court struck down as unconstitutional a minimum-wage law for women that was similar to a number of state laws for which the National Consumers' League had been lobbying following its success in the area of maximum-hours legislation and litigation. Freedom of contract was deemed a controlling factor by the court. While hours might be regulated due to physical differences between the sexes, as in Muller, the regulation of wages could not be similarly justified. The court majority in effect declared women to be men's equals in the question of individual or collective bargaining for wages and left their determination to the market, but let stand distinctions in laws for which a biological difference could be ascribed.[63]

In addition to laws regulating women's hours and wages, prohibitive legislation barred women altogether from certain occupations. Women were not permitted in one or another state to work as molders, coal miners, metal polishers, bartenders, messengers, meter readers, letter carriers, or taxi drivers. Unlike the regulatory laws which were initially violated at will or legally circumvented by many employers, the restrictive laws were strictly enforced. Strong craft unions made sure that employers did not hire any women for jobs that were legally specified for men only. In practice, prohibitive legislation protected men's jobs from female encroachment and reinforced the gender-segregated pattern of the American labor force. Even during the First World War, when labor shortages developed in many occupations by 1918, women who entered nontraditional jobs were confronted by the formidable obstacles of legal restriction and/or organized opposition from male wage earners. As a result of these barriers and the postwar demobilization, women pioneering in men's jobs had no alternative but to return to traditionally female work soon after the war.[64]

Very little is known about the attitudes of women wage earners toward protective legislation. Women's responses were at least as diverse as the nature of the laws. If women did not lose any wages with the reduction in their hours of work, they looked favorably upon the hours laws. When their pay was adjusted downward to compensate for the loss in hours of work, then women disapproved of the laws. Female wage earners who were denied access to male-dominated jobs resented the restrictive laws that barred them from employment opportunities. The same was true of skilled women who could not compete on equal terms with craftsmen because of night-work laws. The Women's Bureau reluctantly reported in 1928 that some sixty thousand women had lost their jobs as a result of restrictive laws. Female trade unionists generally sided with social reformers like Butler and favored labor standards laws as the only way to protect young, unorganized women from ruthless employers. A few trade unionists disagreed, arguing that unionization was the only equitable way to protect both women and men from the hazards and exploitation of wage work.[65] As a rule of thumb, the more women had to lose the more critical they were of protective laws. And the reverse was also true. The more women stood to benefit from the laws, the more they approved of them.

The debate over protective legislation as ultimately more helpful or harmful to women dates from Butler's time and continued into the 1960s. From Butler's point of view, one positive value in protective laws, which transcended the principal of gender classification, was that protective legislation helped to establish the precedent for government intervention in the setting and enforcement of labor standards.[66] As economic circumstances, labor organization, and social attitudes have changed over the past three-quarters of a century, the relevance of legal protection for women workers has gradually undergone modification. Protective laws were not appreciably extended during the 1920s, but the unprecedented economic depression of the 1930s brought about the passage of new labor laws for both women and men.

Labor Laws Since the 1930s

The Fair Labor Standards Act, passed in 1938, established a national standard for forty-four (later forty) hours of work per week and payment at a rate of time and a half for overtime work; it also provided for minimum wages. The new law exempted many women and men employed in service trades and local industries by covering only persons engaged in interstate commerce, but it did represent legislative removal of the gender test in hours laws and helped to regulate wages. Officially men and women were to be treated equally, although gender-specific protective laws continued in force. The Second World War simultaneously brought about the massive influx of women into the labor force and the suspension of state labor laws to meet production quotas. A fundamental shift in attitude toward the early twentieth-century protective laws followed from the equal application of some depression-era social programs to men and women, and women's increased involvement in the labor movement during the 1930s and 1940s. The advocates of protective legislation for women began to question the necessity of the old labor laws.[67]

A further shift in attitude occurred in the 1960s as the federal government began to respond through legislation and executive orders to the large increases in the labor-force participation of women. At the same time, from the black civil rights movement women—especially white, middle-class women—borrowed the rhetoric of equality and were forming the women's liberation movement in the middle 1960s. The 1963 Equal Pay Act announced new terms for women in the labor force across the board —with the notable exceptions as yet of domestics and farm workers. Only with the passage of the Civil Rights Act of 1964, which banned discrimination on the grounds of race, religion, ethnicity, and sex, did working women acquire the legal basis for combating gender discrimination. Between 1964 and 1970 the courts applied the Equal Pay and Civil Rights Acts to strike down numerous protective laws. A new era in the legal protection of women workers had been ushered in. The 1960s witnessed the greatest challenge to the legitimacy of the many state laws that Butler and her generation of social reformers had worked so hard to secure.

III
CHANGES AND CONTINUITIES IN WOMEN'S WORK

During the seven decades since the publication of Butler's investigation of working women in Pittsburgh, much has changed in the contours of women's employment, the composition of the female labor force, and the status of women wage earners before the law. At the same time women have remained in some ways as economically disadvantaged as Butler had observed of them so long ago.

Over the course of the twentieth century a demographic revolution has occurred in the female labor force. In 1910 the typical woman worker, young and single, worked a few years before marriage and then left the job market permanently to raise a family. Women reentered the labor force only when they faced economic hardship due to desertion, divorce, or a spouse's layoff, work accident, or death. In 1980 the typical woman worker was married, divorced, or widowed, usually with responsibility for the economic welfare of preschool or school-age children. Increasingly, women remain in the job market as full- or part-time employees following marriage and even after they become mothers.

This shift in the composition of the female work force is due to many factors. Over the course of the twentieth century compulsory school laws and the legal prohibition of child labor have decreased the economic contribution of children to their families. Children ages ten to sixteen or eighteen have been legally obliged to stay in school, in part because the number of jobs for the unskilled has decreased dramatically during the twentieth century. The decline in the birth and infant-mortality rates has also encouraged married women to seek jobs outside the home. The rise of the consumer society has since the 1920s redefined the American standard of living, making consumer durables affordable through credit purchasing. Home ownership, automobiles, domestic appliances, large varieties of clothing, vacations, and commercial entertainment have become essential to the "good" life. The more that has become available for purchase, the greater has become the need for two adult incomes to keep up the new standard of living. Lastly, women's personal aspirations regarding jobs and careers have changed since the women's liberation movement in the 1960s brought about new job opportunities for women in male-domi-nated fields.[68]

The legal guarantees for equitable treatment in the labor force have also increased since the 1960s. The Equal Pay Act of 1963, Title VII of the Civil Rights Act of 1964 (which resulted in the establishment of the Equal Employment Opportunity Commission and affirmative action programs), and the Pregnancy Discrimina-tion Act of 1978 have educated women about their rights at the workplace.

But change has not been uniform on every front. Gender segre-gation has been such a thoroughgoing aspect of the organization of the American economy that some scholars have argued that it would take a social revolution to integrate women into male-dominated fields of work and men into female-dominated fields. Unequal pay has been one result of the historical pattern of job segregation. "Equal pay for equal work" has been an ineffective banner for bringing about pay equity between women and men because women have not performed exactly the same work as men. The new feminist slogan is "equal pay for comparable work," which implies that women should be paid the same as men for work demanding comparable skills, education, accreditation, and respon-sibility. The realization of pay equity remains an active item on working women's public agenda.

If Butler were alive, few of these changes or continuities in women's work experiences would have surprised her. She under-stood only too well the positive and negative employment trends of her own time. Her masterful contribution to the Pittsburgh Survey will speak to future generations as long as inequality remains a persistent characteristic of American society. The clear exposition she offered her readers of the dilemmas facing Pittsburgh's working women and the women in male workers' families suggests parallels and continuities as well as notable differences in current work and family settings. Her model research and her passionate commitment to her subjects combine powerfully as examples for contemporary students, scholars, and observers of the interface of labor, gender, and family in American life.

IV
LEWIS WICKES HINE,
DOCUMENTARY PHOTOGRAPHER

Lewis W. Hine, pioneer in the field of documentary photography in the United States, was responsible for all of the pictures in the six volumes of the Pittsburgh Survey. Born in Oshkosh, Wisconsin, in 1874, Hine studied stenography, drawing, and sculpture at the State Normal School and worked over the course of seven years in an upholstery factory, clothing store, water-filter company, and local bank in Wisconsin before he turned to photography in 1903. Hine was first attracted to photography as an innovative aid for teaching botany and nature studies at the Ethical Culture School in New York City, an institution dedicated to the improvement of humanity through individual moral conduct and social responsibility. By 1907, when he was hired by Paul U. Kellogg as photographer for the Pittsburgh Survey, Hine had, in his own words, shifted his "educational efforts from the school-room to the world."[69]

During the course of his career as a social photographer Hine received most of his assignments from the National Child Labor Committee and *The Survey*, which brought him into contact with the most important social reformers of his day. He also worked at one time or another for the National Consumers' League, the American Red Cross, the Amalgamated Clothing Workers' union, and several agencies of the federal government during the 1930s. His career flourished from 1907 until 1920 after which Hine found it increasingly difficult to make a living as a photographer. His photographic style had by then fallen out of fashion. He died poverty stricken in 1940. Only in the last two years of his life did Hine receive public acclaim from professionals in his field for his outstanding contribution to American documentary photography.

A humanist photographer concerned with the "common" man,

woman, and child, Hine actively sought the acceptance of realism as a style of photography and an impetus to social reform. During his career Hine photographed immigrants at Ellis Island, urban slums, child labor, the construction of the Empire State Building, then the tallest building in the United States, and small-town life. During the immediate aftermath of World War I Hine traveled abroad to record the destruction of Europe. So powerful and moving are Hine's photos that they have become an important part of the American heritage, reprinted in many sources without identification of the author.

LEWIS WICKES HINE
Lewis W. Hine Collection; U. S. History, Local History & Genealogy Division, The New York Public Library; Astor, Lenox and Tilden Foundations.

Hine's greatest achievement was the extensive documentation of the nature of life and labor for America's heterogeneous working class. His photos include men, women, and children, blacks and whites, foreign- and native-born, young and old. They document the degrading and difficult conditions under which workers earned their livelihoods as well as the strength of workers' spirit to survive.

Employers only unwittingly opened their doors to Hine who disguised himself in numerous personas to gain access to workplaces barred to less enterprising social reformers. In the guise of a fire inspector, postcard vendor, Bible salesman, hard-luck school teacher selling insurance, or industrial photographer, he entered many a factory or mine, recording for posterity the stark reality of paid labor in the twentieth century.

Hine's assignments took him all over the United States. To glass works in West Virginia and New Jersey. To woolen, cotton, and silk mills in New England, North Carolina, Alabama, Mississippi, and Virginia. To the street trades in Connecticut and Delaware. To oyster packing and tobacco production from Florida to Louisiana. To canneries in upstate New York. To coal mines in Alabama, West Virginia, and Pennsylvania. To farmlands in Texas and California. Hine's thousands of carefully rendered black and white photos earned him the well-deserved reputation as the most "successful photographer of social welfare work in the country."[70]

HINE'S PICTURES OF WOMEN WAGE EARNERS

The forty-three photos in *Women and the Trades* superbly illustrate the nature of women's work in different settings. From the assembly-line bottling of food in Pittsburgh canneries to the stripping of tobacco in the Hill District sweatshops, Hine restates in picture form the major themes in Butler's book. Gender segregation is visible everywhere. With few exceptions men appear as the supervisors of female operatives, as in the stogy factories, laundries, telephone exchanges, and metal-working plants. The rigidity of work processes are well documented. The photo entitled "A Telephone Exchange," for example, captures the highly refined system of surveillance, known euphemistically as "team work." Supervisors walked up and down behind the operators to insure that they performed their prescribed duties. Behind the supervisor sat monitors at an observation board connected to every position in the exchange; from here the monitors could listen to any operator and follow her work in detail. Behind the monitor stood a male supervisor who oversaw everyone, an elaborate hierarchy which made telephone operating one of the most stressful female occupa-

LEWIS WICKES HINE AT WORK
International Museum of Photography at George Eastman House.

tions. The routinization of labor is underscored in pictures like the full-room photo of female coil winders at Westinghouse showing long rows of the same machine as far as the eye can see, with each woman seated straight-backed at her assigned place. Glancing at the photo for a minute, one sees the mass of workers, lights, coil winders and metal superstructure fuse into an indelible image of the machine worker under industrial capitalism. In other photos Hine took great pains to focus directly on the individual worker. The smiling olive bottler. The neatly dressed laundry checker. The disheveled and fatigued tobacco strippers. Hine never let his viewers forget that the motors of the American economy were fueled by the fortitude, effort, and skill of individual people.[71]

Pittsburgh, 1984

NOTES

1. John R. Commons and William Leiserson, "The Wage-Earners of Pittsburgh," in *Wage-Earning Pittsburgh*, ed. Paul U. Kellogg (New York: Survey Associates, Russell Sage Foundation, 1914), p. 119.

2. The Survey volumes in order of publication are: Elizabeth Beardsley Butler, *Women and the Trades, Pittsburgh, 1907-1908* (New York: Charities Publication Committee, Russell Sage Foundation, 1909); Margaret F. Byington, *Homestead: The Households of a Mill Town* (New York: Charities Publication Committee, Russell Sage Foundation, 1910); Crystal Eastman, *Work-Accidents and the Law* (New York: Survey Associates, Russell Sage Foundation, 1910); John Fitch, *The Steel Workers* (New York: Charities Publication Committee, Russell Sage Foundation, 1910); Paul U. Kellogg, ed., *Wage-Earning Pittsburgh* (New York: Survey Associates, Russell Sage Foundation, 1914); Paul U. Kellogg, ed., *The Pittsburgh District: Civic Frontage* (New York: Survey Associates, Russell Sage Foundation, 1914).

3. Paul U. Kellogg, "The Pittsburgh Survey," *Charities and the Commons* 21 (January 2, 1909): 525.

4. Edward T. Devine, "Results of the Pittsburgh Survey," *American Journal of Sociology* 14 (March 1909): 660-67. Brief summaries of the Survey's findings can also be found in Roy Lubove, *Twentieth-Century Pittsburgh: Government, Business and Environmental Change* (New York: John Wiley & Sons, Inc., 1969), pp. 6-19, and Clarke A. Chambers, *Paul U. Kellogg*

and the Survey: Voices for Social Welfare and Social Justice (Minneapolis: University of Minnesota Press, 1971), pp. 37–38.

5. Lubove, *Twentieth-Century Pittsburgh*, p. 8.

6. P.U.K., "Elizabeth Beardsley Butler," *Survey* 26 (August 19, 1911): 744. P.U.K. stands for Paul U. Kellogg, the editor of the *Survey* and the director of the Pittsburgh Survey.

7. Chambers, *Paul U. Kellogg*, pp. 39–40.

8. Devine, "Results of the Pittsburgh Survey," p. 661; Paul U. Kellogg, "The Social Engineer in Pittsburgh," *New Outlook* 93 (September 25, 1909): 167.

9. Lubove, *Twentieth-Century Pittsburgh*, pp. 20–58.

10. Concise portraits of Florence Kelley, Grace Abbott, Josephine Goldmark, Crystal Eastman and Julia Lathrop can be found in Edward and Janet Wilson James, eds., *Notable American Women, 1607–1950: A Biographical Dictionary*, 3 vols. (Cambridge, Mass.: Harvard University Press, 1971). For information about Pauline Goldmark, see her obituary notice, *New York Times*, October 20, 1962. Butler is mentioned, for example, in Lubove, *Twentieth-Century Pittsburgh*, p. 11, and Chambers, *Paul U. Kellogg*, p. 35.

11. Elizabeth Beardsley Butler, *Saleswomen in Mercantile Stores, Baltimore, 1909* (New York: Charities Publication Committee, Russell Sage Foundation, 1912). Butler's articles include "Cobden of To-day," *Charities and the Commons* 20 (September 5, 1908): 648–54; "New Jersey Children in the Street Trades," *Charities and the Commons* 17 (March 16, 1907): 1062–64; "Sweated Work in Hudson County, New Jersey," *Charities and the Commons* 19 (December 21, 1907): 1257–64; "Sharpsburg: A Typical Waste of Childhood," in *Wage-Earning Pittsburgh*, pp. 279–304.

12. *Survey* 26 (August 19, 1911): 743–44.

13. John Rousmaniere, "The Cultural Hybrid in the Slums: The College Woman and the Settlement House, 1889–1894," *American Quarterly* (Spring 1970): 45–66; Mary Roth Walsh, *"Doctors Wanted: No Women Need Apply": Sexual Barriers in the Medical Profession, 1835–1975* (New Haven: Yale University Press, 1977); Jill Kerr Conway, "Women Reformers and American Culture, 1870–1930," *Journal of Social History* 5, no. 2 (Winter 1971–72): 164–77; Kathryn Kish Sklar, "Florence Kelley: Resources and Achievements" (paper delivered at the Fifth Berkshire Conference on the History of Women, Vassar College, June 1981).

14. Margaret W. Rossiter, *Women Scientists in America: Struggles and Strategies to 1940* (Baltimore: The Johns Hopkins University Press, 1982), pp. 29–50.

15. Alumnae Records, Wollman Library, Barnard College; *Survey* 26 (August 19, 1911): 743.

16. Allis Rosenberg Wolfe, "Women, Consumerism, and the National Consumers' League in the Progressive Era, 1900–1923," *Labor History* 16 (Summer 1975): 378–92; Jacob A. Lieberman, "Their Sisters' Keepers: The

Women's Hours and Wages Movement in the United States, 1890–1925" (Ph.D. diss., Columbia University, 1971).

17. *Survey* 26 (August 19, 1911): 743–44.

18. Ibid.

19. Ibid.

20. Paul U. Kellogg, "Field Work of the Pittsburgh Survey," in *The Pittsburgh District: Civic Frontage*, p. 496.

21. Irvin G. Wyllie, "Margaret Olivia Slocum Sage," *Notable American Women, 1607–1950*, vol. 3, pp. 222–23.

22. Blanche Wiesen Cook, Introduction to *Crystal Eastman on Women and Revolution* (New York: Oxford University Press, 1978), pp. 1–38; see Byington's obituary notice, *New York Times*, August 19, 1952.

23. Kellogg, *The Pittsburgh District: Civic Frontage*, pp. vi–x.

24. Joseph A. Hill, *Women in Gainful Occupations, 1870 to 1920*, U. S. Bureau of the Census, Census Monograph no. 9 (Washington, D.C.: Government Printing Office, 1929), pp. 75–84.

25. Alfred Chandler, Jr., *The Visible Hand: The Managerial Revolution in American Business* (Cambridge, Mass.: Harvard University Press, 1977).

26. Peter R. Shergold, *Working-Class Life: The "American Standard" in Comparative Perspective, 1899–1913* (Pittsburgh: University of Pittsburgh Press, 1982), pp. 66–68.

27. Butler, *Women and the Trades*, pp. 287, 232, 239.

28. Ibid., pp. 62, 77, 22–23, 26.

29. Ibid., pp. 26, 22–24.

30. Ibid., p. 188.

31. Ibid., pp. 34, 209, 242–45, 226, 164, 76–79, 65, 237, 95–96, 289–90.

32. Ibid., p. 50.

33. Ibid., p. 27.

34. Ibid., p. 96.

35. Ibid., p. 337.

36. Ibid., p. 237.

37. Ibid., p. 306.

38. Shergold, *Working-Class Life*, p. 70.

39. Hill, *Women in Gainful Occupations, 1870 to 1920*, p. 36.

40. David M. Katzman, *Seven Days a Week: Women and Domestic Service in Industrializing America* (New York: Oxford University Press, 1978), pp. 44–94.

41. Janet M. Hooks, *Women's Occupations through Seven Decades*, U. S. Department of Labor, Women's Bureau Bulletin no. 218 (Washington, D.C.: Government Printing Office, 1947), pp. 75, 78, Table IIB: p. 227.

42. Shergold, *Working-Class Life*, pp. 69–70.

43. Margery W. Davies, *Woman's Place Is at the Typewriter: Office Work and Office Workers, 1870–1930* (Philadelphia: Temple University Press, 1982), pp. 156–62.

44. Butler, *Women and the Trades*, p. 303.

45. U. S. Bureau of the Census, *Historical Statistics of the United States, Colonial Times to 1970*, Bicentennial Edition, Part I, Series D 182–232, pp. 139–40.

46. Leo Wolman, *The Growth of American Trade Unions, 1880–1923* (New York: National Bureau of Economic Research, Inc., 1924), p. 105.

47. Butler, *Women and the Trades*, pp. 68, 202.

48. Ibid., pp. 292–94.

49. Susan Porter Benson, " 'The Clerking Sisterhood': Rationalization and the Work Culture of Saleswomen," *Radical America* 12 (March–April 1978): 15–32.

50. Maurine Weiner Greenwald, *Women, War, and Work: The Impact of World War I on Women Workers in the United States* (Westport, Conn.: Greenwood Press, 1980), pp. 202–07.

51. Patrick Lynch, "Pittsburgh, the I.W.W., and the Stogie Workers," in *At the Point of Production: The Local History of the I. W. W.*, ed. Joseph R. Conlin (Westport, Conn.: Greenwood Press, 1981), pp. 79–94. Thanks are due Steve Sapolsky for reminding me about the relevance of this essay to Butler's book.

52. David Montgomery, "The 'New Unionism' and the Transformation of Workers' Consciousness in America, 1909–22," in *Workers' Control in America: Studies in the History of Work, Technology, and Labor Struggles* (New York: Cambridge University Press, 1979), pp. 91–112.

53. Butler, *Women and the Trades*, p. 138.

54. Tamara K. Hareven, *Family Time and Industrial Time: The Relationship between the Family and Work in a New England Industrial Community* (New York: Cambridge University Press, 1982); Virginia Yans McLaughlin, *Family and Community: Italian Immigrants in Buffalo, 1880–1930* (Ithaca: Cornell University Press, 1977); Dorothy Schwieder, *Black Diamonds: Life and Work in Iowa's Coal Mining Communities, 1895–1925* (Ames: Iowa University Press, 1983), esp. pp. 59–111.

55. Butler, *Women and the Trades*, pp. 39–41, 200–01, 264, 108, 68, 300–01.

56. Ibid., pp. 180, 263, 215, 202, 234.

57. Ronnie Steinberg, *Wages and Hours: Labor and Reform in Twentieth-Century America* (New Brunswick, N.J.: Rutgers University Press, 1982), pp. 74–78; Alice Kessler-Harris, *Out to Work: A History of Wage-Earning Women in the United States* (New York: Oxford University Press, 1982), pp. 180–84.

58. Steinberg, *Wages and Hours*, pp. 78–81; Kessler-Harris, *Out to Work*, pp. 184–86.

59. Louis D. Brandeis and Josephine Goldmark, *Women in Industry: Decision of the United States Supreme Court in Curt Muller vs. State of Oregon Upholding the Constitutionality of the Oregon Ten-Hour Law for Women, and Brief for the State of Oregon* (New York: National Consumers' League, n.d.).

60. Steinberg, *Wages and Hours*, p. 82.

61. Kessler-Harris, *Out to Work*, pp. 199–201.

62. U.S. Department of Labor, Women's Bureau, *State Laws Affecting Working Women*, Bulletin no. 63 (Washington, D.C., Government Printing Office, 1927), p. 6.

63. Adkins v. Children's Hospital of the District of Columbia, 261 U.S. 525, 43 S. Ct. 394, 67 L.Ed. 785 (1923).

64. Greenwald, *Women, War, and Work*, pp. 123–24.

65. Ibid., pp. 106–13; Kessler-Harris, *Out to Work*, pp. 189–214.

66. Steinberg, *Wages and Hours*, p. 86.

67. Ibid., pp. 109–18.

68. Winifred D. Wandersee, *Women's Work and Family Values, 1920–1940* (Cambridge, Mass.: Harvard University Press, 1981), pp. 7–26, 55–66; Frank L. Mott, "Women: The Employment Revolution," in *The Employment Revolution: Young American Women in the 1970s*, ed. Frank L. Mott (Cambridge, Mass.: The MIT Press, 1982), pp. 1–18.

69. Quoted in Alan Trachtenberg, "Ever—the Human Document," in *America and Lewis Hine: Photographs, 1904–1940* (Millerton, N.Y.: Aperture, Inc., 1977), p. 125.

70. Naomi Rosenblum, "Biographical Notes," ibid., p. 20.

71. Several books provide useful overviews of Lewis Hine's career. Judith Mara Gutman, *Lewis W. Hine, 1874–1940: Two Perspectives* (New York: Grossman Publishers, 1974) reprints Gutman's 1967 essay on Hine's photos coupled with a new commentary on Hine's work from the 1920s and 1930s. A bibliography of Hine's work can be found in Judith Mara Gutman, *Lewis W. Hine and the American Social Conscience* (New York: Walker and Company, 1967), pp. 52–61. *America and Lewis Hine* includes three commentaries on Hine: a foreword by Walter Rosenblum, biographical notes by Naomi Rosenblum, and an essay by Alan Trachtenberg. A selection of Hine's photos on women wage earners can be found in *Women at Work: 153 Photographs by Lewis W. Hine*, ed. Jonathan L. Doherty (New York: George Eastman House, Rochester, in association with Dover Publications, Inc., 1981).

Most of Hine's photos in this edition of *Women and the Trades* are reprints from a 1909 copy of the book. A thorough search of institutions known to possess Hine's original photographs turned up only four of the pictures found in Butler's book. These few photographs are reprinted with the permission of George Eastman House.

ACKNOWLEDGMENTS

This essay benefited from the help of many people. My special thanks to Frederick A. Hetzel, Director of the University of Pittsburgh Press, for offering me the opportunity to write the introduction to this reprint.

The following individuals aided my intensive search for biographical information about Elizabeth Beardsley Butler: Adelaide Weir Sukiennik, Women's Studies Bibliographer, Hillman Library, the University of Pittsburgh; Frank Zabrosky, Curator, Archives of Industrial Society, Hillman Library, the University of Pittsburgh; Edward Skipworth, Department of Special Collections and Achives, Archibald Stevens Alexander Library, Rutgers University; Barbara Dunlap, Chief, Archives and Special Collections, the City College of the City University of New York; Yvonne Untch, Alumnae Office, Barnard College; Patricia K. Ballou, Archivist, Wollman Library, Barnard College.

My thanks go to Martin A. Greenwald, Ileen A. DeVault, Diana M. Wood, and Ann B. Jannetta for suggesting ways to broaden and sharpen my introduction to Butler's book.

I sought the advice of experts on Lewis Wickes Hine for my search for vintage photographs or negatives of the pictures that Hine took for the Butler book. Naomi Rosenblum, Alan Trachtenberg, and Judith Mara Gutman suggested essential, albeit disappointing, leads for my inquiry. The staffs of the following institutions diligently searched their holdings for the Hine photographs of Pittsburgh women wage earners: the Local History and Genealogy Division, Arts, Prints, and Photographs Division, Manuscript Division, and Picture Collection Division of the New York Public Library and the Social Welfare Archives Center, University of Minnesota. Tom Beck, Curator of the Edward L. Bafford Photography Collection, the Albin O. Kuhn Library and Gallery, University of Maryland, Baltimore County, single-handedly searched five thousand Hine photos, unfortunately to no avail. David Wooters and Barbara Puorro Galasso of the International Museum of Photography at George Eastman House, respectively, located and reproduced the only existing vintage photographs from *Women and the Trades*. Nina Rosenblum, filmmaker, graciously sent me photocopies and film clips of photographs of Hine as a young man.

Mary J. Hamler typed the original manuscript and its successive drafts on a computer. Her outstanding clerical skills and good humor considerably eased the task of revising this work.

WOMEN AND THE TRADES

Photo. by Hine

GLASS DECORATORS
By polishing the glass on a revolving wheel
the decorator brings out the brilliancy of the ruby color.
International Museum of Photography at George Eastman House.

RUSSELL SAGE
FOUNDATION
—

WOMEN AND THE TRADES

PITTSBURGH, 1907–1908

By

ELIZABETH BEARDSLEY BUTLER

FORMER SECRETARY, CONSUMERS LEAGUE OF NEW JERSEY

THE PITTSBURGH SURVEY

FINDINGS IN SIX VOLUMES

EDITED BY

PAUL UNDERWOOD KELLOGG

NEW YORK
CHARITIES PUBLICATION
COMMITTEE . . . MCMIX

PRESS OF WM. F. FELL CO.,
PHILADELPHIA

INTRODUCTORY

ONE of the first acts of the trustees of the Russell Sage Foundation was to make an appropriation of $7,000 for the work of the Pittsburgh Survey. Other appropriations followed during the year, that made a total sum of $27,000.

The plan of the survey proposed a careful and fairly comprehensive study of the conditions under which working people live and labor in a great industrial city, and a fair public statement of facts discovered. It was hoped that these facts would lead to the prompt application of some practical measures, whose value to the community would be readily recognized, and that with respect to such conditions as are firmly rooted in custom and convention, they would afford a basis for efforts to secure legislative or other remedies. It was hoped, too, that they would constitute a body of evidence, such as we had never had, bearing on our national civilization, and that they would supply a foundation for further study in a deeper and more comprehensive way of conditions whose consequences are little understood, although they affect vitally our whole community life. These anticipations have already been realized. The appointment by the Mayor of Pittsburgh of a Civic Commission composed of eminent citizens and specialists in various lines, to devise and advocate measures to promote the welfare of Pittsburgh's people, and to advance their standards materially and spiritually, may in itself prove a sufficient justification and return for the effort and expenditure put into the survey.

These volumes will present a vivid picture of certain phases of life in Pittsburgh. We do not claim that it is a complete picture nor that it is entirely free from error. But we believe that it presents fairly and justly dominant elements in the lives of many individuals who form a large and important proportion of Pittsburgh's population. We believe that the facts are not

1

only representative of the life of Pittsburgh, but that in large measure they are matched in all our bigger cities.

The Pittsburgh Survey had been planned by the editors of "Charities and The Commons" before the organization of the Russell Sage Foundation. The Charities Publication Committee accepted and assumed responsibility for the project. The financial co-operation of the Russell Sage Foundation permitted the work to be begun more promptly and with a larger staff of investigators and advisers than would have been possible without it.

The work was under the immediate direction of Paul U. Kellogg. He also edits the volumes containing the reports of the investigations.

JOHN M. GLENN
Director Russell Sage Foundation

EDITOR'S FOREWORD

IF second sight were the gift of the economic investigator, all that is put down in these pages might well have been read between the lines of any one of a hundred Pittsburgh payrolls, where the names of girls and immigrant women are entered beside those of boys and men, or are crowding them out entirely. As it is, this volume presents the findings of a year of exacting inquiry among employers, foremen and operatives as to the 22,000 women employed at wages in Pittsburgh, and the conditions under which they worked in the manufacturing and mercantile establishments in 1907 and 1908.

In an inclusive sense these women make up a new labor force such as employers of an earlier generation would not have hired, for they had not the instruments to use it economically; nor would they have had social sanction for doing so. The group may be regarded as a great fragment, torn off from the traditional occupations of women in the home; or as an entering wedge of a new and changing industrial order in which an increasing share of the efforts of factory production will be expended by women. In either case the articulation of this group of human beings to the processes, buildings, tools, wages, hours and health environment of modern industrial plants, becomes a matter charged with importance far beyond the numerical strength of this company of wage-earning women. They complicate every industrial question; and on the other hand, the conditions and tendencies affecting their employment cannot adequately be dealt with apart from the general problems of the community.

As a thing by itself Miss Butler's investigation has been the first general survey of the women employing trades of an American city. A close study was made of some four hundred establishments. No intensive study was attempted of the women in any particular occupation, nor of the scientific problems, such as factory sanitation and health, opened up by the field work. To

3

such specialized inquiries, wherever made, this general review should supply framework and background.

The investigation was, moreover, an integral part of a larger undertaking, the Pittsburgh Survey, which was carried out in 1907-8 under the Charities Publication Committee with funds supplied by the Russell Sage Foundation. This Survey as a whole attempted a diagnosis of an American industrial district along social and economic lines, and included within its scope such subjects as sanitation, public health, dependency, assimilation, wages, hours and organization of labor. Beside this general work, four special inquiries were carried on throughout the year. The findings of the staff will be issued in six volumes; these volumes will be consistent and related, but they afford the writers a larger individuality of treatment than would be the case were they parts of a formal report.

As a contribution to a city's self-knowledge, this report is a piece of joinery, bringing together for the first time the experience of employers and employes in many Pittsburgh industries. It supplies a record of labor adjustments and technique in factory work such as neither mechanical nor business training afford the individual manager. Let me illustrate by the case of one of the higher officials of a great Pittsburgh manufacturing establishment. Young, enthusiastic, a man with engineering training, he had shown a party of investors and others through a department where expert mechanics were at work on a new turbine. Next a room was entered where hundreds of girls were employed at high-speed machines. These workers, he said, were paid $20 per week. There was nothing in the look or dress of the girls to show such prosperity, and surprise was expressed by one of the party, the headworker of an East Side settlement whose large staff of nurses visits every section of the New York tenements. The official was confident and called for the payroll of the department. The earnings of the women were found to be for the most part $5.00 to $7.00 a week. It was the forewoman who was paid $20. He had carried this figure in his mind and believed it true of them all.

My point is not so much the meagreness of the actual wages, as the disparity between the technical equipment of this official and his ignorance of the human factors in production. He had at

4

his finger tips the threads, the measurements, the temper, the revolutions per second—all the factors that were going into the new turbine. Yet here was human machinery, more delicate, more sensitive, of finer metal than his propeller shaft. And of this he was ignorant.

One of the several points made by Miss Butler is the need for vocational training of the girls, many of them crude and undisciplined, who go to work in Pittsburgh. No less real is the need for a more practical working knowledge of these new recruits to industry on the part of their employers; or, as a more immediate suggestion, the need for an interchange of such working knowledge as there is. For if a conference were called of those who have dealings with working girls in Pittsburgh, there are in the city pickle canners, cracker makers, electrical manufacturers, laundry owners, department store managers, a good company of them, who could contribute methods and experience which, if combined into a standard, would put a new meaning into the day's work, —a standard which physicians, educators, and social economists, no less than the general public, could set seal upon; as today they cannot in conscience nor in thrift.

As a beginning toward this common knowledge, Miss Butler's survey is offered. It is an interpretation of an industrial situation which is repeated over and over in American cities. Wherever it is repeated, and the longer it is repeated, it gruels health and numbs the faculties upon which industrial progress no less than the fuller life depend.

PAUL U. KELLOGG
Director Pittsburgh Survey

TABLE OF CONTENTS

THE CLEANING INDUSTRIES

METALS, LAMPS AND GLASS

MISCELLANEOUS TRADES

THE COMMERCIAL TRADES

LIST OF ILLUSTRATIONS

11

LIST OF TABLES

13

WORKERS AND WORKROOMS

CHAPTER I

WORKERS AND WORKROOMS

PITTSBURGH as a workshop for women seems a contradiction in terms. Workshop this city is, but a workshop which calls for the labor of men. To dig crude ores, to fuse and forge them, are not among the lighter handicrafts at which women can readily be employed. Look down from Mount Washington at the merging of the two dull brown rivers, at the irregular succession of bridges, at scows and small river craft slowly finding way from wharf to wharf; and on either shore, at the black enclosures, gleaming now with leaping flames, now with the steady white-hot glow of Bessemer converters, but everywhere swarthy from the rising columns of black smoke. The cry of the dwarfs under the earth, the first metal smiths, rings again in the blows of the miners' tools and in the shouts of gangs of furnacemen and engine crews in the recesses of the mills.

Nevertheless, in this city whose prosperity is founded in steel, iron and coal, there has come into being beside the men a group of co-laborers. If we listen closely enough, we hear the cry of the dwarfs not only from gangs of furnacemen, but from the girl thread makers at the screw and bolt works, and from the strong-armed women who fashion sand cores in foundries planned like Alberich's smithy in the underworld. And if we listen still more closely, we shall hear answering voices in many other workrooms, in the hum of machines in a garment factory, in the steady turn of metal rolls in a laundry, and even in the clip of the stogy roller's knife in a tenement loft. For Pittsburgh is not only a great workshop, it is many workshops; and in these workshops women stand beside the men. Forced by individual and group necessities, they have found a place in industry in the steel district of the Alleghenies.

Various selective forces have played a part in recruiting these women, in the teeth of the tonnage industries that shut them out. The influence of climate, the commercial wants of a rich producing district and the demands of a great laboring force as consumers, can readily be seen in tracing the development of the trades which employ them. As the shopping center of a nest of mill towns, Pittsburgh gives employment to over 6,000 saleswomen. The city is also an office center for plants and mines; and the printing trades, alive in every city, have taken on character, and with almost no edition work, turn out the ledgers and office paper of the big companies. In walking through the business streets, you are impressed by the number and size of the commercial stationers. They fairly flourish on every corner, and the function of Pittsburgh's pressrooms and binderies is to supply them. Pittsburgh's location and its knot of railroad lines have made it a distributing point within a radius of 200 miles for articles of use and wear. Scattered industrial plants make brooms and brushes, caskets, trunks and suit-cases, and cork. The manufactories of foodstuffs (canned goods, crackers and candy) were first called into being by the demands of neighboring counties in Ohio, West Virginia and Pennsylvania, but now they supply national markets. The success of the stogy industry is traceable in large measure to the demand for cheap tobacco of workingmen who for forty miles along the rivers are busy at metals or coal or steel. Similarly, garment trades came into being to supply cheap jeans and railroad jumpers by the hundred thousands. Moreover, no making of fine garments, no textile manufacture, could persist in this region of smoke-clouds. The city sets its seal upon fabrics. They survive by their wearing qualities and by their ability to withstand smoke and grime and fog. Although the growth of the city and of neighboring towns developed a market for a greater variety of goods, workmen's overalls are still the staple article of trade.

All of these Pittsburgh industries have recruited women as wage-earners. As occupations, some of them, such as the mercantile employments, differ but little from the forms they take in other cities. Others, like stogy making, printing and the garment trades, bear a distinctive stamp. From a national standpoint, the trades of far-reaching significance are those in which we find women molding metals, shaping lamps and making glass. Here women's work has reached the midst of the mechanical industries upon which is founded the city's wealth.

Altogether, 22,185 women wage-earners, excluding agricultural and professional workers and domestic servants, are employed in Pittsburgh. These figures are based on a careful census of the women-employing trades, made during the winter of 1907-8. This working force is distributed in 449 factories and shops and stores. The following table gives the trade groups in the order of their numerical importance:

TABLE I.—DISTRIBUTION OF WOMEN IN TRADE GROUPS*

1.	Mercantile Houses	7,540
2.	Food Production	2,726
	Canneries	
	Confectionery	
	Crackers	
	Molasses	
3.	Cleaning Industries	2,685
	Dyeing and cleaning	
	Laundries	
4.	Stogy Industry	2,611
5.	Metal Trades	1,954
	Electrical appliances	
	Screw and bolt works	
	Miscellaneous trades	
	Machine shops and foundries	
6.	Needle Trades	1,494
	Garments	
	Awnings	
	Mattresses and bedding	
	Gloves	
	Millinery	
7.	Miscellaneous Manufactures	1,137
	Cork	
	Paper boxes	
	Soap	
	Caskets	
	Paint	
	Brooms and brushes	
	Trunks and suit-cases	
8.	Lamps and Glass	864
9.	Telephone and Telegraph	777
10.	Printing Trades	397
	Total women workers	22,185

* This study deals only with part of the working women tabulated in the U. S. Census. The Census of 1900, for instance, groups women's work under 5 headings: (1) Agricultural pursuits, (2) Domestic and personal service, (3) Pro-

This table is in a sense an arithmetical summary of the results of the selective processes of the industries in drawing girls into them. In order to understand fully the place which women have taken, we should need to know more than has been written of the industrial history of the "forks of the Ohio," from trading post and frontier settlement to mill town, and to the complexly developed city of today. We know a little of the life of women pioneers, who were themselves producers of goods; and have hints here and there of household industries, such as weaving and stogy making,* in intermediate decades, which helped make the lives of women in miners' households active and significant. There are gaps in our recorded knowledge of the process of change, of the forces that little by little have called into the factories high-strung girls of American birth along with young exiles from Russia, fieldworkers from Austria, and fair-haired Poles—a call away from the four walls that sheltered the industries of the home and out to mills and shops, to division of labor and to specialization of work at a machine.

One fact significant of the situation in Pittsburgh today is the excess of male over female population, a trifle less than ten thousand, according to the United States Census of 1900. When the industries of the district first drew on Europe for laborers, it was the men of Ireland and Germany, of Italy, Austria and Poland, who came. Later in smaller numbers the women followed. They came because their husbands and brothers were here, but not often for the purpose of forging out a life of their own. Similarly the women of the later immigrant races, the Slavs and the Southern Europeans, are lagging behind. Giuseppina keeps the little Italian cottage, sure that Pietro will return or will make his way before he sends for her. Life in America for her

fessional service, (4) Trade and transportation, (5) Manufacturing and mechanical pursuits.

In this table (1) Agricultural pursuits and (3) Professional service, are excluded; also (2) Domestic and Personal Service, with the exception of the cleaning industries. The cleaning industries in Pittsburgh engage 2685 women, 12.10 per cent of the number we are considering. Under the census grouping of (4) Trade and Transportation, would come saleswomen, telephone and telegraph operators in Pittsburgh to the number of 8317 (37.4 per cent). The remainder, 11,183 women (50.4 per cent), are engaged in (5) Manufacturing and Mechanical Pursuits.

* Abbott, Edith: Employment of Women in Industries. Cigar Making. Jour. Pol. Econ., 15: 1–25.

is not a settled destiny. It is a growing probability, to be sure, for all those populations whose demands exceed the productive power of the soil; but even to the strong it remains something of an experiment, something for which peasant women must await the issue before they follow in numbers equal to the men.

Length of settlement becomes a measure, then, both of the domestic life and of the industrial success of an immigrant group. Irish and Germans, in fact, we no longer think of as immigrants. Their households are as much wrought into the fabric of the nation as those which we are pleased to called American. Jewish immigrants from Austria and Russia have trebled in numbers with the recent religious persecutions, yet they have been part of the life of the city for so long that among them there is a distinct family grouping, and a nearly normal proportion of men and women. This is in part due to race tradition, as well as to length of settlement.

In the congested Italian neighborhoods, on the other hand, women are but an unimportant factor. Sections of the city, of course, such as the Hill district,* contain streets of Italian families where the women still honor the custom of life in the household. A scattered few roll paste-smeared tobacco leaves into tobies after the Italian fashion, or follow with painstaking docility the signs of the forewoman in a garment workshop. But there are, after all, few of these forerunners of congregate activity among the Latins. Ties of tradition that keep the girl to her house and to early marriage are too strong for more than a very few to break. Pittsburgh offers small opportunity for them at once to preserve their self-respect and to earn money by sewing at home. The smoky air bars out flowers of delicate tints and fine embroideries, such as are made by their countrywomen in New York tenements. Such outwork as there is dates back before their time; it fell naturally into the hands of Irish and Germans, whose homes are scattered in early settled regions in the coal-filled hills.

In the mill neighborhoods and in outlying districts, within

* This general name is given to the old residence district on high ground above the main business quarter of Pittsburgh. The Hill district is now one of the most congested portions of the city and is largely tenanted by Jewish immigrants. Italians, Greeks, Assyrians and Negroes have each their particular section of the Hill.

reach of railroads and mines, still fewer women are to be found among the colonies of young Italian laborers, whose numbers contribute largely to the excess male population of the city. Among still later immigrants, the situation is intensified. For example, near the Pressed Steel Car Works, there are streets of two-story houses, each house exactly like every other, and each filled with its family of "boarders," single men who club together or rent a room jointly of a boarding-boss in order to make their pay serve both for their own support and for the help of those in the old country. The majority are Slavs—"Hunkies." They are underworkmen in mill, mine and machine shop. Some of the first comers have worked up from the subordinate jobs, and have brought their wives and families. Some few sisters and friends, with the desire to try a new fortune, have come too, leaving their families behind. But this boarding-house population is in the main made up of single men who are Slavic immigrants.

It would seem that the families among the Slavs have tended to settle rather in the glass-making district, or near factories which turn out steel products and which make use of quick fingers as well as of strong and untrained arms. Here the women have not the conservatism which keeps the Italian girl at home. They have not the same standard of close-knit family relationships. There is flexibility in their attitude toward life and toward their part in it. Already in numbers and in work these Slavic women are to be reckoned with in industry.

From this raw material, native born and immigrant, each woman-employing trade in Pittsburgh has drawn its characteristic racial group, and in some cases a secondary racial group. At the same time, of course, women of the same nationality may be found in several trades. No other occupation seems so desirable as "clerking" to the girl with some personal ambition, but without the training necessary for an office position. The saleswomen are for the most part native born, of Irish or German parents, but among them is many a bright Jewish girl whose deep-seated dislike of noisy machines has kept her away from factories.

The stogy factories and the garment factories, like the mercantile houses, are employers of Jewish girls. In all three industries many Americans are to be found, but they are in the more

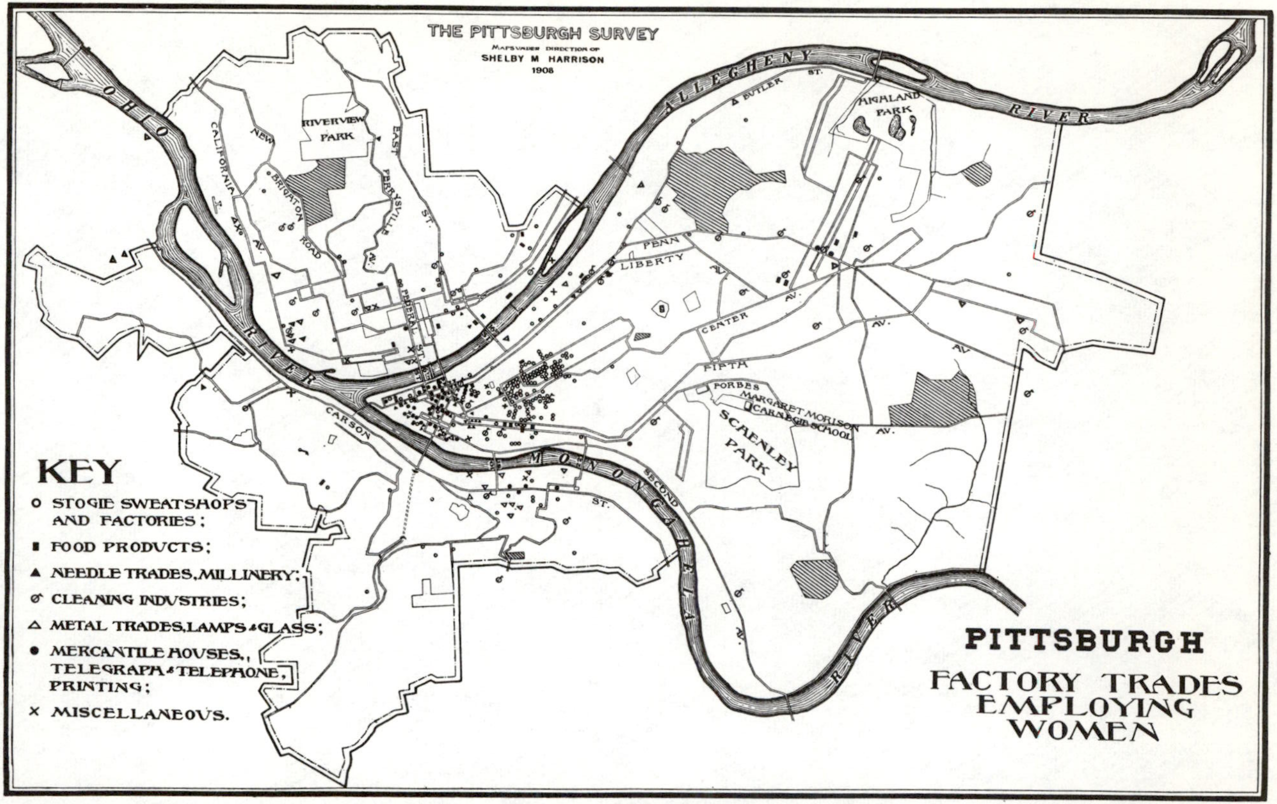

THE PITTSBURGH SURVEY
MAPS UNDER DIRECTION OF
SHELBY M HARRISON
1908
KEY
o STOGIE SWEATSHOPS AND FACTORIES;
■ FOOD PRODUCTS;
▲ NEEDLE TRADES, MILLINERY;
♂ CLEANING INDUSTRIES;
△ METAL TRADES, LAMPS & GLASS;
● MERCANTILE HOUSES, TELEGRAPH & TELEPHONE, PRINTING;
× MISCELLANEOUS.
PITTSBURGH
FACTORY TRADES EMPLOYING WOMEN
OHIO
RIVER
ALLEGHENY
RIVER
MONONGAHELA
RIVER
RIVERVIEW PARK
HIGHLAND PARK
SCHENLEY PARK
MARGARET MORISON CARNEGIE SCHOOL
CALIFORNIA
AV.
NEW BRIGHTON ROAD
EAST
PERRYSVILLE
AV.
ST.
FEDERAL ST.
BUTLER ST.
PENN
LIBERTY
AV.
CENTER
AV.
FIFTH
AV.
FORBES
AV.
CARSON
ST.
SECOND
AV.

Location of Establishments Employing Women

desirable positions, and in the better-class shops which make provision for light and air. Americans have the nervous readiness to learn new ways, the adaptability and measure of skill which tend to bring them both the better work and the better workplaces. The Jewish girls predominate in the cheap and hustling shops. They put up with the drive in rarely cleaned upper rooms, where between narrow walls faint daylight finds its way toward the machines, and where drifting lint and ten hours' stooping over a power-driven needle come in time to affect the strength of even a girl with rugged generations behind her. The newcomers cannot choose either workshop or wages. With the subordination of the industrially unadjusted, they crave a chance to learn, whether it be by the whirr of the needle or by team work at cheap mold stogies to supply the workingmen's demand.

The least desirable work in the needle trades does not fall to Jewish or American girls, but to a different group. When garment manufacturers of Pittsburgh were spurred to production by the increasing army of laborers who bought their wares, they gave the jeans and railroad jumpers to Irish or German women who would make them at home. The sweating system, as old and older than the ready-made trade, adapted itself to the city, and took on a form scarcely recognizable to one familiar with the contract shops among the Italians and Russians on New York's East Side. There is no contract system here. Rather, the outwork entrenched itself in individual homes before the present day immigrants had settled into districts, when the only available outworkers were the wives of workingmen in Carrick and Lower St. Clair. Even today, it takes a rambling journey along muddy footpaths, across brooks and fields and along the edges of the barren hills, to bring you to the sweated district. The workroom here is not a crowded tenement, but a small wooden house with six machines filling the living room, and every member of the family, from father to baby, steadily occupied. Outworkers pay the driver a percentage on every dozen that he brings, according to the distance from town. As the driver knows the people and often gives them the chance to work, his position is in some respects that of a middleman. A seemingly inaccessible hill country within the city limits, wooden shacks swarming with chickens and children, a whirr of machines audible from the field below—these contradictions characterize the sweating system in Pittsburgh.

The garment factories, then, employ Jewish and American girls, while Irish and German women, the hill-dwelling wives of the miners, hold the subordinate place. The inferior work of stogy factories falls to Slavic women, some of them married and others raw immigrant girls. The least desirable occupation in this industry is tobacco stripping, pulling the stems out of the moist leaves, weighing and tying them in pounds for the rollers. In tenement shops you may find these strippers in a cellar, their backs against a damp wall, working by a flaring gas jet. In a large factory they sit in low stalls, row behind row, stemming and weighing and throwing the waste to one side. "They would work all night," a foreman said to me, "if I would give them the chance. We never have any trouble with them. We can't give them enough work to do." In this case they were married women; but the rule holds good, and the Slavic hands in a stogy factory seldom make trouble. They are there too much on sufferance for grievances to be worth their while. They have entrenched themselves in the stripping room, and are found now and then at a bunching machine, or rolling stogies at the suction table; but stogy-rolling, in that it requires more dexterity and is in consequence more desirable, is still largely in the hands of American and Jewish girls.

But women of the Slavic races have already pushed their way into a wider circle of industries than have the Jewish girls. A close study of the service of this one race to the different industries would be as significant as such a study as has just been outlined of the actual racial make-up of the needle and tobacco trades. For the most part, the Slavic women in Pittsburgh are limited by lack of training, trade indifference, and a stolid physical poise that cannot be speeded at the high pressure to which an American girl will respond. They accept factory positions that girls of other races regard as socially inferior. They consent to do the rough and unpleasant work, work that leads and can lead to nothing except coarsening of fibre and a final break in strength. They change from one place to another with an irresponsibility, an independence, born perhaps of long-slumbering memories of revolution in their own land.

In canneries and cracker factories, to be sure, the Slavic girls are fair, light-handed, delicately built. They have the nervous energy to pack or to fill jars at high speed, to stand beside the traveling conveyor which carries cans of beans, and to slip a bit of pork into each can as it passes. Without turning their heads or changing their positions, working with high concentration and intensity, they can keep pace with the chains. While the majority do mechanical work, hulling and stemming berries, preparing fruit, filling and labeling cans, the Slavs are found also among the bottling girls, on whom the responsibility for the looks of the finished product so largely rests. Each pickle or piece of preserved fruit is put in place according to model. The girl uses a grooved stick to slip the pickle into place, and is obliged to be accurate as well as quick, for she works under inspection on a piece basis. If she misplaces an onion in a jar of mixed pickles she is required to do all the work over at her own expense.

Possibly between the Slavic girls in the canneries and their kinswomen in the metal trades there is the difference between the child of the city and the child whose life and the life of whose parents has been close to earth. With knee and hand and metal-centered glove, these rough-skinned stolid women open the sheets of tin still warm from the furnaces of the sheet and tin-plate mill; they screw nuts on bolts by a fish-oil process, and carry heavy trays in foundries where they have displaced men. They are the packers in glass factories, the riveters and foot-press operators in lamp works. They have a hundred miscellaneous things to do, no one of which is a trade or can be a trade so long as a shifting group of women, women with muscular strength and readiness to do disagreeable things, is at hand for the odd jobs about a factory. They learn to operate one machine, but they are not among the hands who know the ways of the shop and work up to the better occupations. Either through the barrier of language or in part through their own indifference, they are still used for the less desirable work in such occupations as in a measure they have made their own.

Slavic girls of both types are to be found in laundries, but

25

in most cases they are employed only in the mangle room. Their work is to feed in sheets under the metal rolls, to shake them out before feeding, or to receive and fold them at the other end, while the steam rises from the hot metal and from the huge washing cylinders below.

To complete my racial analysis of industries employing women: in the candy factories, the miscellaneous manufactories, telephone and telegraph offices, the wholesale millinery houses, and the printing trades, the employes are largely English-speaking. Telephone and telegraph work, like "clerking," is socially desirable, and by reason of this, claims the American girl. The same is true of the millinery workroom in spite of irregular hours and short seasons. Perhaps a reflected "odor of sanctity," an association by proxy with clerical work, has made the pressrooms and binderies favored above more obviously manufacturing pursuits. Perhaps, too, location of the binderies in the business section of the city has given them American employes, for the Slavic girl, like her Jewish co-worker, is limited in her imaginings to factories and shops within the few streets that make up the sum of her experience. Yet, to a limited extent, pressrooms and binderies employ girls of foreign birth, and in the cork factory also many of the sorters are Slavs. The candy trade is in high esteem among women workers and is largely in the hands of Americans.

Surveying the city, then, we see English-speaking girls holding the positions for which a few months' training and some intelligence are needed, a knowledge of English, or of reading and writing. The Italian girl, hindered by tradition, scarcely figures, but within a limited circle of industries, immigrant Jewesses hold positions beside girls of native birth. We see much inferior and unpleasant work yielded to Slavic immigrants, and we see these newcomers, sometimes by sheer physical strength, sometimes by personal indifference and a low standard, competing on the basis of lower wages for men's work which otherwise would never have been given to girls to do. Workrooms that would not long be tolerated for American women have been regarded with indifference for the Slavs, perhaps because of our inability to share the sensations of a foreigner. The place of the Slav, scrubbing floors and sorting onions for canners, packing crackers, stripping tobacco for stogy makers, and trimming bolts for the metal workers, is lowest industrially among the women workers of Pittsburgh. It is the place of the woman who is fighting her way, but has not yet thought where she is going. Marriage is not suffered to act as a hindrance. A determination to work and to earn is uppermost.

Our survey of the city shows us more than this. We see that since the days of settlement and mill town, Pittsburgh has become an industrial center whose workrooms give hire to more than 22,000 wage-earning women. These women have left household work and home industry for the field of collective service. From doing the whole of a thing and from knowing the user, the younger generation has gradually found its work more and more minutely subdivided; the individual worker makes not even a whole hinge, but a tenth part of it, and knows neither the use nor the destination of the finished product. She does not know the relation of her fraction of the work to the other fractions nor to the product as a whole,—and she works with a speed unknown to the houseworker. These younger women have pushed past the traditional activities of cleaning and cooking and sewing. Relatively few are occupied even by the congregate form of these industries, such as the laundries and garment factories. They have not only gone into pressrooms and binderies, into cork factories, and workrooms where candies are made and fruit is preserved, but they help to finish the glass tumblers that the men in the next room blow, they make the cores for the foundrymen, they are among the shapers of metals for lamps and for hinges and bolts and screws. In a district that is pre-eminent for the making of steel and iron and the products of steel and iron, women have gained a foothold in industries that seemed wholly in the hands of men. If mere numbers were the criterion, in the discussion of occupations which follows the Pittsburgh saleswomen should demand our first attention; but it has been the task of this investigation to consider primarily these factory trades where women are extending the boundaries of their industrial activity.

Pittsburgh as a city of wage-earning women is seen in all this to be not a contradiction in terms, but an actuality. From river to river, women have rapidly come to share in the modern industrial life of the city. It is a movement 22,000 strong. An industrial movement which makes for cheapness, or for efficiency, or for the utilization of a hitherto only partially utilized labor force, cannot be turned back by any theory as to its inappropriateness. But our survey shows us still other and more fundamental issues to be reckoned with in this situation. Many of these women are put to work at wages below the cost of subsistence, for hours longer than the measure of their strength, in buildings and at ill-constructed machines which cannot but injure their health, and at processes which must handicap heavily the development of both body and mind. Industrial movements and practices which lead to such consequences may not easily be stayed, yet they may be directed and controlled by law and by public opinion grounded on considerations of the social welfare. To this end the investigation has sought more thorough knowledge of conditions under which women work in the industries than has hitherto been available to the public, to the progressive individual employer, or to the women themselves. The study has thrown light on how the occupations of women and of men are related, how far women have reached the point of self-support, and what the social effect of their work seems to be.

The numbers of women workers in competitive industry are greater, not less, than they were fifty years ago, or twenty-five years ago, or ten years ago. There is every indication that these numbers will continue actually and proportionately to increase. We have no reason to think that the problems presented by the industrial employment of women will be solved by a cessation of that employment. But there is reasonable prospect that through change in the conditions of their labor much that seems evil in it may be done away, and the participation of women in industry may become a force of permanent value.

FOOD PRODUCTION

CHAPTER II

THE CANNING INDUSTRIES

THE commercial use of electricity has fairly revolutionized methods of transportation and manufacture in the dominant industries of Pittsburgh. Yet nothing short of that change will serve, by way of comparison, in estimating the effect industrially upon women of the transfer of much of their work of production from houses to factories.

Little by little the nineteenth century has seen one home industry after another gathered out of its individual relations into a collective impersonal unit. At the beginning of the century, brewing and baking, cooking, cleaning and sewing, as well as much spinning, knitting and weaving were done within household walls. The family was not only a social but an industrial unit. Today the bakeshop, the brewery, the laundry, and the garment factory have in large measure supplanted the housewife's ovens, vats, washtubs and sewing baskets. Little by little, as these industries passed out of the home the women followed them. From being all-round artisans, many became, for example, packers of candy, of crackers and fruit, operators of ironing machinery and power sewing machines. Others have gone farther. Many who entered the doors of the factory in following after their home occupation found their way into industries which had left the home so long before that the line of descent seemed broken if it ever existed. In Pittsburgh they have gone into cork and soap and paint factories. They have learned to grind and melt and paint the edges of glassware, to bore and rivet metal, to sort the corn for brooms, to put threads in screws and bolts on nuts, to wind coils for electric motors and to tear apart the sheets of tin still faint-red from the furnace heat. Into these industries we shall follow them. We shall find the women workers of Pittsburgh in great groups of factory trades—food production, the needle trades, the cleaning industries, stogy making, lamp and glass making and the metal trades. To understand the significance to women and to the community of this industrial change, we shall need to consider in connection with each industry what work it is that the women employes do and what tools they use, how long and for what wages they are employed, what is likely to be the physical effect upon them of this work, and what is the reaction, socially and intellectually, of their factory environment.

Food production in Pittsburgh as a factory employment for women falls into three main trade groups: the canning industry, the making of confectionery and the cracker industry. The two largest canneries in Pittsburgh may be seen from the Allegheny river. They are in the built-up city district. By quality of output, as well as by abundant advertising, they have extended their reputation so far that vegetable and fruit preserving and pickle bottling are known everywhere as characteristic Pittsburgh industries, no less than the mills and furnaces whose smoke is the insignia of the city. Food production in such an atmosphere would seem full of risks, yet the cool green country near the farms whence fruit and berries come, apparently an ideal site for a cannery, cannot compare in transportation facilities with this point at the meeting of rivers and of railroads from east and west. The raw fruits gathered in along a hundred converging lines from Michigan, Illinois and Indiana, are transformed by industrial alchemy and sent out in bottles and tins to innumerable local centres. The commercial advantage is with the city cannery.

In the country canneries long, low sheds are grouped about the main buildings; a vast but irregular force of employes comes and goes with the seasons; farmers' wives and daughters work a few hours a day in berry time; troops of Italians, coming by families in carloads from the cities, live in shacks near the sheds, and work early and late until the chill of winter sends them back. Often women after a day in the fields come to the sheds at night to prepare the fruit they have picked. Often padroni contract to supply the labor force. The very out-of-door atmosphere of the work, whether in shed or field, the bright scarfs of the Italian

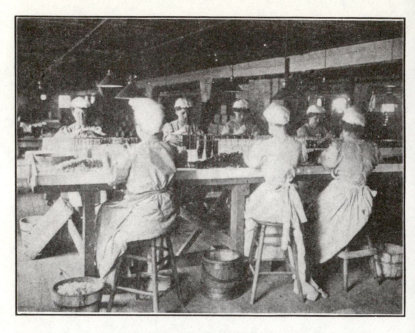

BOTTLING PICKLES AND ONIONS

Photos. by Hine

WHERE JARS ARE WASHED AND STACKED

women, the children asleep on benches, the interchange between indoor and outdoor days—all these things give to the country cannery a character almost primitive, suggestive of some old-world industry in the fields of Austria or Italy; an aloofness from industrial developments as we know them in the larger cities of the United States.

With these city canneries, however, we meet a different situation. Here there is no background of rolling fields and foreground of low, open sheds with the wind sweeping through. There are no rude frame shacks close by for intermittent occupation by a foreign labor force. Instead, there are brick buildings, enclosed, with tight windows, and a fairly permanent force of workers gathered from throughout the city or from neighboring towns. The gay colors of the Italian women are missing. The little children asleep on the benches are not here. When children come, they come as individuals to work and carry their earnings home with them. There are few mature women in the canneries. Instead, there are young girls, sixteen to twenty, sometimes older, seldom coming back as married women to the trade. The American girls are omnipresent, although compared with girls of Slavic origin they are a minority. Many of the processes, such as washing bottles, scrubbing floors and paring fruit, are near of kin to domestic service. For this reason, perhaps, American girls are often reluctant to take positions in a cannery; when they do, they tend to enter departments which require the higher degrees of dexterity. Now and then there is a Russian or Hungarian girl, and still oftener the quiet, steady German. Most numerous are the Poles, Hungarians, and Croatians—slight, fair-haired girls with low foreheads, high cheekbones, and a dull patient look about their blue eyes. "They are the best workers I have," said one employer, of four Hungarian girls who pared quinces in a little cage of a room, "they keep at it just like horses."

There are seven canneries in Pittsburgh. Three of them employ 1350 of the 1400 workers in the trade. Some of the factory buildings are small wooden structures, with dark beams, much-washed floors, and narrowly subdivided interiors. Some are crowded with barrels of syrup and stained with decaying fruit. One of the larger canneries, which stands between railroad track and river in a dip of the hill, is a five-story brick building which has gathered its various processes into wide cool rooms connected by long corridors. Above storage cellars and offices, on third, fourth, and fifth floors, is the actual factory work. Another factory, the largest in Pittsburgh, occupies eight buildings. The walls of light brick, scrupulously cleaned, stand out against the murky background of the city; and within doors, the light walls, wide windows, and spotless white of work tables bear out first impressions that the management has high standards both for the surroundings of its work-people and the quality of its product. From the central building, bridges connect with the neighboring buildings on upper floors; and allied processes are grouped together in common units of space. Tin cans are made in one building, boxes and barrels are nailed together in a second, and in a third pickles are sorted, bottled and labeled preparatory to shipping; in other buildings fruits are stemmed, hulled, washed and sliced, mustard grains are ground in mechanical presses which crush a slow yellow mass into the receiving tubs, beans are baked and prepared for shipment, and the cooking and sealing for a condiment-loving people go forward with speed and ingenuity.

Although the canning of vegetables in factories is not preeminently a woman's trade, women are in the majority. They numbered, in 1907, 55.8 per cent of the total cannery workers, 728 altogether as compared with 618 men. The men, however, do all the responsible work, such as the actual cooking and preserving of fruit, the pickling of cucumbers and the baking of beans. They make the boxes and barrels when the cannery is large enough to have a box factory or a coopershop of its own; they attend to the shipping and plan new methods of sale and of process. The women workers do not compete with the men, but have a division of the trade distinct and characteristic. They wash bottles and scrub floors and help about the kitchens. They sort and bottle pickles, prepare raw materials, label and fill the jars of preserves. Their work, in other words, is secondary and comparatively mechanical. Graded from most to least skill, the main processes in which women employes take part are bottling, sorting, labeling by hand, labeling by machine, tin-can cutting and preparation work.

34

OCCUPATIONS OF WOMEN

Bottling pickles requires the highest dexterity. Blue-gowned, white-capped girls sit at long tables in rows transferring pickles from bowls to squat, thick glass bottles that signify vinegar and preserves to the mind of the retail customer. Each girl holds in her right hand a grooved stick which she thrusts into the bottle, then with her left hand she starts the pickle along the groove to the precise spot which, according to the model, it must occupy. The model jar shows how every pickle is to be placed. Bottles of olives and pickled cucumbers are planned to economize space, and bottles of mixed pickles are so arranged that each bit of color will be just right to make a harmonious whole. After the bottles are filled, they are inspected and compared with the model. The quick, sure touch with which the bottling girls follow the pattern and manage their tools is not learned in a day's apprenticeship, but must be acquired by continued practice.

Sorters of onions and of pickles, but especially of pickles, have a task that also requires a quick eye. The onion sorters sit on long benches with groups of boxes in front of them into which they throw onions of different sizes. The small work is done by a series of sieves in a machine. Pickles are sorted entirely by hand. Each sorter stands by a table with the pickles in front of her, and behind her eight boxes for eight different sizes of pickles which she throws over her shoulder with an intuitive aim that strikes the right box every time. All the boxes are inspected and any imperfectly sorted lots sent back. She has need for quick judgment in order to make the day's work pay, for there is no time allowance for hesitancy. A second's hesitation, a careless toss of the hand, means a decrease in her possible earnings.

Labeling is done by hand on jars of applebutter, jellies, preserves or mustard, or bottles of pickles, olives or gherkins. On each jar four labels are pasted,—two side labels, a third on the top, and a fourth around the neck,—and when the jars stand finished in a symmetrical row, the labels, too, must appear symmetrical, every one placed exactly alike. To do this work well, to pick up the right label from the different piles, to fix it so exactly in the right spot that it can pass a critical inspec-

35

tion for perfection of appearance—this also requires a good eye, a sure hand, a neat touch, and time in which to learn.

A labeling machine is used for cans of beans and soup. In the middle of the machine are the labels dipped in paste. The cans are placed on belts and carried over the paste-dipped labels which they pick up en route, going on to be stacked at the other end. The operators place the cans on the machine and stack them when labeled. Six or eight girls are required for each machine to keep the cans racing in unbroken succession.

Tin-can cutting is a subsidiary occupation. Boys were formerly used for this work, but they were found to be careless and accidents were frequent. The girls who now run the foot presses are paid no less than the boys whom they succeeded. Ten tops for cans are cut from each sheet of tin. The foot-press operator places the sheet in the press and gauges it so that it will fall evenly and exactly and the tin will not be wasted. A slight, quick pressure of the foot is required to clip the tin for each top, and this slight, quick pressure is repeated forty times a minute, 24,000 times a day. Soldering of tins is done by machine. The operator passes a rolled tin (the side of the can) over the arm of her machine, which revolves horizontally around a pivot under a soldering iron, carries the soldered tin back to the point of starting, and drops it into a traveling chain which in turn leads to another part of the room where the top is put on. The work of the tin-can department, arranged not according to the estimated demand from year to year, but simply from week to week, varies with the volume of business and the demand of other departments. This living from hand to mouth, as it were, implies, of course, considerable irregularity of work. Since orders are executed as they are received, a week of overtime until nine o'clock nightly is often followed by a week when the entire department is laid off.

Lowest in the industrial scale of a cannery is preparation work. This is of various kinds. Some of the new hands assist at the machines which put lids on catsup bottles. Three girls work at each machine, one putting the bottles underneath while the lid is automatically clamped on, one washing the bottles, and the third removing them and putting them into a basket. Some girls pack bottles in the sterilizing retorts; some wash bottles and

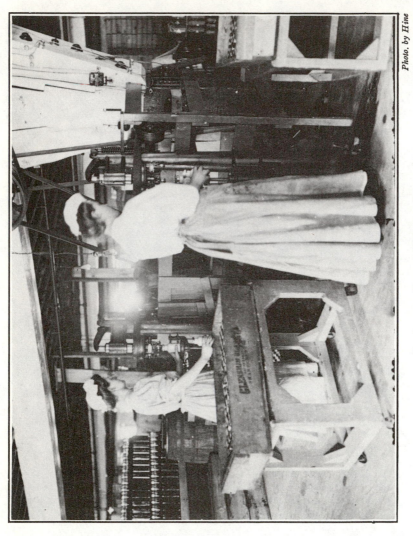

FILLING AND CAPPING MUSTARD JARS
International Museum of Photography at George Eastman House.

scrub floors; others pare and cut fruit. Occasionally pickle cutting occupies an entire department. Women, with their fingers bound with cloths to break the slip of the knife, sit at long tables emptying tubful after tubful of pickles at a fierce rate of speed. The pickles are cut lengthwise or crosswise according to their shape. Hand knives are used, but the incessant downward motion of blade and fingers looks like the vibrations of a machine. A blind haste that allows not a moment to look up or away spurs the nerves of the workers from early morning until night.

The beanery girls, also, have work which requires a low grade of dexterity. The beans, which are cooked on an upper floor, slide through a shute to the floor below into a traveling chain of cans which passes automatically beneath the shute. This chain carries its freight past a row of girls who put slices of pork into the cans as they pass. Each girl serves as an extra arm of the machine. The chain is not set to her pace, but she must adjust herself to the pace of the machine, at a speed which is hard for tired arms to sustain. She cannot turn her head or change her position, or she will miss a can, and fail to slip in a slice of pork. The chain is inexorable. A moment's idling means waste of the product.

The main points to be noted about women's work in canneries, besides the general character of the processes, are the number of women in each, the wages paid, and the seasonal overtime. All women employes, and especially the unskilled, are liable to be shifted from one piece of work to another. In describing the processes, I roughly grouped them according to dexterity. The following table summarizes the distribution of women in occupations in order of numbers in each:

TABLE 2.—OCCUPATIONS OF WOMEN IN PITTSBURGH CANNERIES

Occupation	Number of Women
Sorting pickles	48
Wrapping	50
Preparation work (stemming, paring, shelling, etc.)	67
Filling cans	70
Tin-can cutting or soldering	75
Bottling	179
Labeling	293
Total	782

WAGES

Under several heads in this table there is both work that requires dexterity and work that is totally mechanical. Wages in canneries, although determined by the location of the plant and the occupation of the individual, tend to fall within certain fixed limits of variation. One suburban cannery pays $7.00 a week to each of its women employes, "because," said the clerk, "we have to pay higher wages than most of them or we couldn't get the girls out here." Another firm guarantees its girls $6.00 a week, and then if they earn more than $6.00, allows them something extra on a piece basis; most of the girls make under $7.00. In a third plant the usual rate is $3.50, and none of the girls earn over $4.00. This plant is so far out on the edge of the hills that there are few industries to compete with it. Half the force is laid off from October until May, and even in the busy season there is no opportunity for extra earnings, but the factory is able to obtain all the employes it wants, on its own terms.

The three large canneries pay most of their women employes by the piece. New hands are usually given a day rate, as also are some of the machine hands (such as operators of labeling machines) whose output could not readily be calculated. The standard pay for a trained and dexterous girl is $1.25 a day. This does not mean that this pay is never exceeded, but rather that the average output of employes is calculated in departments which demand the most careful work, and the piece rate fixed with reference to this standard. If at times a girl exceeds the standard pay, it is usually attributable to a "run of good material." For instance, in one factory the bottling girls, who are generally the best-paid workers, make from $1.30 to $1.50 a day. In another factory where a premium of 5 per cent to 10 per cent of each bottling girl's total earnings is added to her pay every six months for neatness and general excellence of work, one of the more successful girls received $18 in July, 1907 (at 10 per cent), which represented $180 earned in half a year, or an average of $6.92 a week. Bottling is enough of a trade to warrant a higher level of wages. High dexterity, like skill, can only be acquired by time. Whereas some of the older hands exceed the

38

standard pay, many others are not able to earn more than $ .90 to $1.00 per day.

This is as true of sorters and labelers as of bottlers. Pickle sorters, on a "good day," when the pickles are well-shaped and firm, can earn $1.83. On other days they make from $1.00 to $1.25. Labelers are paid $ .03 a dozen for pasting four labels on mustard jars. In one plant, the fastest girl in the department, who has had four years' experience, can finish sixty dozen jars a day. Yet, although she can often earn $1.80, neither of the girls beside her can earn more than $ .98.

Tin-can cutters, machine labelers and many preparation hands are paid day rates. The foot-press operators in the tin-can department are paid $1.25 a day, and the machine labelers are paid $ .60. Some of the beanery girls and some of the preparers are paid $ .75 to $ .85, and some few are paid $ .95. On the other hand, some are paid $ .40 to $ .50 a day. In general, it is girls under sixteen years of age who get $ .60 down, and the older ones who earn from $ .70 to $ .85. Even this rate of wages marks an advance for the beanery girls due to the difficulty in getting hands even for regular work. In 1906 the maximum price for unskilled labor was raised from $ .60, which was formerly the standard, to $ .85 a day.

To sum up the wage groups in canneries: a majority of the bottlers, all the sorters, and a third of the labelers are earning $1.25 a day, and sometimes more. This third among the labelers are hand workers who have had experience; so, too, are the sorters and bottlers. Contrasted with these 324 girls, comprising 41 per cent of the women employes, who are earning $7.00 and half of them $8.00 a week, are the remaining 458 girls (59 per cent) who are earning $6.00 or less. In both groups, accuracy and some dexterity is needed, and in both the work is done at high speed.

HOURS OF WORK AND OVERTIME

Overtime is a condition characteristic of the canning industry. The regular working day, in every cannery but one, is from seven a. m. to six p. m., but during the busy season four of the canneries work every night until nine, and the others work at least two nights a week. This makes a working week of 72 hours, although the legal limit for women is 60 hours per week. Even the factories which work but two nights a week are exceeding by four hours the maximum working week allowed by the Pennsylvania law.

The busy season begins in May and lasts on through the summer, reaching its climax from early September to late November. Vegetables and fruits come into the yards in quantities. Crops of berries, fruits, peas, corn, beans and tomatoes follow each other in rapid succession, and with increasing heat the necessity for the quick handling of raw material becomes more urgent. The carloads of perishable foodstuffs must be cared for at once or they will be unfit for use, a loss to the company.

The problem of the factory management is to deal with these raw materials without loss of time or of product. The management does not know when the carloads of fruits or vegetables may arrive, and hence cannot plan far ahead for temporary increase in the numbers of its employes. Overtime is habitual in country canneries, in spite of the elastic labor force at their command. The labor force available for city canneries is less elastic. A few women can be called in from the neighborhood, children can be used after school hours for simple preparation work, and there is always a residuum of the unemployed. One cannery, by arrangement with a neighboring parochial school, systematically employed school children from eleven to fourteen years of age during the months of May and June as berries came in. As many as 200 children could be obtained for afternoons on a moment's notice to tide over the difficulty, by hulling strawberries by the quart, under direction. Other canneries feel, however, that the extensive employment of children is inadvisable. Progressive educators certainly do.

Sometimes a rush of work is met by the transfer of workers from one room to another. Pickles yield precedence to strawberries for a day, and half the pickle department is set at hulling and sorting the perishable fruit. Yet such transfers of sections of the working force can be effected only to a limited extent, as orders for all departments are constantly coming in and must be finished and shipped without undue delay. In general, and in-

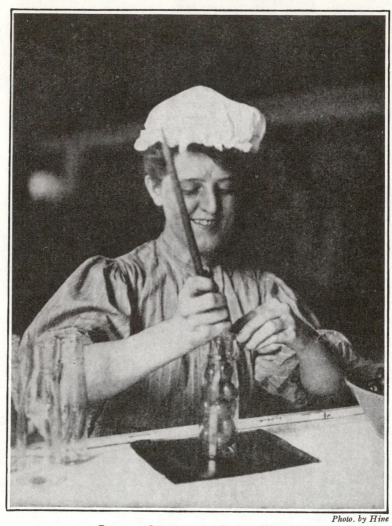

BOTTLING OLIVES WITH A GROOVED STICK
International Museum of Photography at George Eastman House.

variably when these meagre sources of extra labor supply fail, the situation is met by the management by requiring continued overtime work of the factory force.

There is not a cannery in Pittsburgh of which this is not true. It is difficult to say how much effort is actually made to secure extra hands when needed. Neighborhood women available for such irregular and impermanent employment are few. Those who need to earn a living wish steady jobs. For the others, the cannery does not offer money enough to induce them to leave their housework. It would seem, however, that more successful efforts might be made to reach the girls in other seasonal occupations who are laid off in summer, and that the system of transferring workers from one department to another might perhaps be developed further.

It is worth noting that in the bottling room there is almost no overtime. Whenever possible, the girls are sent home not later than six p. m. To a less extent, this is true of the hand labelers, but when we get to the more mechanical processes, such as machine tending or the stemming and paring of vegetables and fruits, overtime is ordered by the management without hesitation. The managers in this industry do not say, like makers of stogies and confectionery, that overtime is simply a loss because the girls do poorer work the next day, and that if it were not for the unregulated demand of local dealers, the trade would be glad to get along without ever working over hours. Stogies and confectionery are lines in which the appearance of the finished product depends on the alertness of the employes. This is so far recognized that the managers regard overtime as a regrettable necessity. Similarly, in bottling pickles, and some labeling, much of the appearance of the finished product depends on the worker. In these two departments in the canneries, overtime is rare. But preparation work, tending machinery, or filling cans, affects the appearance of the sales package only to a very limited degree. It can be done by women without training or experience, and by women who are already jaded by twelve-hour days behind them, and by a ten-hour day just passed. So far as the sale of the product goes, overtime in these departments makes no difference. The first concern of the management is to handle the raw material and the orders, with overtime if necessary, not to eliminate in some way the long weeks of night work in the fall.

The average tenure of position, both among skilled and unskilled workers in canneries, is less than two years. This instability and brief trade life is a result of two untoward factors in cannery work as it is carried on in Pittsburgh. Overtime admittedly involves danger to health and nervous strain. The other factor is that the pace of many workers is pitched high by a piece rate, or set to follow a machine with a gear which entails excessive strain. This pace setting runs like a black line through many industries.

THE CANNING OF MOLASSES

With the other canneries should be grouped a special factory where molasses is tinned. Pittsburgh's location at the headwaters of the Ohio, which reaches down to the canefields of the South, may account for its development; for with its sixty employes, forty of whom were girls, it was in 1907 one of the largest factories of its kind in the world. Girls are employed for everything in connection with the canning of molasses, from cutting the tin to putting tops on the filled cans. The women who fill the cans work, four at a machine, in a dark room, where floor and walls, machines and girls, are sticky with the exudations of syrup, and a visitor can scarcely walk without being fastened like a fly to whatever spot he touches. The stickiness is of course in the very nature of the business. The room and the machines are cleaned once a week, but a far greater degree of comfort could be obtained, as in some of the sticky departments of the fruit canneries, by the constant service of a staff of attendants armed with boiling water and strong brushes.

Molasses comes in a continuous stream from the spout of the machine and spatters the girls as well as every exposed spot of floor or wall nearby. One girl pushes the cans under the spout, another takes them out and puts the tops on, a third clamps the top at another machine, and a fourth puts the can on a chain which takes it to the labeling table. The machine which puts the tops on the cans is difficult to adjust, yet if it is a sixteenth of an inch out of gear, the molasses splashes all over the girls and the floors. Two girls in another part of the room sterilize and label the cans by hand.

On the floor above, there are twenty girls who cut the tin and solder sides of cans. Soldering is done by hand, each girl having an assistant who puts the tin on the iron, takes it off and replaces it instantly with another. The solderer simply goes over the side seam with the iron. On the same floor other girls run a machine which presses screw tops into screw-top cans. This operation is similar to that of clamping into place the tops of cans which have been filled. The four soldering girls are considered the most skilled and earn the best wages, from $8.50 to $10 a week. Most of the others, solderers' assistants and employes at machines, earn $4.00, $5.00, or in a few cases $6.00. Hours of work are ten daily with half an hour for rest at noon.

The girls employed at the disagreeable work of filling cans are Slavic, and the girls at the relatively clean work on the upper floor, German or American—a typical circumstance in this small compact factory, which will be found repeated over and over again in the broad groupings of nationalities and occupations in the other industries of Pittsburgh.

CHAPTER III

CONFECTIONERY FACTORIES

VERY small people, from Kate Greenaway's time to Miss Daskam's, have thought of candy only as a beautiful confection to be sucked at in supreme disconcern. Grown-ups, of more serious bent, have put forth much critical writing on the subject of candy making, but almost invariably from the standpoint of the consumer. We have been informed of dirty workrooms, of candy dippers with sores on their hands, of glucose and paraffin and aniline dyes. From this point of view, the confectionery trade acquires an interest painfully acute. What touches our digestion, concerns us nearly. Yet there is a third point of view with regard to the trade, no less significant. I have nothing to add about adulteration of materials, and shall say very little about the uncleanliness of workrooms, but much of candy making as a trade from the standpoint of the girls who are working at it, and whose occupations are in wider variety within the limits of the city of Pittsburgh, than even the lively imaginations of small people with a liking for sweets would consider possible.

Among the seventeen candy factories in Pittsburgh some firms deal only in hard candy, others incline to salted peanuts and prize bags, and a majority manufacture the classic caramel, chocolates, and creams. The number of employes ranges from two to 400, only four exceeding the hundred mark on their payrolls. Of 1240 people engaged in the trade in 1907, 372 were men and 868 were women.*

TYPES OF FACTORIES AND KINDS OF WORK

The types of building are various. Here is a single, roomy workroom above a retail store, there a little shed where Polish

* If the chewing gum factory be included in this enumeration, the number of men in the trade is 374 and the number of women 966.

44

girls prepare cheap goods for some of the foreign shops; here a dingy third floor of a factory building, and there a square brick structure built for the sole purpose of candy making. With the exception of two small workrooms in the East End and three medium-sized plants on the North Side, most of the factories are located in the old business section of the city near the low ground where the two rivers meet. Narrow streets radiate out from "the Point," narrow buildings seek a few square feet of frontage, narrow workrooms grasp at uncertain daylight from windows at either end, and even these windows, meagre as they would be for purposes of ventilation, are kept closed. Candy as a food product must be protected from the smoke which makes the city picturesque to a non-resident. Yet the means adopted to protect the product from outside impurities involves serious harm to the workers. The atmosphere indoors is cloudy from boiling kettles and cooling candies; the need for fresh air is urgent. Some of the small workrooms are well kept and well aired, it is true, but the type of room most in evidence is steamy, dark, and narrow, with windows tight closed.

One plant which illustrates several kinds of manufacture is in a five-story brick building not far from the freight yards. A small jobbing and retail selling business is carried on on the first floor, above are stock and warerooms, and on the fourth and fifth floors the actual manufacturing is done, generally by six men and fifteen girls, but with the number of girls increased in the rush season to eighteen or twenty. There is a roar of trains and a puffing of black smoke outside the windows at either end of the long room; inside, there are steaming copper kettles, white-aproned men who pass back and forth, and the quick, silent movements of a tableful of girls, dipping chocolates, wrapping and packing, or filling prize bags. It has long been declared that men make the best cooks. In recurring instances, when cooking is for a critical public, and not for an indulgent home, some rule of survival selects the undomestic sex to do the work. The whole-sale making of candy is no exception. Men are the cooks, the makers. In this factory, on the fourth floor, they preside over the open furnaces where the chocolate is melted and the caramel is prepared; they bake the peanuts; they have entire charge of the hard candy making, with all its wonderful possible variations of peppermint canes, round kisses with red stars in the middle, suckers and chips in green, white, and red. With the poster artist's eye for color, they lift the great, white vanilla slabs, and cut them into fives; knead the translucent wintergreen into a ship's anchor, set the vanilla slabs pillarlike about it, and bind the gay sweetmeat with a ring of crimson. Then comes the pull, the quick cuts of the knife, and, strange to behold, the huge pink anchor is transformed into a thousand little anchors, each with its five-pointed white star and its crimson ring. A ship's feast is made from the contents of one kettle. All this the men do. The girls wrap candies and dip chocolates at the other end of the room.

The wrappers twine waxed paper about the peppermint canes, and twist the peanut kisses with a little rosette at each end. There are nine girls to handle the output of three furnaces; they work here by the week, because the kinds of candy change so frequently that at piece rates they would not be able to make anything. Half of them were laid off in February, but in March the sudden popularity of peanut kisses brought in so many orders that the wrappers had to work overtime every night for three weeks.

Separated by piles of boxes and cases of stock are six chocolate dippers, two of them experts. Their work is more nearly a trade than that of the other girls, and they are respected accordingly. As one woman said to me, who had been employed at teaching new girls in factories from Boston to Denver, "You can't just teach a dipper. A girl's got to have a natural talent for it, or she'll never succeed. It's like millinery, an art that you're born with." The girls sit at a table with pans of the hot melted stuff in front of them. Each girl has a mixing board, and beside her a square of waxed paper, indicating where the chips are to be put, and how many each paper is to hold. Taking the chip in her left hand, she dips first the top and then the bottom in the chocolate, and with her right hand puts it on the waxed paper and finishes by a ridge or other decoration. She is paid by the hundred pounds. The packer takes the waxed sheets of chips from the table, and puts up the candy in half-pound boxes, crediting each dipper with her amount, at $ .01½ a pound. The two expert dippers can usually turn out 100 pounds a day, which means a total pay of $9.00 a week. The visitor carries away a picture of a little workroom shut in by rough boards and sooty walls; of deep pans emptied and refilled; of squares and squares of tempting brown chips arranged by the packer; and of chocolate cooling and reheated, stirred, kept in motion and at the right temperature by the vigilant right hand of each girl at her place.

Upstairs two girls fill prize bags, ugly little paper packets which retail for a cent apiece and contain four or five peanuts, two pieces of cheap candy, and a prize—a tin cockade, a two-inch American flag, or a wooden whistle. For children of country towns where life holds few possibilities of excitement, the prize bag is a wonderland. Wishfulness for happenings such as are not put down on the routine calendar of one's daily life, the reckless gambling instinct that expends a penny for one knows not what—all this idealistic pursuit of the unknown is gratified by the mottled little bag on the candy counter of the country store. And the girls who pack the bags? They stand at a table with boxes before them, from which they take peanuts, candy, and prizes with quick automatic motion. They turn down the two corners of each bag, and string the bags when full in long bulky curls of seventy-two. The pay is $ .04 a hundred, and the faster of the two girls turns out 3000 a day. With ten hours' work, that means 300 an hour or five a minute. At that rate, when work is steady, she can earn $7.50 a week.

One of the large Pittsburgh firms recently put up a new building which illustrates some of the best features of factory construction, demonstrating anew that whereas a small concern is apt to cling to a close economy to the detriment of both employes and goods, a large concern, with industrial imagination, can house both on lines dictated by far-sighted economy, which is after all synonymous with the best conditions. Built square on a large lot, facing toward the river and with windows on four sides, with high ceilings and large light rooms, this plant makes comfort possible even on a hot day.

Cleanliness in candy factories is recognized as axiomatic. The guilty unscrubbed factory is likely to close its doors to visitors. But sufficient air, pure air, circulation of air, are essentials to health which are not axiomatic, and the absence of which is met with at every hand. A minimum air space in cubic feet means little when the air is vitiated and unchanged from day to day. Even this minimum is not always enforced in the candy factories. There is reason for congratulation then, when good and sufficient air is found voluntarily provided, as in the case of this factory whose square rooms with long rows of windows and high white ceilings give breathing space even when there are 100 girls in the room. In the dipping department the air is changed at frequent intervals and artificially cooled to about 60 degrees, so that the chocolate will be kept at the right heat. Upstairs in the hard candy department cold water runs under marble slabs on which the candy cools. This quickens the cooling process and lessens the workers' discomfort. The emphasis is on quality of output, and a spirit of consideration runs through the relations of the firm with its employes. There are neither fines nor bad work, nor rate cutting if "the girls make too much." Instead, the rates are in many cases a little better than those of the other factories, the attitude of the managers is a little more liberal, and the result is the retention of the best candy makers in the Pittsburgh trade.

WAGES AND OCCUPATIONS OF GIRLS

In taking up the range of wages in the candy factories, the table on page 49 showing what work falls to the girls in the different plants, will afford a basis for discussion.

The first thing that stands out in this summary is that 473, or nearly half the girls in the trade, are engaged in wrapping, labeling, and packing. Many of the packers are entirely unskilled. Some by long practice have acquired that speed and accuracy which is a high degree of dexterity. In one factory, where work is done for local stores, a few packers earn more than dippers, but their work is to put up fancy boxes, selecting from the different kinds of stock, and combining sizes and colors. Even here the planning of the boxes is not left to their judgment, but pattern styles are given them to follow. The bulk of the output from Pittsburgh factories is not candy of the highest grade, and a majority of the packers merely wrap in tin-foil or waxed paper.

TABLE 3.—NUMBER OF MEN AND WOMEN AND OCCUPATIONS OF WOMEN EMPLOYED IN CANDY FACTORIES

No. of plant	No. of Men	No. of Women	Occupations of Women			
			Wrappers, Packers and Labelers	Cream Dippers	Chocolate Dippers	Miscellaneous
1	3	6	3	..	..	3 *
2	2	6	4	..	..	2 †
3	3	10	3	..	7	..
4	35	75	75	..	..	..
5	1	10	5	2	3	..
6	4	18	6	6	6	..
7	100	15	15	..	..	..
8	1	2	..	..	1	1 ‡
9	10	89	59	..	30	..
10	6	15	11	..	4	..
11	2	10	8	..	2	..
12	35	20	20	..	..	..
13	9	31	13	4	14	..
14	100	300	100	50	103	47
15	10	60	50	..	10	..
16	1	1	1	..	..	..
17	50	200	100	25	75	..
Total §	372	868	473	87	255	53

* Hard candy Department.
† Cooking Candy.
‡ Salting nuts.
§ Total, 374 men and 966 women if chewing gum factory is included.

As packing demands speed and not judgment or skill, it is not as a rule highly paid. Sometimes all are paid a flat rate of $5.00. The minimum runs from $2.50 to $4.00, and in one case to $5.00. In six factories, three-fourths of the packers do not earn over $5.00, and in two factories $6.00 is the highest amount ever paid to a packer. Wages vary considerably, however, according to the dexterity of the hands. For instance, in one factory, all the girls are packers. Seventy-five of them work in a bleak, square room fronting on an alley; the light shut off by high buildings set back from the street beyond, the walls dirty, and the floors unswept. They sit at a long table, working at a nervous pace. The piece rate is $ .01 a pound for kisses and

$ .01¼ for caramels, the number of candies per pound varying with the different kinds. One caramel runs 60 to the pound, and at this work the best of the wrappers reached a maximum of 150 pounds in ten hours, that is, 9000 caramels a day, with a pay of $1.87. Others in the same department cannot wrap more than fifteen pounds a day. The superintendent states that an industrious worker ought to be able to make $6.00 a week. In general, $7.00 is the maximum for all packers except forewomen.

What is true of packers is true of the miscellaneous hands. Many of these are transferred to the packing department for seasonal work. Before Easter, packers are set at tinting rabbits or filling the centres of nuts, and in December these unclassified workers are set to wrapping and packing. Some of them during the rest of the year salt nuts; two Polish girls cook candy. Others spend most of their time thrusting little wooden sticks into penny suckers. These latter are paid by the box; in each box are 72 rows with 12 suckers to a row, that is, a total of 864 candies into which handle-sticks are to be forced while the candies are still soft. The girls are paid $ .03 a box. They could finish twenty-five boxes a day, the manager estimates, if they kept at the one task, but they are usually transferred to some other piece of work before they have a chance to develop speed.

The wage basis for both the packers and the miscellaneous hands is on the whole the same, and that same is extremely low. Of the 526 girls in the two departments, only twenty-one are earning $7.00 a week; the majority earn from $4.00 to $5.00. Among the dippers, however, we may expect to find a different situation.* Here we have seen that real skill is needed, or if not skill, a knack that everyone does not possess. Sometimes a girl can learn to dip in two weeks; again, it will take six months, and there are some who never learn. The chocolate curls, hearts, and bands on top of creams are marks of hand-dipped work, and it is the pride of a good dipper to make exact decorations on piece after piece, gauging each time the right amount of chocolate. She must be able, too, to gauge the temperature both of chocolate and of creams and to estimate the quality. Creams must be dipped

* For range of wages in different occupations, see Appendix B, p. 384, Table 38.

immediately or they will grow stale, but after dipping they mellow by keeping. If the cream is too cool when dipped, the butter in the chocolate hardens and it will not dry properly; the dipper must understand this to prevent waste and arrange for to be reheated. If the chocolate itself is either too hot or too cold, it cannot be used, and if when dipped, one hot streak be left on the outside of the chocolate, it will not dry and the piece will be worthless. The dipper must keep adding hot chocolate to her board from the steam-heated pan on the table to keep it at the right working temperature; moreover, she must see to it that the air in the workroom is dry, or the chocolate will be sticky and cannot be worked easily. The cold-air system which has been spoken of in connection with one Pittsburgh factory does this for her, but in the other plants the responsibility is on the dippers themselves to keep their windows closed most of the time.

The tendency in Pittsburgh seems to be for most of the girls to dip by hand rather than with a fork. Ordinarily a certain amount of chocolate is supposed to cover a given number of creams, and a fork dipper is apt to use too much chocolate. Almonds and some other small work of the same kind are still fork dipped. Four factories have dipping machines. Two girls place the white centers on a continuous belt, like pawns on a running chess board, and as they pass under the glass screen of the machine, these whites are drenched by a stream of liquid chocolate until they finally emerge in hostile livery, to be straightened and set to rights by a girl at the other end. Here the machine has proved itself. It saves time and labor, it does its work accurately and cheaply; 46 girls who tend dipping machines turn out nearly all the smooth work made in Pittsburgh. The growth of machine work, however, does not seem to threaten the hand dippers' trade. Even very cheap wafers have a ridge across the centre which is put on by hand, and this is true of the great majority of chocolates sold, except "penny creams."

The dipping of creams in cream is an occupation distinct from chocolate dipping. There are only 87 cream dippers in Pittsburgh, although two large factories and three small ones have a department where this work is done. The cream is thicker to handle than chocolate. Chocolate dippers can usually work in cream without much difficulty; but a cream dipper who attempts to work with chocolate has to learn over again. The earnings in either case are about the same.

We should expect, in work which demands some skill, like cream or chocolate dipping, and which demands invariably both deftness of touch, not possessed by every one, and sureness of judgment as to temperature and quality of material, that the rates of pay would be high enough to attract girls abler than the majority of operatives in factories. What is the case? There are 342 dippers. In six factories they are paid by the week, and in three by the piece, while two factories have both systems in use. Where week wages are paid, we find head girls earning a maximum of $9.00 a week; in three cases the maximum wage is $7.00, and in one case a flat rate of $7.00 is paid to all hands. One employer pays his two best girls $6.50 a week and the other ten girls sums ranging from $3.00 to $5.00. Another factory which employs 30 dippers pays 24 of its girls $5.50.

With piece payments the case is no different. Almond dipping is paid at the rate of $ .01½ a pound in some factories, $ .03 a pound in one. The rate for pecans is $ .04 and for creams $ .01 to $ .05. Marshmallows, which are very light, are paid for, not by weight, but by time. The number of dippers who can earn over $7.00 a week is small, as the girls are held responsible for bad work, and output at high speed one week is likely to mean a slackening of pace the next. Possibly this is because only a small proportion of those who come into the trade have the "natural talent" for it which seems necessary. The woman quoted before, a teacher of dippers in a chain of factories, now herself an employer, told me that not more than 2 per cent of the learners become really expert enough to earn $10 or even $9.00 a week in the piece-work factories. The other 98 per cent either remain at low wages or change to some other occupation. In Pittsburgh I found that 112, or one-third of all the dippers, earned wages of $6.00 and under a week. One hundred eighty-eight of them earned $7.00, and 66, or less than one-fifth, earned weekly wages of from $7.00 to $9.00.

HOURS AND OVERTIME

The hours of work in candy factories vary with the seasons. During three-fourths of the year twelve of the seventeen factories in Pittsburgh have a ten-hour day and five have a nine and a half-hour day. December overtime is universal. It comes about very simply. The holly-trimmed box carries Christmas good-will with a natural readiness. It has a spontaneous holiday air that suggests "best wishes," and it sometimes seems the only solution to a puzzled purchaser whose gift-giving imagination has failed. In spite of the wide varieties in possible gifts, candies continue to hold their popularity. Retail dealers, zealous to be well supplied, order two or three times as large a stock as during the rest of the year. Wholesalers, eager to meet the retail demand, increase on the volume of these orders in sending to the factories. The factories meet the situation as best they can. For much of the work, especially for dipping, they cannot use untrained hands; the number of experienced hands is limited; and, therefore, to fill orders on time, the trained employes work often unlimited hours at night in December. In half of the factories there is in addition frequent night work from September until the first of the year.

One manager told me, with a twinkle in his eye, that his girls worked 75 hours a week for two months every year, and that in a neighboring factory they worked 80 hours a week; "but," he said, "the inspectors don't interfere with us. They usually come around in September and then again after the holidays and they never see any overtime. This year I guess somebody had stirred them up and they came later, not till the first of November, but they didn't *see* us working at night and nothing was said. I don't think they mean to interfere with factories where the other conditions are good. They know it's a business matter with us and that we don't like it any better than they do." The girls in one workroom which supplies a well-known caterer have been kept nearly all night just before the holidays, and a little factory in the Polish district on Penn Avenue keeps open at night for four months in order to assist its neighbors in a proper celebration of Christmas. Overtime

53

is found to the greatest extent in the chocolate and cream-dipping departments, and among the packers of all fancy makes of candy. Hard candy making does not require overtime for the girls who work at it. For example, one firm has found it practicable to confine all overtime to the men employes. The men do the making, boiling, squaring, coloring, cutting, and packing in pails. The girls merely pack the peanut bars in boxes, and by a little rearrangement of work they can keep up to the men's output without staying later than six o'clock at night.

There is not a manufacturer in the trade but will admit that overtime is a bad thing. It is no longer questioned that long hours mean inferior work the next day, and that the Christmas trade, upon which the prosperity of the industry so largely depends, means a long pull and a physical strain not to be counterbalanced by extra pay and easier work afterward. The gratuitous overtime which once existed—a redoubling of efforts toward increased production, a speculation almost, taking at the flood the public's impulse to buy—is no longer found among the candy manufacturers in Pittsburgh. On the contrary, managers are alive to the fact that this seasonal rush must, as far as possible, be diminished. There would seem to be two ways of meeting the situation: one of them suggests itself naturally from the experience of other trades. Salesmen in many lines of Christmas specialties arrange with local dealers for Christmas orders during the early part of the year. This has not been done in the candy industry, in part because of inertia, and in part because the goods are perishable. Were Pennsylvania's prohibition of overtime for women less flexible, and were factories in consequence unable to meet late-coming orders on time, such an arrangement and re-distribution of orders would clearly be necessary. At the present time, instead of ordering their Christmas goods six months to a year ahead, retailers have a panic as fall wears on lest they shall not have a large enough stock on hand. They order too much at the last moment, and then during January and February send in no orders at all. The factories, unable to plan ahead, are congested by the rush of incoming orders.

This congestion of work, however, cannot be avoided by a redistribution of orders alone. A second solution lies in carrying to a further point methods of handling materials, which are already familiar to the technical men in the industry. By further studies of the keeping qualities of candy it is not impossible that much candy made in the spring can be used for the fall trade. To a certain extent this is already done in the case of chocolates. A good chocolate mellows by keeping and has a better taste six months after it is made than the day after. The cream inside is protected from the air, and so remains in good condition. If orders are but given in advance, experienced candy makers hold that it will in time be entirely possible to make up in the spring chocolates for the Christmas trade.

Creams present a different problem, for no way has yet been found by which they can be kept any length of time without deterioration. The trade in them is lighter than the trade in chocolates, and could possibly be handled in the fall without inconvenience if the other goods were largely made up in the spring. The situation is at least hopeful enough to warrant the belief that there is no intrinsic need for an interminable succession of years with overtime work, wearing out the strength of one group of working girls after another.

THE SLACK SEASON

The obverse side of the fall rush is the summer depression. In January and February there is a slack season in the hard-candy trade, but in most of the factories the dull time comes during the warm months, beginning sometimes in May and lasting well through August. There are several reasons for this. People do not eat quantities of chocolate in summer. The same impulse which sends them to a candy store when it is cool, sends them to a soda fountain when it is warm, and if they do buy candy, it is of the less substantial and less perishable kind. Further, it is difficult in summer to induce either chocolates or creams to harden properly. Manufacturing is confined to filling daily orders. One factory keeps its dippers to make up stock for the winter, but in most factories the girls are laid off in large numbers.

This long slack season brings up questions of wages. Is a candy maker's skill so slight that the girl will fit readily into some other equally unskilled occupation when the dull season comes? And does the dull season come at a time when other trades are busy? Or, if the opportunity for subsidiary occupation is small, are the wages received during the year sufficient to carry a wrapper or dipper through a possible two months of unemployment?

We need not touch on the girls in the packing departments, because very evidently they are a less dexterous and less characteristic element in the trade. But the dippers have a specialized dexterity which does not fit them to enter other occupations, such as canneries, on an equal level. Furthermore, their dull season comes at a time when most other trades are also dull. Some few find employment selling candy in the parks or at places of amusement near the city; the majority have to count most of the summer as lost time.

This relation of wages to the slack season becomes acute in view of the proportion of girls in the trade who are obliged to be self-supporting. In the smaller factories the girls come from homes in the neighborhood, but a majority of the girls in the larger plants come from towns nearby to learn the trade, and are paying board in the city. For instance, one forewoman who directs about 100 chocolate dippers states that most of them are from homes outside of Pittsburgh, and that at least a third board with strangers. Yet less than one-fourth of the dippers (one-thirteenth of all the women in the trade) are earning wages that give them even a slight margin over living expenses. Even if we were to suppose that this slight margin is sufficient to carry a girl who is laid off through her season of unemployment, we could scarcely take it for granted that it is the more fortunate or able girl who is laid off. On the contrary, when forces are reduced, it is the girls with less ability, less accuracy, and a smaller output per day who go. It is the $7.00 girls, and the girls whose earnings are below $7.00. In part, of course, the girls return to their homes, and their families bear the loss due to seasonal unemployment. But in part the cost, in undernutrition, in unsocial employment, is borne, as ultimately every individual human loss is borne, by the community of which the chocolate dippers are a part.

Despite slack seasons and Christmas rush the trade is a

popular one among working girls. It attracts girls of good appearance, of quiet ways, usually of good physical development. In the first place, it has a reputation among the girls for healthfulness. Windows are closed, it is true, and this is undesirable, but there is no dust about the work, and a majority of the rooms are clean and well scrubbed. Perhaps the very handling of sugar and the eating of it help to make so many of the girls plump and round-armed. The desire to make so pleasurable a thing as candy plays its part. In choosing factory work (supposing a girl does not choose whatever happens to be next door or across the street), she is more likely to think well of a place where interesting things to eat are cooked, than of places in which impersonal things are made for a great unpersonified public. There is a third reason, which, I think, enters with the others, to select the type of girl found in these factories. That is the element of manual dexterity. In that there is a challenge, though often unacknowledged, to the girl who even by a generation's right can call herself American. She has a pride in doing the thing that the "Hunkies" without her four or five years in school are less apt to do. Here is an undeveloped germ-like sense of craftsmanship.

With the reputed healthfulness of candy making, the pleasure of it, and the challenge of a necessary slight degree of skill combining to draw into the trade a desirable class of girls, it is possible for wages to remain at a relatively low level. Such indeed is the case in the absence of effective demand on the part of the employes. Managers say that they have more applicants than positions, and that there is never a lack of girl apprentices. Once in a candy factory, the girls tend to stay. They do not marry until they are twenty-two or twenty-three years old, which is three or four years later than with a majority of unskilled factory operatives. The percentage of change from this trade to others and within the trade itself seems remarkably low. Some managers can point out girls who have been in their employ for eight or nine years. "Once a chocolate dipper, always a chocolate dipper," they say.

CHEWING GUM

A chewing-gum factory at the rim of the woods at the west end of town belongs logically in this chapter, although the work differs enough from candy to make a separate description necessary. A hundred employes work in a large, light building with square rooms and bright windows. Many of them come from the North Side, where the factory was formerly located, but a minority live nearby, in tiny weather-gray houses, along the unpaved roads, or farther in toward town, at the foot of the hill.

The making of chewing gum, like the making of candy, is done by men. Chickel comes in hard blocks, and has to be ground, pulverized, mixed with other things, and cooked in vacuum kettles, before it can be rolled thin and cut by the girls. A slab of gum, twelve inches square, is fed in and out under the rolls until it is as thin as the commercial piece of chewing gum. The cutting machine marks it into oblong pieces six inches by twelve, and a girl breaks it along the marks made by the machine. Next her, at a wooden table, sit four "breaking-off" girls, who gather up the narrow lengths of gum and break them crossways into pieces short enough to fit into the slot machines.

From here, the gum is taken to the packing girls. They sit at long tables working in pairs, the first girl covering each piece of gum with waxed paper and a printed outside wrapper; the second girl wrapping five sticks in a package, and putting five packages in a box. When this department is running full time there are 57 girls here, all of them piece workers. Some of them earn $7.00 a week, but the majority do not make more than $6.00.

On the second floor is the Chu-Chu department—a name given to a brand of popcorn that is put up in prize packages and sent out to the neighboring towns. Here the product suggests that of many candy factories, but the work is on a larger scale, and the machinery different. The Chu-Chu is put up first in a waxed cardboard package, which is afterward inserted in a colored card wrapper. One end of the wrapper is machine glued, and sent on a traveling chain past the girls who stand at benches close by. As the colored wrappers pass them the girls slip the waxed packages of popcorn into the conveyor, which takes the packages through the machine a second time, to be glued at the other end. There are 35 girls here. One little girl explained to me with much detail what she did with every box. She put the prize in, picked up a tiny strip stating what the prize was, pasted the strip on the box, put the waxed paper on, and ironed the waxed paper smooth. She was paid $ .03 for twenty boxes, and "though I just sweated at that work," she said, "I couldn't make more than $ .30 a day." This is, of course, extreme, for most of the girls creep up to $5.00 and some to $6.00 after they have had enough experience to gain speed.

Summer is the harvest time for this factory, and in the very months when the candy factories are laying off their hands, the chewing-gum and popcorn packers are working at night to supply the demand from circuses and pleasure parks and shows.

CHAPTER IV

THE CRACKER INDUSTRY

IT is a far cry from a pan of biscuits in a solitary kitchen to a seven-story factory, whence food-stuffs are shipped to all the United States. Individual bread baking is still with us, but individual cracker baking has become an anachronism. Gradually cracker bakeries have been combined into chains of factories under the National Biscuit Company, reaching from coast to coast, with careful arrangement for the making of this product here and that product there, and with large economy in labor, freight charges, and machinery. Co-existing with this chain of factories are local independent plants which send out goods within a radius of a hundred miles. Crackers in their numberless varieties are not only an occasional convenience to the housewife who still struggles with her cook stove, but a staple food to the host of roomers and lodgers who have drifted into the city to forge out a way of life.

A bewildering and irrepressible inventiveness characterizes the cracker-planning mind. Not only are we given more and more improved styles of the soda cracker, the ginger snap, and other friends honored by length of acquaintance; but we are given hitherto unimagined varieties of cracker-cakes, marshmallows and chocolates, grated nuts, and Scotch oatmeal cakes with an ancestry of flat stones behind them, but now, like their confrères, of the progeny of the oven. Even such changelings as cheese sandwiches have made their appearance among the rest. The trade list of products for a small factory makes a magazine-sized pamphlet with four pages of fine type, and for a large factory, the catalogue assumes the proportions of a small book.

Bread baking in Pittsburgh is done by men, but the cracker industry stands fifth in the employment of women. Of its 1810 employes in 1907, 928, a little more than half,

60

were women.* There are five factories. One little four-story plant has stood looking out at the river for twenty years; it does much of its work by hand now, as it did in the beginning, and employs 25 women and 13 men. A huge seven-story loft building has been rearranged and forcibly adjusted to turning out every variety of oven product, at the hands of 1100 employes. A more modest but newer five-story building boasts a force of 175. In these three plants are stratified, as it were, the different stages in the growth of the industry and in its adaptations of factory construction.

Less than ten men mix the dough for all this output. They know the formulæ and the secret combinations on which every manufacturer builds his faith in his business success; they are the only skilled workers in the plant. In one factory they are paid from $75 to $100 a month. In the very largest plant there are only three of them; in others, two or one. Men are employed also to tend the ovens, to work in storerooms and shipping departments, to polish cans, and to carry the heavy trays of dough.

The women's work is to tend the cracker machines, to pack, to ice the cakes, and to mend cans. They are kept as a rule in one department, not because this is a trade which they have learned, but because the attainment of maximum speed requires physical and mental concentration on doing one thing, the repetition of one operation a thousand times in a day, ten thousand times in a week, and that over and over again from month to month. A girl is given a job in a cracker factory, and in an hour's teaching may be able to do the thing as she is told; but it will be a week, perhaps a month, before she can do the same thing as many times in a day as the experienced girl who was there before her. Her muscles have to be taught to keep pace with the machine. Her senses have to grow accustomed to the smell of the dough if she works near the ovens, to the heat of the cooling crackers if she is a packer, and to the sight of the chains constantly traveling beneath her eyes. For the most part, the work is done standing and at high speed. New girls come and go. Seldom do they acquire individuality in the eyes of their employers; they work in numbers too large, and at operations too me-

*See Appendix B, p. 385, Table 39.

chanical, for that. Where they come from or where they go to the men who deal with them do not know. They may drift to the mangle rooms of laundries, or to some of the screw and bolt works, or to packing other kinds of food-stuffs in canneries or candy factories. They have the speed equipment to do any of these things, but they will not be found in lines of work that require judgment, skill, or a strong physique.

The cracker factory girl is of different type, both in nationality and age, from the girl in the candy factory. Seven out of nine girls in the trade are foreign born; some few are Italians, but most of them Poles. Race prejudice is strong, and the knowledge that the "Hunkies" are in a trade is often enough to keep native-born girls away. In the packing room and the icing room the work is of such a nature that girls as young as fourteen years can be used, and, in consequence, it is a possible first employment for a child who has just secured her working papers. As such, it is to her mind and to her mother's less a permanent calling than a two or three years' interlude, during which experience is gained, and a small addition made to the family wage.

TYPES OF FACTORIES AND KINDS OF WORK

The primitive factory offers an introduction to the industry. Here the icing girls have no machine with which to keep pace. They work by hand, placing round crackers under a hole in a board a quarter of an inch thick. With a scraper they brush icing over the hole, so that the cracker is decorated symmetrically. On square cakes, the girls spread the icing with their fingers, using no tools at all, but proceeding with their work in a reflective and leisurely manner as if no such things as machines and a minimum output had ever been known in the world. On the floor below, in the cracker-making department, there is the same absence of haste. A woman here for twenty years has done nothing but lift the great heavy masses of dough from the tray to the squeezer of the cracker-making rolls that flatten and stamp them. Two other girls brush flour over the dough, and keep the raw crackers straight on the trays. In the same room there are fifteen girls packing. They have no conveyor, no traveling chain of boxes with which to keep pace, and although they work quickly, they work without overstrain.

In the wareroom there are girls, too, doing such work as in other factories is done only by men. They fill the orders that come in, lifting the heavy boxes of crackers, and packing them in crates, lifting the great square crates on trucks, and putting them on the freight elevator to be taken down to the drivers. The three girls here are pale and anemic, with an older look than the rest. They earn $7.00 a week. I talked with one of them as she took me through the factory. She had been working there twenty years and had never worked anywhere else. I asked her if she thought the work unhealthful, and she said, "Oh, I don't know as it is, but it's tiresome. I always think I'd never work in a cracker factory again if I had to start over. Yet the girls has it easy now. We used to work until seven-thirty every night, and often until nine, without any extra pay, but now the girls get out at five-thirty, and when they work at night until nine they get paid extra. They don't get paid by the piece either, but by the week, and they don't have to work nearly so hard."

In three other of the Pittsburgh cracker factories employes are paid by the week, but in the largest, where 450 girls are employed, almost half of all in the trade in Pittsburgh, the piece system is in use. This largest factory, one of the chain in different cities, illustrates a different type. An old building has been made over to house it. Large and square as it is, with narrow frame stairways and a single fire-escape along the side, its interior construction and few exits suggest constant danger for the thousand employes, half of whom are on the upper floors.

By starting at the top floor of the factory we shall get the clearest idea of the arrangement of departments. On the seventh floor are the cracker ovens. Here the dough is mixed by huge metal blades, shaped like the wings of a windmill. It is rolled, cut into thin sheets, and fed into the cracker-making machine, which stretches almost from end to end of the room. The first roller flattens the dough and stamps on it a pattern; the second roller is simply a brush roller, which shakes on flour and prevents the raw sheet from sticking to the metal; the third marks the dough with the lines into which it is to be broken for separate crackers.   At the second roller sits a girl whose duty it is to brush on the flour.   The motion of her arm is quick and incessant, as following the moving line of dough she keeps the rolls dry and flour-filled.   At the end of the machine the crackers are slipped onto trays to be taken by oven boys, who, with their flannel shirts thrown open, pass back and forth in the intense heat carrying the trays.   On either side of the machine at this end are two other girls.   They straighten the crackers and throw the scrappy, unformed edges of the dough into a tin to be fed with fresh dough into the funnel at the other end of the room.   Their workplace is not six feet from the ovens.   The men say that not many of the girls can stand the work for long.   In the excessive heat, with the smell of the dough, they must stare at the trays which pass slowly, continuously, beneath their eyes.   They become light-headed and ill.   I saw one who had been in the place three years.   She was white, with a faint look about her mouth, but the clerk said that she stood the work well.   She was an Italian, and they had advanced her to $5.00 a week, "for it's worth while to keep a girl who really stands the work when once you get her."

Directly below the cracker ovens, on the sixth floor, crackers are packed and fancy cakes are made.   The factory has a small trade in special orders, such as pies, crullers, or wedding cake, which are made by hand.   Fifteen of the 20 girls in this department are scullery hands, busied at cutting apples, washing pans, or sugaring crullers, but the others have the more important task of icing and decorating the fancy cakes.   These hand cake-makers and other "specials" hold their positions insecurely.   Trade is variable; they stand in constant likelihood of being laid off through the year, and are certain of unemployment in July and August.

On the same floor, in another room, there are 200 packers.   These are piece workers, folding and filling boxes of soda biscuit and other crackers at high speed.   The boxes pass on a narrow traveling chain which runs parallel to a second conveyor, on which the crackers come from the floor above.   The girls stationed at the conveyor gather handfuls of crackers and fill the boxes as they pass rapidly by; further down the room other girls wrap the sides and still others the ends. The pace of each worker is pitched to the highest point. I noticed especially one small girl with flushed cheeks and white lips who was folding the ends of soda cracker boxes and putting on each end a red stamp. She earned $ .01 a dozen, and if she could make a hundred dozen a day, she would get $ .10 bonus, altogether $1.10. Her teeth were set, and her breath came hard, like that of an overspent runner at the end of a race; yet it was only ten o'clock in the morning. Her arms moved irregularly, jerkily, as if she were spurring her nervous energy to its limit. The office boy who was standing near watching her, said casually, "She's lucky if she makes her bonus. I was in this department a while ago and I seen these girls get so tired their arms was ready to drop off at night but they wouldn't make no hundred boxes." Yet she was not an exception. The others were working at top speed and many, like her, were forcing themselves to keep to it.

In the icing room on the fifth floor, where the fancy crackers are made, the machinery does most of the work. Continuous chains pass from floor to ceiling, across the room, then down to the floor again and across. Carried along each chain at intervals of a few inches are wire trays, each with a series of spikes on which cakes are so fastened that they come in contact with nothing, and have an opportunity to become dry on all sides. The icing is made and measured by a man at the far end of the floor, and there is a uniform process of dipping which the girls follow without the need of using much judgment of their own. As the chain passes, the girls at the starting point lift off the trays and dip them, with one motion covering all the cakes. I was told that the girls here are considered the most skilled in the factory, because they have to know how many times to dip the various kinds of cakes; they are paid not more than $6.00 a week, and most of them not more than $5.00. In the next room are more girls packing like those on the floor above, and adjoining is a room where old tins sent back by customers are repaired. Damage to a can is usually charged to the customer. The company repairs a can, puts in new glass, repaints and polishes, before sending it out for use again. This room is noisy with the rattling of tin, and now and then with the crash of broken glass as the old pieces are thrown away and new pieces slipped into place. Some of the girls simply paste on labels and freshen rough edges, but most of them work on the tins themselves. All the buffing is done by boys in another part of the room.

Below this floor are more machines and more packing, and on the third floor are the bread ovens where only men are employed. But the heat from these ovens affects not only them but the hundreds of girls on the floors above, where the work, at best, is done in a high temperature and under the double pressure of a piece-rate system and pace setting by a machine. Here, then, in broad lines, is a striking contrast to the old-time, primitive cracker bakery near the river.

Two other factories are housed much like this one; the fifth Pittsburgh factory is constructed on a different plan. Here there is the same division of work between men and women, but there are more American girls than Poles. On the sixth floor of the building, above not below the other departments, are the mixing department and all the ovens. A high ceiling, with open windows on three sides, even without forced ventilation affords good circulation of air. The ovens are of recent make, and the heat given off is less than that in the baking rooms elsewhere. A sweep of breeze from window to window makes work in this room tolerable, even to the people nearest the ovens. The height of the ceilings protects the workers on the lower floors from the heat; even on the floor directly below it is scarcely noticeable, and the ovens do not affect the temperature in other departments at all.

In the icing department on the fifth floor about 20 girls are employed. Some of them are at the icing trolleys, and others, marshmallow girls, squeeze liquid marshmallow out of cheesecloth bags. Still others sprinkle grated nuts on the marshmallow cakes as they pass. The girls in this department are shifted frequently from one sort of work to another, but the marshmallow girls are ordinarily kept at the job, for it takes at least a week to learn and sometimes a month or two. At the other end of the trolley there are girls to remove the cakes and pack them away in tins.

The cracker packing is on the fourth floor. From the ovens

the trays of crackers pass slowly on a conveyor through the two floors, and at the point where the conveyor dips into the packing room, moving horizontally across it, electric fans are set so that the crackers will be thoroughly cooled by the time they reach the girls. This has a two-fold effect, keeping the crackers in better condition after they are packed, and making the work of the packers less disagreeable. Each girl is supposed to lift from the passing trays a certain share of the crackers, so that by the time the conveyor has passed a given number of girls it will be entirely empty. Sometimes it is six months before a new girl has learned how to pack the different styles of crackers and to manage her share of the conveyor. There is a second conveyor in this room, which carries the filled boxes to the girls who wrap and label them. When the wrapper has covered a box, she replaces it and the conveyor carries it away to the shelves to be stacked.

Below the packing room there are two floors of storerooms and offices, and on the first floor, which is really a basement, a tin-can room where cans are labeled, stamped, and freshened.

IMPORTANCE OF THE BUILDING PLAN

As I have already pointed out, these three factories may be taken as three broad types of different phases in the development of the industry. It is in the old factory with limited equipment that women are doing heavy lifting in the order room and at the machines. It is there, too, that one gets the impression of leisure, and that cake-icing is carelessly done in an unsanitary way. The volume of trade is small; the manager is easy-going and makes little effort to increase it. There may be some slight advantage to the employes in an "easy-going boss," but though the packers do not work at high speed, they work in the same room with the baking ovens, in a deadly heat that is never stirred nor lifted by a breeze.

The huge building which the largest factory has adapted to its uses is crowded with machines and with workers, for maximum output from available space. When an oven was needed, an oven was put in wherever there was room, without reference to the number of employes working above it, and without regard for possible devices for deflecting some of the heat from the upper floors. When a new department was needed, a new department was introduced where there was room. The unvarying emphasis has been on the saving of space. There has been a meagre compliance with the orders of the factory inspection department in the erection of fire-escapes, and in some other primary demands of the law. Beyond this there is no standard save the one of output. Yet it can scarcely be other than costly economy to work 450 women and 200 men on floors above the bread ovens, where they must stand on scorching boards, unrelieved by currents of air between the low walls or by any system of forced ventilation to carry off the heat from above or below. It is an economy which is one cause of the instability of the women workers; it is certainly a cause both in men and in women of lowered vitality which can mean only industrial inefficiency and social unfitness.

That a better building plan is possible is evidenced by the fifth factory (see Table 4, "Standard"). Here the ovens are on the top floor with its open windows. The artificial cooling of the crackers results both to the advantage of the firm commercially and to the increased comfort of the packing girls. The building of the factory on large lines, with wide rooms and many windows, with high ceilings and ample space between floors, seems a partial recognition of the fact that for each industry must be worked out a special standard of ventilation and sanitation if it is to be adequate. The factory law specifies a volume of air space per person with the intent of assuring individual workers the quality of air necessary to health. This is a minimum. It may be sufficient in some trades; in other trades where the air becomes readily vitiated, it is far from sufficient. Conceivably, less air might be needed in the packing room of a candy factory than in the overheated packing room of a cracker factory. Only where the volume of air is sufficient for health is the intent of the law observed. This fifth factory has set a standard in observing the spirit of the law. It has shown that such a standard is commercially practicable.

How far the other Pittsburgh cracker factories are at variance with this standard will be clearer by a schedule which gives,

68

comparatively, the arrangement of departments. I have put first the factory which has been described as showing the best building plan:

TABLE 4.—ARRANGEMENT OF FLOORS IN CRACKER FACTORIES

Floors	Factory No. 5 "Standard"	Factory No. 1	Factory No. 2	Factory No. 3	Factory No. 4
7	..	..	..	..	Cracker ovens
6	Cracker ovens	..	..		Packing; fancy cakes
5	Icing dept.	..	Packing	Packing	Icing dept.
4	Packing	(Candy)	Ovens	Mixing; packing	Packing
3	Store-rooms	Icing	Packing	Ovens	Cracker ovens; bread ovens
2	Store-rooms; offices	Ovens	(Candy)	Icing dept.; offices	Warerooms
1	Tin-can room	Offices	Offices	Tin-can room.	Offices

The schedule does not show that in the four other factories the ceilings are low and the buildings overcrowded, that a few windows are made to do duty for a large room, and that forced ventilation is not provided. But the schedule does show a clear failure of these factories to meet the intent of the law, which is the conservation of health among workers.

HOURS, WAGES AND CONDITIONS OF WORK

As in other manufacturing industries in Pittsburgh, a ten-hour day is customary in cracker manufacture. For soda wafers and other crackers of the same order, the season of picnics makes unflagging demand, and packers the year round are steadily employed. The icing girls are sometimes kept on short time for a period of two months, and the girls on special work are likely to be laid off altogether, but aside from this the trade is steady. There is little seasonal overtime. Night work is resorted to to fill a rush order or to get out work when there is unusual demand. The mother of one girl told me indignantly that her daughter had to work three nights a week overtime during the month of July without any time off for supper; and that if she worked until exactly nine o'clock she received $ .25 extra, but if she stopped a few minutes before nine, she did not get any extra pay at all.

Rates of pay in specific instances have already been mentioned. There is no apparent distinction between departments, but a general flat rate of minimum, advanced, and maximum pay.* One firm starts all new hands at $3.50, and after a little advances them toward $5.00. Fifty of its 300 girls are considered experienced enough to be making the maximum pay, which is $5.50. No one, except a forewoman or two at $8.00, earns more than this. Factory number 5 pays a new hand $3.00 or $3.50 at the start, according to her size, and, "of course," said the superintendent, "we shouldn't think of starting a girl who was twenty years old, for instance, at less than $4.00." Packing and icing girls are advanced to $5.00, sometimes to $6.00. The head girl earns $7.00. These cases are representative of the rest. The highest pay of any of the regular hands is $7.00, and 700 of the 900 girls are earning weekly wages of $4.00 to $5.00, or $5.00 to $6.00. They are without opportunity for advancement or for developing any quality except speed.

The following table shows the distribution of work among women employes in the five factories:

TABLE 5.—DISTRIBUTION OF WORK AMONG WOMEN EMPLOYES IN CRACKER FACTORIES

No. of Plant	Packing	Icing	Tin-can Room	Cracker-making machines	Specials	Order Room
1	15	4	..	3	..	3
2	40	6	6	1	..	..
3	245	16	30	2	2	5
4	300	50	50	30	20	..
5	70	18	8	2	..	2
Total	670	94	94	38	22	10

So far as number of employes is concerned, packing is the important process in a cracker factory. Two-thirds of the women

* See Appendix B, page 385, Table 40.

are working at the traveling conveyors, rapidly lifting the hot crackers, and filling box after box to be shipped fresh from the ovens. Most of the icing girls' work is done while sitting and at a relatively even pace, under more pleasant conditions than those of the packers. It is the girls at the cracker machines, few though they are in number (only thirty-eight altogether), who stand out in the industry as deserving of most serious social concern. The ten hours that they spend close to the intolerable heat of the ovens is given over to work which demands neither judgment, skill, nor speed. Consider, by way of comparison, that in machine shops a lathe that bores in oil is supplied with the oil mechanically. If women were not available for work at the cracker machines, a way might be found to supply the flour for the brush roller mechanically, and to remove the scraps of dough and carry them to the funnel at the other end of the room. In other industries there are self-feeding machines and machines which adjust themselves to waste at the sides.

With respect to girl-saving machinery, as with respect to the lay-out of buildings, a little ingenuity and consideration for health have done much for the cracker industry, and would do far more were they given wider application.

THE STOGY INDUSTRY

SORTING AND PACKING STOGIES BY THE THOUSAND

CHAPTER V

THE STOGY INDUSTRY

THE explanation of the stogy industry is the workmen's demand for a cheap luxury, for the companionable dissipation of a "smoke." To clerk, mechanic and laborer, no less than to the business man, it is at once a source of complacent enjoyment and an occasion for fellowship. The aroma of the brown leaves is a symbol of the good things in the leisure hours of life. But to the tenement tobacco worker the stogy is grossly materialized. With the lessening of leisure hours, with the steady monotony of isolated work, it is reduced to lowest terms, an object of barter and sale.

Wheeling, where the stogy industry started, and Pittsburgh, where it shortly took root, are recognized as the two centres from which it has spread through many towns of West Virginia, Western Pennsylvania, and Ohio. The original stogy, or toby, was a long, loosely rolled cigar, made only of crumpled filler leaf and smooth, fine wrapper. The binder leaf was left out to lessen cost both in time and material, making it possible to sell the best stogy for from half to a third the price of the cheapest cigar. Changes in the trade have blurred this distinction. There are still many undoubted stogies on sale, but beside them in larger numbers are short filler "mold stogies," indistinguishable from cigars in size or shape. The district has given continuity to the name, and through all this section of the middle west, stogies of either brand still have a selling price which meets the needs of men who want a cheap smoke.

The industry gives an impression of complexity and varied development. Some of the skilled craftsmen, hand stogy makers, work systematically in large factories; others, in their little shops in the tenement districts, use a room or two for the entire process of manufacture, sometimes putting wives and children to work

75

at the preliminary stripping, sometimes exploiting a newly arrived compatriot until he learns wisdom and establishes a shop of his own. Of the women workers, some are craftsmen, too, but most of them are employed at subordinate occupations in the trade, such as rolling or bunching. Barely one in fifty of them is engaged in work demanding a high degree of skill. The women outnumber the men nearly three to one. Factories, sweatshops, home workshops, working in part at cross purposes and in part developing the industry along different lines—all these are of immediate interest to us, both as avenues of employment for more women than any other one factory trade in Pittsburgh, and as illustrations of varying industrial tendencies which are found in more than one American city.

There were in 1907, in what has become greater Pittsburgh (Pittsburgh and Allegheny), 32 stogy factories and 203 sweatshops,* a total of 235 work places. The sweatshops employed 400 women and 453 men; the factories, 2211 women and 463 men; 3527 workers in the trade as a whole, 916 of them men and 2611 women.

A TYPICAL STOGY FACTORY

The best means of introduction to the industry is to follow step by step the process of stogy making, drawing our description from departments in different factories. Departments could be cited which are better, others much worse; therefore this description may be considered even more representative than if one factory were described throughout. Little bunches of rich brown leaves are spread out in the drying room on an upper floor to mellow and grow soft and workable. They are "air dried" for the finest work. This takes a month or two, sometimes a year for work of the best grade; sometimes, when there is haste, not more than a few days. In any case natural drying without heat produces leaf more responsive to the touch of the shaper.

In another room close by, tobacco may be drying by heat; the windows are closed, and a stove keeps the room at high tem-

* For tables, showing in detail conditions in the industry, see Appendix B, pp. 385–388, Tables 41–45.

perature. Fine dust from the brittle leaves sifts through the air, and the leaves themselves are so dusty and burnt that they seem scarcely akin to the mellow things in the next room. This heat-dried tobacco is for mold stogies. It is shaped artificially by a quick process, and can be used when so dry that hand work upon it would be impossible. Since time and space are both saved where mold stogies are made and air drying is unnecessary, the cost to the consumer is greatly reduced.

Both drying rooms are tended by men, old men, worn out at their trade, but still with the feel of tobacco in their hands. In contrast, the basement is full of women. There you see a roomful of strippers, perhaps a hundred in number. Each woman sits low in her little stall, and leans against a piece of rough board; her lap is full of tobacco, and close beside her are a scale and a low rounded stand. Light from the windows hardly reaches all parts of the great square room, but the work is so purely mechanical that light is almost unnecessary. The stem of filler tobacco is pulled out, the leaf is thrown into the scales, and tied pound by pound. The wrapper leaf, and sometimes the binder, is wet and smoothed out over the rounded stand. Care must be taken to cut the stem without tearing the rest of the leaf, but aside from this, the work presents no difficulty. Its very simplicity has drawn into it women of a type different from the others in the factory. Many of the strippers are mature women, coming into a trade which they have not learned. There is a peasant look about their faces, a something near the soil and the growing of dark leaves out-of-doors. Some of them are young girls, a little stupid, a little inefficient, here and there with a defect of sight, here and there with a slightly deformed body, nearly always in some respect physically below the standard strength that keeps pace with a machine. Some of the strippers belong to yet a different group: they are wrecks of the trade. Once they worked upstairs bunching or at the suction tables. Others who had started with them married. These kept on until the day when their pace began to fall off and their output to diminish, and at length they dropped back among the older untrained women, the young girls whose physique is below par, and the Slavic girls whom race prejudice bars out of every room but this.

On the floor above are the hand stogy makers. All of them are men, craftsmen. They sit opposite one another at long tables which run the length of the room, although at the far end there is little daylight and no provision for artificial lighting. They manifest their skill in the close cutting of the leaf, in their choice of exactly the right amount of long filler, in the rolling, molding, and final loose curling of the head. The best stock is used. The worker's deft hands are here the most important factor in production. The men have had an apprenticeship of at least a year, and they have a craft which still holds a strong position in spite of the encroachments of cheaper and more mechanical methods of manufacture.

Team work among women in the making of mold stogies is the rival of hand work among the men. Both rolling and bunching are done with the help of a machine. The buncher stands with her foot on the treadle, puts on the horizontal plate of the machine her handful of scrap filler and her bit of binder leaf, and presses the treadle; canvas rolls wind about the leaf and release it, making a bunch. This bunched leaf is placed in one of a row of cigar-shaped transverse grooves, six to eight inches long, cut in a wooden board. When the rows are full, a second matrix board is faced down on the first and the two are put under a press until the bunches are molded permanently into shape, ready for the rollers.

Some rollers work by hand, cutting the wrapper and shaping it around these molded bunches one by one, finishing either with curl or paste head. Each girl has her little cutting board, her knife, and her clipper to cut the end. These tools are the stock in trade which the stogy maker carries with her from place to place. The demand upon her for training of the eye and hand is greater than upon her neighbors at the suction table, who are also called rollers, but who have scarcely any responsibility left. They spread the leaf over a little metal stand which is so arranged that the leaf is drawn out and held in place by suction. The operative cuts the tobacco after the guide line on the metal block, always the same shape and size, then rolls it round the bunch and puts it into the box beside her. There are perhaps three times as many rollers as there are girls at the bunching machines, but all

STRIPPING TOBACCO BY THE POUND

of them work with a degree of intensity which is the joint result
of a piece rate and untired youth. These girls are young, seventeen, eighteen, sometimes twenty. The oldest among them have
worked for four or five years, and will perhaps keep it up for
another year or so. Many are Jewish girls, who would rather be
in a quiet workplace than in factories where actual muscular
effort is more in demand. Nervous energy they expend freely.

The packers are like unto them. They stand beside tables,
ranged in front of the windows, and beside them are stools, not
for the girls, but to hold the box of stogies from which a packer
sorts out light, medium, and dark into piles in front of her. Some
she packs on end, a hundred at a time, into round tins; others
she puts in square boxes in rows of ten. By the help of a sloping
board she slips one row after another into place, cuts short the
time of shrinkage by vigorously squeezing the stogies together
under a press, nails down the cover and ties—all this with a sureness of sight which discriminates unhesitatingly between different colors and a quickness of hand which the watcher can scarcely
follow. The bander across the room takes some of the boxes apart,
unpacks and pastes bands on the stogies, row by row. Then she
repacks them just as they were before and again nails and ties.
High speed is in the atmosphere. There is no stopping to rest
or to think. Evidently the girls are working by the thousand.
Most of the packers are Americans; they stand the pace better
than the occasional Jewish girls, therefore preference is given to
them.

In every factory and in every sweatshop these branches
of the trade are duplicated in one way or another. There are
strippers, bunchers and rollers, hand stogy makers and packers.
Given these constant factors to be reckoned with, it is left for
us to see how factories and sweatshops group themselves, where
they are found and how constructed, what wages and hours
of work they offer, and how they have been influenced by the
unions, the trust, and the labor laws of the state. A word must
be said, too, about the displacement of men by women, and of
hand work by machine work, and about the physical effects of
the trade as it now is compared with the possible physical effects
under a somewhat different method of factory construction.

HILL FACTORIES AND SWEATSHOPS

The factories and sweatshops are scattered widely as the limits of the city allow, but in some districts there are colonies of shops, partly as the result of nationality groupings, and partly on lines of business convenience.* In a number of shops the advantage is with "the Hill," where the bulk of the immigrant Jewish population lives, and where nine factories and 124 sweatshops employ nearly a third of the workers in the trade. These workers are Austrian and Russian, sometimes German Jews. The only Gentiles are the handful of Italians who make stogies as it is done "in Napoli." A majority of the Jewish men are foreign born, but many of the women were born in this country of foreign parents. A newcomer gravitates naturally to the shop of a friend, and the girl whose life is bounded by the circle of a few streets is not likely to go to some unknown downtown factory, when she can find employment for such hours as she likes in the little workroom next door.

The typical Hill factory is a small place, not over two stories high. With the exception of one plant owned by the trust and an independent factory of some size, there are no pretensions to large output or to an extensive business. The old buildings are often L-shaped, adapted and readapted for their present uses, and reeking with the disabilities which come of age and unfit construction. In contrast are a few trim little brick structures of recent erection, small enough to be well lighted, and comparably well aired. These small factories on the Hill deal to a large extent in mold stogies, which are cheaper to manufacture than hand-made stogies, and equally sure of sale. At best they are unimportant competitors of the large concerns, although more sharply pushed, in that they bid for a wider market than the sweatshops in the neighboring dwellings, whose entire commercial life may begin at the leaf wholesaler's store across the way, and end at the cigar-seller's on the corner.

* The distinction made for the sake of clearness in this study between factory and sweatshop is based solely on the uses to which the whole building is put. Where stogies are made in a building constructed or otherwise used for business purposes, the place is called a factory, as distinguished from a sweatshop, which occupies part of a dwelling-house.

It is in the Hill sweatshops that most of the hand stogy makers are found. The types of shop are as various as the prosperity of the owners. Simplest of all, the primitive cell of the organism of stogy manufacture, is the kitchen workbench, such as that of Joseph Lebovitz, who, soon after he came from Russia, was taken in hand by his neighbors and trained to be a stogy maker. He is rather thin, but still brown of face and tall, and with the help of his wife earns enough at stogies to live and to pay the rent of two rooms on the first floor. His bench and bag of tobacco are close to the one window. A little farther away stands the cradle of the new baby, rocked between times by the little Russian mother in the moments that can be spared from housekeeping and stripping tobacco for her husband. Lebovitz is under bond, of course, to the revenue office. Now and then he has to go down to the great stone building and buy stamps for his boxes of stock, but otherwise the Hill is large enough to supply all his needs. There is a box factory a few squares away; in the very next house is the man who sells leaf to half the small shops on the Hill. The cigar-seller on Centre Avenue deals with his neighbors in preference to the big factories that demand a large amount of trade.

In this district there are twenty of these home shops, where no outside hands are employed. Sometimes the little place has continued for years in the same way until it has absorbed children as well as parents, and expanded without breaking the family tie. I caught a glimpse of one such group of workers through the foot-high window of a cellar where the utmost economy of space and lack of air were combined with that marvelous neatness so expressive of the righteous German soul. The dark cellar was so full of cases of stock as to tax the ingenuity of any one who sought entrance. Inside there were two rooms, perhaps eight by eight, with a seven-foot ceiling. Here Fritz Rosenberg, a patriarchal gray-bearded German, worked with his wife and daughter at a table set beneath the tight-closed wire-screened window. A foot below the ceiling hung a wide wooden rack. Finished stogies were drying on it, and tobacco leaves were heaped high on a sofa at the rear of the room. Although I wondered how such an overrun place could ever be cleaned, there was evidence of care in the clean floor and benches. But freedom from scrap cannot compensate for lack of air.

In many cases such a workshop is operated in connection with a retail store, but more often it is independent. The first outsider to be brought in as trade expands is another man to help, a girl to strip, or a small child after school. The girl will sometimes be shared by several shops. If more workers are added, just here the point of divergence in method usually comes. Sometimes there will be three or four men making only hand stogies, with one or two girls to strip for them. More often, however, it happens that as the shop grows its policy changes, girls and cheaper men being taken on to work at molds. I have come upon such a transformed workshop in a half cellar, reached through an alley-way from the rear; or under a low sloping roof on the third floor; but more often than not, when I found a license sign at the door, and walked boldly through the family parlor and up the dark staircase in the middle of the tenement, at the top I would encounter the odor of tobacco leaves. The stairs would have to be climbed in total darkness, for the doors at either side are always closed, but behind one of them would be my workshop. Within, the atmosphere is businesslike; there is no furniture that has not its use for the manufacture of stogies. The rollers have their benches against the two front windows, and the bunchers work at the dark side of the room; the round white finished boxes are piled ceiling-high against the walls, and in the corner which no one happens to be using there are little heaps of tobacco spread out to dry. Three of the rollers are strong peasant types, immigrants, whose forebears tilled fields in Austria. The other roller and two of the three bunchers are men. Both of the strippers are women. They work next the bales of tobacco and the case of stems, in a little corner of the cellar which is not heated in winter or dried in summer. Unless the heat is unbearable, windows are not opened, because tobacco is injured by a too variable temperature.

In general, the workplaces on the Hill are characterized by a lack of cleanliness, by overcrowding (as low as 150 cubic feet of air space to a person in some shops), by an absence of ventilation and of sanitary accommodations. Dirt and scrap are heaped

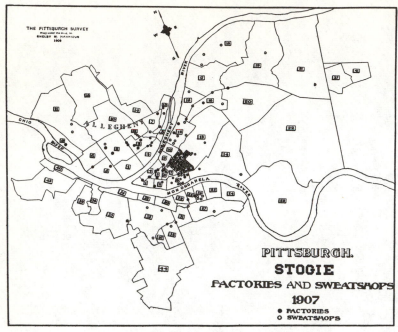

LOCATION OF STOGY FACTORIES AND SWEATSHOPS, 1907

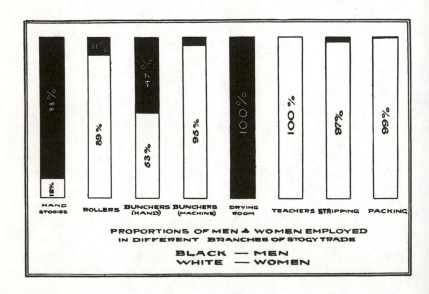

under the tables.   In two-fifths (53) of the shops visited tobacco was dried in the room, sometimes on the floor, sometimes at the side or overhead, in part breaking into dust as it dries, and in part weighting down the atmosphere with nicotine—for both reasons a potent cause of ill-health among the workers.

In the smaller shops the strippers are discriminated against, so far as workroom accommodations are concerned.   Whenever a cellar is used, they work in the cellar.   When the upper part of the house is used, they work at the staircase landing, or at the entrance of the dark room where tobacco is stored.   They are sometimes Negroes, sometimes Slavs, sometimes Jews of a lower grade than the molders of the leaf, and they take such places as are provided.   I went into one cellar opposite a Hill factory where two women and one man, all Negroes, were stripping in a room less than seven feet in height.   The only source of air was a narrow door leading by a flight of steps up to the street.   A tiny slit of a window at the far end was close barred, and two-thirds of the cubic space in the room was occupied by bales of tobacco and cases of stripped stock.   Pools of muddy water stood on the earth floor, and the air was foul beyond endurance.

Nearby, in another cellar workroom, three low-grade Polish girls and a feeble-minded man worked behind a closed door in the underground dampness.   Steps led down from the yard to a room not over eight feet square.   On dark days a flaring gas jet helped to exhaust the oxygen.   Except for the gas jet there was no way of heating the place in the winter or drying the damp floor and walls in summer.   Such conditions are not exceptional. They are the workplaces of the inert or least vigorous, of the children, the old women, the girls broken down with illness who have lost their speed, the unskilled women too ambitionless to learn something that pays better, too spiritless to combat exploitation.   Elsewhere in the city, the genesis of sweatshops has been along the same lines, although sometimes one finds that the proprietor is an ex-resident of the Hill who has moved away in pursuit of space and light and air.   The Jewish stock predominates, but there are groups of tenement shops to be found in the straggling unpainted Italian streets in the East End or among the colonies of Slavic and Celtic people on the South Side, three downtown, and others among the Germans of the North Side—a total of 30. Of the 69 shops outside Hill district, 43 are operated in connection with retail stores. A double business of this sort indicates deliberate, purposeful choice of occupation, rather than the chance employment, the eager learning of the nearest thing at hand, characteristic of the Jewish immigrants in the congested district. The standard of cleanliness and sanitation is higher.

The majority of the large factories are near the business center of the city.

RATES OF PAY

Before discussing earnings in the stogy industry it is necessary to have a general understanding of rates of pay and the causes which affect them. "Equal pay for equal work" is the rule in factories and tenement shops alike, but, as we shall see, there are variables in the system of payment which lead to speeding as readily as in industries where rate cutting is frequent.

Rates of pay are as follows:

TABLE 6.—RATES OF PAY IN THE STOGY INDUSTRY

District	STRIPPERS			MOLD STOGY MAKERS				HAND STOGY MAKERS
				Rollers		Bunchers		
	Filler per lb.	Binder per lb.	Wrapper per lb.	Paste per 100	Curl per 100	Hand per 100	Machine per 100	
Hill	$ .01½	$ .02	$ .04	$ .11	$ .12	$ .08	$ .03	$2.00 per 1000
North and South Side	.01½	.02–.03	.05	.12	.13	.08	.05	$3.00–3.50 per 1000

The rate of pay, of course, gives no clue to actual earnings. There are always natural differences of speed among the workers, but there is, besides, much variation in the quality of stock. A leaf that is old or weak in fibre is likely to break in handling and takes two or three times as long to strip as "Kentuck", which is heavy and tough, as tobaccos go. Similarly, the difficulties of rollers and bunchers are increased. When the stock is poor, the

84

problem of cutting without waste checks the speed and output of even the best workers, and to the less efficient it is disastrous. Sometimes a "run of poor stock" comes to the roller as a matter of chance, and sometimes it is a deliberate means of cheapening cost. The large factories are more apt than the small shops to cut down expenses in this way because they can use scrap at a profit, whereas small shops attempt to keep a few customers for goods of even quality rather than to bid for a varied trade. This is a generalization, however, with many exceptions. Irregular hours, no less than difference in speed and quality of stock, affect the amount earned. An estimate based on a nine-hour day in a factory could not be equally true for a ten- or twelve-hour day in a sweatshop; nor could an estimate based on high-pressure work be equally true in a shop where the pace is relatively even and unstrained.

PREMIUMS AND SLIDING SCALE

There are eight factories which employ a hundred hands or more. In each of them, as well as in some smaller plants which approach them in size, there are speed requirements. For instance, while no sweatshop falls below the $ .11 rate for rollers, one factory pays only $ .09 a hundred if a roller turns out less than 6000 stogies a week. In other cases emphasis is placed on close cutting as well as on speed. The following regulations are posted on a workroom door:*

TABLE 7.—POSTED RATES FOR ROLLERS IN A NORTH SIDE STOGY FACTORY

Pump Handles (Cigars)

All rollers getting an average of below 275 a pound will receive 13 cents a 100.
All rollers getting an average of 275 or better will receive 13 cents a 100.
All rollers getting an average of over 325 will receive 25 cents additional to their week's pay.

Little Havana Specials

All rollers getting an average of below 325 a pound will receive 12 cents a 100.
All rollers getting an average of 325 or better will receive 13 cents a 100.
All rollers getting an average of over 375 will receive 25 cents additional to their week's pay.

* This factory is on the North Side where thirteen cents a hundred is the standard rate.

It is true that were there no requirement of the sort, many girls might become careless and waste an unnecessary amount of leaf. It is also true that such a requirement greatly increases the worker's expenditure of nervous energy. She is pulled in two directions, urged on the one hand by the necessity for speed if she is to have a good sum at the end of the week and keep her place in the factory, and urged on the other hand to slacken her pace on each stogy in order to increase her output per pound. In four of the larger factories the scale is as follows:

TABLE 8.—SLIDING SCALE FOR ROLLERS IN FOUR STOGY FACTORIES

No. per pound	Rate per 100
300 stogies	10 cents
325 "	11 "
350 "	12 "
375 "	13 "
400 "	13½–14 cents

A higher pace with economy of material can scarcely be obtained. The girl's goal is both the highest total number of stogies each day and the highest total number cut from each pound. Every girl is kept by this double tension at her maximum. That maximum means minimum cost to the firm. In one case the forewoman said to me, "Every one of my girls makes 1400 stogies a day." I asked her how that was possible, and she replied, "If she does not make 1400 a day, she is discharged."

Further, premiums are given in some factories to stimulate speed. I have been told that one factory which employs 300 girls pays a biweekly premium of $ .50 in four departments (long filler rolling and bunching, and scrap rolling and bunching) to the two girls in each department who have the highest total, both in the actual number of stogies made and in the number cut from each pound of tobacco. The girls whose speed and number of stogies per pound have come nearest to that of the premium girls are paid the regular rate, but the blow falls on those at the foot of the list. By an ingenious but not wholly clear process of reasoning they are fined $ .30 to $ .35 a pound for their scrap, although this is more than the wrapper tobacco costs retail, and the scrap is by no means a total loss to the management.

86

Tobacco Stripping in a Hill Sweatshop

Without placing too much emphasis upon this instance, it is within the facts to say that the tendency in the larger factories is to stimulate the speed of the workers to a high pitch within the working day; in tenement shops as a rule there is a slower going atmosphere of taking things as they come, but working overtime at will. These differences of tension, of stock, and of natural ability must be considered, as well as rates of pay, in estimating actual output and earnings in the several branches of the trade.

To begin with the lowest industrial grade: among strippers I found every variation, from the curly-haired little boy of five who could strip "zwölf Händel" a day, to the expert whose average at filler work is between 60 and 70 pounds. Tobacco is weighed after the stems are out. The filler is stripped least carefully because it is crumpled and rolled inside the other leaves. The output of one of the best filler strippers on the Hill for a week was as follows:

TABLE 9.—OUTPUT OF AN EXPERT FILLER STRIPPER DURING ONE WEEK

Day	Pounds
Monday	79
Tuesday	24
Wednesday	67
Thursday	56
Friday	58
Saturday	89½
Daily Average	62⅓

The general average of filler strippers is 40 to 60 pounds; the pay is $ .01½ per pound. Binder strippers turn out 30 to 50 and wrapper strippers have an average of not more than 20 pounds a day ($ .80 to $1.00). In the following schedule of an unusually rapid stripper the gaps and variations in the day's work show how statements of individual high output in this trade must be discounted. Tessa with natural optimism would tell you that she could strip 34 pounds, but she reached this maximum only once. Often she fell much below 30. On days that are blank she was sent home because there was no work, and several times she had to battle with poor stock.

TABLE 10.—OUTPUT OF AN EXPERT WRAPPER STRIPPER DURING FOUR WEEKS

Week of August—, '07.	*Pounds*	*Week of September—, '07.*	*Pounds*
Monday	33	Monday	32
Tuesday	33	Tuesday	25
Wednesday	..	Wednesday	..
Thursday	31	Thursday	27
Friday	31	Friday	33
Saturday	12	Saturday	..

Week of September—, '07.	*Pounds*	*Week of September—, '07.*	*Pounds*
Monday	19	Monday	6
Tuesday	20	Tuesday	29
Wednesday . . .	31	Wednesday . . .	13
Thursday	34	Thursday	..
Friday	..	Friday	23
Saturday	..	Saturday	23

From these four weeks we get a daily average of 18.9 pounds, or (at the rate of $ .05 per pound) $ .94. An old stogy maker who has worked with several generations of girl strippers says that not one of them can average over $5.00 a week, and that a fair estimate, counting in seasons of dull trade and of overtime, would be from $ .60 to $ .80 a day. Stripping is almost entirely in the hands of women. Of 523 strippers, only 18 were men. Of these, four were colored, two were feeble-minded, three were boys; the rest were too old to be trusted with any other work.

Machine bunch makers are a step higher than the strippers. Earlier in this chapter, one kind of bunch making by machine was mentioned. Among the various types in use is a large power-driven machine operated by two girls, who with good stock turn out 8400 bunches a day. One girl feeds the filler, and the other the binder, but the machine makes the bunches and carries them on a conveyor the length of the work table to seven rollers whom it keeps constantly supplied. Each machine girl is paid $ .17½ per 1000 bunches, or about $1.40 a day. In tenement shops is found an old-style foot machine for short filler work. The funnel is filled with scrap; the operator presses the treadle, and in so doing opens the funnel just enough to let a handful of scrap fall on the leaf to be wound about it. Incidentally a cloud of dust flies out into the room. From 3000 to 5000 bunches a day can be made on such a foot machine, and this work is paid for at the rate of $ .03, and sometimes $ .05, per 100.

Bunches for long filler work are made by hand at the rate of $ .08 per 100 in the small shops and in many factories. With high endurance and prolonged working hours, some men can earn as much as $2.00 a day, and for this reason probably we find twice as many men bunching as rolling. In each branch of the trade, however, the number of women is greater than the number of men. A woman of moderate ability does not turn out over 1400 a day, with earnings of $1.00 to $1.20. I learned of no woman who had reached the record of one man on the Hill, 2000 bunches.

Among rollers of mold stogies who have learned their trade,* daily output varies widely because of difference in stock and in market demand, and sometimes because of high speeding one day with exhaustion the next. I have heard of one woman who made 2000 a day, but she stood alone in the experience of the boss who knew her. The consensus of opinion seems to be that 1000 is a good output for an experienced roller, and the following schedules, taken from the payroll of six experts for the same week, show a daily average of 930. According to these schedules, an experienced hand can expect to earn $1.00 to $1.30 a day. In some cases, with additional night work, the girl's total income is brought up to $10 or more a week.

TABLE II.—OUTPUT OF SIX EXPERT MOLD STOGY ROLLERS DURING ONE WEEK

	No. 1 Lbs.		No. 2 Lbs.		No. 3 Lbs.
Monday .	800	Monday .	1300	Monday .	600
Tuesday .	400	Tuesday .	1400	Tuesday .	600
Wednesday.	1000	Wednesday.	1500	Wednesday.	1100
Thursday .	1000	Thursday .	600	Thursday .	1000
Friday .	1000	Friday .	1000	Friday .	1000
Saturday .	1200	Saturday .	1600	Saturday .	300

	No. 4		No. 5		No. 6
Monday .	1400	Monday .	1300	Monday .	400
Tuesday .	1400	Tuesday .	1400	Tuesday .	1200
Wednesday.	1400	Wednesday.	1300	Wednesday.	1700
Thursday .	1500	Thursday .	1100	Thursday .	500
Friday .	1500	Friday .	..	Friday .	..
Saturday .	..	Saturday .	..	Saturday .	..

* Each roller, when learning her trade, has the initial expense of $1.35 for tools.

Trained packers at piece rates ($ .07 to $ .50 a 1000) turn out at the lowest rate not less than 14,000 ($ .98) a day. Banding is paid at the rate of $ .25 a 1000. There are so many different styles of packing stogies that there is little opportunity to acquire speed with accuracy in a single line, and pay by the week has often been found more satisfactory. Seven-tenths of the 209 girl packers earn week wages of $3.00 to $10, the large majority being paid $4.00 to $6.00 for their 56 to 60 hours' work.

The hand stogy makers, with whom the trade started, are its best paid workers. On the Hill they are paid $2.00 a 1000; on the South Side, where the union influence still persists, $3.00 to $3.50, and in a very few shops $3.75 per 1000. The output of an experienced hand stogy maker at dry rolling is 1000 a day. Italian women are employed in one factory to make stogies after the Italian fashion, smearing the board with paste and carelessly rolling the leaf without finishing either end. They are paid $1.75 a 1000, and often do not make over 500 a day. The rest of the women hand stogy makers are found in small shops, working with their husbands in most cases. Counting factory and home workers, there are not more than 56 of them altogether, as compared with 392 men.

Turning now to the effect of hours and seasons of work on wages: in the tenement shops, as stated before, there is a decided tendency toward irregular hours, night work being optional with outside hands, but often a matter of course with the families. Half the shops which employ outsiders confessedly work at night. The largest Hill factory is open until ten p. m., but no compulsion is exerted to keep women employes after six. As a rule, the factories work overtime only for the Christmas trade, twenty-two of them having a ten-hour day during the year. The rest, with one exception, have a working day of seven and a half hours to nine and a half. Overtime is admitted to be a failure. Comparatively few men in the trade willingly keep their hands at night during the rush from August until December. For every night worked, poorer work is done during the day. This fact has so far won recognition that in seven factories there is no overtime at all; in others, night work is reduced to two nights a week, or three at most. Yet since factories are run according to orders

WORKING AT THE SUCTION TABLE
International Museum of Photography at George Eastman House.

received and since dealers do not order long ahead, there comes an inevitable rush and crowding during the fall months, succeeded by utter deadness of trade in January and February. It rarely happens that a factory shuts down in the slack season, but instead the payroll is reduced materially by continuous use of bad stock. Sometimes in a week's pay strippers earn $1.00 less than when trade is normal, and rollers $1.50 less.

DISTRIBUTION OF WORK

This discussion of rates of pay and output in general brings us to more specific consideration of the relation of women's work to the trade. Are the women craftsmen or machine operators? Are they competing with men for the same work at the same pay or for different work at lesser pay?

A graphic statement will give the best basis for an answer to these questions:

TABLE 12.—DISTRIBUTION OF WORK AMONG MEN AND WOMEN IN STOGY FACTORIES

Type of workplace	Strippers		Rollers		Bunchers (Hand)		Bunchers (Machine)		Packers		Hand Stogy Makers		Drying Room		Teachers		Total	
	Men	Women	Men	Women	Men	Women	Men	Women	Men	Women	Men	Women	Men	Women	Men	Women	Men	Women
Sweat shops	13	148	88	147	118	56	5	1	.	4	224	44	5	.			453	400
Factories	5	357	77	1185	190	289	4	161	1	205	168	12	18	2			463	2211
Total	18	505	165	1332	308	345	9	162	1	209	392	56	23	2			916	2611

The figures show that stripping, the most mechanical and poorly paid branch of the trade, is almost exclusively in the hands of women. In team work by hand or by machine, women outnumber men nearly four to one, whereas there is only one woman among seven men at hand stogy making. So far as numbers go, it is clear that the women in the stogy industry are not craftsmen. Overwhelmingly they are machine operators or engaged in preparation work.

We have found that wage rates are general, not special according to sex. Where men and women enter the shop together to do the same work, they receive the same rate of pay, and the employment of one or the other is largely a matter of chance. They are regarded in sweatshops as equally desirable, and are employed in about equal numbers—453 men to 400 women. The real competition is between higher skill and lesser skill, hand work and machine work, men hand stogy makers and women mold stogy makers doing work of cheaper grade for lower wages. It is in rolling and bunching that the numbers of women loom large, in considering their competition with or displacement of men. Men who do rolling and bunching are comparatively few, because as laborers they can earn more elsewhere after they have learned the ways of the country and found themselves. There are no trustworthy figures to show whether the group of hand workers has actually, as well as proportionately,* diminished, but the point on which we can be certain is that the great increase has come among the less skilled machine workers, who put out a product which by its very cheapness has a strong hold on the market. This distribution of work shows absolutely the displacement in the industry at Pittsburgh of men at a handicraft by women at machines.

INFLUENCE OF THE TRUST AND OF UNIONS

The growth of the tobacco trust in Pittsburgh is closely bound up with this change in the character of the industry. Within the last few years the Union American Cigar Company has acquired four of the largest factories in the Pittsburgh district to turn out a cheap grade of mold work, mainly for the western trade. Three of the factories use machines for rolling and bunching, and in one case stripping machines have been installed. The fourth factory, where mold work is done without

* The proportion of hand stogy makers to the total number of workers in the trade is 1 : 7.87.

machines, employs 50 women and 50 men; but in the other three, all but ten of the 1025 employes are women. The impetus given by the trust to trade in machine-made goods can hardly be overestimated. Of course, back of this action is the constant demand of the consumer for a lower purchasing price, and of the investor for a lower cost of production.

The apprentice system is not found fully developed in the independent factories, although most large plants will take an occasional learner. In the factories of the Union American Cigar Company, however, apprentices are regularly employed in each department, and trained for the work. A learner is given no opportunity to become familiar with more than a single branch of the work, and her apprenticeship is mainly a speed-developing process. For the first week she receives a premium of $2.50 in addition to what she earns. Each week her premium is reduced by $ .25* until the tenth week, when she is supposed to be able "to make her time." It is by no means true that she can acquire high speed in rolling (unless by machine) in so short a time, but merely enough sureness of touch to warrant her being trusted on the various sorts of work. The apprentices are usually young girls not much over fourteen. They fit into pace-setting ways and in a couple of years reach their maximum output.

The only active opponents of trust methods have been the labor unions, but their history in the stogy industry is in large measure characterized by ineffective action, disunion, and internal quarrels. Within a single year I came across shops belonging to four different labor organizations, no one of which controlled an influential portion of the trade. The Industrial Workers of the World and the Cigar Makers' International Union were no longer represented in this trade in Pittsburgh in 1907. The National Stogy Makers, an offshoot from the Knights of Labor, have been unable to duplicate here their wonderfully successful work in Wheeling, where their boast is that "there is not a trust factory, and every stogy maker in town has his union card." They control one Pittsburgh factory, but the other union shops are under the Knights of Labor. This latter organization has its strongest hold among German shops on the South Side which use the label,

* In one case by fifty cents.

although the workmen are charged with taking what wages they can get even if the rate is below the regular scale.

Hand stogy makers have always been sought after most by the union. At one time a number of women mold workers were organized, but the women accepted pay below the scale from one manufacturer. Men in the shop remonstrated with the firm, and then went out on strike to force up the women's pay, but the women would not go. Meanwhile a hostile union came in and organized the shop while the old employes were striking. Since then the enthusiasm of the union for women members has waned. Five or six women still belong to the local Knights of Labor, but by the constitution of the National Stogy Makers they are definitely excluded. Among the Jewish shops every attempt at organization has failed. The rate of pay on the Hill is a third less than on the South Side, but union men have been powerless to break through the barrier of clannishness and suspicion characteristic of shifting immigrants.

A third outside influence, which besides the unions and the trust organization has been brought to bear upon the industry, is the state factory law. There are no clauses having especial reference to stogy making, but this industry, like others, is affected by the general prohibition of excessive hours of work for women, and of unsanitary buildings.* That twelve hours is the maximum working day for women undoubtedly has influenced the attitude of the larger factories toward overtime.

CONDITIONS AFFECTING HEALTH

Poor lighting, overcrowding, and lack of sanitary accommodations are found here as in other trades. Insufficient ventilation in the factories of a dust-producing occupation calls for especial comment. In 101 factories and sweatshops, tobacco is dried in the workroom. Thirty-one of this number keep the brown leaves heaped on the floor, but 17 have racks overhead, and 53 have racks built at the side of the room.

---

* Also of child labor. In 1907 there were ninety to one hundred children from five to twelve years old stripping tobacco in tenement sweatshops in Pittsburgh; and double that number stripping after school.

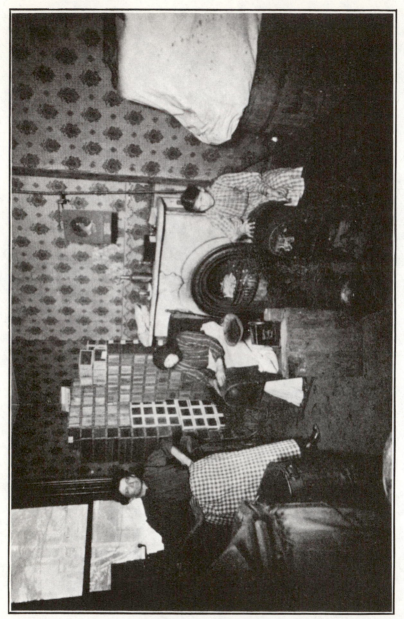

A Sweatshop Proprietor and Two of Her Employes

This economy of space is a source of danger to the workers. The air grows heavy from the nicotine exhaled by the mellowing leaves, and thick with the dust of pulverized scrap and brittle edges. Yet because of the uneven climate, windows are kept closed. The possibility of artificial ventilation does not seem to be recognized, and with few exceptions factories large and small are offenders against health by their lack of pure air.

Tenement shops are frequently the worst offenders, but these seem to be diminishing in number. In Wheeling, the force which has been effective in preventing sweatshops has been the union. In Pittsburgh it seems to be the trust. Combinations among leaf growers, packers, and manufacturers had doubled the price of leaf in 1907 within the year, until a point was reached so far prohibitive to small dealers that twenty-four had left the trade and more had cut down the number of their employes. Yet with tenement shops eliminated, the problem of health in the stogy industry would still be unsolved. There is no conclusive evidence that disease is caused by working in tobacco, but evidence is abundant that the long hours during which the roller sits at her bench in one position, the tight closed windows, the dust sifting through the air, tend to produce diseases of throat and lungs, in many cases tuberculosis. Danger is increased by dry sweeping during working hours and often by requiring the girls to clean their own work benches. No brushes are provided, and the girls sweep the dust and scrap into each other's aprons and faces. In some factories the rollers bite the ends of their stogies instead of cutting them, but this is sharply looked after by the management. The danger of infection is increased by the custom of placing workers opposite one another to save space, instead of facing them in the same direction. The law would be strengthened by specific legal prohibition of drying tobacco in workrooms, by more definite requirements for ventilation and for a higher minimum of air space per person.

Serious as the menace of tuberculosis is, even more serious is the threat to racial vitality by the nervous exhaustion of the girl workers. The two react upon each other. I have spoken of the double tension on the stogy maker, who must cut close and at the same time have a high output. To earn the wages they wish at the rate set, the girls speed themselves; the company's sliding scale per pound of material makes that speeding tense and exhausting. "No girl can keep up her pace more than six years," said the manager of one large factory to me. Others put it that the girls get tired of working and do not take the same interest, while some think that the nicotine makes them sluggish. The majority admit that except for girls of the most robust physique, the tension seldom can be maintained. Cases are cited of rollers who have worked ten years (in one instance, sixteen), whose output has not diminished and whose general health has no appearance of having suffered from any nervous tension due to the work. But against these cases could be cited many where the reverse is true. Sarah Cohen, a stripper, twenty-one years old, is an instance of this. I should have thought her a woman of thirty-five. The first break in her strength came from typhoid, four years ago, but she never has been able to regain the speed which she had at sixteen. With overtime rolling, she was able at one time to earn $12 a week. She has to-day dropped behind into the stripping room of an alley sweatshop where she cannot finish in a day over fourteen pounds, at $ .05 a pound. This means an income of $4.20 a week. Rose Bernstein, a slight little girl with drooping mouth and sloping shoulders, told me that in three years her output had dropped from 1000 to 700 stogies a day and that now she is losing perceptibly. Such instances are too numerous to be put aside or denied by anything short of a thorough medical inquiry as to the condition both of the girls in the trade and of those who have left it.

Where there is such nervous loss its cost is not borne by the industry. Most of the girls marry at twenty or twenty-one, just at the time when their speed breaks. Some of the cost is borne by the homes into which they go. This social waste, more serious by far than the destruction of the individual, we have not yet had means of estimating. Those who know these factory workers intimately know only that in case after case the industry is taking young undeveloped girls, lifting their speed to its highest pitch, and wearing them out. They know, too, after the gap of a few years, their unfit homes and undervitalized children. In a city where typhoid and bad housing have been general, as

TOBACCO STRIPPERS

in Pittsburgh, it would be rash to conclude that any one thing is wholly responsible; but we may be sure beyond possibility of doubt that a trade which often causes nervous exhaustion is at least a factor.

To sum up: in the large factories, the emphasis in women's work is on output rather than on craftsmanship; on a high rate of cheap production rather than on a moderate rate of superior production. The growth in numbers has come among team workers and to a large extent among workers at the machine. In the tenement shops there is less emphasis on speed and more laxity as to hours, but there are counterbalancing disadvantages of frequent night work, congested workrooms, and unsanitary as well as unventilated buildings.

The brown stogy, that symbol of fellowship, social intercourse, and the good things of the leisure hours of life, has become socially a costly thing to produce. No small share of this social cost is needless waste.

THE NEEDLE TRADES

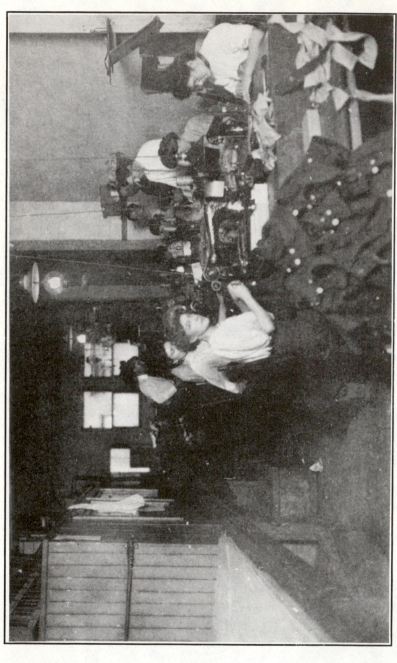

A Prevailing Type of Garment Workroom

CHAPTER VI

THE GARMENT TRADES

FACTORIES

GARMENT making, among all the industries which have left the home and ranged themselves in the factories, is perhaps of the first importance. It is impartial in the employment of men and of women, and it numbers its employes the country over among the hundreds of thousands. It has reached out and gathered one garment after another beneath the metal guides of its power sewing machines.

In Pittsburgh, however, garment making has been sharply limited by circumstance. The black smoke of the mills has determined the scope of the industry. No Pittsburgh factory would risk the making of shirtwaists and gowns.* There remains the making of men's clothing—coats, vests, trousers, overalls, and shirts, but even here the atmosphere has curtailed the field in which the industry thrives. It is goods dark in color and coarse in material which are made up in bulk for the ready-made trade. Jeans and corduroys, overalls and coarse shirts, are the staple products of the local factories. The demand for these goods, which alone can be kept in stock in the midst of the Pittsburgh smoke without undue harm, begins at the very doors of the garment factories in the vast numbers of workmen employed in the tonnage industries within a radius of two hundred and fifty miles of the city, and extends throughout the Ohio Valley.

The plants in which garments are made divide themselves into factories and workshops. As a working definition for the terms as used in this chapter, the establishments which occupy buildings used only for business purposes and in which power machinery is installed will be called factories; when the shop

---

* The work of individual dressmakers is not considered in this study.

occupies a building used also as a residence, or when although in a business building, it makes use of foot power and hand work, it will be called a workshop. The factory side of the industry concerns us first, next the workshops, their occasional degeneration into sweatshops, and the outwork system.

PHYSICAL CHARACTERISTICS OF FACTORIES

Garment making in factories may be thought of as a single trade in which people work at power machines, making different kinds of clothes, or it may be thought of as an aggregate of different lines of production. The several branches of the trade, such as the making of coats and vests, trousers, overalls, and shirts, are alike in much of the machinery that they use and in many of the working conditions. To some extent, however, they are different in their demands on the workers and in the specialization of machinery. As the number of factories in each division of the Pittsburgh garment industry is small, we shall think of it primarily as one trade presenting characteristics common to each of its component divisions; and indeed these similarities are more striking than the differences.

As you mount the narrow staircase of a downtown overall factory and open the door, you are greeted with a roar of wheels and a quivering of the floor that bear witness to the harnessing of the sewing machine. The sewing machine itself we think of as a late development. Many among us can remember when we hailed it as a time saver, a burden bearer of our individual cares. It is just at this point that the further development has come. By the application of steam power to the sewing machine principle, work is done for the community instead of for the individual home. The possibilities of ready-made garments, both for men and women, are increasing yearly. The demand for them, too, is increasing. More skill among the cutters, new modifications of the machines, a higher standard in the work that is turned out, suggest for this industry a growing future.

As you enter the workroom, in addition to the roar of wheels and the quivering of the wooden framework, you hear the unmistakable sound of many needles being driven through cloth.

Breaking upon the light, steady, determined whirr of the steel, come the clamp of a button stamper and half a dozen other abrupt utterances of the power, momentarily released in some new machine. The long high-ceilinged room is keyed to quick production. The power carries with it its own tenseness. The operators feel the spur and never relax. Near the door are long tables stacked high with piles of cloth just sent from the cutting room below. They are arranged in bundles so that a lot can be easily carried away by each girl to replenish the pile she has finished. Because of the seventy-five-foot distance between front and rear windows, the center of the room is dim in spite of the electric bulbs hung over each machine. The walls are dull grayish from dirt and old paint; the floor, which is swept weekly, has thread and scraps of cloth and dust scattered about it.

At each end of the room is a row of machines. The girls who are farthest from the windows use continuously the electric bulbs above their needles, and on dark days the girls at the rear must also do so; the high buildings fronting on the next street cut off a good share of their daylight. Outside are brick walls. Inside are two double rows of tense women, facing each other, and bending forward over their machines with eyes fixed on the glint and flash of the needle and the dark seam of the cloth. No girl who is incapable of concentration can stay in a garment factory. No girl who is so unambitious as not to care whether she drives her piece wages up to $6.00 a week can hold her place at the machine. Others whose needs sharpen their ambition are waiting for her place. There are young girls here, but they are not irresponsible. Like the older ones, they are eager and single minded, as they give light touch to the treadle and turn out piece after piece their dozens of garments.

In numbers of firms represented, shirt making is the most important of the garment trades in Pittsburgh. Of the twenty-one factories, eight in 1907 made shirts alone, four of them as feeders for retail stores operated by the same firms, while three made both overalls and shirts. Two made overalls only and five made pants only. One made pants, coats, and vests, and one made vests only. In one factory muslin underwear was manufactured.

STRUCTURE

Two factories have put up eight-story buildings to accommodate their large stockrooms, cutting rooms, and warerooms; another firm has a six-story and another a seven-story plant. Each of nine other factories occupies an entire building, but in contrast these buildings are usually small, not more than three stories high, and have been used indifferently for various manufacturing purposes or for warerooms. Eight factories simply rent floors or small workrooms in business buildings. Even in the larger plants, the actual manufacturing occupies only a small part of the space.

With the exception, then, of the four plants first noted, the workrooms in general are small and have been adapted to their present use. Their other physical characteristics will stand out more clearly in a summary of lighting, cleanliness, and the guarding of machinery.

TABLE 13.—PHYSICAL CHARACTERISTICS OF GARMENT WORKROOMS

Grade	ARRANGEMENT OF WINDOWS	No. of Workrooms
A	Large room; windows on four sides, or three sides and skylight	3
B	Square room; windows on two sides	3
C	Long room; windows front and rear or at one end	13
D	No windows; inadequate skylight or dark basement windows	2
		21

	USE OF ARTIFICIAL LIGHT	
A	None; daylight sufficient	6
B	Shaded light above machine	8
C	Electric bulbs shining directly on needle	2
D	Workroom dark, but no provision for artificial light	5
		21

	CLEANLINESS	
A	Excellent *	2
B	Good †	9
C	Fair ‡	6
D	Bad §	4
		21

	GUARDS IN FRONT OF MACHINES	
A	Complete protection	0
B	Narrow boards in front of all machines	10
C	Narrow boards in front of some machines	3
D	No guards	8
		21

* Room swept daily; walls freshly painted.
† Room swept daily.
‡ Room swept weekly.
§ No specified time for cleaning room; accumulated dirt on floor.

Clearly the type of workroom most in evidence is the commercial loft, or the room in an old building, long and narrow, with windows at either end and the machines set toward the windows. Such a room is the antithesis of a factory planned on a large scale with provisions for growth and comfort. There is an element of chance about it; it means that the tenant has had to content himself with things as he found them. For a small plant comfort may be possible under such conditions, but one cannot wisely assume that a business will always remain of the same dimensions. The row of machines will be added to until finally there are three rows of machines reaching from the two narrow windows well into the room, and so crowded together that one cannot pass between. Even if the business does not grow to this extent, this type of workroom is often at the mercy of its neighbors. A large building directly opposite, another one in the rear, a gradual filling up of the vacant bits of court space, and the clear ample daylight that once came in through the windows has vanished.

A small square room with windows at two sides is likely to bear some of the same disadvantages, but there is always this in its favor, that light has not so far to travel from side to side of the room, and artificial lighting is less likely to be essential.

Of the two garment factories that I have put in the lowest grade structurally, one is a shirt factory on the third floor of a small building. There are two windows at one end which is partitioned off and used as the office, so that no light reaches the rest of the room. Two-thirds of the remaining air space is taken up by piles of cloth, made-up stock, and so on. The machines are stationed at the dark farther end, lighted only by a small and very dim skylight just above them. Artificial light is imperative here, and ventilation is almost impossible. Take out of the cubic air space in the room the bulk of the piles of material, and less than the legal minimum per person remains. There is a wholesome hatred of this place among the employes, and its reputation among garment workers is far reaching.

The other factory is practically a cellar: over two-thirds of the workroom is below ground. Light comes from small basement windows in the rear. In the front are only the house wall and the furnace. The machines are near the back, where the windows are, and the light, although never bright, is nearly sufficient on a clear day. When the weather is dark outside, it is difficult to see how the eight girls employed manage to do their work at all. The place has a dry floor and is thoroughly clean, but even so, with its eight-foot ceiling and imperfect light, it cannot be adequately ventilated and healthful. At the time of my visit the proprietor stated that it was a temporary expedient, but the room had been in use for a number of months and there was little probability of change before the season of summer heat.

On the contrary, when a business has become so well established that the management can venture to plan large, and to build a garment factory, as such, there is better promise of workrooms arranged on lines of comfort and efficiency. The trade in Pittsburgh is fortunate in having two new and excellently planned factory buildings, one for the manufacture of stock shirts and one for coats, vests, and pants, neither one of which has as yet reached its maximum capacity for output. In these it has become possible to develop a better type of workroom. There is not the same menace of encroachment by neighboring buildings. The ceilings are fourteen feet high. Light comes from all sides through large windows set close together along the wall, and in addition there are skylights with shades adjusted.

ARTIFICIAL LIGHTING AND CLEANLINESS

Turning now to the next category in the schedule,—arrangements for artificial light,—it is noteworthy that only two factories use the method of fastening unshaded electric bulbs to the individual machines. By this method, the glare falls directly on the needle and is reflected back into the eyes of the operator, causing serious eyestrain. In the other eight factories which provide electric lights, the bulbs are hung above the machines and usually are covered with a green shade. This method of lighting offers this advantage, that a bright steady light is thrown on the work and not in the eyes of the worker.

Eleven factories have no artificial light. This does not mean that in these eleven factories the workrooms are flooded with

daylight; on the contrary, in five cases the reverse is true. Manufacturers of stock or custom goods for discriminating customers
must provide sufficient light for their employes so that the work
will be turned out well, but when the articles manufactured are
of cheap quality the standard of finish is low, and light in the workroom becomes of less importance. In the former case daylight
or well-planned artificial lighting has a commercial value; in
the latter case its value is considerably lowered. That this
kind of economy results in eyestrain among the employes does not
go down on the ledger of the business.

Sunlight and cleanliness are nearly parallel in the extent of
their effect on health, and in a garment factory both are important.
The goods are dusty, lint sifts to the floor, strips of cloth and
threads fall from the machines, all becoming nuclei for the
accumulation of dirt. In the schedule I have called two shops
"excellent." This means not simply absence of dirt, but a manifest cleanliness, occasional lanes of sunlight through the windows,
the movement of fresh air, newly white-washed walls and ceilings, a floor that is scrubbed as well as swept. Nine other shops
are "good." While they have not the newness and freshness of
these two, they are swept daily and are free from accumulation
of dirt; the management has a standard as to workroom conditions. In other shops, where conditions are not so good, there
are weekly sweepings. This does not mean cleanliness. It means
that the management has either failed to realize the quantity of
dust produced by a score of power sewing machines running at
full speed through an eight- or ten-hour working day, or else has
failed to assume responsibility for meeting the situation. In
four cases the best that can be said is that cleanliness is absent.
Scattered about the floor are undisturbed accumulations of rub-
bish, and the lighting is so poor that there can be no possible dis-
infection by sunshine. One-fifth of the garment factories show
such evidences of neglect.

GUARDING OF MACHINERY

Adequate guarding of machinery is no less important a
factor in work environment in trades where power is used. In

the garment trade there is obviously not the danger of serious accident that there is in many others, but the notices posted by cautious employers are significant. The machinery of immediate interest is the row of power sewing machines connected about six inches from the floor by a revolving shafting to which small wheels are attached at intervals. As the girl sits at her work, her skirts may catch in the wheels of the shafting. This is guarded against by a narrow board so placed in front of the shafting that while the girl is occupied in sewing there is very little likelihood of accident. Whether or not such protection is complete, it puts the maximum probability on the side of safety.

It does not prevent a girl from stooping under her machine to pick up a spool and having her hair caught in the wheel. This recently happened to a girl who was partly scalped and badly cut about the head. Her employer ascribed the cause of the accident to her carelessness. Undoubtedly it was due to her carelessness. "Carelessness," however, is not an ultimate cause, but a resultant from any one of a multitude of things, one of which is the haste and disregard of personal risk resulting almost inevitably from a piece-work system. I have seen a girl stoop down and slip into its place on a rapidly revolving wheel the belting which had become loosened. Had she been hurt, the accident, judging from past instances, would have been characterized as carelessness. Yet the machine was totally without protective devices.

In eight factories out of the twenty-one, when I visited them in 1907, no skirt board was provided. Some employers were apparently ignorant that it is necessary, and obviously the state factory inspection department had failed to demand it. Other employers attempted to shift the responsibility for accidents to their employes. One man, for instance, who employed ninety girls, had placed this placard on the wall: "Girls must not work at any machine without board over shaft." On the day of my visit half the girls had been laid off, but of the remaining forty-five, there were twelve girls at one side of the room working at unguarded machines. The other side of the room was so much in the dark and crowded with girls that I could not count how many machines were guarded. Ordinarily, in the other factories skirt guards are attached to the machines, although a guard is occasionally missing.

Ventilation in garment factories has been impossible to tabulate. There are no systems of forced ventilation in use in these Pittsburgh factories, and in the absence of such definite provision for fresh air, the quality of the air is a matter of degree rather than of kind. The need for ventilation in this industry is especially urgent. The materials are full of lint and dust, the workrooms are often crowded, and the operators are bent for eight or nine hours daily over their machines. Windows are unreliable as a source of fresh air, because they create a draft. Sometimes, of course, the windows are opened, and sometimes the ceilings are high, but even so the atmosphere in these rooms is often heavy and unsafe to breathe. In one workroom, by way of contrast, the upper parts of the windows are opened systematically at intervals, and in this workroom in which there are windows on three sides the quality of the air is noticeably good.

In summing up the physical characteristics of garment workrooms, I find it impossible to say categorically that so many are good, so many are fair, so many are bad. I remember one as intolerably and inexcusably bad on all counts; another as showing care in arrangement, a general excellence at every point far beyond what is required by the law or even by the common standards of the industry. Of most of the factories it can be said that they have some good and some bad qualities, according as the managers have been able actually to plan their workrooms for garment making, and as they have reckoned with the commercial value of a healthy and contented working force.

SYSTEM OF WORK

What work falls to the men and what to the women in these workrooms next concerns us, and how the women's work is subdivided into minor tasks. The factory trade at its height in 1907 engaged 1006 persons in the twenty plants. One hundred and thirty-eight of these were men and 868 women, a proportion of one to six (6.2) in favor of women workers. Leaving the cutting rooms to men, contesting in part for the pressing departments, women have in their own hands the work of garment making by the entire garment system, or, under the section system, the operating of single-needle and special machines. These divisions will have more meaning as I take them up one by one.

The cutters arrange the cloth, and in large factories sometimes cut through thirty-two ply at a time with their electric knives. Their work, which is the best paid of any occupation in the trade, requires knowledge of material, judgment in the layout of the cloth, and some muscular strength in the use of the knife—qualities not generally possessed by the women employes. Assistant cutters sometimes make as little as $12 a week. In time, however, as they are given responsibility, they can earn from $20 to $30. In the muslin underwear factory, where a coarse grade of goods is made, the forewoman does the cutting. Another woman cutter is in a small shirt factory, where she acts as assistant to the proprietor, who himself does the more important cutting. At one time the assistant was a girl who had been trained in an eastern factory, and who earned $14. Now the employe is an inexperienced girl who cuts out cuffs and collars under direction by the use of brass forms, and who is paid $7.50 a week.

With these minor exceptions, all the cutting of garments is done by men. Where vests are made also the men have the main part of the work to do, and you see the immigrant of not many years back cutting and pressing and machining the entire garment, with women compatriots to help at the finishing. Men of this type, however, are found more generally in the smaller factories and in the workshops. In Pittsburgh most of the garment factory employes are "genuine Americans," they will tell you, and they have learned much of their power to bargain since the days when the trade was of less importance. Indeed, it is common report that a few years ago men were kept at work machining for eighteen hours at a stretch and were even locked in until the boss was willing to let them go. That was before the union was started and before the workers had really found themselves. Three of the largest shops have now signed trade agreements with the union which has brought about a reduction of hours to nine daily, with a half day Saturday, and has increased the wages of week workers $2.00 a week. The cutters have organized a separate local, but they coöperate with the other local in helping Americanize newcomers and in getting them out of the sweating work and into the factories.

The pressing department, on the contrary, is a contested field between men and women. Pressers have charge of shrinking cloth goods, and, following this, of seam pressing and garment pressing. Frequently new hands are given only seam pressing to do until they are familiar with the work. Although electric irons are sometimes used, in Pittsburgh gas irons are more usual. As contestants for this work, men have the advantage in muscular strength, women in the cheapness of their labor. The fine custom work is done almost entirely by men. Sometimes heavier irons are used for work of this kind, and invariably more care and experience are needed in handling the goods than when the work is of cheaper grade. As the quality of the work cheapens, women tend to enter the pressing department. In three factories where men's suits are made, both men and women pressers are employed, the men for the better grade of work and the women for the inferior grade. For the same kind of occupation on a different grade of material men are paid $16 a week and women $6.00 to $7.00. In another similar factory women do all the pressing on goods of all grades. Seam pressers start at $4.50 a week, and in time may work up to $10 or $11. Although men in the department assert that women have not strength for the work, it does not appear in four out of the five pants factories, for instance, that the cheaper material on which women are employed is in reality any lighter than the goods the men handle. Twenty-six of the thirty-seven women pressers in the trade are employed on work of this kind, apparently for the sole reason that it requires less skill and can be done by cheaper labor.

In shirt and overall factories the situation is somewhat different. Most of the shirts are laundered outside the factory, and only a few pressers are needed for inside work. Unquestionably, too, the work is light, the irons are easily handled, and the degree of skill required is less than in pressing fine custom suits. In consequence women have full possession of the department in plants where articles of this kind are manufactured. Four shirt or overall factories employ six women pressers, the largest shirt factory employing three women pressers, and the others one each. The muslin underwear factory employs five women pressers.

OCCUPATIONS OF WOMEN

More important numerically than this contested field are the various occupations held solely by women. The basis of all later specialization is the single-needle, power-driven machine, which still sews most of the seams and puts together most parts of the garments. A touch of the treadle starts the machine and no further foot motion is involved. Of the 591 women engaged at single-needle work at the time of the investigation, 205 (34.6 per cent) worked by the entire garment system; that is, each girl did all the work on one garment that can be done by a machine of this kind. Each factory, of course, must have a few special machines for buttonholing, button sewing, or clamping. The entire garment system is of advantage to the girl in that it equips her to do different kinds of work if she changes her position, and makes it less difficult for her to fit into another place. It is of advantage to the factory in that it places emphasis on accurate work rather than on speed. It is quite as likely to be used in large factories where 160 hands are employed, as in small factories where there are only eight operators, and is found quite as frequently in one line of the industry as in another. The experience of each shop decides the owners on the plan of work most profitable.

Yet, although no one line of manufacture shows a distinct tendency toward the adoption of the section system, certain individual plants have abandoned the entire garment system in its favor. Sixty-five per cent of the factories, and of the operators in fact, did only section work in 1907. Undeniably speed is gained by minimizing the work done on a garment by an individual, and where inspection is thorough, this speed is not gained at the expense of accuracy. Since the system is used by a majority of the factories and a majority of the operators, it probably secures the highest output efficiency.

The section system may perhaps be understood best through some specific cases. In one shirt factory one operator makes the bosoms, one the cuffs and neckband, and one seams and closes the shirt. This latter is the best paying work here, but in another shirt factory nearby the best girls do the trimming; that is, make the cuffs, neckbands, and bands for the bosom. In a pants factory, the division of work on the cheaper grade of goods is as follows: (1) making fronts and putting in pockets; (2) joining seams; (3) hemming bottoms; (4) putting canvas in and belt on; (5) putting in curtains (hand work). The best grade of goods is made in three sections only, and belt and canvas as well as curtains are put in by hand.

After the single-needle work has been done, some sections of the garment must be finished on special machines. The number of these machines varies according to the kind of work and the size of the shop, but in all cases there are only two distinct principles of operation. Either a touch of the treadle releases the power and starts the machine,—as in machines for buttonholing, button sewing, tacking (for ends of pockets), serging edges of seams, and all double-needle work,—or the work is done without power by forceful pressure of the treadle. Everything that must be clamped in place, such as hooks and eyes, buttons for overalls, and so forth, is clamped by a machine operated on this second principle. Often it is necessary to have three or four different machines for different kinds of buttons, and in a small shop one operator may run several of the "specials"; but in the large shops there is a girl for each machine.

Except in a few custom shirt workrooms, button-sewing machines are universal. The operation is so simple that the machine is often run by a young girl. The button is inserted in the jaws of the machine, the garment is fastened in place, and by a touch of the treadle the needle moves rapidly back and forth until the button is firmly fastened.

Chief among the "specials," however, is the double-needle machine. This is of two kinds, either a "flat-bed," set in the table like any of the single needles, or a "cylinder," standing out from the table and made so that the arm or leg of a garment may be passed over it. The cylinder double needle is used for closing the sleeves of shirts or for the long inner seams in overalls. The flat-bed, which is somewhat less in evidence, is used in the larger factories for putting in sleeves. The advantages of the machine are, of course, that a double seam can be made by one operation, and that there is saving both in time and in number of employes. The operator is an expert hand, and among the best paid girls in the factory. But even quite large shops do not use more than one or two machines, and the very largest uses only eight, so the demand for operators is relatively small. In pants factories, double needles are not required. As a vacancy at this work is usually filled by the forewoman until one of the other hands can be trained, it follows that a skilled girl would not have many opportunities for employment.

Buttonholing is now done by machine much more generally than it was two years ago, as improvements have been introduced which make it possible to operate without injury even to very fine material. Buttonholes are worked by hand only at the request of the customer. Many manufacturers do not consider the hand buttonholes more desirable even for the best grade of custom shirts; while for trousers or other cloth goods they are not used at all. By the introduction of a control for the knife in a buttonhole machine, it has become possible so to regulate it that the cloth is not cut until the operator wishes, the value of this being that if the thread tangles, or there is any other imperfection of finish, the buttonhole can be remade before any cutting is done.

HAND FINISHING

With these machines in use there is less occasion for extensive hand finishing of shirts, which formerly led to so much outwork. Even manufacturers for the most exclusive trade use machines for much of their work and have the rest hand-done inside. Similarly, the hand finishing necessary for pants has been greatly reduced, and the five plants where hand finishing is needed at all are so organized that finishing is done within the factory.

There were in 1907, 87 inside finishers in the trade, 74 of them at work on pants, putting in curtains, loops, and sometimes belts and canvas. In the union shops finishing is a recognized part of the manufacturing process, and as such has the scale of prices regulated and fixed, so that possible earnings may run as high as $10. In the non-union pants factories, finishers, who earn at most $4.00 to $8.00 a week, do not fare so well. Coats and vests require more hand work, but there are only two factories of any size where they are made. Other manufacturers who deal in them give out the contract to some one of the small tailor shops on Smithfield Street, or Sixth Street, where in most cases, although the work is done on the premises, the conditions are anything but desirable.

In shirt factories expert hand workers of buttonholes rarely succeed in earning over $5.00 or $6.00. In one case, where in addition to the buttonholes the customer's initials have to be embroidered on each shirt, the income of these girls with their unmarketable skill does not average over $8.00 a week the year round. Clearly, the demand for hand finishing is waning, and in cases where it still seems an integral part of the work, it is being systematized and brought under factory control.

Most factories employ examiners or inspectors to pass upon the complete articles, as a check to possible carelessness. Sometimes this is held not as a separate position, but in conjunction with other work, and it rarely commands such wages as can be obtained by expert machine hands. In shirt factories, articles after being laundered are re-inspected.

Trimmers, folders and boxers are among the other employes in this department. The trimmer's duty is to clip the threads left long by the operators. She is usually a young girl paid by the day, $ .65 or $ .70, but in one place the forewoman has developed a different system. Instead of four trimmers at day rates, there is now but one, who is paid by the piece and earns as much as $9.50 a week. The girls at the machines were raised $ .01 on their work and encouraged to clip their ends more closely, so that they too are able to earn more.

WAGES

Although some departments in nearly all factories are paid by time, the piece-payment system is far more prevalent. Time payments are, of course, necessary for folders, trimmers, boxers, and examiners; frequently, also, the same system proves most convenient for pressers, and, when the kind of work constantly changes, for buttonhole operators and button sewers. Two factories, however, both small and both making custom shirts, pay all their employes by the week. In one there are only two girls and each does several kinds of work, so that a calculation of piece rates would be almost impossible. In the other, where nine girls are employed, section work is the rule, but so much attention is paid to finish that the firm prefers to pay by the week, and to raise wages when good work is turned out rapidly, rather than to put the emphasis primarily on speed. Under the piece-payment system in the other factories, checks upon carelessness, such as inspection, and the rule that girls must remake bad work without pay, are relied on to keep the output up to standard. One employer summarized the disadvantages of each plan after this fashion: "Piece-work girls are apt to hurry," he said, "and to set the machine for long stitches in order to get out more work; but, on the other hand, week workers are likely to be lazy and have to be watched constantly." On the whole, the piece-work system with inspection seemed to him more efficient. By requiring a minimum output from each section, and by keeping after hours any section that is behind with its work, he has secured a record for high speeding.

There is little advantage in giving in detail the various piece rates on which wages are based. For the different qualities of goods, for the different articles, and for the different sections of each article, there are special rates. One garment may be much easier to do than another apparently like it, and often a higher wage is earned on a piece of goods that is easy to handle than on the same section of heavy goods, for which a higher rate is paid. The points to be noted are the possible range of wages* between slow workers and fast workers, the sums earned by the majority, and the pressure brought to bear upon them in getting out their work. A summary of the payrolls of a few typical factories may serve to illustrate these points:

*For range of wages in each garment factory see Appendix B, p. 389, Table 46.

TABLE 14.—PAYROLL: FACTORY NO. 1.   ARTICLE MANUFACTURED:
PANTS

Number of Employes: Men, 15; Women, 70.   Total, 85.

Occupations of Women	No. of Women	Weekly Wages (piece system)		
		Minimum	Maximum	Majority
Single-needle operators .	28	$4.00	$9.00	$7.00
Specials	13	..	..	..
Buttonhole . . .	..	..	7.00	..
Button stamping . .	..	..	4.00 (wk.)	..
Button sewing . .	..	..	6.00	..
Serging edges of seams .	..	..	7.50	..
Pressers	10		..	..
Seam presser . . .	..	5.00	6.00	..
Shrinker	..	..	7.00	..
Others	..	6.00	7.00	..
Examiners	7	4.00 (wk.)	8.00 (wk.)	..
Hand finishers . . .	12	4.00	8.00	6.00

Factory No. 1 is a non-union shop in which the wages were
reduced by a 15 per cent cut during the business depression in
1907–1908.   For the next summary, one of the large union shops
has been taken:

TABLE 15.—PAYROLL: FACTORY NO. 2.   ARTICLES MANUFACTURED:
PANTS, COATS, AND VESTS

Number of Employes: Men, 65; Women, 95.   Total, 160.

Occupations of Women	No. of Women	Weekly Wages (piece system)		
		Minimum	Maximum	Majority
Single-needle operators (pants and coats) . . .	76	$6.00	$12.00	$9.00
Specials (several machines operated by one girl) . .	2	5.00 (wk.)	8.00 (wk.)	..
Pressers	4	8.00	11.00	10.00
Hand finishers (pants) .	1	7.00	10.00	8.00
" " (coats) .	7	7.00	10.00	8.00
Vest makers (each worker does all work on vest, even to the pressing)	3	8.00	11.00	10.00
Examiners	2	5.00	8.00	..

The scheme of work and wages in one of the overall factories* is shown in the next schedule (Factory No. 3). This is in a part of the city where there are few competing industries. Most of the girls live in the neighborhood and accept a slightly lower wage because of the convenient location which enables them to save carfare. An interesting thing about this plant set on the slope of a hill is that it was originally built for a school-house, and the machine hands have inherited the fine square rooms, lighted by high windows, and in summer the free sweep of air to lessen the burden of long hours.

TABLE 16.—PAYROLL: FACTORY NO. 3. ARTICLE MANUFACTURED: OVERALLS

Number of Employes: Men, 2; Women, 38. Total, 40.

Occupations of Women	No. of Women	WEEKLY WAGES (piece system)		
		Minimum	Maximum	Majority
Single-needle operators .	32	$5.00	$8.00	$7.00
Specials . . .				
Double-needle operators	3	8.00	12.00	9.00
Buttonhole machine .	1	..	7.00 (wk.)	..
Button-sewing machine	1	..	4.50 (wk.)	..
Presser and folder . .	1	..	5.50 (wk.)	..

The advantage which double-needle girls have over their co-workers in this factory is true of the other overall factories. When a girl once has the knack of the machine, she can easily bring her pace to a pitch which totals a good sum weekly. The long seams closing the legs and the short seam across the back are paid for in union shops at the rate of $ .09 a dozen. In one place, the present operator, who is not an experienced girl, is able already to make twenty dozen ($1.80) a day, and her predecessor earned, as a rule, $2.70, the pay for thirty dozens.

The schedules of one small shirt factory with a custom trade, and of a large one which manufactures goods for stock, will fairly

* In this factory, the entire garment is made by one girl. No section work, except special machining and pressing. Non-union.

give the range of possibilities in this branch of the industry. The
smaller of the two follows:

TABLE 17.—PAYROLL: FACTORY NO. 4. ARTICLES MANUFACTURED:
SHIRTS (CUSTOM AND STOCK)

Number of Employes: Men, 1; Women, 9. Total, 10.

Occupations of Women	No. of Women	Weekly Wages (time system)		
		Minimum	Maximum	Majority
Single-needle operators .	5	$7.00	$11.00	$9.00
Specials				
Buttonhole machine oper-ators	1	7.00	..	..
Hand finishing (fine em-broidering of initials) .	3	5.50	6.50	..

In this factory, where wages are paid by time instead of by piece,
the gross sum does not vary greatly from that earned by piece
workers. Yet there is not that nervous intensity which characterizes the face and manner of the garment worker. Stress is
laid on quality of output rather than on speed, wages are secure
whether material is good or bad, and a girl is not so much at the
mercy of the whims or favoritism of the forewoman in her department. The complaints of some girls on this score in the other
factories give evidence that there is often genuine ground for ill
feeling.

The last of these schedules (see page 120) is for the largest
of the shirt factories, whose building and equipment are in many
respects model, and whose management is notable for small
courtesies toward its workers.

Here the forewoman finds that there are always half a dozen
girls who earn $13 or $14, and below them about twenty others
earning $10 to $12. The per cent earning $10 or over is remark-
ably high, but the girls have no reason to fear having their wages
cut if they make too much. They have been allowed to share in
the firm's progress. For instance, when a few years ago new
buttonhole machines were introduced which could do the work
formerly done by four machines, the operators, each of whom was

TABLE 18.—PAYROLL: FACTORY NO. 5. ARTICLE MANUFACTURED: SHIRTS (STOCK)

Number of Employes: Men, 5; Women, 75. Total, 80.

Occupations of Women	No. of Women	WEEKLY WAGES (piece system)		
		Minimum	Maximum	Majority
Single-needle operators . .	51	$5.00	$15.00	$8.00
Specials				
Double-needle, flat bed .	4	6.00	12.00	7.00
Double-needle, cylinder .	4	6.00	12.00	7.00
Buttonhole	3	5.00	15.00	..
Button-sewing . . .	2	5.00	6.50	..
Examiners	4	6.50 (wk.)	11.00	..
Pressers	3	4.50 (wk.)	10.00	..
Trimmer	1	..	9.50	..
Folder	2	6.00 (wk.)	..	..
Boxer	1	6.00 (wk.)	..	..

turning out at the new machine a third more work, were paid at the same piece rate as before and consequently were able to earn much higher wages weekly. A less far-sighted firm would immediately have cut the rate. The members of this firm, however, feel that some of the profit from a new invention should go to the girls as well as to them. Much has been gained for the girls, too, through the influence of the forewoman, who takes more than a commercial interest in her charges. "I see them more hours than their mothers do," she says, "and I want these hours to count for as much as possible to them."

The foregoing tables illustrate the wages that can be earned at special machines, as well as at single needles. Clearly, among specials the double-needle operators are in a class by themselves with an earning capacity of $4.00 to $5.00 a week more than the operators of buttonhole, button-sewing, or button-stamping machines. Whereas these others earn for the most part $4.00 to $7.00 a week, the button stampers being paid the least, double-needle operators can earn as much as $12. This rate of earnings is exceeded only in one instance among specials, by a buttonhole operator who makes $15 a week. This case, however, is exceptional, and in general it may be said that the double-needle operators earn the highest wages obtainable at special work.

As the single-needle operators are much more numerous than the specials, and as their occupation is really the determining characteristic of the trade, a detailed summary of the wages paid them in each of the Pittsburgh garment factories may be of interest:

TABLE 19.—RANGE OF WEEKLY WAGES OF SINGLE-NEEDLE OPERATORS

No. of Plant	Article Manufactured	No. Single-needle Operators	WEEKLY WAGES		
			Minimum	Maximum	Majority
1	Shirts . . .	15	$6.00	$12.00	$7.00
2	Pants . . .	114	4.00	14.00	9.00
3	Muslin underwear .	34	4.00	10.00	7.00
4	Shirts . . .	1	..	10.00*	..
5	Shirts . . .	3	8.00	10.00	8.00
6	Overalls . .	15	1.00	12.00	8.00
7	Shirts . . .	24	6.00	8.00	8.00
8	Shirts and overalls .	39	4.00	12.00	8.00
9	Pants . . .	37	3.00	12.00	8.00
10	Overalls . .	34	5.00	8.00	7.00
11	Pants . . .	6	3.00	9.00	7.00
12	Pants . . .	28	4.00	9.00	7.00
13	Shirts and overalls .	26	6.00	10.00	8.00
14	Shirts and overalls .	75	6.00	10.50	7.00
15	Shirts . . .	5	7.00*	11.00*	..
16	Pants . . .	10	4.00	9.00	8.00
17	Pants, coats, and vests .	49	7.00	12.00	9.00
18	Shirts . . .	18	7.00	14.00	10.00
19	Shirts . . .	51	5.00	15.00	8.00
20	Vests † . . .	..	..	..	..
21	Shirts . . .	7	6.50	12.00	8.00

* Time wages.   † Women do only hand finishing.

It is evident from this table that earnings vary less according to the article manufactured than according to the policy of individual shops. The majority of the operators reach the same point, $7.00 to $8.00 a week. In shops 2 and 16 which are the largest in this local of the United Garment Workers, they have reached a higher point, $9.00 a week. Shop 17, however, which is non-union, has the highest majority earnings; the policy of the firm has brought more upward pressure to bear on the wage-scale than could a delegation of union representatives. Yet this case is exceptional, and for the trade as a whole it seems a fair inference that the union has been able slightly to raise the general level of wages.

HOURS AND SEASONS

The longest regular working day in any of the factories is nine hours and a half; this obtains in one of the unorganized pants factories. In seven other factories the hours run from nine to nine and a quarter daily. In 60 per cent of the factories, however, the working hours daily are less than nine. The characteristic working day in the trade is comparatively short.

Sometimes overtime occurs as a matter of individual policy. One proprietor, for instance, requires a stated minimum number of pieces to be produced daily by each section of his factory workers. If the girls in one section fall behind in their output, they are obliged to stay after hours and finish. This system in reality operates to secure from each section the maximum output, rather than a minimum to which all can without too great effort attain.

Under the same circumstances in other firms the situation is handled not by requiring the belated section to stay, but by giving some of its work to a more advanced section, so that by the closing hour all the employes may have completed the desired amount.

The exaggerated alternation of slack and busy seasons in garment factories has become almost proverbial, but in this respect the trade in Pittsburgh, by its stability, is distinguished markedly from the same trade as carried on in the east. Not one of the Pittsburgh firms depends for its success on goods made of expensive materials. Although garments of good quality are made to some extent, and although in the demand for them there is some fluctuation, the staple articles of manufacture are railroad jumpers and workingmen's jeans. Since the kind of clothing worn by workmen in the Pittsburgh district varies but little from season to season, the rough goods are put on the market steadily without reference to seasonal change. The probable demand for these goods can be calculated from year to year, and production so distributed that the workers are steadily employed. Save for three days' stock-taking the first of the year, the pants factories and all the overall factories except one have steady work the year round. There is no off season in which they can shut down and lay off their hands. One overall factory closes for two weeks in summer.

Seasonal overtime occurs occasionally in several lines of the trade. The pants manufacturers who supply the local ready-made trade in medium and high-class goods sometimes have night work as orders come in during the fall and winter. The largest of these firms works overtime until nine o'clock for three months in the fall. Another which had the heaviest record for overtime work in 1907, worked two, three, and four nights a week from September to March, at times reaching a working week of sixty-six hours. The vest factories have four months of night work during the winter, and when times are prosperous, the custom shirt factories have two months of night work in the fall. Yet, taking the trade as a whole, overtime is exceptional in Pittsburgh, and in some of the most important plants, where only cheap goods are manufactured, it is never required. Individual proprietors freely express their disapproval of the practice. For instance, one man who runs a small shop for the ready-made trade said on this point, "No, we never have overtime. Nine hours is enough for the girls and they can't stand it if we keep them at it any longer than that. The work is hard enough for all day, but at night it is too much."

Thus, just as overtime in a majority of the garment trades in Pittsburgh has been minimized, so the slack season, because of this balancing influence of a steady trade in cheap goods, has been largely obviated. The making of custom shirts and of the finer grade of stock shirts, however, is more subject to seasonal variation and sensitive to changes in the money market. Seasonal change is of less importance than change in general business prosperity. In summer, because customers are away, the trade is always dull and the girls may be laid off for from two weeks to three months, although usually this summer cessation of work, which is ordered whenever the demand for work fails, is not for more than three or four weeks. Changes in business prosperity, on the other hand, may occur at any time, and with any dullness or insecurity of the market the volume of business in the shirt factories instantly shrinks and the girls are threatened with a period of idleness. During the depression in 1907–08 one-fourth of the women in the trade were laid off, and others were kept only on part time. This represented an exceptional condition, however, and cannot rightly be compared with years more nearly normal.

But the making of custom shirts engages only a small fraction, less than 7 per cent, of the women in the Pittsburgh trade. The representative line of garment making—cheap jeans and railroad jumpers—is subject to none of these vicissitudes, and of the trade as a whole it may be said that few plants require overtime, slack time is almost unknown, and work in general is steady the year round.

SUMMARY OF TRADE CONDITIONS

The final point to be noted about a trade is the personnel of the workers in it, for through them often may be made the clearest estimate of its opportunities.

Some of the women in garment factories are Jewish; others are native born of Irish or German stock. Almost no Italians have come into the trade. One man prefers Jewish girls because they make the quickest workers. "Italians marry too young," he says; "one no sooner teaches them the work than they leave to get married, and we want girls who will stay with us a few years at least." In seven factories none but Jewish girls are employed. Other employers object to them, especially to immigrant Jewish girls, because "they don't take to the work as well as American girls; they're not used to factories and they complain about the work being hard." In five factories Americans and Jews are employed in equal numbers, and in the rest the majority of the girls are American.

They are not of the shifting type, who go from factory to factory, from one kind of work to another. They have a trade, and they stay at it. A girl with a grievance has always the possibility of obtaining work with some other firm; yet these girls are far less hasty in parting with a place than are others in occupations that demand less skill. There is no room for one who will not work hard, and who does not keep up to a certain minimum pace.

Repeatedly one hears the statement, "If a girl can't make $6.00 a week, we don't want her. Her place at the machine is worth more than she is." From among the hosts of applicants and trial hands, there are sifted out the quick, steady girls with a capacity for concentration and endurance.

The type is fundamentally good, but some years of the work seem to make the girls thin and nervous. Few leave the trade in less than two years; many are engaged at it for six or seven years, and some for more. They stand the work, as a rule, without any slackening of their pace. "Of course, they are tired," said one forewoman, "but no more so at this than they would be at any other thing." One manager who has had longer experience does not altogether agree with the foregoing. He manufactures pants; has worked at a machine himself, he says, and knows that it is hard. "A girl might work for $5.00 or $6.00 a week all her life and stand it, but when it comes to earning $8.00, that wears her out. Many a time an ambitious foreign girl has come over here, only to be worn out and have to drop the trade after three years; the pace is too high." That one hears less testimony of this sort in the larger shops is no doubt due to the fact that mere numbers are a screen to the wearier ones, and that they may drop out with little comment in the course of the year's work.

Among these girls, sifted out for speed and endurance as they are, the life outside the workroom is in part determined by nationality. Girls of American stock with few exceptions live with their parents, and their earnings are a contribution to the family income. Not less than 38 per cent* of the women garment workers, however, are boarding with strangers. Most of these homeless girls are Jewish, of foreign origin. They have left their families in the old country, and through agencies of their race, have gradually come into the trade. Their problem is distinctly different from that of the girl who is one of a family group. In most cases they must learn the trade here and manage to live either on savings or by the help of others, until they have worked up to a good weekly income.

Past experiences of girls who came to a factory with no

* This percentage is based on the statements of forewomen in each of the 21 garment shops.

intention of learning the trade, took their week's wages and left, have made employers cautious in paying apprentices. The larger factories will take apprentices; the others want experienced girls. From four employers only may a beginner look for payment by the week while she learns. Elsewhere, the beginner is paid what she makes and she must shoulder the disappointment of having earned a dollar after a week's work, if she wants to keep on and in time earn more. Estimates vary as to how long it will take her. "After a week or so, she ought to know how to run the machine," says one employer, but the forewoman says, "four months at the very least, before she can earn good wages, and often six months." Theory may be acquired in a week, but not dexterity. It is of interest to know that in the factory with the largest proportion of foreign Jewish girls, apprentices are paid weekly instead of by the piece from the start. In view of the large number who are here without family connections, it is significant that practically none who stay at their work earn less than $6.00 a week, and that half of these earn over $7.00.

CHAPTER VII

THE GARMENT TRADES

THE SMALL SHOPS AND OUTWORK

THE factory trade where goods are made by the hundred dozen would seem to be easily marked off for study. But when we come to consider its ramifications, we realize how verily rootlike it has grown, now here, now there, through a chain of small tailor shops in lofts and stores, out to women in their homes in the Hill district, in the slums of the North Side among the coal hills of Carrick, and as far as Millvale and Crafton.

With the exception of custom shirts, most of the garments made up in factories are "ready made"; that is, they are turned out in wholesale quantities after patterns in stock sizes. Some of these factories which sell entire suits, make up in their own workrooms perhaps only one of the parts which go into the suits. This leads to the further puzzle of workrooms to all outward appearance factories, in which no manufacturing whatever is carried on save the cutting of cloth, but from which finished garments are turned out each week by the hundreds. We may sum up our queries and deal with them one by one: When a pants factory undertakes to handle orders for whole suits, where and how are the coats and vests made? How is the custom work of the city handled? Where are garments made and finished for the workrooms in which there is no machine equipment, and in which cutting only is done?

When thousands of orders for suits are handled by a pants factory, the genesis of vests and coats is to be found in Smithfield Street, Sixth Street, and on Liberty Avenue. A factory that is not equipped to make coats and vests gives the order to a small shop in the neighborhood.

The contract system, as known in the seaboard cities,

does not exist in Pittsburgh. We do not find here a chief contractor who gets the order from the factory, cutting out the goods and giving the machining to a subcontractor, who in turn may give out the buttonholing, felling, and other finishing to a second subcontractor, who, as another link in the chain, may turn over much of the handwork to women in the tenement households. Contracting in Pittsburgh is of a different sort. Instead of this complex subdivision of work and profits, we find that the subordinate contract shop which depends on factory orders for its existence has itself a force of perhaps from eight to twelve people, sufficient to make up the goods inside.

These small shops are technically factories, and as such are subject to inspection. Being located for the most part in business buildings, they are not technically "sweatshops," for in the Pennsylvania law that term is applied only to a workshop in a tenement or dwelling in which articles are manufactured for sale by others than members of the family which rents the room. Yet in make-up and characteristics they fall within the meaning of the term as it is employed by those who know the slums of our manufacturing cities, where populations, largely immigrant, throw out their frail defenses against the threatening encroachments of high rent and intolerable living conditions. The word stands for a system of work which may or may not be legally assailable, but which in itself is at least definite, vivid, and industrially indefensible. In this sense, contract shops belong to the sweatshop type.

One of them can be reached from Strawberry Alley by climbing three flights of narrow, dark stairs. You pass the retail cigar store on the ground floor, the dingy Chinese restaurant on the floor above, and above that silent warerooms. Pausing for breath at the blind landing just below the roof, you see through the half-open door half a dozen stocky, undersized, foreign-looking men passing from stove to table with their irons, or machining at the far end of the room. In the corner of the room near one window, where the ceiling slants, a group of women in blousy, ill-fitting wrappers bend over lapfuls of coats into which they are putting the linings. The ceiling is nowhere more than eight feet high, and by the window it is only six and a half feet. The handsewers and the two or three machine-workers get what light there

is from the street. The cutters and pressers work on tables farther away. Near the door is a small gas stove, partly broken down,
on which all the irons are heated. In the other corner, also near
the door, is an unpainted and battered tin basin with a disabled
faucet; this serves as a lavatory. Such machinery as there is is
of the most primitive type, foot-power sewing machines, hand
shears, hand knives. The workers, too, are in a sense primitive;
they have served apprenticeship neither to the life of the city
nor to the standards of industrial work. The men are Jewish
immigrants from Russia and Roumania; the women are Neapoli-
tans. Both for the men and for the women this is their first attempt at factory production.

Other of the contract shops are variations on this type.
One, even more primitive, occupies a three-cornered room in an
old building on Fifth Avenue. This room boasts one window,
one table, and two or three broken chairs. The laths of the walls
are exposed in places where the plaster has broken away, and the
floor is littered with the decay of old boards and discarded scraps
of cloth. Three men and three women are employed here. The
women finish by hand, one man cuts, another presses, and a third
machines the goods.

Such shops as inhabit the upper and cheaper floors of old
buildings are characterized in general by low ceilings, by poor
light through one or two small windows, with occasionally a
flaring gas jet to help out the far dim end of the room, by walls
gray with neglect and floors burdened with refuse. In contrast
I could take you to shops that are clean, light, and well-managed,
but they are exceptions. Colonies of undesirable workrooms are
the distinguishing feature of the streets where small contract
shops prevail. Men, and men only, recent Jewish immigrants
from the Slavic and Balkan countries, work at the machines.
Women, some of them the wives of these men, and others from
southern Italy, finish the garments by hand. The shops have
neither regular hours nor regular wages. Each individual strikes
his bargain with the proprietor, who is often an immigrant only
a few years in advance of his employes, for pay by the week if
the proprietor cares to run the risk, or more often for pay by the
piece. Sometimes the piece rate will be for making and finishing

a garment entire, and at other times it will be split up into smaller piece rates for work on different sections. Sometimes two of the employes work by teams and pool their earnings. In general, the men make $7.00 to $9.00 a week, the women $4.00 to $5.00, although even in a workshop of this type, an exceptionally efficient hand may forge ahead and secure a much larger sum for the week's work. The ambitious have an opportunity to make extra earnings, through longer hours than are permitted in larger factories. Here the day begins at seven o'clock if you wish. The lunch hour is a casual interval, often omitted. The close of the day comes sometimes at six, sometimes at nine, sometimes at ten; in fact, whenever the work is finished. If the work is not too pressing, those who wish may go home by nightfall, but when a rush of orders calls for it, employes are tacitly obliged to stay. Whereas none of the garment factories has a working day of more than nine and a half hours, the contract shops have a working day of ten to fourteen hours. Whereas the garment factories employ English-speaking, frequently native-born girls, who by their unions have secured for many of their number a living wage, the contract shops employ immigrant labor at rates which often enable them to underbid factory production.

The check to the trade of the contract shop is in many instances the necessarily inferior quality of the output. Yet contract shops are found which not only handle stock coats and vests of the cheaper grade for factories, but which take over from these same factories their finest grade of custom work. The factory equipment may be unsuited to the filling of special orders, or it may be suited for the filling of special orders only in part. The rest of the orders which the customer has no doubt arranged for with great particularity of detail, may go with the lump order for stock suits, to be made in one of the contract shops dependent on the factory. That part of a suit is made under fair conditions implies nothing as to the rest of it, and the mating of a well-equipped factory with an unsanitary workshop, in their joint contribution to a customer's outfit, is a matter of daily occurrence.

CUSTOM TAILORING

This brings us part of the answer to the second question, as to where and how the custom work of the city is done. The contract shops handle much of the custom trade that comes through factories. The rest of it, and by far the larger portion, is carried by the merchant tailors, who number 1500 in Pittsburgh and the North Side. It has been beyond the possibilities of this investigation to attempt to cover statistically the work of women in these shops. As most of them employ one or two women each for hand finishing, the estimate of an old tradesman in the district that 2000 women are used in this tailoring work is probably not far wrong. The conditions of their employment are as various as the parts of the city where they work. You find the wife of a small tailor increasing the family income by saving the wages of an employe, but herself receiving no payment and having no regular hours for the work. You find efficient hand finishers who are employed spring and fall by a larger merchant nine hours a day for a sixteen weeks' season at $9.00 a week. On the other hand, you find hours and wages which more nearly approach the sweatshop conditions, and you find women workers of the immigrant type. In workrooms, there is every gradation from the clean, light, well-equipped room back of a well-built store to dim basements where two or three men and women work at the same task with poor tools and for uncounted hours.

There is still to be answered the third question, as to the making of garments that are cut out by so-called factories which have no machine equipment for putting the cloth together before selling it in suits. In this category also falls the residue of cheap garments ordered through fully equipped factories, but which they cannot turn out in quantities sufficient to meet the demand.

This question is answered primarily by the scattered outworkers in different parts of the city. On Iten Street, where a straggling little row of houses clings to the edge of a North Side hill, I found two women in rooms reached by an unsteady outside staircase. Once within, the clean oilcloth and carefully scrubbed sink bespoke the neat German housewife, whom no amount of work and poverty can deprive of her inbred tradition of scrupulous cleanliness. The $7.00 rent gave them only two small rooms. One sister took in two washes a week and both worked on trousers. At the sewing they made not over $3.00 a week, although when the price was higher they used to make $4.80. When they started in, there had been a sick mother to care for, a small brother and sister at home, and the two older girls felt that they could not work in a shop. The mother had died since then, the brother and sister had married and gone away. These two who were left had kept on at the only trade they knew. One of them went to the factory last year to see if she could work inside, but the noise and dust made her ill; so she went back to the old way.

Spring Garden, beyond the end of the car line, has some colonies of such outworkers, and still others are in the down-town section of the city. In a back street whose six frame houses are alike without paint or plumbing or sewerage connection, I found a little gray lady, a vest maker, on the second floor. There were no numbers and no bells, but children playing outside gave me the clue. A glance at the room showed that a fight for a standard had been made here. The surroundings were not wholly clean; the garments were finished with a nervous haste that could not keep pace with lowering of prices. When Mrs. Neil's husband died fifteen years before, she took the insurance and tried to keep a store, but failed. There was a little daughter, then only four years old, and there was apparently no resource but the trade that she used to work at long ago, vest making. She found that by taking the vests home and working several hours in the evening, as well as during the day, she could make a dozen and a half in a week, which paid her $6.30. This meant doing the entire work on each vest, even to buttons and buttonholes. After a while the pay was cut from $ .35 to $ .25 for a vest. To make up the difference and earn as much as before, Mrs. Neil redoubled her energy, but beyond a certain point, speed can be increased only for a spurt, not for a steady pull. The result was a fall in output below the amount that she had made at first. Her limit is a dozen a week now, and no matter how hard she works, it seems to her impossible to do more. The $3.00 which she earns is supplemented by the earnings of her daughter. Together they manage to meet the $7.00 a month rent for their two rooms and to provide food and clothes.

"But it's a pull," said Mrs. Neil to me, "and it's taken the life out of us both."

THE OUTWORK DISTRICT

As you go farther beyond the built-up portion of the city, this question as to the manufacture of garments is answered more fully. One early spring morning I set out with the secretary of the Cutters' Local to find the further answer. We rode through the factory district of the South Side, past streets of small brick houses to the end of the Carson Street line, and then walked for perhaps half a mile along a muddy, unpaved road, the Allegheny River at our left and on our right an irregular, broken line of hills. After a while, we climbed an embankment along which ran the narrow track of a railroad. Twice the busy little engine passed us, carrying coal direct from mine to river. At length we came to a steep wagon road leading into the hills. These hills are full of little settlements, made up of groups of people who have taken houses near the mines in order to be near their work, who have left the city to get cheaper rent, or who, farming in meagre fashion, have never known another sort of life than this isolation, unlovely and sordid as only country slums can be. This district is within the city limits of Pittsburgh, but to all appearance it might be away a hundred miles. The houses, scattered wide apart, are tiny, broken-down affairs, dilapidated and unsightly. The statement that "as a rule one family occupies a house" must be taken with due consideration of the size of the house. Three rooms, one of which is the kitchen, shared by a household of nine or ten, may mean as much actual congestion as three rooms shared by two families.

At the left of the first wagon road were perhaps half a dozen houses. The whirr of machines from within doors broke in louder than any other sound upon the stupor that seemed to hang over the invisible life of the street. This whirr of machines, repeated from house to house, told of the presence of garment makers whose scattered forces, if drawn together, would more than outdistance the working force of the largest Pittsburgh factory in this trade. In one tiny gray cottage I found a family of three. The son is a miner, home that day and lying helpless from a fall of rock in the mine some weeks before. The old German mother and her daughter make jeans, they told me, at $1.10 a dozen, and have done this work for years. It helps out during good seasons, and when the son is out of work, or hurt, as now, it keeps them going. The driver brings the goods from the city and they pay him $ .07½ a dozen for hauling, which comes out of their profits. The thread is furnished them and the goods are cut at the factory, but they are expected to send the garments back completely made, finished even to the buttons and buttonholes. Although the price for this work has gone up, they cannot be sure what they will receive. A few years ago, before the union was strong, the makers of cheap jeans received not over $ .70 a dozen. That was in the days when the scattered workers among the hills were so many cogs fitting into the machine that brought prosperity to the employer, so many uncomplaining profit makers for the big firms in the city.

Yet a few years have made a great difference in the trade. The United Garment Workers, who were organized in 1900 in one of the large factories with the idea that the union label would secure additional trade to the firm, proved capable of standing their ground and bargaining for their own advantage. The union then began to deal with this menace of the outworkers, to make them, too, a coherent part of its growth. When there was a vacancy at a factory machine, the union tried to bring in one of the hill girls to fill the place. When a factory was to be enlarged, the union men went out to the forlorn little groups of houses, and told the workers how much more they could earn and how much better places they could work in, if they would come into the city and belong to a union shop, instead of toiling at a foot-power machine day in and day out for a week's earnings of $4.50.

Now and then a girl went into the city to test the truth of what the union men had told her, and once at a power machine, she stayed. Others followed, until by degrees the outworkers' contingent began to lose its younger members. Naturally, it was the more ambitious and more efficient who broke their traditions and went down to the city. Behind were left the pale, tired girls who would not break into the old ways of their life by a new routine, the mothers whose duties kept them to the house, and the families in which each member, old and young, was so utilized that imagination proved powerless to suggest, should their forces be scattered, other means of obtaining equal earnings.

Thus the union sifted out possible factory workers, but this process could not be continued indefinitely. Against the women of these three groups who still manufacture in their homes, the most logical arguments proved futile. They felt apparently that some of the logic was on their side. Yet the campaign of the union was not without its effect upon them. They had learned what the union prices were. They had learned about wage scales, and when a neighbor's daughter went to the city and came back with $12 a week, being paid at the rate of $1.35 a dozen for jeans, there began a counter-reformation. The little factories that gave out all their work, saving expense in rent, machinery, and lighting, but competing for orders with "closed shops," were forced to reckon with the hill-women. For fear of losing their outwork employes these shrewd employers found it expedient to raise the rates for making goods. Pay for making jeans went up to $ .85, to $ .90, and finally to $1.05. This was for the cheaper grade of work. Material a little better, which required more care, paid the workers $1.10, and heavy jeans with pockets were rated at $1.25. Of course, the output of a foot-power machine can never approach the output of a steam-driven machine, but with this increase of prices the pay for the finished piece of goods, done by unorganized outworkers, was beginning to approach the pay for a finished piece made by a union girl. The union prices were still about 25 per cent higher, but the increase to the outworkers meant that the union was to be reckoned with.

The two German women in the little gray cottage knew the union arguments, but the mother spoke no English; she was used to her housework and to her quiet seven or eight hours of sewing day after day. She had her son's earnings and did not have to work unduly hard. Why should she go into the city? And her daughter? A girl to whom the idea of a factory is terrible. The noise, the rush, the exactions appall her; she too is used to the quiet daily work at home and wants no other. Mother and daughter together do not make more than five dozen pairs a week in summer, but in winter they can make six or seven dozen. They work only in the daytime. Trade is always steady, for out work, like factory work in the district, is free from alternating seasonal rush and slack times.

Across the road from the gray cottage the hill goes steeply down into a hollow where are other houses. One, a long, gray, weathered shack with a porch of decaying boards, is the home of two more outworkers. Close to it runs a creek, and opposite is a little whitewashed building of some nondescript material, built like a stable. Here, too, through the dull white walls, I heard the sound of a machine. The driver never takes the trouble to go down so far with his bundles, but throws them somewhere over the hill, and the woman, or a child or two, comes out of the house, wades through the creek, and carries home the load of clothing to be.

To reach one house that day we had to strike through the fields, across a brook, and finally to trust to a footpath that led along the steep slope of one hill out to the summit of another. There, a brief little road with its end and beginning not more than a quarter of a mile apart, boasted two houses. At the first I stopped. It was small, one and a half stories high, and built of gray boards. At the rear the hill sloped upward. In front was a tiny yard fenced in, and as I unfastened the sagging gate and stooped under the drain-pipe which ran diagonally across the yard, a family of children came to the door to greet me. All of them seemed undersized, for the mother told me that the oldest boy was nineteen and the girl seventeen; the slight little fellow who had worked in a glass-house all the fall was fifteen, she said. The enumeration ran through a series of six or seven youngsters, down to the littlest one who could only just walk, but was very dexterous at pulling threads. The mother herself fitted in with her surroundings. Had she been older and grayer, her spare figure and sunken cheeks might have belonged to one of the scrub-women who clean our city offices in the dark of the morning. But she was brown-haired and her fingers were quick and nervous.

The house was small enough to show all its possibilities at once. Two rooms and an attic housed a family of nine people, six ducks, and twenty-four chickens, the latter living contentedly in the kitchen. In the other room were six machines, and there the family slept—I could not see where, unless it were on the piles of clothing. The attic was reserved just then for one small boy, about whom I did not hear until a little girl up the road called out to me, "Say, did you see Johnnie? He's got the measles orful and he's getting worser."

Mrs. J. has worked on jeans for twenty years, she told me. Her husband used to be in the mill, but one of his hands was crippled and he lost his job. The children were little then. The rent for the crazy little shack was only $3.50, but food was a serious item. The result was that husband and wife began to make jeans at home, and as fast as the children could hold a needle they were pressed into service. Besides the two oldest children, the second boy and a girl of thirteen now work at the machines, and the others who are still younger sew on buttons, make buttonholes, and pull out threads. The hours of work seem incredible; from four in the morning until nine at night, one steady drive for every member of the household. The output is only fifteen to twenty dozen pairs of jeans a week at best, which brings an income for the family of $16 to $22. It is no wonder that the bare floors seem never to have been cleaned; that the children are ragged, ignorant, uncared for; that for mere life everything has been sacrificed to the dark piles of clothes on the floor.

"Sometimes I think I'd do better by goin' out washin' onct or twict a week," said Mrs. J., "but then washin's hard to git regular and I'm used to the pants."

Here is not the only household in which the steel mills have thrown the burden onto the women. Farther down the hill, where dwellings are set together more thickly, a small red house is built behind its bigger neighbors. Here, too, the family has six machines, and here, too, father, mother, sons, and daughters bend over a joint task, the making of jeans. "He had to do it," said Mrs. Freude, "he vas hurt in de mill and ve could both vork together and make somedings, but he couldn't get vork nowhere else." It is a far cry from the great half-lit spaces of the mill, and from handling the unfinished rails which glide white-hot through the dusk, to living in the back room of a little red cottage and working by the hour at a sewing machine. This is one way in which the handicapped from the steel industry have placed themselves. The two sons and two daughters of this family have grown up to the work since babyhood. By allowing no time for cleaning the workroom or for care of the house, by working twelve to thirteen hours a day, they turn out forty-five dozen pairs a week, and sometimes as many as fifty dozen. They have kept at work even when every one else was unable to secure the goods. Just as I came through the gate the driver's heavy wagon stood outside and he tossed one bundle after another down the alley in the direction of the red house. Down they tumbled from muddy step to step, until the ex-mill worker picked them up and threw them on the floor.

The scattered city workers carry their bundles back and forth from the shop, but in Carrick the business is managed by a system of drivers. There are two or three men, rough old Germans, who know every inch of the hills and all the women on them, and who can be trusted to drive off each trip with their thirty or forty dozen pairs of cut-out jeans to be made up somewhere and called for later on. The owners of the cloth themselves do not know where the drivers go. Sometimes the women come into the city for the money, and in that way become known to their employers, but often the driver is a go-between and to all intents is himself the women's employer. The rates charged for hauling, which might in a sense be regarded as a commission, vary with the residence of the outworker. Whereas $ .06 or $ .07 a dozen is charged for hauling to fairly accessible places, the women far up among the hills must pay $1.50 each trip, whether the goods are many or few.

Seven of the Fifth Avenue shops send out all their work, and for five factories a part of the work is done outside. The total of these home workrooms, when times are prosperous, ranges up to three thousand dozen pairs of jeans a week.

A third of the work is made up in Lower St. Clair, and another third in Millvale, or elsewhere near the city. That it is cheap work does not mean that it is carelessly made or that any sort of machining will pass. There is inspection enough to insure precaution on the part of the women, and there is enough poorly cut work sent out to tax their ingenuity. This is not true in the larger factories. There the cutters are allowed an extra two to four yards of goods on each lot. In the little shops, on the other hand, the policy of saving is carried to an extreme. "It would cost us far more," said one man, "to have the women inside. We would have to rent another floor to make room for their machines; we would have to buy the machines, and we would have gas and heat, and then have to pay them more, may be, into the bargain." He did not add that the cost of material would be increased, because no operator can make speed at a power machine if there is much piecing to be done. The time of the outworker, however, does not concern the owner of the shop. Consequently, on each lot of cloth he can save a good deal by having it cut short and compelling the women to piece it out themselves. This is the regular custom, the women claim, in six out of seven of the Fifth Avenue shops, and takes away not a little from their total possible earnings. A standing grievance with them is the hours that they have spent piecing, when they might have been going ahead on straight work and earning more. "An' it's always the worst paid work that has to be pieced the most," they say.

Altogether, between 150 and 180 families are engaged in home manufacture. There could scarely be a sharper contrast to the modern city factory than this outwork. The factory itself is a gathering place for women engaged at the same task. However ill kept and gloomy it may be, there is always the background of the city itself, with its centres for social activity, its light and movement, and the meeting together of kind with kind. But in Carrick, or in the nameless lanes of Mount Oliver, there are none of these things. This is not country, if by that we mean farmland instinct with life. These are coal hills, green at times, but often the gray brown of an exhausted soil, unproductive, unpromising, scarred. The dwellings are casual, unrelated, and too far apart for common work or intercourse. When men have worked since daylight in a mine, and women since the day's beginning have sewed seam after seam with unrelaxed energy, it is not enough that social opportunity is not difficult; it must be distinctly easy. To accomplish this in wholesome ways is one of the problems of the city. Out in these wayplaces, where the pulse of life is low and the succession of days is void of meaning, even the social impulse seems numb. The struggle to live is reduced to its lowest terms. All that we have read into the words "to live," all the color and richness that we think of as an integral part of tolerable life, is absent. Factory work has its evils, but such outwork as this is no solution of them. Where it is not regulated, as here, it carries those evils out into the hill shacks, and, as in the case of outwork in the tenements, puts a check to the wholesome growth of family life. Though the amount of work given out has been cut down again and again, the sum of it is still great enough to show that among these barren hills is a stronghold of sweated work and cheap labor for some years to come.

CHAPTER VIII

THE MINOR NEEDLE TRADES

WHAT I shall call the minor needle trades in Pittsburgh, millinery, glove making, mattress and awning manufacture, are minor only in the sense that fewer plants and fewer people are engaged in their work. In contrast to the 868 women employed in making garments, in 1907 these four branches of the trade together employed 629. Like the garment trades, three of them, awning, mattress, and glove making, are needle trades which have further adapted and specialized the power sewing machine. Two of them, the glove and millinery industries, are again like the garment trades in that they produce articles of wear, millinery continuing largely as a hand industry, while the glove industry has involved a specialization of machine work. With the exception possibly of glove making, they all inherit some of the seasonal characteristics of the prime industry. The women employes in these minor needle trades are with few exceptions American.

MILLINERY

The retail millinery trade, like dressmaking, is without the province of this study. The wholesale trade, however, comes well within its boundaries in that large numbers of girls work together in a single plant under the direction of a single firm.

Wholesale millinery houses have established themselves in long, narrow buildings along the business streets of the downtown section of Pittsburgh. These buildings are usually five stories high, well lighted both with shaded electric bulbs which can be turned upon the cases in the showrooms, and with high wide windows. Freshly painted walls and light board floors reflect the light and add an impression of cleanliness in dainty contrast to

141

some of the contract sweatshops in the same district. The hat shapes are piled on tables in the centre of the workroom and the work is done near the windows.

When visited in June, such a workroom is almost empty; the downstairs rooms are deserted, and the elevator boy leisurely considers possible alternatives before rising to answer the bell. The only models are a couple of forlorn remnants of the season just closed, which rest on their forms with an air of general indifference. There are a few boxes of unused flowers and draped and vacant shelves. Half a dozen girls are working without haste or interest on the last order. Visit the place in mid-August and you will find the workroom so crowded with seats between the tables that there is scarcely room to pass. This seasonal change of the two midsummer months is the great fact in the wholesale millinery trade. For such a millinery house is much more than a factory; it is a sales centre. Through the open door in the season you get glimpses of shelves upon shelves of flowers and plumes, of alert buyers examining the trimmed and untrimmed models, and of attentive clerks. You must go past floor after floor devoted to flowers and plumes before you find the girls in their workroom at the top.

The progress of a hat, in all its absurd contortions of shape, from factory workroom to wearer, through the hands of shaper, maker, and trimmer, has given rise to a set of trade conditions in some respects unique, and to a group of workers unlike in training and in opportunity to the workers in the other needle trades. In the regular seasons the women in the five wholesale houses of Pittsburgh number about 400.

The Pittsburgh trade stands in contrast to that of New York and Philadelphia, where the making of cheap stock hats is of first importance. Recognizing that this field is held secure by eastern houses, the Pittsburgh wholesalers act as distributors of French hats, and of medium-grade American models, to smaller local centres within a radius of 200 miles. To a limited extent, they act also as agents for the cheaper hats. But as manufacturers they confine themselves almost entirely to hats of the better sort. Their business is not large. Their opportunity for expansion lies in the field where the personal element enters, where orders are relatively small but flexible in the expression of local preferences. In two houses straw hats are made, but in the others straw and felt shapes are bought from factories and trimmed in the workrooms. The number of makers, relatively skilled hands, in Pittsburgh houses, judged by New York standards, is disproportionately large, and the preparers who assist them are frequently given the opportunity to do dainty bits of work. Instead of being stifled by a mechanically subdivided section system, in which one trimmer keeps two dozen preparers busy, personal ability has a chance to show itself. In New York, many of the workrooms are really factories where women are paying for the cheapness by life itself, and hats are turned out by the thousand. Pittsburgh does not compete with this price and section system, but pays by the week and places the emphasis on quality of work.

The Pittsburgh wholesale millinery house which most resembles the New York type employs 76 girls in mid-season. Forty of them are sewers of straw foundations—work that elsewhere is done frequently by machine. These girls start their spring work before Christmas, and their season lasts longer than that of the trimmers—on into June. All the sewing is done by hand and pay is by the piece, $ .25 for making an ordinary hat. The difference in cost to the wearer is not in the making but in the fineness of the straw, and the girls get the same rate for coarse hats and fine. Thirty out of the 40 girls are able to make about $6.00 a week, and the others range upward toward $10, with the exception of five "drapers," who are on salary. These "drapers" loop or drape the crown of the hat over the brim; they have had longer experience and training than the piece workers and are paid $10 to $12 a week.

The trimming room in this factory shows us at a glance the main occupations in the trade. There are 36 girls in regular employment. They sit 12 at a table, with the three trimmers in charge. These three trimmers—the forewoman and her two assistants—do all the actual planning and much of the trimming; below them are six copyists, two at a table, who follow out their plans and do much of the secondary work, while to assist the copyists there is a force of 24 makers and preparers.

OCCUPATIONS AND WAGES OF WOMEN

The following summary, ranged in order of most to least skill and of most to least wage-earning opportunity, shows the distribution of women in occupations in the Pittsburgh millinery trade as a whole:

TABLE 20.—DISTRIBUTION OF WOMEN IN VARIOUS OCCUPATIONS AMONG WHOLESALE MILLINERY HOUSES

Kind of work	No. of girls
Trimmers	49
Expert makers	68
Copyists	41
Straw hat makers	70
Preparers and inexpert makers	161
Apprentices	17
Total	406

Regular trimmers in a wholesale house can command from $15 to $25 a week, the majority earning not more than $18. They plan the stock hats and do all original work on the models. The line between a maker and a copyist is not always clear. In one factory there are no girls called copyists, but trimmers and makers work together, the maker copying the first under parts of a hat, and the trimmer copying or finishing the rest of it. Where there are copyists distinct from makers, they are paid from $10 to $15, and the expert makers from $8.00 to $10. Even the best maker cannot command more than $10, and she, too, must have ability to seize an idea and execute it—"the unteachable quality of being a good milliner." It must be remembered, however, that the inexpert makers are greatly in the majority and that they, with the girls engaged in preparation work, are earning from $4.00 to $6.00, or sometimes not more than $3.00. The trade at the height of the season shows the larger percentage of girls to be inexpert. Counting preparers and the poorer makers, apprentices and many of the straw-hat sewers,* there are 288 (56 per cent) whose weekly earnings are $4.00 to $6.00 or less, 83 earning between $8.00 and $10, and 95 earning above $10—altogether

* Fifty straw hat makers earning $6.00 or less.

178 girls (43.87 per cent) earning $8.00 or more. These wages are not for the year round, but during the season only.

APPRENTICESHIP

Millinery apprenticeship lasts for two seasons. The newcomer to the trade is expected to serve through the spring and the fall term without pay, doing odd jobs, sewing bandeaus, and tucking chiffon—and if the forewoman looks out for her, really learning something of how hats are made. As a rule, however, after she has learned a few fundamental things, she is a convenience to the rest of the employes and the process of her own education is a secondary matter. She has to stay in the wholesale workroom for a much longer time than the term of her apprenticeship before she has learned enough of the trade for her to be useful to a retail dealer. One firm, contrary to the custom in the wholesale trade, pays its apprentices. The forewoman reasons that if a girl is not worth $3.00 a week, she is not worth her place at the table, and that if a girl shows ability before the end of her apprenticeship, she should be given the opportunity to advance. Here one apprentice works at each table, and in the course of the season she is initiated into one process of hat trimming after another. She is allowed to undertake work as fast as she shows capacity for it. One girl, for instance, was taken as an apprentice at Christmas time, and by May she was placed with a retail firm as an expert copyist at $12 a week.

HOURS AND SEASONS

The hours in the trade are not so long as they have been in the past, for there has come a reaction, in some cases, at least, against overtime. The hours in one house are from eight to five-thirty, although this is shorter by half an hour than elsewhere, and the workers had only two nights' overtime during the season. Another house had eight nights' overtime. These two represent the advance guard, however, in the reaction against night work, for in other cases "night work was frequent," and one firm ordered night work three times a week during February, March, and April. In the millinery trade, overtime for girls on salary does not mean extra pay. There is a rush to catch the tide of business at the flood, and every hand in the workroom must do her share. The experience acquired in a wholesale house is far too valuable to be lightly thrust aside even though it be gained at the cost of much-needed rest and essential hours of sleep.

The fall season is from August first until December first; the spring season, from January first to the middle of May—in some houses until Decoration Day. The condition of work as well as the hours and the number of employes fluctuates with the seasons. In mid-August there are at least 500 milliners in the wholesale workrooms. Many are trimmers who come for a week or two at a time until the wholesalers send them out to retail establishments, for these girls find it easier to get season positions in this way and the retailers insist on sending to wholesale houses for girls. The smaller dealers think that the girls who have worked a week or two in a large establishment will have more ideas and will do better work. But to the wholesalers this demand of their customers is a source of much annoyance. They complain that the girls come merely to fill in time and get the $1.00 a day that they command, and do not try to learn the ways of the house nor to do good work. The vagrant trimmers, it is claimed, are in many cases quite inefficient and frequently spoil good material, but they are sure to be taken on year after year because of the demand of retail firms.

Toward September, the workrooms thin out a little; three firms have a force of 100, but they are likely week by week to lay off girls, until some have as few as 25 at the close of the fall season. The number in the trade varies too much to justify an inflexible statement, but at least the limits to its variation can be stated from one part of the season to another. After the irregular force of trimmers had passed into the retail workrooms, there remained in the five wholesale houses in 1907, 406 girls in regular employment. By December first, the end of the autumn season, this number had fallen to 280. After the lapse of a few weeks, the number is again as large as it was in September, until the season wanes once more and workrooms close for the summer. This leaves a blank of six weeks in winter and of two months in summer which the more expert girls fill in when possible by a few weeks at the retail trade. The retail season lasts two weeks later in winter and a month later in spring, so the period of enforced idleness is reduced to six weeks for such of the girls as are placed in a retail firm at the end of their wholesale season. Necessarily, this possibility is only for the few from each house. In December some girls clerk in the stores for two or three weeks, but even this leaves them with an idle two weeks at the beginning of the year.

In view of these gaps in the working year, it is of interest to learn how many of these girls have families within reach. Those who come from small towns to learn the trade seem to be much in the minority. It is more usual for a girl to be apprenticed to a retailer in her own village and then to come in for what is practically a second apprenticeship at a wholesale house. These girls do not stay in the city, but use their time there rather as a means of increasing their local trade after their return. There remains, however, a contingent of girls who have not their families back of them in time of stress; how many there are, the forewomen do not definitely know.

The term "milliner" suggests immediately that quality of taste, that sense of color and form, which cannot be taught to her who lacks them. A trade in which a natural gift is the fundamental need, carries with it inevitably social esteem in higher degree than a trade in which success is open to large numbers. No distinction is made by outsiders between the girl with real ability and the girl called by the same trade term who is merely a routine hand. The millinery worker has a certain standing which makes other factory workers envy her, and to gain this standing girls are willing to accept the low wages and irregular work in the trade. Although the trimmers and copyists are sure of the longest seasons and of fairly steady work, few even of them earn enough wholly to support themselves between seasons. Unquestionably, also, the less expert makers and those who are below them are not only unable to earn enough for the dull two months, but in many cases receive wages inadequate for their support when the season is at its height. For the expert trimmer, with an instinctive sense of form and color, there are possibilities of $50 a week with some retail firms, but for the girl of inferior ability there is scant possibility of an income adequate to carry her through the year. The forewoman in one of the large houses was contrasting the trade in Pittsburgh with the trade in New York; she had the enthusiasm born of instinctive love for the work and insisted that it was good trade. "Yet, even so," she said, "although it's a better trade here than in New York because we pay week wages and not those ridiculously low prices for piece work, it's only the few who can make good wages, and only the exceptional ones who can make wages that are at all high. The trade is full of inefficient girls who would never make steady hands, and who are entirely without the natural gift to develop into experts even at mechanical processes."

GLOVE MAKING

Unlike the millinery trade, which has never secured a foothold in the making of cheap stock goods, the glove industry in Pittsburgh has distinctly served the demands of the wage-earning population. Just as the lines primarily important in the garment trades are overalls and jeans, so in the glove industry the chief and indeed the only lines of goods put on the market by the local factories have been cheap gloves, in canvas, leather, and heavy sheepskin. Fine gloves can be imported or shipped in from the east, but these gloves made close to the point of sale are not for decoration of the hands but for protection in hard work. They wholesale for $ .50 to $1.00, and they are sold to the miners and millmen who in so many of the Pittsburgh industries create the effective demand.

In this district the glove industry is young; it is represented by only two firms, the larger of which shut down completely during the depression of 1907–08, throwing 100 girls out of employment, while the smaller, with its force of eight employes, ran on short time. The experience of the larger factory in putting inexperienced girls on piece work is significant. The manager of the factory proposed to pay the girls $4.00 a week at the start, then to raise them every two weeks until they were making $1.00 a day, and to keep them on this until they could work rapidly enough to be put on piece work. "For a dollar a day," he said, "you can get any number of girls in Pittsburgh, but if they don't make that much they get discouraged and want to try something else. When a girl isn't making a dollar a day, she is likely to go off all of a sudden and get married; but if she is making that much or more, she will think twice." The firm, however, was unwilling to pay beginners time wages for more than two weeks. The girls were told that in two weeks they ought to be able to make $1.00 a day easily; but when they found that instead of $1.00 they could not make more than $ .40, they usually lost interest and gave up the work. The result was that within a few months more than 500 different girls were engaged to fill the 100 positions at the factory.

As you look down the workroom, in this larger factory, the machines in rows seem a bit like the machines in a garment factory, but there are variations and adaptations for different sorts of work. One glove goes through six or eight different hands in the making, each section being finished by a special machine. There are single-needle machines, and flat-bed double needles, and a four-needle to put the fancy stitching on the backs of gloves. There is a binder for the bottom of gloves, which puts on the binding with one operation. This was formerly done by stitching the binding on one side with a single-needle, then turning the rough edge under and stitching down again. A dozen gloves could not be bound in less than half an hour in the old way, whereas by the new method they can be bound in fifteen minutes. There is an overstitch machine for putting the leather decorations on the flap of the glove, and a "walking-foot" machine for stitching thumb and fingers. The single needle is used to put lining and outside together, and the double needle to stitch together the flap and the main part of the glove.

The smaller factory belongs to the International Glove Workers' Union. The owner, who has been a union man himself, has required the girls to join and to keep in touch with union doings, although he recognizes that success at the machine depends on many conditions unspecified in the union scale. Banding and binding, for instance, are paid at a certain price, but the scale does not specify whether the binding be done in one operation or by a series of operations. Neither does the scale differentiate between materials, whether leather, or heavy sheepskin, or fine sheepskin. Yet the quality of material and the way in which the glove is cut and sewed obviously affect the possible speed rate of the operator. All the cutting is done by men, and if it is poorly done, the difficulty of machine work is greatly increased. Cutters have had to be brought from other cities, but the operators are usually either from Pittsburgh or from neighboring towns. Machines, power, and needles are furnished to the operators. There is no tenement work in Pittsburgh in this trade.

There is undoubtedly a large market in the locality for the development of a really strong glove-making business. How the industry will work its way through the difficulties of a general trade depression, it is hard to tell. Up to 1908 there were other difficulties in securing labor and training girls unused to this trade, for the city had no available force of experienced glove makers. Lack of judgment among girls whose education is defective and who have gone to work too young, is a subject of frequent complaint by the management. No girl can become expert in less than a year, but after that she should earn, one manager says, not less than $9.00 a week. Were a sufficient force of operators paid on a wage basis that would enable them to keep at work until they had learned, there is reason to think that this industry should take its place with the other needle trades, as one in which the opportunities for fair wages and steady work are relatively good.

AWNINGS AND MATTRESSES

The making of awnings and of mattresses are omnipresent industries. There are few large factories in these lines; establishments in the different cities seek for a local trade and alike are prosperous or idle according to season. The reason for this trade restriction, however, differs in the two industries. The awning industry is confined to the filling of orders. Windows and shop fronts are of too many sizes for a manufacturer to be able advantageously to meet the demand from his made-up stock. He must delay starting his machines until shop-keepers send in orders for the kinds of lettering and stripes and sizes that they want. In the mattress industry, on the other hand, the reason for small local factories and for a seasonal trade lies in the fact that mattresses cannot well be made up for stock. If they are piled on top of one another, they flatten, and if they stand on end, they become uneven—in either case, unsaleable. They must therefore be made to order and shipped while still fresh from the makers' hands. The busy seasons in the two industries fall at about the same times, from March through June, when new houses are being rented and when shop fronts are being redecorated; and again in September, the second renting season, and the time when tarpaulins are looked over for the winter. In the fall, the awning industry becomes a tarpaulin industry and lasts for only a few weeks; the mattress factories continue their customary work until November. During winter and summer, both industries are dull.

Of the eight awning companies in Pittsburgh, seven,* in 1907, had workrooms of their own. A room above stairs, or in the rear, served for the power machines. The eighth had a small business and no workroom in connection with the shop. The workroom has often an accidental appearance, a look of unpremeditated staying on through the habit of the thing, rather than from any real appropriateness or fitness for the work carried on there. Dim windows and crowded floors, narrow passageways, machines excessive in size for the floor and air space, piles of tarpaulin and canvas—and somewhere in the midst of all these you find five or six women who have learned this branch of machine operating. In one case only does the workroom seem to have been built for the purpose. In the others, there are varied degrees of crowding and of imperfect light.

Fourteen women, nearly a third of the women in the trade, are employed in one factory, which is an extreme illustration of the chance use of a building. On the first floor are office and storeroom. You mount to the second by a totally dark and very dirty staircase, over which hangs an unlighted electric bulb. Except for cases and scrap, this second floor appears not to be used, but across the room and close to the next flight of steps a

* See Appendix B, p. 389, Table 47, for number of men and of women in each factory.

four-inch wide power belt, unprotected, rises diagonally. The staircase has no railing, though protection is needed from the rapidly moving belt, and a part of the steps is cut away to allow ropes to pass through, so that the actual space for walking is very narrow.

At the top is a triangular workroom, with three dim windows along one side. Little light can pass the grimed and cobwebbed panes; each machine must have its electric bulb or the girls would be unable to work at all. The operators are not young girls who have learned the use of power here and the handling of cloth, but older workers who for one reason or another, perhaps because work of other sorts failed, have come into this less desirable trade. They are seasoned to nine hours a day over the flashing needle. For four months in the spring and two months in the fall the full force is employed, but after that the number is reduced to seven, and sometimes to three or four. During the season, the trade is steady, but whether in off seasons the girls fit into other trades the owner of the business did not know. For years, this factory has been in the same place. With growth in business and in reputation, the little haphazard workroom has not grown or changed. In a building not planned for the use of power, nor adapted skilfully; in a room not designed for long rows of machines, with poor light and air, even with absolute uncleanliness, orders continue to be filled successfully. You can only guess how this loft chanced to be used in the first place, but from the unfit appearance of the room today you judge that the first chance usage has crystallized into an unhealthful permanence.

In contrast, one awning factory, recently erected, has adequate provision for the present scope of the business. The workroom is on the second floor, above storeroom and offices. In the dull season not more than two girls besides the forewoman are employed, but in spring there are as many as seven. A row of open windows fronts on the street and invites the river breeze.

The equipment consists of five single-needle machines and one double-needle, and a press for putting in staples. By use of the double-needle, the work of five girls is saved, congestion in the workroom is avoided, both floor and window space being economized, and the factory is able to turn out more work with fewer hands. Nevertheless, this is the only instance where a double-needle machine is in use. The other factories have all their work done on single-needles. One girl is used for finishing. The others work by sections, some sewing the goods lengthwise, others putting the ends on, others the curtains, or flaps, in front. A "sleeve" or opening must also be run in the curtain for the rod. The firm will not take an inexperienced girl. The main difficulty is in handling the goods, which are heavy, bulky and awkward to manage. This is especially true of the winter work, the stiff unmanageable tarpaulin for wagon covers which are made up during two months in the fall.

WAGES AND HOURS

In the first factory mentioned wages are paid by the piece. The operators can increase their earnings by occasional overtime, but even so, few make more than $6.00 a week. Elsewhere wages are paid by time.* A beginner is started at $5.00 or $6.00 and advanced to $7.00, $8.00 or sometimes $10. Although the work is hard in any case, the girls are worn out much more quickly under a piece system—some of them in three years, the forewoman says. She herself has been in the trade six years, but she thinks that if she were making a fresh start she would never go into it again. "It takes too much out of you," she says.

In one factory the hours of work are ten a day, but in four others the operators work nine, and in three cases only eight hours a day. Yet overtime from March until July often brings the total up to 12 hours a day and 72 a week for weeks at a time. Orders do not come in until the warm weather begins; then, with the first warm days, all the customers order at once, and the girls have to stay night after night so as to comply as speedily as possible with the demand. Here would seem to be a case in which business might be distributed more evenly throughout the year if tradesmen would order in advance. Were this done, it would be a great gain to girls in the workrooms. Two of the smaller awning companies have been able to reduce their overtime to a few nights, but in the others through May and June,

* See Appendix B, p. 390, Table 48, for range of wages in each factory.

often from March to July, the power runs until nine o'clock at night.*

In August, and after the brief fall season, there is wholesale dismissal of hands; in 1907, 30 out of the 41 in the trade were obliged to seek other positions. In summer they can scarcely hope to place themselves, but in the winter there are more opportunities. Some make draperies and others take advantage of the longer fall season in the mattress factories to seek work there.

MATTRESS MAKING

In mattress factories, to turn to the final branch of the needle trades, the unfit conditions of buildings and of workrooms which are to be found in the awning factories are repeated outside and in. The walls seem dingy and worn-out, innocent of paint, crusted with accumulations of lint and dust, and on the windows is the residue of dust-making processes—cotton-picking, filling, closing. The cotton is prepared for use by a picking machine, which unless there is an exhaust equipment, fills the air with fine particles. This machine is managed by men; they also tuft the filled mattresses, forcing long needles through and pulling the twine fast; then forcing the needle through in the opposite direction and pulling the twine again, until rows of knots are made from end to end. In some cities, this work is done by women, but not in Pittsburgh. Here women close mattresses, however, often in rooms where the air is bad, and sometimes with their machines placed directly beside the filling machines. Other girls† make spring beds or knot wire springs. Some of them stand at a form, start the wire and clip it at the end, the machine itself intertwining the wire, and forming it. No special training is required. Inexperienced girls who do not earn over $6.00 a week can be used for this work. Some managers say there is jealousy between them and the sewing girls who make the ticks and who of necessity have been longer in training and have greater dexterity. This

---

* Fourteen hours a day, 84 a week, in one factory. See Appendix B, p. 390, Table 49, for hours of work in each factory.

† See Appendix B, p. 390, Table 50, for division of work among women in mattress factories.

may be an instance* not unlike what we shall find in the laundry industry, of class distinction within a factory. In some cases the sewing girls use a binder single-needle machine, although one factory owner states that this kind of machine is really not so satisfactory, but simply enables a firm to make use of inexperienced girls. The test of an experienced girl is the ability to sew binder and tick in one operation, and when she has learned this she can work more quickly with an ordinary single-needle.

Pay is by the piece quite as frequently as by the week, but under either system the mattress workers earn far more than the workers on awnings. The rate of pay varies from $ .08 to $ .12½ for a tick, and the girls are expected to earn something over $1.00 a day. In one case, when a manager was asked how long it took the girls to learn, he replied that he had a girl who was unable to make more than two ticks in a week, but that even beginners could usually work more quickly. One firm pays time wages of $4.50 a week for three weeks, and then puts the girls on piece work, with the understanding that if they do not make more than $4.50 they will be dropped.

In other cases, the minimum for experienced girls is $7.00 a week and the maximum $10. Forty-eight of the 71 girls in the trade in 1907 earned $8.00 to $9.00 a week. Although the number of women in the trade is small, this percentage (67.6 per cent) earning more than $7.00 a week is highest among factory trades.

The hours of work are longer in this industry than in the awning factories,—usually nine to nine and a half and ten hours, and in three out of four cases there is occasional overtime. But the overtime is not so long continued nor at such high pressure, and the slack season does not mean such wholesale dismissal of hands. Two factories do not lay off their girls at all; others dismiss only three or four. One firm keeps all its girls on part time, half the force working one week and the other half the next. Although in the awning factories three-fourths of the girls are out of work five months in the year, in the mattress factories three-fourths of the girls are at work the year round. The work is heavier in spring when old things are discarded and houses refur-

* Cf. class distinction in laundries, p. 188.

nished, but even in summer and mid-winter the trade does not fall away entirely. It is doubtful whether the girls who are laid off are able generally to place themselves with other firms. One man says that he does not think that any of his girls find positions, as very often he calls them in during the summer for special orders; that one girl does dressmaking between seasons, and the others have families with whom they can stay. Contrasting with the awning industry, which wears out its girls so rapidly, these factories draw the mature steady type of American girl who works at a power machine, often for ten years, until she leaves to be married. One firm employs a few Italians and says that they keep at the work better than the Americans, but this opinion is apparently not shared by the other firms, among whose employes there are few changes.

Competition with family workshops among the Hill tenements has almost died out, and in Pittsburgh, at least, mattress making is now a factory trade. Two of the small home shops were burned and did not reopen. There is one which is still turning out cheap work in limited quantities, but it is negligible in comparison with the trade of the larger factories. The making of awnings is altogether a factory trade.

These two industries, so similar in many of their working conditions, are notably unlike in their effect on their employes. The work both in mattress and awning factories is productive of dust and lint; in both industries the workrooms are in general makeshift and haphazard, and in both industries the work fluctuates with the seasons. The great advantage which the mattress industry has over the awning industry is the relative lightness of the work. Ticks for mattresses are light and easy to handle; awnings and tarpaulins are stiff and difficult. It is in this difference in the character of the work, perhaps, that an explanation is to be found for the marked contrast between the three- or four-year working life of the awning maker, and the ten-year working life of the mattress maker. To this, too, as well as to the greater extent of underemployment in the awning industry, may be attributed the difference between the types of workers in the two trades. Heavy work inevitably draws a lower grade of worker— the woman of coarser physique, less industrial stability, and a lower wage-value. It acts in two ways to shorten the awning maker's working life, both by wearing her out physically and by making her lose interest so that she seeks the first avenue of escape. The mattress maker, on the other hand, because she has to rely less on physical strength than on dexterity, gains wage-value, and in consequence tends to stick to her trade. In the one case, better workrooms and a more even distribution of work might do much to mitigate the unpleasant features of the industry and to improve the grade of workers; in the other, in spite of dust and lint and unpleasant workrooms, the greater opportunity offered has selected a desirable type of employe.

THE CLEANING INDUSTRIES

CHAPTER IX

LAUNDRIES

WASHING, MANGLING AND STARCHING

SOLITARY washtub and red-armed washwoman as industrial types are passing as surely as individual loom and shuttle have passed, and the individual dye-vat for cloth. The type in the ascendant today is the low stone building with its washing machine, mangles and steam ironers of a dozen kinds, its system of marking worked out in minute detail, and its network of agencies and drivers' routes to gather in trade from hotels and factories, from railroads and private houses. Here and there circumstances give added reasons for the growth of the newer type. A railroad center with its stream of travelers demanding quick, efficient service, its stations and Pullman cars with their immaculate porters, its hotels and cafés sending out wagon loads of table linen—these are consumers who seldom can wait until it is the whim of the sun that their linen be dried. The commercial laundry is the only possibility.

The knot of railroad lines, the travelers, the hotels, have helped make the industry prosperous in Pittsburgh, but the best allies of the laundrymen have been the black smoke and the smoke-filled fog. From the lower city to the East End there were in 1907 no less than 32 steam laundries, four of them in charitable institutions, but all of them commercial, with a force of 2402* employes, of whom 2185 were women. As employers of women, exclusive of clerical work, the laundries stand third. Mercantile houses rank first and the stogy industry second.

* This total is exclusive of drivers and of office help. It represents the number employed in the actual manual work of checking incoming clothing, washing, starching, drying and ironing it, and finally sorting it out and wrapping it to send away. See Appendix B, p. 392, Table 54, for number of men and women in each laundry.

Corner sites which allow for a maximum number of windows have frequently been made use of in the newer buildings. A considerable minority of the laundrymen, however, still occupy small structures in the middle of business blocks, overcrowded, and in large part shut out from light and air. If you walk along Chartiers Street near seven in the morning, you may see the girls coming down the street to their work. Bleak and dull red and square, the low buildings of a laundry stand against the gray light. A single driver's wagon is in the alley-way. Several men, high-cheeked Slavs, have just gone in, but close behind them come half a dozen American girls, collarless and rough jacketed. There is pride in their look, but none of the almost defiant independence which one instinctively reads into the stubborn pace of the three Polish girls who follow. These are linked together in the spirit of "we against the world," even if "we" be only three feeders at a mangle, and the world that large impersonal thing represented by the foreman. There are young girls, too, girls out of school only a month or two, lacking the training of eye or hand or brain which might set them a step higher at the start. A rough-armed Irishwoman, a grandmother, walks with them. With the loss of her early strength she has lost the customers for whom she worked by the day, and has found here her only chance to get a steady job. Some of the workers are women who have spent their youth too quickly, and have sold their strength at a little price; others are women worn out at other trades. Lastly, there are girls with fresh faces and bright eyes, girls who step quickly, surely, with the pride that comes from the consciousness of a trained hand and a clear brain. There are only a few of these, but of the others there are many. The whistle from a neighboring factory shrills out the hour, there is the slow sound of an engine starting, a gathering whirr of belts and wheels, and the last girls disappear to take their places at the machines.

Before we discuss the work a word must be said about the managerial side of the business. The apparent prosperity of the industry has not resulted from a trade combination. The various plants have worked in the main as individuals, and therefore suffered somewhat both from the rise in prices of materials and from the expenses of competition, without being able to save duplication of running expenses. The price of wrapping paper, twine, soap and starch has gone up 15 to 20 per cent even within a year. Wages, too, have advanced. Employers are of the opinion that the demands of their employes have become exorbitant, out of all proportion to the profits of the business. "Fifteen years ago when I started," said the owner of one plant, "you didn't have to pay the best girl in the laundry more than $6.00 or $7.00 a week, and you could get an inexperienced hand for $2.50. Now they won't start work for less than $4.00, and you have to raise them to $5.00 pretty quickly, or they leave you and go somewhere else." This was in a district where many opportunities of employment are open to girls. It is true, however, of laundries which employ the cheapest help, that ten years has seen an increase of 30 per cent in the wages of women employes.

Steam laundries, by ancestral connection with the washtub, have shared the difficulties of individual housekeepers in obtaining hands. In the years immediately before the trade depression of 1907–08, laundry workers were known to be an unusually independent group, ready to leave in an instant if they fancied themselves offended, and ready to increase their value by bargaining now with one employer and now with another, until their wages showed a high absolute and proportionate increase. Many a manager complained of brother laundrymen who would waylay his new shirt girl, for instance, as she came from work, and ask, "How much are you getting at ———?" "Five dollars." "Well, come to us and we will give you $6.00." The desire for advancement, too, has prompted many a girl, paid $4.00 at one laundry, to ask for a job at another laundry a few squares away. "Have you ever worked before?" "Yes, at———." "How much did you get?" "Five-fifty." "All right, we will give you that and more if you make good."

Competition for drivers has been another managerial difficulty. An able driver is as important a source of trade as the traveling salesman for a commercial house. He often is paid a commission, and is responsible both for keeping the customers on his route and for getting more. With eager desire to gain the market, rival managers forced up the wages of drivers and even bribed men to leave former employers and bring customers to them. The increase of this practice produced a chaotic state of affairs. From Friday night until Monday morning, no man felt sure that his drivers and his agencies might not have seceded to a competing firm, and left him without means of keeping his trade. Some firms, in order to get business, had recourse to a desperate cutting of prices. Employes became notably unreliable, and seemed to lose all sense of the relation between service given and wages earned; between competitors there was constant irritation and suspicion.

Price cutting and increasing expenses finally led to the formation of the Laundrymen's Association in 1901. The Association does not attempt to district the city, although this would mean great saving in the cost of drivers and agencies, nor does it attempt to fix the wages of employes, and to prevent one plant from outbidding another for its more valuable hands. Its jurisdiction extends only to a flexible arrangement with regard to prices charged, and to a working agreement against "stealing agencies" and drivers.

The division of labor in a laundry is carried far as in a factory. There is specialization for speed. Most of the women are young, as factory girls are young. Women are found in the washroom— a few of the older women, bending over hot tubs of dainty clothes; at the mangles—young untrained girls shaking and folding and feeding the flat work into the machines; in the starching room— young girls still, dipping the pieces by machine and rubbing them smooth by hand; in the ironing department—raw newcomers and seasoned machine hands, operating a dozen different presses and heated rolls; and in the checking and sorting room where the work is in part clerical.

WASHING DEPARTMENT

At the preliminary processes* of washing, mangling, and starching, place is found for the beginners and the girls of lowest grade. The washroom is usually on the first floor or in the cellar, its location being partly for the convenience of drivers and partly because of tradition, referable perhaps to the location of washtubs

* The four institutional laundries will be considered separately in Chapter XI.

in the kitchen. This is preëminently the man's part of the laundry, and the few women who work here are employed on fine work which can more conveniently be done by hand. The washermen, frequently American, and the wringermen, who are nearly always Slavs, have full charge of the washing machines—huge cylinders full of hot water and steaming clothes, and of the extractors, which twist the clothes and fling out the water by centrifugal force. With haste always at their heels, the men do not wait to let all the water run out before they lift the dripping garments into trucks and wheel them over to the metal wringers. The results are a wet floor and a cloud of steam, which affect the workers not only here, but on the floor above.

From this point of view, the washroom is the most important department in a laundry. The health of workers in all parts of the building is dependent upon its location, its drainage, and its provision for the escape of steam and forced ventilation. (Table 21 on the following page shows the location, as well as other physical characteristics, of the washrooms, in the twenty-eight Pittsburgh laundries.) Yet there is only one laundry in Pittsburgh in which the washroom is on a floor above the other departments. One other has a second floor washroom, but the rest choose first floors or cellars with fine disregard of the discomfort and positive ill health that may result.

We might expect that even if location were not considered carefully in the arrangement of departments, such means would be provided for the escape of steam and for adequate ventilation as to make the workrooms more tolerable. But in considering provision for the escape of steam, we find a situation characteristic of Pittsburgh. In only one case is there any outlet except through the windows, and on a foggy day windows are useless. For the Pittsburgh fog is not the fog that a coast town knows; it is moisture permeated with coal dust and grime, perilous to the eyes and throat of the pedestrian, and of a fatal, penetrating quality wherever open door or window gives it a chance to enter. It has to answer for the spoiling of many a lot of clothes on their way from washing machine to extractor—a mishap not discoverable until they reach the ironing room and have to be sent back ignominiously for a second washing. What wonder, then, that orders are issued for doors and windows to be kept closed? What wonder that in seven cases the washroom windows are so small and low, not over three feet by three, that steam has small chance to fly out; or that in three cases there are no windows or other openings at all?

TABLE 21.—PHYSICAL CHARACTERISTICS OF WASHROOMS *

Grade	Location	No. of Workrooms
A	Second floor	2
B	First floor	13
C	Basement	6
D	Cellar	7
		28
	DRAINAGE	
A	Gutters; drainage good*; floors convex	3
B	Gutters; drainage good	6
C	Gutters; drainage imperfect †	16
D	No gutters; floor drainage ‡	3
		28
	ESCAPE FOR STEAM	
A	Windows	17
B	Windows, small and low, 3 x 3	7
C	Shaft to roof	1
D	No escape §	3
		28
	VENTILATION	
A	Exhaust fans—adequate	1
B	Inadequate	9
C	Iron pipes admitting outside air	1
D	Shaft to roof	1
E	No provision for ventilation	16
		28

* *Gutters; drainage good.* Gutters run length of machines. Floor is flat, but most water is carried off.

† *Gutters; drainage imperfect.* Gutters have not sufficient slope to carry off water. Floor is flat, worn, with numerous holes. Water stands in pools.

‡ *Floor; no gutters.* Water that is spilled remains on floor; opening to drain only at one point..

§ *No escape.* Cellar entirely closed in, without windows or other access to outer air.

But to the girls standing just above, the hot boards seem scorching. The steam works its way through cracks and crevices, and attacks them like a vicious thing until in dismay they give up their jobs and try what chance may have for them elsewhere. One girl told me that as long as she worked in a laundry she went home by a back street so that no one should see the old shoes

* See also Appendix B, p. 393, Table 55.

which she had to wear. Tight-fitting shoes were unendurable. "I never knew anyone who worked in a laundry long," said another girl, "the work's too hard, and you simply can't stand the heat."

Sometimes electric fans are placed by the slit of a window at the far end of the room or near the stairway, but one or two fans are but a feeble defense against clouds of steam rising from two to six boiling cylinders, ten hours a day. Even iron pipes to admit outside air, a device used in one basement washroom, are powerless in the presence of a hot six-roll mangle and a row of washing machines, cellar-wide.

Good drainage would make ventilation less difficult. In all but three cases, gutters run under the washing machines to carry off the waste, and where the floor is convex, there need not be much waste water under foot, if reasonable care is used in lifting the clothes. But in a majority of the rooms, nineteen cases, I found that the floor was either flat or sunken and filled with holes, and that the water stood in pools. Sometimes the ill-drained washroom was in a cellar, closed in by rough, damp stones and lighted by a flaring gas jet: sometimes it was on a first floor, a few steps away from the mangle room and just beneath the ironers. Often it was in a basement, half lighted by small, dim panes of glass, damp from steam that had risen and cooled upon them for months, and foul with the odor of soiled linen. To the women, and to all the other workers in the plant, the location of the washroom below rather than above other departments, the imperfect drainage, inadequate ventilation, and lack of provision for the escape of steam, make work unnecessarily hard, and take too great a toll from their store of strength.

One washroom which is a strong contrast to the usual type in Pittsburgh, contains all the good features which most of the others lack. It is on the top floor of the building, shut off by concrete walls. The flooring, which is of slate, is graded down toward the gutters, and the gutters are sloped toward the drains. The window space on one side occupies over 60 per cent of the wall area, and fans are placed at the windows to draw off the steam. Even in the midst of work, the air in this washroom is not oppressive.

The point of danger in the washing department is the extractor. In loading the wringer, the goods must be distributed so that the weight and therefore the outward pressure will be the same at all points. As the machine rapidly revolves, the water in the goods is thrown by centrifugal force out at the perforations in the sides of the inner basket, caught in the outer can, and carried down to the drain. The basket is made of steel or copper, reinforced by iron bands, strong enough to allow for a limited margin of overweight at some point, in the event of careless loading. If this margin is exceeded, there is danger that the basket will strike hard against the case and break, and be hurled about the room by the great force with which it is revolved.

For the women in these washrooms, there are few mitigating circumstances. No women are employed regularly in twenty of the laundry washrooms. But in eight laundries thirteen hand-washers, and more under extra pressure of trade, are regularly employed. "You can't get a young woman to do this work," managers say. The hand-washers are women whose strength has gone at other trades, mainly housewifery. For $1.00 a day they work ten hours over the tubs, at flannels and socks and bits of finery that would need to be handled by an extra machine if they were machine-done. From the record of a visit to one laundry, I have taken the following: "Cellar washroom; eight men employed. Two women hand-washers for flannels. The firm finds that its trade in articles of this kind has doubled since it began to do this work by hand. The washroom is not well drained. Gutters beneath washing machines, but the floor is flat and has sunk in places. Windows are small, three feet by three. Ceiling low, less than ten feet. No escape for steam, and the air is foul." It is incongruous to find this survival of the home industry, with its discomforts, incorporated in a department of a factory industry imperfectly developed. It is questionable whether this survival is necessary. Some laundries succeed without it, even treating fine goods en masse without undue wear and tear. It would seem, in any event, that some solution other than this hand work would be needed when the present generation of old women has passed away. Recruits are not readily found among the younger women, with whom the factory tradition, the idea of collective work, is fundamental.

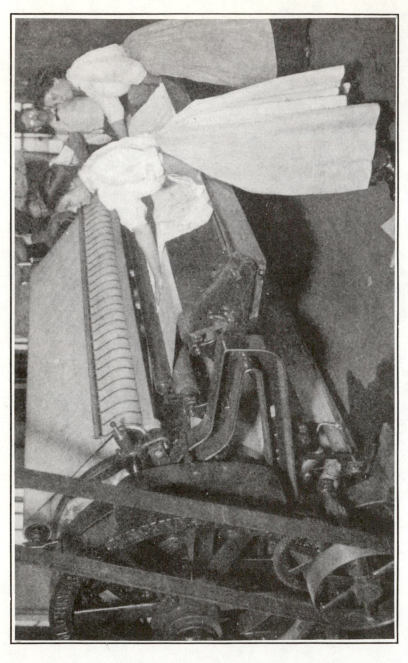

THE FEEDER AT A CYLINDER MANGLE

MANGLE ROOM *

Opening out of the washroom or on the floor just above it is the room where the mangle stands. The size and weight of the machine are reasons for placing it on the first floor. Then, too, by close connection between mangling and washing departments, flat work can be speedily finished, sorted and given to the drivers. Under the steam-heated metal rolls, or around the steam cylinder of the great machine, winding in tortuous ways through inner recesses, go table and bed linen, towels and all manner of flat things, to come out smooth and dry at the farther end. There is a fascination in watching the even pace of the continuous apron that carries the sheet along, the developed efficiency of this socialized household ironing day.

The mangle department as a whole still has some disabilities. In addition to the steam from the nearby washroom, the mangle itself is a steam-producer, as it dries and irons articles that pass through its rolls. The point at which invention has been taxed is in arrangement for sufficiently long contact with a steam-heated surface, and at the same time for intervals of exposure to the air, to allow for the escape of steam. If the article travels over too short a heated surface, it will need to be passed through the mangle several times. Similarly, if the steam has too little chance to escape, the article will still be damp and will need to be ironed again. For economy of time, fuel, and machinery, a mangle must be so constructed that the articles shall be ironed in as few operations as possible. Chest mangles are constructed with a series of heated rolls, seldom less than four, above a steam chest. One firm has two six-roll mangles, each with a capacity of ten sheets a minute, dried perfectly in once passing through. Cylinder mangles, in which a traveling apron passes under heated rolls around a steam cylinder, are also built on large lines, to allow for a long heated surface, and ample provision for the escape of steam. All this means that steam, much steam, is inevitable in the mangle room. The point for laundrymen to solve is how to take care of it.

Nineteen mangle rooms have no forced ventilation whatever.

* See Appendix B, pp. 393–395, Tables 56–58.

Some others set ventilating fans at the windows, but these fans draw the steam through the room on its way to the escape and do not greatly decrease the clouds of vapor about the operators. An open skylight and fans directly above the mangle have been sufficient in one case to carry away the steam. Two laundries, however, meet the situation effectively without a skylight. Galvanized iron hoods leading to exhaust pipes are placed about five feet above the rolls; and although this apparatus is expensive both to install and to operate, by increasing the comfort of the employes it greatly increases their efficiency.

Sometimes the mangle room is in a cellar, damp with overflow from the washroom, and the air is further vitiated by sputtering gas lamps. Scarcely better are the seven first floor mangle rooms which are not separated from the washrooms at all, or the nine mangle rooms placed directly above the washing cylinders and exposed to rising heat and steam.

The actual work in the department is done by machine. The responsibility on the girls is relatively small. First of all, goods come to the shakers-out. Near trucks full of tightly twisted knots of clothes stands a group of young girls and tired-faced women untwisting, unknotting, shaking out piece after piece, so that they may be fed into the mangle. Sometimes there is a wooden "tumbler" to make the work easier. Shaped like a washing machine, it untwists the clothes by revolving rapidly with a reversible motion; but only a few laundries provide these machines, and as a rule all the work of standing and shaking out falls on the girls. This occupation nowise involves training or skill. The shakers-out have not even responsibility for the appearance of the finished product; they stand between washers and ironers, their only care being not to interfere with the work of the one, nor to undo the work of the other. This is the first process at which a learner is put; it is sometimes the last process for a woman worn out at other trades. Some earn $4.00 a week, but the greater number, whether young girls or older unskilled women, are paid $3.50 and $3.00. For the younger ones, at least, there is opportunity for promotion.

The first step of advancement in most mangle rooms is to the position of folder, but as this is the third process, I shall speak of the feeders' work first.   The feeders stand at one end of the mangle and push the flat goods over the metal apron until the rolls catch the goods and relieve the feeders of further responsibility.   One girl can feed in towels or other small pieces without help, but for table linen, or wide pieces of the sort, two and sometimes three girls are needed, so that they may hold the piece at several places, and feed evenly under the rolls.   The work requires some care and attention, to keep the linen smooth and secure the desired finish by placing the proper side uppermost. Yet here, too, the process needs no skill, and but little training. It is learned in an hour, and thereafter the feeder needs only to give attention to the work to do it well.

The feeder is marked out from other laundry workers by the dangerous nature of her work.   Some years ago, when mangles were in process of development, it happened that as the flat piece was pushed over the roll, the roll frequently caught more than the cloth; it caught fingers and hand and arm of the girl operative.   Fingers and hand and arm were crushed flat as the cloth that they had been guiding, for there is no halting in the perfect mechanism of the mangle, no stopping place before the length of the rolls is reached unless the belt is shifted and the machine thrown out of gear.   This meant not death, but hideous suffering.   From an economic standpoint it meant that the girl's wage-earning capacity was irreparably lowered even if it were not altogether at an end.   Accidents of this sort increased to the point where employers considered it advisable to guard the machine.   Today one never finds a mangle unguarded.   A small roll, two and a half inches in diameter, is sometimes set at a space of four to six inches from the heated rolls, so that its weight, which could not seriously injure the girls' hands should they go under it, yet might serve as a reminder to them.   Sometimes this unheated roll is so connected with the belting that lifting the roll throws off the belt and stops the machine.   In one case a large roll, four inches in diameter, is set at a distance from the heated rolls.   Five mangles are guarded by upright bars placed directly in front of the rolls.

In twenty-one of the laundries the small roll is used, because it serves the purpose of partly straightening the cloth as well as of guarding the feeders, and in consequence is more popular with laundrymen than a bar which has no use so far as the goods are concerned. Yet we may realize that this small roll is not wholly adequate, by comparing its diameter with that of the large steam heated rolls, two and one-half inches against twelve. The feeder works ten hours a day at least. Hour after hour and week after week she goes through the same operations. She loses respect for the danger of the thing which she seems to know so thoroughly. If the guard roll were set close to the heated rolls, it would tend simply to draw in her hand: set at a distance from the heated rolls, it leaves a space unguarded,* and if there is a space between small roll and large, and the sheet is started unevenly, what more easy than to straighten it before it reaches the large roll, in the perilous space between? To obviate this, one foreman had the small roll removed and an upright bar put in its place. The bar was set at the height of an inch above the metal apron, and the feeder had to depend on her own alertness quite as much as before. Three weeks after the change of guard, her attention slackened, and her fingers were crushed. Yet since a four-inch bar covers more of the heated rolls than a small roll possibly can, if it is set so that there is not space beneath for fingers to go through, an accident seems improbable. It seems to be the safest form of guard that up to the present has been put to commercial use.

The wool and canvas covering of the rolls is changed at frequent intervals, often once a week. The guard is removed for this operation which is so admittedly dangerous that although sometimes done by the girls, it is more often a duty of men employed about the plant.

It is not my purpose to arraign the mangle departments of laundries for a record of maimed hands and arms. Indeed, as far as can be learned, the percentage of accidents yearly is not over 3 per cent of the total employes in the department. The point to be made is that accidents still occur, and that it is possible to prevent them. One could wish that as much thought had been

* A large guard roll is open to the same objection—that the space between guard roll and heated roll makes an accident possible. The laundry of an institution near Pittsburgh guards its mangle by a heavy wire screen (removable for cleaning) over the rolls. This screen was designed and set up immediately after an accident at this laundry, and since the screen has been in place there has been no further accident. No commercial laundry, however, employs a safeguard of this sort.

RECEIVING OPERATORS AT A MANGLE

given to making a mangle accident, one of the most horrible of non-fatal accidents, impossible, as has been given in bringing to perfection the mechanical details of the machine. The one form of guard which seems generally to be effective, the upright bar, is in use in only five of the laundries; the guards more generally used depend for their effectiveness on the alertness of the employe. Yet should an accident occur and the injured employe bring suit, she could not recover, under the imperfect employers' liability law of Pennsylvania, if the machine were guarded by any of the methods described, for it could be shown that the employer had taken "all reasonable care," had used the guards that are customary, and the operative would therefore be judged "careless."

The work of the folder, or receiving operator, may sometimes be dangerous, but it is not usually so. She sits in front of the shelving on which the goods fall from the machine. If she reaches up to catch an article that is being carried through the machine a second time, there is much chance that her hands will be caught. As a rule, however, the sheets drop from the rolls, and she has only to receive them and fold them to convenient size. Responsibility for the attractive appearance of laundered articles rests on her. She is usually the only girl in the mangle room who can be seated, although in one laundry stools are provided for the feeders.

On the whole, the mangle girls rank lowest among laundry workers. They are the most unstable, the most difficult to manage. Socially they form a group by themselves. Where there is marked difference in ages, it is the mangle girls who are the youngest, and where there is difference in nationality, they are of the immigrant group. Their work, which requires least training, is paid at the lowest rates, in a third of the laundries at $3.00 to $4.00 a week, in half of the laundries at $4.00 to $5.00. Except in the position of head girl, no mangle girl is paid more than $6.00.

One plant which does nothing but flat work is in several important points an exception to what has been said. It was originally started by the Pullman Company to handle the linen used on sleeping and dining cars, but changed hands in 1891, and has since been privately operated. The bulk of its work is for the Pullman Company still, but it also has the trade of a large café, and of a local towel company—all of them customers who require perfect work. The building is old, and in some ways ill-adapted to laundry purposes, but so much has been done to make it comfortable, that it is preferable to many newer buildings. There are exhaust pipes over the mangles, and fans in the wall; and there are windows along the side. The feeders are seated while handling small work and the folders have comfortable benches. The two great six-roll mangles have a capacity of ten sheets a minute, the sheets being perfectly dry after once passing through, and the girls are trained to feed in and fold the goods with absolute accuracy. Slight imperfections are not tolerated. From the folders at the machines the articles go to eight especially expert folders who make bundles—ten napkins or ten pillow slips, etc.—of the small work. A knife placed along the edge of the bundles would not show the smallest measurable irregularity.

Wages correspond to the greater exactness required. Although in other laundries few mangle girls earn more than $4.00 a week, in this plant all but four girls, shakers-out, are earning more. A few are paid $4.50 and the rest $5.00 to $6.00. The head girls at the mangles are paid $8.00. The eight expert folders and the four coat girls upstairs earn $7.00 and $8.00. The wages of employes are usually advanced each spring—a custom general in many other trades, but not so among the local laundries. "We expect good work," said the manager, "and we make it worth the girls' while to give it and to stay with us."

That the wages in this laundry are somewhat higher than those in most other mangle rooms, does not altogether account for the rare degree of contentment and stability among the girls. It must be remembered that with the exception of the four coat-ironers, all the forty to fifty girls in this plant belong to the group which in the trade as a whole has been characterized as shifting, unreliable, unstable. All with the exception of those four are employed at the mangles. Their wages, while far better than those of the majority, are yet not better than those of some of the other laundries, and their hours might be considered harder, since they have six ten-hour days each week. One factor in producing this greater reliability is unquestionably the spirit of consideration evidenced not only in exhaust pipes and seats at the mangle, but in sympathetic friendliness on the part of the managing head. The other factor is the summoning into action of all the dexterity and care which these girls can give. Poor work will not pass. There is a challenge in that. Wages are not paid by the piece but by the week, and except through rank carelessness, the girls do not lose. Yet in keeping to the standard set by this laundry, there has become involved a point of honor— a point which the employes have seemed to recognize and wish to maintain.

STARCHING DEPARTMENT

The order of promotion is from mangle room to starching department. Here machinery is less in evidence, and hand work assumes prominence once more. As you pass through the room, you can see half a dozen girls, collarless, their waists turned in at the neck, faces flushed, sleeves rolled high; you see a few small machines with pans of boiling starch, a great square dryhouse, half as big as the room, with its chain of hooks moving slowly, steadily, in and out, and a long table where three or four other girls stand rubbing hundreds of collars smooth. The dryhouse is placed directly above the boiler, so that the pipes may run in a straight line, sometimes for the distance of three floors. This often means that the starching room is pushed into a corner of the building formed by an inside partition on one side and the dryhouse on the other, with light from the outside windows completely shut off. Yet in this room movement of cool air is especially important to the workers, because there is heat from the dryhouse as well as from the washroom on the lower floor. In a few cases electric fans have been set up, but otherwise there is no forced ventilation to the rescue.

As to the work itself, shirt and collar starching are of the most importance. The principal machines are three: a collar starcher, a shirt bosom starcher, and a band starcher. The band starcher has two rolls about four inches wide, the lower one resting in a starch pan that is kept at high temperature by a steam chest underneath. Pressure of a treadle lifts the lower roll out of the starch, causing it to revolve against the upper roll, around which the article is placed, and in this way to rub in starch for as long a time as the pressure is continued. Attached cuffs and collars, neckbands, wristbands, are starched at this machine. The pressure required is light, and the machine so largely automatic that little skill or experience is demanded of the operator.

The same principle is applied in the shirt bosom starcher, but here there is only one roll, usually of cupped rubber. This roll rests in a steam-heated starch pan, until treadle pressure causes it to revolve backward and forward over the oval wiping board on which the shirt bosom is placed. The operator holds the shirt in position. Injured fingers often result from unintentional contact with an inflexible cylinder and with boiling starch.

The collar starcher is more complex, but among the many different kinds in use there stand out only two distinct types. In all machines for this purpose the operator feeds in collars or cuffs, which are then carried by the conveying apron into contact with rolls immersed in hot starch; the starch is rubbed in, and the collars are brought by the conveying apron out to the receiving table at the other side. In twenty-two of twenty-eight laundries, wiping girls follow the work of the collar machine by rubbing in the starch with their hands, and then wiping the collars smooth with a cloth. To do this work properly the girls have to acquire a firm, even pressure and to use judgment as to the amount of starch.

In this department, more than elsewhere in laundries, the similarity between the factory process and the household process is apparent, but this hand work is passing too. At least the change is clearly on its way, for four laundries use a new style collar starcher, which itself does the rubbing and wiping that in other cases the girls are required to do. There is no resemblance here to a former domestic process, for somewhere in the recesses of the machine the thinking is done, and the collars are rubbed clear before they reach the receiving table.

The dryhouse* is operated automatically. Collars and cuffs hung by their eyelet holes on hooks are carried on a continuous chain through a series of loops in the closed, highly heated room.

---

* Three laundries have an old style drying room. Collars have to be taken from the hooks by hand. Instead of a traveling chain, there are heavy wooden frames which the girls push in and out at need.

Starching by Hand

As they reach the outer air again they drop automatically into a basket and are taken away to be dampened and ironed. Shirts and larger articles are in another compartment; they are hung from hooks attached to sliding frames which can be pulled out when the door is opened.

Machines for dampening shirts and collars are built like small mangles. The articles are carried by a conveying apron to inner rolls (one of which is constantly immersed in water), and after passing over the moist surface to the receiving table, are placed in an enclosed dampening press which keeps them evenly moist until they are ironed. In the case of the shirt dampener, the articles are fed directly between the rolls. Serious accidents formerly caused by this machine have led to the partial enclosure of the rolls by a wooden shield, and as the dampener is in use only intermittently in all but the very largest laundries, the danger from careless handling is minimized. Even in large laundries the dampener is seldom in constant use.

One duty of the starching girls is to keep the conveyor (the traveling chain of hooks) clean. Early Monday morning, before the other girls are at work, they come to scrub to a state of shining perfection the long chain that hourly carries its freight of damp, starched clothes. This is a difficult piece of machinery to keep in good condition, for every hook of it must be gone over scrupulously. Yet, this extra duty notwithstanding, the wages* of starchers are still low. In many cases they are the same as those of the mangle girls. A tendency is observable, however, toward a little higher level. Although the wiping machine reduces the work in this department to a mechanical series of processes, this machine has not yet made sufficient headway to have affected wages. The hand work with the judgment needed for good results has brought the wages above the point reached in the mangle room. More of the starchers are earning $4.00 and $5.00. Some in time are advanced to $6.00, and in some instances where the head girls are old employes they are earning $7.00 and $8.00.

* For table of wages of starching girls, see Appendix B, p. 396, Table 59.

CHAPTER X

LAUNDRIES

IRONING, SEWING, CHECKING AND SORTING

THE preliminary laundry processes—washing, mangling, starching—were grouped together partly by order of occurrence, and partly through the grade of skill required by them. Ironing by hand and by machine, and the semi-clerical work of checking and sorting, demand as a rule still greater dexterity and are better paid.

IRONING DEPARTMENT

As you enter the ironing room on an upper floor of a laundry, you hear a rush of belting, the irregular sound of reversible rolls, and the sharp quick clamp of a metal press. A machine is set next each window, and others adapted for various uses stand one behind another toward the centre of the room. The girl ironers are specialists. This one adjusts the metal clamp to a neckband; a second forces a cuff press into position; a third steps back and forth with steady treadmill motion as the rolls of the body ironer before her revolve and reverse, revolve and reverse, incessantly. No girl irons a whole article. Instead, she irons a sleeve, or a cuff, or yoke, or perhaps one side of a collar. In small laundries the girls are often taught to use all the machines, but more generally the operator is trained for speed and maximum output in one line of work.

The ironing room is usually on the second floor. In twenty-four of the twenty-eight laundries, it is well lighted, with clear large windows, and often with skylights in addition. The ironers need to see well in order to do good work. They can do good work, however, without breathing fresh air. Ironing room, no less than starching room, feels the effect of steam from the washing cylinders below, and in addition, each of its dozen or more

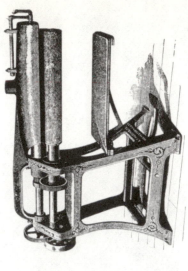

The Body Ironer, Protected and Unprotected

At the left is the unprotected machine in use in American laundries; on the right, the protected machine made in America for the export trade to Great Britain

power-driven machines produces steam by drying garments, and when gas-heated, itself radiates heat. The ironing room, therefore, is a trial in summer to the most robust; but ventilating devices for carrying off the excess heat are expensive, and laundry managers, as a rule, keep such expenses down.

TABLE 22.—VENTILATION IN IRONING ROOMS

Good *	Fair †	Inadequate ‡	None §
4	2	7	14

* Air clear and of moderate temperature.
† Fans and outlets for steam, but air hot and heavy with steam.
‡ One or two fans.   No perceptible effect on temperature.
§ No ventilation except through windows.

One plant has a shaft from its ironing room to the floor above, a method which scatters the steam but admits no fresh air. A few have temporized by placing fans in the wall. One laundry has thirty-three electric fans inside and two ventilating fans in the wall, but so much machinery is crowded into a small room and so much heat is given off by the machines that even this system is ineffectual. One laundry which has many disadvantages,—crowded rooms, unsatisfactory light due to location in the midst of a group of buildings, a site in a part of the city where dust from the mills renders open windows impossible,—has yet been successful in securing good ventilation. A shaft opening at each floor runs from basement to roof, and on the roof a large ventilating fan is placed. This provides an escape for the steam, and the temperature of the ironing room is not oppressive in spite of the crowding. In a few cases, though the system of ventilation is not elaborate, the air is good, simply because of high ceilings and space between machines; but this can be true only in the laundries recently erected and large enough to admit of increase in trade for several years to come. Otherwise, crowding seems to be general, and a more drastic mode of dealing with the steam, as in the instance cited, becomes requisite.

There are two main groups of ironing machines: the steam presses and the rolls. For sleeve and body ironing a machine is built with two hollow metal rolls, the upper one heated by interior gas jets, the lower one unheated and usually padded. The garment is placed over this lower roll, which is lifted by pressure of a treadle into position against the constantly revolving upper roll. Where a reversing mechanism is secured by belts or gears, double treadle action is required. With the left foot the operator presses on one treadle heavily enough to lift the lower roll into close, continuous contact with the upper. The pressure must be steady, for the moment it is lessened the roll will drop. To reverse the motion of the upper roll, the second treadle must be pressed by the right foot; and these two motions are repeated until the garment is ironed. The rolls of a sleeve ironer are not more than six to twelve inches long, but in a body ironer the rolls are twenty-two to thirty-four inches in length, with a diameter of seven and one-half inches for the heated roll, and five and one-fourth inches for the padded roll. The metal is not less than three-fourths of an inch thick. Operation of the machine does not involve simply release of the mechanism, but a continuous muscular exertion to keep the contact of the two rolls complete and even. One foreman remarked naively that unless a girl weighed 180 pounds, he would not hire her for the body ironer.

Fumes from the gas* are a constant annoyance, and in Great Britain have been considered so serious a menace to health that the law specifically requires vents or protectors to be provided for the operators.† In the catalogue of the American Laundry Machinery Company, issued in September, 1906, page 110, I find the following statement:

"This particular style of body ironer is manufactured more especially for the export trade, and is extremely popular in Great Britain, though it can be used to good advantage anywhere..... An iron hood lined with magnesia forms a covering for the heated roll. This is provided with a vent pipe at the top, through which the excess heat and unconsumed gases escape, thus protecting the operator. This latter device is attached in order to comply with the factory laws of Great Britain."

This ironer, although it is heavier and its dimensions are

---

* It is stated by laundrymen that a roll machine cannot well be heated by steam because of the difficulty of keeping the revolving rolls at as great a temperature as is required.

† Factory and Workshop Act, Aug. 17, 1901, Ch. 22, Sec. 103 (1 Edw. 7).

greater than the others, is not listed at a higher price. The extra expense of setting it up is slight, yet not one of the Pittsburgh laundries has such a device, nor does one protect its operators against the inhalation, ten hours a day, of the fumes of gas. The American Laundry Machinery Company states that there is no sale for this kind of body ironer in this country.

Roll ironing of shirt bosoms seems to be falling into disuse because of the popularity of the "domestic finish" produced by the steam press. Yet eight laundries still use roll shirt polishers altogether, and three use them intermittently for certain kinds of work. Instead of a lower roll, the polisher has a slightly rounded padded board shaped like a shirt bosom, and an upper steam-heated metal roll at the head of the board. Treadle pressure causes the board to pass backward and forward under the metal roll. This machine, now largely superseded, is the most difficult to operate, but, in spite of the great difference in process, the wages formerly paid to the operator are now in most cases paid to the operator of the bosom press.

The action of the bosom press is in the main automatic. Two padded boards are turreted on the same post, so that the operator does not need to change her position as she adjusts the shirts. The neckband ring is adjustable, and the shirt is fastened by metal plates which keep the shape exact. While the operator is fastening a shirt to one of the padded boards, another shirt is being ironed by pressure under a steam chest; with a touch of the release treadle the two boards are swung around, the clamps that held in place the shirt that has just been ironed are automatically pushed off, and another shirt can be adjusted. Some men estimate that a girl can learn the work in two hours. There is no doubt as to the simplicity of it, but the capacity of the press is not so great as that of the polisher, the rates of output according to one estimate being respectively 35 and 80 per hour. One laundryman spoke with considerable indignation of the effect of the demand for the domestic finish. "Two years ago," he said, "we used to finish all our shirt bosoms on a roll shirt polisher. The machine cost $175, and the operator, a really unusually good girl, got $6.00 a week. Now to get the finish our customers demand, we've had to buy two bosom presses, $600 each, with a weekly expense of $10 to $14 for padding the boards, and the two girls who operate them we have to pay $8.00 a week each."

Cuff, neckband and yoke* presses, and the wing point tipper for collars, are operated in very nearly the same way. The cuff is placed over the saddle-shaped padded head; pressure of a treadle raises the head against a steam chest, and pressure of another treadle causes the head to drop back as the cuff is finished. Only by violent exertion can hot metal and padded head be forced together. By sheer physical effort, therefore, the operator presses each cuff four times, twice on a side, and the whole body of the girl is shaken by the force which she is obliged to use. In one laundry the manager said: "No American can stand this. We have to use Hungarians or other foreigners. It seems to be unhealthful, but I don't know. The girls don't stay long enough for us to tell." Yet American girls do stand it. I have seen them ironing at the rate of three cuffs (twelve of these violent motions) a minute, making a total of 7,200 treadle pressures in a day. Sometimes, although the rate of output varies, the manager expects the cuff operators to keep up to four cuffs a minute.

In later models a spiral spring supplements the foot pressure, a touch of the treadle releasing the spring and forcing the saddle-shaped head against the steam chest. The cuff remains under the press longer, and the finish is better; the actual ironing, as in the case of the bosom ironer, is done automatically. With less exertion, too, the girls do more work. For instance, one manager says that with a new model machine his cuff press operator can finish 220 cuffs in an hour, which is an increase of 18 per cent over her former output. Each side of the cuff is ironed only once, instead of twice, and as it remains for a few seconds in position, one operator can keep two presses busy, if necessary. All the advantage seems to be on the side of these later models, yet they are found in only four of the Pittsburgh laundries.

The ironing of separate collars, no less than of shirts, bulks large in importance. The actual collar ironer is really a small mangle, but this is the least of the machines concerned, for each

---

* Yoke presses are found in only two or three laundries. Elsewhere other machines are adapted for the same work. Nine laundries still use small roll machines for cuffs and neckbands.

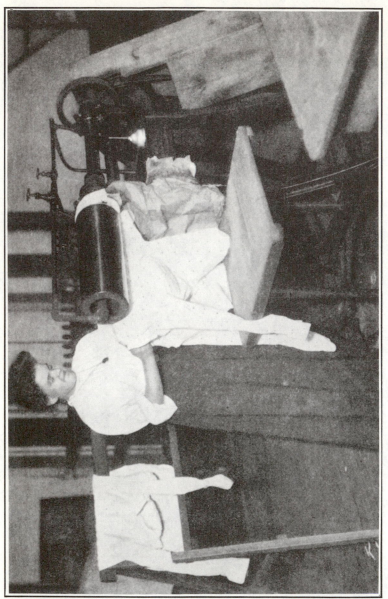

THE BODY IRONER AT WORK

collar after its initial ironing goes through a series of finishing processes. Straight collars must be shaped, and turnover collars must have the seam dampened, must be turned, must have the seam ironed and the rough edges smoothed, and must finally be shaped to fit tightly about the owner's neck. For each process there is a machine, and the four or five small machines used for this type of work are fastened on a table. The work is almost automatic, requiring so little skill and judgment that very young girls, learners, are employed at it successfully.

There is one machine in the collar department which should be described more fully. This is the wing point tipper, found in only three Pittsburgh laundries. The points of the collar after having been seam dampened are placed in the machine, and by pressure of the foot treadle the jaws of the machine are pressed against the reverse side of the points, the right side being in contact with the steam-heated head. A second treadle pressure releases the collar. The motion required for operating the tipper is as violent as that of the old style cuff press, the pressure of either treadle requiring the most extreme physical effort; but in each case where I saw the machine in use, the operator was a young girl not over fifteen years of age, and she was white with the strain. Of one the manager said, "She really is a pretty good worker. Since we put that department on piece rates, she does the work of two girls, and we don't have to pay but half as much wages."

Eight dollars* is the high water mark of wages in the ironing department. Shirt bosom ironers are never paid less than $6.00; more generally they receive $7.00, occasionally $8.00, and in one case $9.00. They are paid more, not less, than sleeve ironers, apparently only because usually they are the girls who formerly operated the more difficult shirt polishers. Between wages paid operators of roll and of press machines there is no assignable difference. The girls at the other machines earn $5.00 to $7.00, and sometimes at the cuff presses fall as low as $3.50. In general, wages are paid to the girl, not to the position. The specific amount depends on the personal appearance of the

* For table of wages in ironing department see Appendix B, p. 400, Table 63.

applicant, her quickness, regularity, and her ability to bargain. For instance, one girl agreed to run four cuff presses, taking the places of four girls who earned, one $3.50; two $4.00; and one $4.50 a week. She did the work of all of them but she was paid $7.00, not $16.

Promotion to the bosom-ironing machine is the climax of a laundry girl's ambition. Sometimes a totally inexperienced girl has been started at cuff or neckband presses, and later has worked up through the series of machine operations to be head girl. At other times an efficient starcher has been promoted to fill a vacancy in the ironing room. Yet although from time to time these opportunities occur, the length of time during which laundry girls keep at their work is so brief, that it is well-nigh impossible for any but the ablest of the under-employes to work up to the better paying positions.

In nine small laundries, which make a point of doing careful work, the girls are shifted from one machine to another as the work comes in, rather than kept steadily at one job. This implies a degree of experience with ironing machinery which the little recruit from the starching room does not often possess, and the lowest wage for ironers in these laundries is accordingly from $1.00 to $3.00 a week higher than in the other plants. It follows that these nine laundries, like so many small factories, will not take apprentices, but leave all the teaching of learners to large and fully equipped plants. They want experienced girls, who have already learned their trade elsewhere, and have the ability to adapt themselves to different occupations.

There is a growing tendency to stimulate output in the ironing department by substituting piece work for payment by the week. Where the force is so small that one girl cannot be kept at one machine, such a system is of course impracticable; and where perfection in finish is sought, it is undesirable because it tends to make the girls hurry too much. Piece work must always go hand in hand with a system of inspection. A single finisher is sometimes held responsible for all imperfect work. In one laundry there are inspectors for each department, and poor work is traced by a scheme of identifying marks, back to the girl who sent it out. The five best paid employes (at $8.50 a week) have no other duty than to fold and pass finally on shirts as they are finished. Piece rates vary in different laundries. For instance, where more responsibility is placed on the ironers and where the system of inspection is simple, $ .35 a 100 is paid for shirt bosoms and $ .10 a 100 for cuffs; on the other hand, where responsibility is in part shifted from ironers to inspectors and where inspection is elaborate, ironers are paid $ .20 a 100 for shirt bosoms and $ .06 for cuffs.

In two cases where the piece-payment system has been thoroughly worked out, the number of employes has been reduced one-half. The management gains both by the reduction of its payroll and by the absence of idling and inattention among employes who are retained. Under this system the payroll rises and falls automatically with the volume of trade; moreover, the burden of a trade depression is by this means automatically shifted to the employes. "Our girls know," the foreman said, "that they are paid for what they do, and if they don't do much they don't get paid much. Now, in some places, where they pay by the week, they cut the girls' wages at a time like this and then the girls don't like it."

The piece-payment system holds out to ambitious girls the possibility of larger wages. Few of them have worked long enough to find out from their own experience the secondary effects of speeding, the ill-health and nervous strain consequent on a high pace in work, and few of them have the judgment and the social consciousness to measure the system by its effect on others. They think well of it, if it makes their own advancement possible. Among unambitious girls, on the other hand, it frequently produces an indefinite discontent. They find that they have to work harder to make as much as formerly, and they are unwilling to increase their pace so as to be paid more.

One woman who has known the laundry business for years, first as a starcher fourteen years old, and later as a forewoman, told me of the time when she ironed shirts by hand, in a laundry where the piece system has been fully developed: "Yes," she said, "it's growing, this tendency to put everything on piece work, and it is possible to make as much as you used to by the week, but I tell you, you have to work hard for it. The first week I was put on piece work at ——'s, I got $ .04 apiece for shirts, and I made $14.05. The next week the rate was cut so that I had to work hard to make $8.00. They fix the rate according to what you used to make and what they want to get out, and I tell you, you have to work hard."

FINE IRONERS

Finishers and fancy ironers are both included in this department, their work being in a measure interchangeable. Their number varies from about 100 in the season from October to May, to two or three times as many from May to early fall. Where machine equipment is insufficient, finishers go over some of the machine-ironed articles by hand, but fancy ironers are employed almost exclusively on women's wear—shirtwaists and skirts, ruffles and lace and frills. They work with gas-heated sadirons, for puff* or electric irons are rarely found in Pittsburgh.

The tendency toward piece work is greater in this department than among the machine ironers. A fourth of the laundries pay their fine ironers a percentage, 20 to 25 per cent of the market charge for the finished article, and by this means they have both increased output and reduced the number in the department. For the piece workers, the schedule of hours is unimportant and the opportunity for a night's work is often welcomed in the busy summer months. At times the fine ironers have even worked twenty-four hours at a stretch. Although under the time-payment system they seldom received more than $8.00, under the system of piece payments with overtime work they make from $10 to a maximum of $15 a week.

Summer is their harvest time, and with the coming of fall their chances of large earnings are few. Even during the busy season there come weeks of not more than forty-eight hours' employment. The trade of the fine ironer fluctuates with the weather and with the fashion. To the extent that washable frills are worn on snowy days, she may be sure of a living during the winter months, but to the extent that thick waists prove popular

---

* It has been found in other cities that the use of puff irons in addition to the use of sleeve irons will go far toward decreasing hand work, thereby making this department more systematic.

A Laundry Ironing Room

in cold weather, she is likely to find that for the time being her services are not needed.

One wonders what becomes of the women who lose employment. They are not like the others in the laundry, neither old as the women in the washroom are, nor of the same type as the girls who have been advanced from one room to another. They have never worked at all the laundry processes. They seem to be women of a different sort, who have first learned in their own homes how to be expert finishers of fine wear. Some are married, and irregular work fits in easily with their life. Many are not. That they do not enter readily into other occupations is evidenced by the fact that so many of them go back to their old places as soon as the warm weather and the influx of ruffled finery begin. "We simply don't know," said a foreman who was beginning to see the case in its serious aspect. "We keep them as long as we can, for they'd starve if we didn't, but what becomes of them afterward, of them and the fifty other women we discharge when work is slack, we don't know."

Fine ironing is not a trade that a woman could look to for permanent support.* The uncertainty of employment and irregularity of earnings even under the best conditions render it a precarious mode of gaining a living. As a temporary expedient in summer, it offers a high return, and in all probability for a number of years fine ironers will be a requisite part of the laundry force. The progress of machine development, however, seems likely little by little to crowd out hand work in this line.

SEAMSTRESSES

The seamstress's hands are the last through which articles pass before going to the sorting room. Not all laundries have a mending department, but here and there one finds the sewing machine, and the patient round-shouldered woman who has taken to this as a final means of support. She is not in touch with the actual laundry work, nor has she the kind of responsibility which would make her an integral part of the collective industrial processes. Like hand washers, she is paid $6.00; in one place, $8.50.

* For table of wages of fine ironers, see Appendix B, p. 401, Table 64.

CHECKERS AND SORTERS

The sorting room, to which articles are sent after being mended by the seamstress, presents a marked contrast to the other departments. Sorting is the last of the laundry processes, and checking is the first, but as both are semi-clerical, the same force is often used in both departments. The girls in these departments are on a different level from the other laundry employes. Between them and the others there is no basis for fellowship, no intercourse, no consciousness of mutual interests. They do not eat lunch at the same time nor in the same room. They do not go to and from work together. Pride of caste confines each girl socially to the group to which her ability has brought her, and makes common action between departments wellnigh impossible. Starchers are a degree above mangle girls, ironers are a degree above starchers, but between the ironers and the checkers and sorters is a sharp barrier. These last are the aristocrats of the trade. It makes no difference whether they work in a corner of the cellar close by the washroom, or in a bright clean room shut away on the first floor. The other departments regard them with a respect untinged with familiarity.

The checkers receive the bags from the drivers, mark each article with the owner's name, and sort out into different baskets pieces that are to be washed separately—colored goods, flat work, shirts, collars, fancy articles, and so on. This involves considerable handling of soiled linen, and frequently is done in a workroom far from desirable. The point of emphasis in planning a laundry has been to arrange for the shortest possible route from one department to another. This has resulted sometimes in a cellar checkroom, to which the bags are sent through chutes from the street or floor above. It has often meant close contact with the washroom, with an atmosphere permeated with steam, the odor of unwashed clothes, and the musty smell from water long clinging to walls and floor.

In one South Side laundry, the cellar checkroom where five girls work is only partly separated from the washing department by a partition. The floor is damp and uneven, the air is dense with steam which has no other outlet unless it forces its way to the floor above. A faint, uncertain light comes through pebbled glass set in the sidewalk, and even the artificial light seems flickering and insufficient. "It is a hard job," the manager explained, "to get intelligent girls, girls who have had more than three or four years in school, to do this work."

One of the largest firms, which operates two plants and pursues about the same policy with regard to its employes in each, has in its two buildings widely contrasted checking departments, due apparently to the accident of different building construction. It so happens, in one case, that the checkroom is practically in a building by itself. There are windows side and front, and the room is bright, clean and sunny. You see instantly the reaction on the employes. The four girl checkers* are as trimly dressed, with evidence of as much self-respect, as clerks in a business office. They do not suggest kinship with the unkempt women who work in the hurry, dirt, steam and bad air of the usual checkroom. In the other plant owned by the same company the checkroom is on the first floor, separated by a half partition of unpainted boards from the mangle room, and directly above boiler and washroom. Pipes from the dryhouse on the floor above run through it. Three unshaded electric bulbs help out the dim light that filters through from two small windows opening on an alley. The floor is so overheated that in summer the girls can scarcely stand, and the air is so oppressive that even in the cool of winter breathing is difficult. A dozen different girls have come and gone within the summer months, but nevertheless the location is convenient for drivers and for washroom, and to the firm no change seems practicable.

In only six cases are the checkrooms† wholly separated from the washrooms, and at the same time not located directly above them. Twelve laundries use electric lights in the checkrooms because the straggling rays of daylight are insufficient for work, and sixteen have no means of ventilation.

Sorters, on the other hand, usually have a light workplace on an upper floor near the ironing room. The work is subdivided

* In one or two cases including this, checkroom employes have high stools, but elsewhere they stand all day at their work.

† See Appendix B, p. 397, Table 60.

189

among several minor groups of employes. "Rough-dry" sorters, for instance, who rank little above mangle girls in skill, have only to put the unironed work into different bins according to driver's route and owner's name. "Flat-work" sorters take charge of all goods that come from the mangle. Wrappers and banders, young girls of fourteen years, pack the finished articles in attractive bundles. The most difficult and exacting work falls to the "collar and cuff sorters." "If our customers' collars should get mixed," said one foreman graphically, "where would our trade be?" I have seen men in this department sort out thousands of collars from memory with remarkable speed and accuracy, but I cannot remember ever having seen a woman do this. As a rule, women are not so quick, but they can be trained to accuracy, although many laundrymen feel that successful sorting requires the discrimination of a man who wears collars rather than the routine work of a girl who has had a perfunctory training in distinguishing marks.

The checking and sorting departments are particularly interesting in that they offer an instance of competition between men and women on the same ground. Of the 191 workers in these departments in Pittsburgh laundries in 1907, 153 were women and 38 were men, a proportion of 4 to 1. The wages of the women run in general from $5.00 to $12; the wages of the men from $12 to $20. Competition here is not based on a rivalry between women and boys, such as we find in printing offices, nor on rivalry between men who do skilled hand work and women who do cheaper machine work, as in the stogy industry. Since there is no machinery, this is not a case where, although women have displaced men as machine tenders, men are still needed to take care of the women's machines. Here men and women are competing for work which requires no physical strength but which does require a common school education, intelligence, accuracy and speed. Nine years ago the work was exclusively in the hands of men. The one plant which had the prestige of a chain of laundries in several cities, began to employ women checkers, and women have now wholly displaced men in fifteen out of twenty-six* laundries, and partially displaced men in five others. The reason for this is not, as we have seen, that women have proved

* Two laundries have no checking or sorting department.

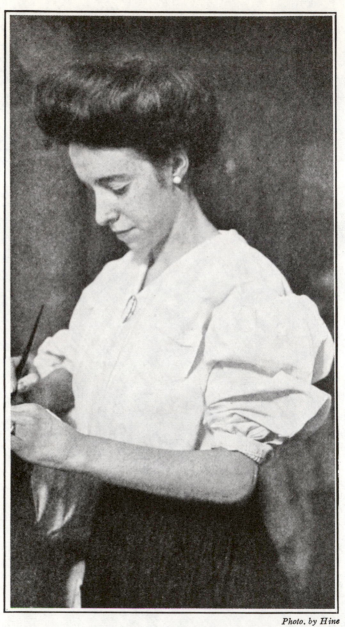

THE HEAD OF THE CHECKROOM

quicker or more accurate. The reason is financial: women are cheap. From the South Side to the East End you hear it said that "You can get two women where you got one man; get twice as much work done, and done just as well."

Of course the men checkers have fought the change. It was not the work of a moment to find women who could act as checkers, and when found, they had to be trained. Some laundrymen planned to introduce one or two women at a time into the checkrooms and by degrees to dismiss the men. This move was unsuccessful. The first women checkers were made so miserable by their co-workers that they speedily left, and employers were forced to plan again. They either dismissed all their men, using the foreman to supervise the checkroom, or dismissed all but one who acted as head checker and sorter, and trained the girls under him. This is the only way in which the joint employment of men and women has been found practicable. Later, women were advanced to the responsible positions and in these, too, they are now in the majority—39 women to 25 men.

The following table gives a summary of the situation in checking and sorting departments in Pittsburgh:

TABLE 23.—DISPLACEMENT OF MEN CHECKERS AND SORTERS BY WOMEN

	Head Checker	Head Sorter	Head Both Departments	Assistants	Reasons for Employing Men		Reasons for Employing Women	
					More accurate	Women hard to get	Cheaper	Cheaper more reliable
No. of plants employing men	11	10	4	3	2	2	..	..
No. of plants employing women	15	16	8	20	..	..	18	4
No. of plants employing men and women jointly	..	..	..	3*		..	..	..

Total number of men, 38.   Total number of women, 153.

* Men and women employed jointly, but in different rooms, at different sorts of work.

There is evidence here that mere cheapness, irrespective sometimes of lesser skill and lesser accuracy, is effective in bringing
about the displacement of one sex by the other.*

The highest regular wages among women laundry workers
are earned in the checking and sorting rooms. The range of
wages in these departments, however, varies widely with the
experience and dexterity of the individual girls. For instance,
one laundry employed four girls in its sorting room. The head
girl received $10 a week and her assistant $4.50 to $6.00. She
left at a time when the company was trying to lower expenses, and
her place was given to a former wrapping girl who was advanced
from $4.50 to $5.00 a week, and was helped out at her new work
by the foreman. Often a foreman supervises, and the best girl
in the checkroom is paid $8.00, the poorest $5.00. Sometimes
women employed as head checkers do not earn more than $8.00
or $9.00 a week, but $10 to $12 is more usual. In no case
does a man, even though an assistant, receive less than $12;
the general rate of pay for men assistants is from $15 to $18
and for head checkers and sorters occasionally $20. In general
a head sorter earns slightly more than a head checker, although
in some cases no distinction in wages is made either between
departments or for the supervision of both departments.

Marking machines have been introduced in four laundries
both as a cause and an effect of the increasing employment of
women. All articles brought to the laundry are marked with the
name of the owner, and sometimes with the route number or other
distinguishing signs. The marking machine combines the principles of the typewriter and of the printing press. The operator
presses down the different keys representing letters, and then
stamps, one after another, all the articles belonging to one person.
Foremen estimate that the machine will do the work of from two
to four girls. It can be operated by a cheap and comparatively
unintelligent employe, thus making possible the use of women
who have had little training, and the permanent displacement of
men.

* See Appendix B, pp. 398–399, Tables 61 and 62.

CHAPTER XI

INSTITUTIONAL LAUNDRIES. THE INDUSTRY AS A WHOLE

BEFORE summing up conditions in the laundry industry as a whole, some account must be given of the four institutional laundries in Pittsburgh which have attempted to combine philanthropy with a business undertaking. One, which does hand work, is run in connection with a relief society. The other three are of the commercial type, one being conducted by a convent which maintains a residence home for working girls, and two in connection with homes for delinquent girls, maintained by a sisterhood. The laundries of these institutions are not installed in separate buildings. In two cases they occupy a cellar, and in the third, rooms on an upper floor. Conditions are described as they were in 1908.

The hand laundry is in a long low building otherwise used by the relief society only for offices, and is maintained largely to provide work for applicants for relief. It is equipped with eight washtubs; the drainage is imperfect and the floor is completely saturated with water. Many of the women who come have had no training or experience in laundry work. They are taught by the supervisor how to wash at a tub, how to starch, and finally how to iron if they make sufficient progress to warrant their being intrusted with customers' clothing. According to the records, they are rarely under this tutelage for more than a month, and during that period are kept on part time, since in order to give as many women as possible these laundry advantages, no one is employed an entire day at a time, but thirty-nine or forty women are employed every week for two or three days each.

The fine ironers in this hand laundry are a more constant group, since to keep its trade the laundry gives most of the ironing to women who really understand it. Many of them, to be sure, have learned in this very workroom, but are now proficient and responsible. These women likewise work on part time. The ironing rooms, in irregular wings of the building, are only partly separated from the washroom, and have no forced ventilation to drive away the steam. The light, however, is good.

The rate of pay to women under training is $1.00 per day. The fine ironers are put on a piece basis which enables them, if they work the week through, to earn $8.00 to $11. On part time they do not earn over $4.00 or $5.00.

The charge has been made by other laundries in the neighborhood, that the society has cut market prices in order to secure trade, but this seems to be unwarranted. Collars, for instance, and a number of other articles, are listed at a higher price than elsewhere. This society deserves commendation in that it has not made a practice of underselling its purely commercial competitors. Moreover, it is attempting to compete in spite of serious handicaps. Its workers are a fluctuating group of untrained women, of low grade in intelligence and ability. Its equipment is of antiquated type,—the type developed by individual, not by collective organization,—and is poor of its kind. Its method, so far as commercial production is concerned, is already superseded.

Judged by business standards, there is every reason why such a plant should fail in entering the competitive market. But judged as a relief measure, other factors enter in. Discussion of relief problems is not within the province of this study; yet in so far as the relief problem is confused with the problem of working women, it demands some brief consideration. The women received into the laundry are in need both of relief and of training to enable them in future to do without relief. If the laundry serves merely as a means of gaining for these women the price of groceries, to obviate supporting them as objects of charity, it is meeting only a part of their need; if it is simply training them to do the work in their own homes better, it is not meeting their immediate economic need at all. Again, if this employment is regarded as the alternative of a pension system, only those women should be selected for the laundry who are not needed continuously at home. Experience of relief societies in general shows that a grave injustice may be done little children whose mother is obliged on the death or illness of the breadwinner to leave them and go out to work. The policy of the society as to the exact purpose of the laundry does not seem to have been thought out. In arriving at such a policy attention must be given both to the present need of applicants and to their problem of future livelihood. In other words, the laundry misses its opportunity if it fails to serve not only for relief, but for practical training to increase the earning power of the women whom it relieves.

To do this effectively, a distinction must be made between women who can work only part time and women who can work full time. The two problems are quite different. If the laundry is designed to meet the needs of women who can work part time, presumably it seeks to equip them to do washing by the day for families. If they are to do this successfully, they must be taught to do ironing as well as washing, and to do both ironing and washing well. This would seem to be the primary field which such a hand laundry can reasonably fill. Yet in the laundry of the relief society, most of the ironing is done by paid employes. The women admitted to its benefits are too irregularly employed and the instruction given them is too unsystematic for adequate training to be possible. Instead of being equipped with a marketable dexterity which they might turn to account as many days in the week as their homes could spare them, they are fitted only for day's work of the most unskilled sort.

If, on the other hand, there are women among them without children or homes, who could work full time, what shall be said of this laundry training? Obviously it fails even more conspicuously to meet their need than that of the part-time workers. They are not equipped to do family washing well. They are not equipped for the modern work in a steam laundry, nor in fact given any kind of trade training which would make them economically secure. Through a confusion of motives they are given occupation with tools which are commercially out of date, and at work which leaves them still inefficient at the close of their period of laundry employment.

The three institutional laundries, which are operated in connection with homes, serve primarily for the production of revenue and are run altogether on a commercial basis, though in the two homes for delinquent girls they serve secondarily as a means of occupational training for the girls.

The methods of the three laundries and their declared objects are similar, but the girls with whom they are dealing are of quite different types and needs. At the working girls' home, the girls are usually from out of town. They are tiding over a period of unemployment, they are too inefficient to secure employment, or through some physical or mental disability they are permanently unable to be commercially employed. Some of them need care and an occupation, which they receive at this home; others need temporary help and training for greater efficiency. Yet the same kind of assistance is extended without distinction to girls of both types.

At the homes for delinquent girls, the girls are young, from fourteen years up, and are in reality prisoners, having been placed there by parents, friends, or by the court for social offenses. It is estimated that in the home where the older girls are kept, 30 per cent are feeble-minded, and a still larger percentage diseased. Few of the girls, before entering the homes, have had regular industrial occupation, and still fewer have had any training by which on leaving the home they could secure profitable work. Leaving out of consideration the girls who are feeble-minded, the others need first of all, while in the homes, an occupation to win their interest. As a second and equally important consideration, they need to be trained for an occupation at which they can earn enough to be financially independent.

Having in mind the types of girls in these homes, I shall speak first of the workrooms, then of the working conditions and of the effect of the work on the girls. All three laundries are run as steam rather than hand laundries; they have washing machines, mangles, and as a rule some ironing machinery. The washroom in each case is in the cellar. The discomforts resulting from cellar washrooms have already been pointed out, but the matter is more serious here in that the upper floors are used for living and sleeping rooms by the occupants of the homes. Men are employed to take charge of the washing machines, but in one washroom five women are also employed to wash by hand. The windows in this washroom are very small, not over three feet by three, there is no forced ventilation and the drainage is imperfect.   In fact none of these washrooms in institutional laundries makes special provision for ventilation, and in only one is the drainage good.

The mangles in each case are also in the cellar.   In one home, the mangle department is walled off from the washroom, but in the others the mangle room is not separate and is full of steam from the machines.   As in other steam laundries a small roll guard is used on the mangles.   The danger with this guard has been pointed out; in the homes the danger is the greater because of the mental incapacity of some of the girls. Unrestricted employment of these girls at laundry work also involves danger to the patrons of the laundry, for where a girl who handles wet linen at a mangle is diseased, as many of them are, she is liable to spread infection to the customer.

Starching in all three of the laundries is done by hand without any machine assistance.

The ironing room in each home for delinquent girls, is in the cellar where the rest of the laundry work is done.   In one case it is excellently equipped with steam-power machinery and electric irons, and is operated by the more promising girls of the home.   In the working girls' home the ironing room is on an upper floor; its equipment is so primitive that it would not serve at all were the trade of the house not largely in flat work.

The sisters of the convent which runs the working girls' home, act as checkers and sorters, and take responsibility for the management.   At the homes for delinquent girls the sisters supervise, but the Magdalens—girls committed to the home who have joined what might be termed a lay order—act as head girls of all departments and as checkers and sorters.

The delinquent girls are of course not paid for their work. Residents at the working girls' home receive, in addition to their board, from $10 to $12 a month; a few of the more expert are paid $5.00 a week, and the chief fine ironer, who does not live at the home, is paid $7.00 a week.   Since most of the girls receive board as well as pay, the rates are not so small as they at first seem; nevertheless some laundrymen feel that this method of hiring employes enables the home by underselling to take unfair advantage of its competitors.   In all three of these laundries

197

there is some evidence of underselling and of individual agreements with customers.

Institutional laundries have frequently been charged with requiring overtime. Undoubtedly overtime work does occur under pressure of trade, but there is no reason to suppose that it occurs more frequently in these homes than in the regular commercial laundries. Former inmates state that they have worked until eleven o'clock at night. Probably this is true occasionally on Friday night, when overtime is general throughout the trade. Midweek overtime which interferes with customary religious observances could occur in religious houses only under exceptional conditions.

The occurrence of overtime, however, is of less significance than the type of work which falls to the girls whom these homes are attempting to benefit. The sisters of the convent provide in their working girls' home an asylum, and an occupation for some of the inefficient. The high grade work which is well paid in commercial laundries they either do themselves or have done by employes living outside. What they are really doing for the underemployed who are capable of improvement is to offer them not profitable training, but solely relief in the shape of an asylum and a temporary occupation. Of the laundries in which delinquent girls are employed, the same criticism may be made. These homes feel that they cannot afford to sacrifice needed revenue for the sake of training their young girls either to be expert domestic laundresses or to take the better-paid positions in steam laundries; still less train them in other occupations more suitable to the physique and personality of some of the girls who come to them. Little really expert work is done by the girls. Such routine work as they do, if followed after they leave the home, would bring them in an income too small to have a salutary effect on their mode of life. It does not appear then, that the laundry work as taught in these homes either stimulates the girls or trains them to economic efficiency.

Finally, it may be said of these three institutions as of the relief society, that they should work out a constructive policy to the end that the training offered might equip those among their inmates who are mentally sound so that in future they would need neither relief nor correction.

THE LAUNDRY INDUSTRY AS A WHOLE

To return to the trade in general:

The laundry girl's week begins late Monday morning and ends late Friday night. Hours vary, of course, in different departments of the same laundry. They vary, too, from laundry to laundry, according to the length of the drivers' routes, the class of trade,—whether it is mainly a family trade or a hotel and restaurant trade,—and partly according to the efficiency of the management. The following schedule is from a small Penn Avenue laundry which employs six men and thirty-two girls:

TABLE 24.—OPENING AND CLOSING TIME IN THE DEPARTMENTS OF
A LAUNDRY

Day of Week	Opening Time		Closing Time	
	Departments	Hour	Departments	Hour
Monday . .	Checkers ⎱ Sorters ⎰	7 a. m.	All	9 p. m.
" . .	Washers ⎱ Mangle girls ⎬ Starchers ⎰	8 a. m.	. . . .	. . . .
" . .	Ironers	10.30 a. m.	. . . .	. . . .
Tues.–Thur. .	All	7 a. m.	All	6 p. m.
Friday . .	All	7 a. m.	All	9–12 p. m.

Washing begins late Monday, because the drivers do not get back from their first rounds in time for goods to be checked in before the middle of the morning. One laundryman who never permits Monday night work in his plant insists on having the bundles brought in early, and says that if this is done the goods can be finished early and no overtime will be necessary. He thinks that overtime is likely to figure less and less in the laundry business. In some places, however, the drivers have routes so long that they cannot make more than one trip a day. Several laundrymen are of the opinion that it would be advisable to district the city so as to confine the trade of each laundry to its own locality, and to do away with the long drivers' trips from one end of the city to the other. This plan, by insuring short routes and the early incoming of work, would go far to obviate late closing on Monday. One laundry has overtime solely on account of some restaurant work which does not come in until three o'clock in the afternoon, and which must be returned the next day. Unquestionably the offer of "one day work" to customers is responsible for much of the night work Mondays. The break between Saturday and Monday means a late start at the beginning of each week and consequent overtime to make up for it. Six laundries at present, either by circumstances of trade or by exceptionally good management, or both, are able to do without night work the first of the week. Some would be glad to do so, but in every other case, late closing is the rule.

The week's work must be finished Friday because customers insist that goods shall be returned by the end of the week. Saturday is the time for cleaning and for padding the machines. With the exception of three laundries all the plants keep open Friday evenings, and six of them work Saturday mornings in addition. "We should be glad not to work Monday and Friday night," said one man, "but the public demands goods on such short notice that we can't help it." The exact hour of Friday closing varies. It may be seven o'clock when trade is light. It may be nine or ten, or it may be later. It is vague and unplanned, dependent on circumstances. "We are in here until we get through," is the general response; "it may be late and it may be early, but we can see the work ahead of us until we finish." Said one foreman, "We stay until nine or ten, or sometimes——" "Later?" I suggested. "Well," he said, "you know the law doesn't allow us to work over twelve hours." Then he added, with a sudden access of frankness, "But every laundry in the city is likely to work more than twelve hours now and then. They know they're violating the law, but they'd rather do that than open up on Saturday." A shirt ironer has told me of working until half past one at night, and several managers have admitted keeping the laundry

BETWEEN THE NOON WHISTLES. TYPES OF LAUNDRY WORKERS.

open until twelve. When possible, they avoid the expense of starting the engines for the short day Saturday.

One laundry has a double shift of women employes, and works night and day. The conditions here are unusual, in that the customers are not private individuals, but four downtown hotels, several theatres and restaurants, all of them requiring short-time work. Theatres and restaurants must have their goods at once. Guests at hotels are likely to be transient and cannot be delayed. The laundry employs 33 picked girls, 12 of them Polish and 21 American. Shifts are not changed from week to week; generally a girl stays on one shift all the time; but the day girls frequently have overtime Mondays and Tuesdays when work is heaviest. Sometimes the night girls are paid slightly less than the day girls, because their work is lighter and their hours not quite so long. As a rule, however, the mangle room is paid a flat rate of $5.00, and the starching and ironing rooms a flat rate of $7.00, with a pay of $8.00 to the head girls. The hours of the two shifts are as follows: day turn: 7–12; 12:45–6; night turn: 6:30–12; 12:45–5. According to the present Pennsylvania law, the employment of women on a night shift is not illegal, as it will be for girls under 18 after the new law goes into effect, January, 1910, but the hours of working women are limited to 12 in one day and 60 in one week. The hours of the day girls in this laundry are 61½ weekly, even when they have no overtime. With overtime, the hours are frequently 66 or more.

In general, not the working week so much as the individual working day is at fault in Pittsburgh laundries. The five-day week would ordinarily cut down the number of hours to a total well within legal limits. But the length of the day is a different matter. It is affected by public demand for quick work; by trade overlapping widely separated sections of the city; by the expense of starting machinery for a short day Saturday when at much less expense it can be kept running for a long day Friday; finally, by a lax factory law which fixes no closing hour for the work of women. Without a closing hour beyond which it is illegal for women to work, the 60-hour limit to the week is easy to evade.

The irregular hours and seasons have unquestionably helped to determine the types of girls in the trade. The types have been determined also by the general low wage. It is true that some women earn $8.00 and more in the checking and sorting rooms, $7.00 and sometimes $8.00 at some of the ironing machines, and $15 as a maximum at fine ironing in heavy weeks. But this last is counterbalanced by long dull seasons, and not more than a sixth of the girls at the machines receive a $7.00 wage. Among the others there are gradations of lower and lower pay, down through starching and mangle room, to the $3.00 beginners. For those who stay and have ability to learn, promotion is possible. But the laundry girls do not stay. Managers give four years as the extreme limit of work at the trade, and many say that they do not keep their girls more than two. The laundry girls change often and marry early; as a class they are shifting and unreliable.*

The reason for this does not lie in the essential nature of the work. The variety of machines in the laundry industry suggests possibilities for the training of expert workers. In the ironing department especially, there is room for a plan of apprenticeship which should equip an alert girl to understand and easily to operate all the machines, and should lay the basis for fair wages.

The reason lies in the physical features of the plants themselves, in the conditions under which the work is carried on, and in the long hours. In earlier chapters the physical conditions of the plants have been described in detail: washrooms so placed below the other departments as needlessly to heat the upper floors; windows kept closed because of the fog and dust; inadequate provision for ventilation. Steam from drying clothes in mangle and ironing rooms, excess heat from the machines, and the fumes of gas, in the absence of vents or other protective devices, add to the general discomfort. One result of the heat and excessive steam is that diseases of the respiratory organs are prevalent among girls who remain long in the trade. Another result is that girls who can choose their workplace do not come into the trade, and that those who do come leave as soon as they can.

* For range of weekly wages in various departments of Pittsburgh laundries, see Appendix B, pp. 394–401, Tables 57–64.

The association of laundry work with domestic service has been another reason for its failure to attract girls who can choose their workplaces. The washtub and all that it implies are irksome to many ambitious girls; the speeding in some laundries under a piece-payment system makes the work still more distasteful. Even under a system of time payments, speed is the point of emphasis. There are few cases where a girl is thoroughly trained in the work of different departments; she is forced rather to acquire speed at a single process and to keep at that.

Finally, the long hours tend to keep desirable girls out of the trade. The very homes which gain a respite from their work through transferring it to the laundry, by their unthinking demands exact late hours of laundry employes.

Such a combination of unhealthful workplace, unpleasant working conditions, and long hours in a trade, cannot but limit its employes to working women who are least efficient, least reliable and least able to choose their kind of employment. With better working conditions and shorter hours, the trade immediately attracts more desirable employes. This is evident in one or two of the Pittsburgh laundries where the working conditions are good and the type of employes markedly superior. The conditions in other laundries tend to intensify rather than to diminish the shifting unreliability of the girls drawn into them.

General adoption of the later devices for the improved action and safeguarding of machines, a rigorous standard in ventilation, the placing of washroom and mangle room so as to make health possible to the workers, an apprentice system which would develop a thorough knowledge of laundry processes and the abolition of night work, would go far to offset the disorganizing tendencies mentioned and to build up a group of employes as a whole stronger, more stable and better poised. These measures are all in line with what the more far-sighted business managers have already done.

CHAPTER XII

DYEING AND CLEANING

THE dyeing and cleaning establishments, like the laundries of Pittsburgh, owe their prosperity in part to mines and mills. Their processes are finer, more individual; their custom is from a different group in the community; but still they are cleaners, removers of dust and grime. That a firm from as far away as Baltimore has opened a competing branch in their midst, is evidence of their success.

Some are large enough to utilize a square of brick buildings and sheds. Others have a little second floor above a shop. How many of them there are, how many prospering establishments and how many makeshifts, there is no trade association record to show. The small family shops where cleaning and dyeing are done might almost be grouped among home industries, and of them no reckoning has been made. Men in the trade estimate that the working force of the larger establishments numbers altogether about 1400 men and 510 women.

The largest of the city plants is a group of two-story brick buildings opening on a yard. The buildings are small and each completely separate from the others in order to reduce fire risks incurred by the use of gasolene. When a garment that has hung in the dryhouse is brought into the cleaning room on a cold day, the electric spark struck off by vigorous rubbing may cause an instant blaze. The probability of fire is less in warm weather, but the work is never danger-proof.

Cleaning by gasolene as well as all scrubbing and wet cleaning in this establishment is done on the first floor by men. Garments and draperies are washed in small tubs, but carpets have to be handled in vats and wrung dry in huge extractors six feet in diameter. On the first floor, too, tapestries are dyed and cleaned.

The ironing room is on the second floor. Men iron the skirts and heavy pieces that require a sixteen-pound iron. Women finish the waists of garments; they rarely use an iron weighing more than nine pounds. Steam-heated ironing machines are only occasionally used, but gas-heated puff irons are continually in demand, now to round the edge of this ruffle, and now to renew the smooth delicacy of that piece of lace. Work of this sort can be learned in a week or in a few months. At least a year of practice is needed, however, before a new hand can be trusted to bring intricate puffs and frills to the perfection of appearance that the patrons of a dyeing and cleaning establishment demand. The waist ironers do not attempt to finish more than six or eight waists in a day, and they work not by the piece, but by time. The requirement is that their work shall be done perfectly. From the beginning, week wages are paid, and experienced girls earn from $7.00 to $10.

The regular day's work is nine and a quarter hours, but during March, April and May, the employes sometimes have overtime for three to five nights a week. The slack season comes in summer. Many employers dismiss their girls, but the policy of this firm is to keep them the year round and thus to avoid the difficulty of securing new and trustworthy hands in the fall.

Seamstresses are employed, too, who are paid $1.50 a day to mend and remake garments. They must take a waist to pieces, if need be, and put it together again exactly as it was before. They must be able with a milliner's skill to retrim a hat after its separate parts have been dyed and cleaned. They must observe the intricacies of a cushion whose surface is covered with impossible contortions of ruffled lace, with bowknots and silk and embroidered letters. They must take it apart, and after the parts have been washed put it exactly together, a feat seemingly possible only for a brain of the circuitous habit that originally conceived the design. These women are not mere seamstresses. In their work there must be the same perfection that is requisite in the ironing of fine garments or in the dyeing and curling of feathers.

In others of the large establishments, women work at gasolene. In one case there are five women doing the actual dry cleaning; in another case, there are two. In unnumbered small establishments, one woman is employed as a general hand for cleaning if need be, or for pressing or sewing, or any other odd job. She may be called on alternately for work at the gasolene tank or over the irons.

In one shop all the employes are French; the three women are relatives of the employer's wife. They press and sew and clean from seven-thirty to six, as the need may be, one of them for $3.00 and her board and washing, one for $7.00 and one for $5.00. How far these wages approximate wages in larger establishments depends in large measure on the quality of the board. Inexperienced girls in general earn from $4.00 to $6.00 and experienced girls $7.00 to $10, as in the large plant described.

The larger places employ many Americans, women of higher grade than those in the laundry industry, and of marketable skill. The work has drawbacks, such as the constant standing, the weight of the irons, the overtime, and the chance of discharge during the slack season. Some of the employes too are totally unskilled; all day long they hang clothes in the dryroom, or wash curtains and shades. The women who handle the gasolene are of a rougher sort than the other girls in the trade.

Yet, when these things are taken into consideration, it is still true that the majority of the workers in dyeing and cleaning establishments are sure of a living wage and of work steady, in the main, throughout the year. Where the buildings are small and separated from each other, as in establishments constructed after the best plan, and where ventilation is adequate, even the ironing room is not an undesirable workplace.

METALS, LAMPS AND GLASS

CHAPTER XIII

THE METAL TRADES

MEN in the Pittsburgh metal trades, in the steel mills, the foundries, the machine shops, are doing work that is both heavy and difficult. They are carrying loads of crude ore, they are running engines, mixing metals in crucibles or operating the levers which move huge, sensitive electric cranes. The product at which they work is measured in tons of metal or reduced to threads and mechanical parts accurate to the thousandth part of an inch. It is shaped into rails and carwheels and tubes, into electric motors and delicate and intricate machinery. Women also have found work to do in these plants, but their product is of a different order. Instead of the brass parts of an engine, they make the sand cores for the molds in which the brass takes form. Instead of electric motors, they make the simplest and smallest of the coils of which the motor is built. Instead of steel rails, they trim the bolts with which the rails are fastened down. They split mica for the insulators which are built by men; they assemble the parts of small metal novelties; they feed light hinges into a machine, or solder tin, or dip pieces of tinware into enamel. They have nothing to do with the great ingots or with the fashioning or assembling of involved machinery; rather they handle the small pieces of brass or aluminum or steel which are needed in such quantities that the process of making them can be turned into a mere series of repetitions, or they tend machines which they do not control or understand. Their product is used either in preparation for the final metal shaping, as in the case of sand cores, or it is finishing work, as japanning, after the metal has been shaped.

Light as the product is, subsidiary as the process often is, the work done by women is a significant part of the metal trades of Pittsburgh. The number of women, too, is significant. Only two other factory trades, stogy making and laundry work, exceed metal work in the number of women employed. Broken up into their several groups, the trades in 1907 ranked numerically as follows:

TABLE 25.—NUMBER OF WOMEN IN VARIOUS DIVISIONS OF THE METAL TRADES

Trade Division	No. of Women
Electrical appliances	652
Screw and bolt works	543
Miscellaneous trades	444
Machine shops and foundries	315
Total	1954

In taking up these trades one by one I shall attempt to state what share of the work falls to the women, and how this work may be measured by wages, by hours and by the character of the process, in its effect on the health and lives of the employes.

FOUNDRIES

Fifty core makers work in the largest foundry core room which employs women in Pittsburgh. All are women. Through the narrow entrance you can see them moving about among wreaths of coal smoke and black dust, working on molds at their benches, or carrying trays to the ovens. Some are Polish girls, round featured, with high foreheads and fair hair; others are peasant women of the Hungarian type, strong and mature, their dark hair roughly combed back, their waists half open and their sleeves rolled high. Muscular and dark of skin, they strike you as an incarnation of the activities of smoking ovens, boiling crucibles and iron soft with fierce heat. The dim light through windows encrusted with black dust hardly reaches to the rows of ovens in the centre of the room, and even the glare of an electric bulb cannot dispel the impression of unreality and remoteness.

The benches of the core makers are on either side of the ovens, ranged through seventy feet of drifting dust. Each girl has her little heaps of different kinds of sand, her mold and shaping tools. She makes the sand cores and carries them, a trayful

WOMEN CORE MAKERS

at a time, weighing sometimes ten pounds, sometimes twenty, sometimes fifty, to the ovens to be baked hard. Her work may be on cores with vents and spikes, or on simple finger-shaped cores which pay the makers $ .10 a 1000. Quick girls can make three a minute or 10,000 a day. The large intricate cores which fit into big machines are not made by girls, but by men in another room.

Altogether the seven core rooms which make use of women core makers employed 159 women in 1907. Some are with brass foundries, some are operated in connection with malleable iron companies, while others are adjuncts to machine shops. In some foundries two or three women supplement the work of men and in others women make all the cores. They are employed irrespective of the kind of foundry so long as the work is not too heavy or too intricate for them to handle. The cores which they make of sand are set in the molds into which the hot metal is poured. In this way a hollow metal shape is produced, lighter and easier to handle than would be the solid metal.

The core room is, of course, but an adjunct to the foundry; core making a subsidiary process; and the convenience of other departments is consulted first in the laying out of the plant. Sometimes part of the foundry itself is used as a core room. Sometimes a space is set apart between machines, or a narrow bit of a room is partitioned off on the floor above. For example, in one case twelve girls work in a loft above a brass foundry. The fumes from the brass find their way up the narrow stairway leading to the loft and out through the one window at the end of the room. The girls stand at their benches in the midst of the dust and fumes. In every core room but one the ovens are either in the room or close beside it. This one plant provides a workplace apart from machinery and dust, in a clean, freshly painted room lighted by side windows and a skylight. High stools are placed at the tables and girls can sit at their work.

The influence of the machinists' union has closed some of the core rooms at 5 : 30 p. m. Others close at five, but all the foundries save one obtain a ten-hour day by cutting short the rest time at noon. Work pressure varies with the seasons, but at different times in different foundries, because the work of each depends upon distinct branches of the metal trade. All of them work on orders. Cores as a rule cannot be made up for stock, as they vary in shape and size according to the molds for which they are used. Overtime is infrequent. In one plant the girls estimate that they have overtime amounting to three months during the year, a week here and a week there when orders are heavy. Much of the work, however, needs daylight for the best results, and in the other plants day hours have with few exceptions been found sufficient.

Unlike men core makers, women are paid by the piece. As trades go, the returns are not high, if we take into consideration the length of time spent in learning. It is two years before a girl is considered expert. In some places, the girls do not earn more than $1.00 a day after they have learned, but $1.25 is more usual, and in two foundries the core makers regularly draw a day's pay of $1.40. An American girl who had worked for five years, said that she usually made from $7.00 to $8.00 a week, although in poor weeks she had fallen as low as $6.00. Once she had made $10.50, and sometimes at long intervals she had made $9.00, but such wages as these were by no means to be regarded as regular earnings. Much of the time her work was on finger-shaped cores with vents, that paid $ .07 a 100, and very often on "round liners" for Kelso couplers. These round liners are finger-shaped with vent and spike. They pay $ .12 a 100, and an experienced girl can turn out from 1,200 to 1,500 a day. These cores are the lightest in weight and are set 13 on a tray, a total weight of not over 10 pounds; but other kinds of cores are set 58 on a tray and weigh from 20 to 25 pounds, if not more. There is a tradition in the core room of this foundry that a girl once made $2.00 a day at a new kind of work and that when the firm found it out, the rate was cut so that no girl thereafter should be able to make more than $1.50, or a maximum, rarely reached, of $1.85. Another foundry has a fixed maximum of $1.75, but 20 out of the 30 women whom it employs do not exceed $1.00 or at most $1.20 a day.

One dollar and twenty-five cents may be regarded as the mean wage of the women core makers in Pittsburgh. For unorganized men, employed on the small work at which girls are otherwise used, the minimum day's pay is $2.50. I am told by men in the trade that there are 500 men core makers in Pittsburgh and the North Side, and that 75 per cent of them are organized. The union rate of wages is $3.50 a day up. That nearly a fourth of all the core makers should be women, would seem at first sight to indicate that this, too, is a trade for which men and women are competing, and that the greater cheapness of women workers is winning them ground. They get $1.25 less a day than the unorganized men; $2.25 less than the union scale. The union, to combat this tendency, admits no women to its membership and prohibits the employment of women in core rooms with union men; its aim is to force women out of the occupation as it increases the number of union shops.

Yet it is only in part true that women in this trade are actively competing with men. A line of cleavage separates the kinds of work at which they are severally employed. The heavy work, the cores of intricate design that require for their making long training and the skill of a craftsman—these cores are made by men. It is the men in the trade who know what kinds of sand to use and how to combine several cores in one. Women are used for the simpler, more obvious things, for the stock shapes of cores which can be learned in a few weeks. The core maker's trade, as men know it, is not by any means in women's hands. No women are apprenticed to learn the work in all its ramifications.

In the more difficult branches of the trade, therefore, there is no active competition between men and women. Yet potentially there is real competition. The small work, as well as the large, was at one time in the hands of men. Except where the union has been strong enough to force a shop to employ only men in the core room, the small work has been given over to women. The proportion of women in the trade is great enough to be menacing, in that they are doing the work at half the price of unorganized, and at a third the price of organized, men. Within a few years they have crept into shops that the public and even people in the trade still suppose to be employing men. They are doing the men's work. They are themselves carrying the trays and handling the tools. Except for the natural limitations to their work on heavy cores and the artificial limitations to their trade apprenticeship, these women core makers are in a fair way to become not only numerically important in the core rooms of machine shops, but economically effective in depressing the wages of the men.

MICA SPLITTING

In connection with one foundry, there is work of another sort which should be mentioned here, although it does not properly come under a discussion of core making. This is a mica-splitting department, which supplies an East Pittsburgh electrical works. One hundred and fifty-six girls, at least two-thirds more than there are in the core room of the foundry, split mica in the room below. In a large square room with dusty windows on two sides, the girls sit at long tables which fill the space to the very center. Electric bulbs above each table help out the imperfect daylight and make the work somewhat less difficult, although in any case it strains the eyesight.

Each girl has her board with the square, stratified block of mica and a knife in front of her, and just back of the board, three boxes for mica of different degrees of fineness. A beginner is paid $ .75 a day for two weeks, then at the third week put on piece work, and expected to "make her time." A few who have been there a long time can make $1.80 a day, and are prevented by rate cutting from making any more, but most of the girls do not run over $1.40 and often fall as low as $1.00. The piece rate is $ .22 a pound for the finest grade of mica, $ .18 for the next and $ .16 for the coarsest. The girl does her own sorting and is paid much or little, according to the amount of fine stock that she can get out of one block of mica. Sometimes the stock may be knotty and almost impossible to split without breaking, and on these days even the piece-work girls make less than their $ .75; but with smooth, well-separated material, they diminish the piles rapidly.

The hours here, as in the foundry, are from seven to five-thirty, with three-quarters of an hour at noon. Ten minutes before closing time the girls are expected to stop work in order to sweep under their tables and around their benches. Men sweep the floor after hours, but the girls are required to do this prelimi-

nary work. The room is always full of dust. Without forced ventilation, with the particles of mica filling the air and the dust from the mica scattered about, this department is an unhealthful workplace.* Reports as to diseases of throat and lungs, sometimes tuberculosis, among old employes, are partial indications of lack of care on the part of the management for the safe-guarding of its labor force.

ELECTRICAL APPLIANCES

From this mica workroom to the Pittsburgh electrical industries that make use of mica is a natural transition. A number of small companies carry on a jobbing and repair business in electrical appliances in the city proper, but of these only a few manufacture, and of these few, but one employs women. Many of the women from the city, however, work in the East Pittsburgh plant of the Westinghouse Electric and Manufacturing Company.

The manufacture of coils, armatures, transformers, motors, requires a force of trained electricians to plan and execute, as well as a force of mechanics and engineers; it also calls for young girls. At East Pittsburgh in 1907 a total of 10,000 workers were employed in the offices and plant which operated with day and night shifts of men. Five hundred of the men in the factory force are apprentices, who work through the different shops and learn the trade, becoming graduate electricians, either in the service of the company, or going out for themselves at the end of their apprenticeship. They are paid little during their term, for this company has more to offer in opportunity than most of its kind in the United States or, indeed, in the world, and to learn here is worth a man's while at a wage of $ .15 an hour or less. The other men in the factory are mechanics, steadily employed in one department, with relatively small chance of advancement.

The 650 women on the force have work less important than that of the apprentices, or of the workmen. They are used for the

* Kober, Dr. George M.: Report on Industrial and Personal Hygiene, p. 20: "Workers in mica dust............are predisposed to diseases of the respiratory passages."

215

execution of a few mechanical processes in building armatures and coils. For them, there is neither trade opportunity nor possibility of promotion. Half of them work together in a huge room, streets wide, and of a length to be counted in fractions of a mile rather than in feet. At one side, men operate lathes and bores; on the other are girls, row back of row, to the number of 300, all of them young and usually pale and a little tired. You guess that from the droop of the shoulders and from the lines about the mouth, not from the pace, for every girl is working fast at winding coils by hand or machine, or at pasting mica at the long tables at the far end. You must speak close to your neighbor's ear for a word to be heard in the midst of this ceaseless whirr of a thousand wheels. The girls' arms keep pace with the power.

PROCESSES

Most of the women are employed at coil winding. The machine process is simple and easily learned, as each girl simply starts the machine and holds in her hands coil and tape, while the rapid revolutions of the wheels wind both together. The power action is so strong that the operator sways backward and forward and is often forced to exert considerable physical strength to keep the tape in place. In a Pittsburgh firm where women are employed only for hand taping, and the machine taping is done by men, the superintendent said that he would never allow women to operate machines, as the pull of the power demands too much strength in keeping the winding right. A different practice is followed at East Pittsburgh, and if any coil is wound imperfectly at these power machines, the girl operator is required to rewind it without pay.

Hand winding is first done with black fish paper, and then with yellow fish paper. Next the whole coil is wound with white tape, then dipped in shellac, and frequently wound a second time with fish paper and tape before being redipped in shellac, and lastly in a heavy black paint. The kind of winding varies somewhat for different uses, but in most cases this general plan is followed. There are eight small foot-power machines for white taping in the East Pittsburgh works, and in their use, too, the pull of the machine and of the coil shakes the whole body of the operator in her effort to keep the tape straight and firmly wound.

The split mica of the Pittsburgh foundry is used here for insulations. Sheets of paper, some four feet square, others smaller and circular in size, are covered with bits of mica pasted on thickly or thinly, according to the use for which they are destined. Girls put the paste on the paper and fix layer after layer of mica firmly in place. Stray girls are employed here and there in other departments. At two presses in the stamping department, four girls are employed to feed into the press small pieces of tin composite which are used to build the cores of transformers. The press is guarded and seems to be in no way dangerous for the feeder, while at the other side, the receiver simply piles the tin pieces together.

In another room there are women who build the cores of transformers by setting one flat piece of tin above another about the center, to the height sometimes of a thousand sheets; setting ten pieces in place and hammering them down, then setting another ten until the core is one compact whole. The work seems purely mechanical, with less judgment and less dexterity required than in the winding room. All the actual assembling of transformers, the assembling and most of the winding of armatures, is done by men. There are some small armatures which are wound by women, the coils being held together by white tape and twisted into place, preparatory to finishing with wire bands. Even with small armatures, this is stiff work.

In some cases women are employed to assemble small groups of coils for motors or other electrical appliances, but the main divisions of their work are the building of the cores of transformers and the winding of armatures and coils. It sometimes happens that men do the heavier winding, but they are never put on the same kind of work for which women are employed, unless there is a rush order and their help is needed temporarily. As the men coil winders are paid exactly double what the girls are paid, it would be a costly policy for the firm to permit the men ordinarily to undertake any of the girls' work.

WAGES

The girls are paid either by the piece or on a premium plan. Learners get $ .08 an hour ($ .78 for a nine and three-quarter hour day) for the first two weeks. They come one day and look on, but after that are given work to do. Premium girls are paid $ .10 an hour, and are given, for example, twelve hours in which to do a specific piece of work. If they can finish it in six hours, they are paid $ .15 an hour, or five hours extra, and are given something else to do in the six hours which they have left. Of course, the time is so calculated that few girls can do their work on a shorter time allowance. To gain speed at any one kind of work takes at least six weeks, but the girls are apt to be transferred frequently from one section to another, so that it is impossible for them to keep up a high rate of earnings. The fastest girls make $1.47 a day, and if this amount is exceeded when a new article is given out, the rate is usually cut. Formerly the base rate was $ .12 an hour, and the girls were able to make $2.00 a day. Two or three of the girls—old employes—are still working at the old rate, but for the others, the rate has been cut to $ .10.

There are other instances of cuts when a girl has earned more than $1.47. A new kind of coil was given out at the rate of $1.25 a 100. Because one girl worked too fast, the rate was cut to $ .75 and she had almost to double her speed in order to make even her usual earnings. In another case, $ .01¾ was paid for winding a new coil, and one of the girls made 100 coils, or $1.75 as a single day's pay. The other girls warned her, but she kept increasing her speed until she finally made 150 in a day, and kept this up for two weeks. The foreman urged her to make more and at length she reached a maximum of 250. Then the firm cut the rate. Now, in order to make her previous earnings of $1.47 a day, the girl has to make 200 of these same coils—exactly double the pace which was considered high even at first. One girl who has been in the employ of the company for three years and is one of their best workers, tells me that her usual pay for two weeks is between $17 and $18. The most she ever made in two weeks was $25, and that was made only by overtime at night and Sunday work. The hours of work, usually from seven to

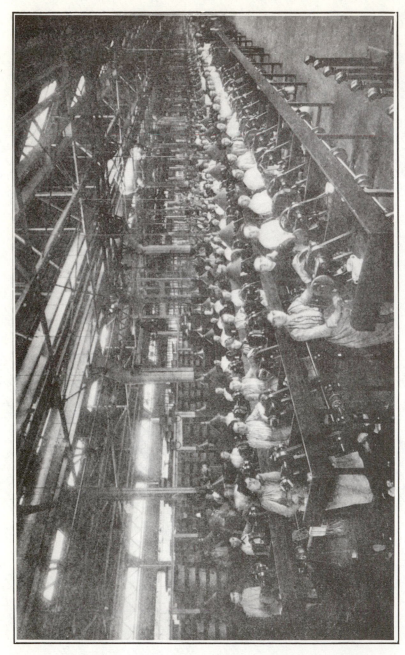

The Coil Winding Room of the Westinghouse Electric and Manufacturing Company

five-thirty (nine and three-quarter hours a day), are extended when necessary to get out orders. Premium workers are paid a time and a half for overtime, and piece workers $ .05 an hour extra. For four months in the summer of 1906, and for a month in the winter of 1907, the girls were kept until eight-thirty every evening. For three weeks they worked on Sundays.

Night and Sunday work, rate cutting, and the consequent high speeding, tend to produce an atmosphere of nervous haste which results both in frequent changes in personnel, and among those who stay, in lowered vitality and overspent nervous force. I am told that not more than twenty-five out of all the women employed at the East Pittsburgh factory have been there as long as four years. In addition to the nervous strain, there is a positive physical effort in much that is given them to do, a physical effort that some men in the trade have considered injurious; furthermore, the women have no professional interest which would keep them at their task if it were not physically and nervously overtaxing. In going through the plant, my guide asked a winder if the coils on which she was working were not for motors of a certain sort, and she replied, "I don't know. We're just told to do them this way." The women do not consciously co-ordinate their work with that of the other departments of the factory, or see in it a significance beyond the mechanical execution of the task allotted. They are operators solely, cheaper than men, who are speeded to the limit of their strength, then dropped for a force of new and as yet untired recruits.

SCREW AND BOLT WORKS

Three Pittsburgh screw and bolt works employed women in 1907—543 in all. From floor to floor, in the midst of the roar of a mill where screws and bolts, nuts and bars and rods are made, I passed by lanes of these women at their work, Slavic all of them, with a native peasant strength which turns as easily to work at a foot press, at a nut-screwing machine, or at a threader in fish oil, as to work in the fields near home. Some I found to be here without their families. Groups of four and five have joined fortunes, in little rooms on the South Side.

Others, members of families, have found work in the same mill with father and brothers. They are of a type different from the young Polish women in the canneries. There is not the same delicacy of feature or slenderness of build. These girls have large features, eyes wide apart, coarse hands and muscular arms. Their faded waists are stained brown from the oil of the machine, their sleeves are rolled high, and their fingers are bound with dirty rags.

In a plant where twenty-five girls are employed, the workroom is on the second floor, just above the mill. Most of the girls stand at their work, but a few sit on rough projecting boards, or on boxes which are oily and brown and never cleaned. They endure the noise and filth of the place as part of the work, for ten and a half hours a day and one or two nights overtime a week until nine o'clock. A short day Saturday brings the working week within the legal limit of sixty hours. The day rate of pay for most of the girls is $ .75; a few old hands are paid $ .85.

Beyond, toward the river, there is another bolt plant where eighteen girls work ten hours a day "in the hole," as the people call the long end of the works set against the hill, with the ground for its floor, and the entrance way for its source of light and air. Some of the girls are painting picks and others work on nuts and bolts.

In the third plant, 500 girls are lost, in spite of their numbers, in the six squares occupied by the iron and steel works along the river front on the South Side. Here are acres of black, half-lighted enclosures where iron rods are made, and of furnaces and rolling mills. In the faint light and the flare of red-hot metal through the smoke, you would not suspect the presence of women workers, but they too have a part in the processes. They are to be found on the upper floors of one or two of the buildings. A few are trimmers of bolts. A girl sits in front of the machine on a wooden stool roughly fashioned from unplaned boards. When she receives the bolt, its edges are rounded, but she fits it into a groove of the machine which carries it under a cutter, where the protruding part is cut off and the end of the bolt is made square. This is the motion of the operator for ten hours a day: she takes the bolt in her left hand from the box at her side, takes it from her left hand with her right and feeds it point downward into the machine. This is repeated at intervals of two seconds, and is paid for at the rate of $ .06 a 1000. The company found that when it paid by the day, the girls missed some of the motions of the machine. If each movement of the press during the day is caught, the girl will have repeated her operation 16,000 times and will have earned $ .96. The pace, while interminable, is not at a speed which makes its endurance impossible for a term of years. Perhaps this is due to the difference of nationality between these Slavs and the American girls who wind coils. "There is no danger in the machine," the superintendent said. "The girl is not obliged to put her fingers under the press; but, of course, toward the end of the day, she sometimes gets careless."

There are other girls, rooms full of them, who screw nuts on bolts under spouts of fish oil. The 200 women in this department stand at their work so that they can do it faster. They are on piece work, too, paid at the rate of $ .40 a 1000, and in some cases finish 4000 nuts a day. The operators who thread the bolts are paid at a lower rate, not over $ .15 a thousand, and turn out 6000 to 7000 a day. They feed the bolts into a machine which puts in the threads. A fish oil compound is used here, too, to make the process easier, and these girls, like those who screw nuts on bolts, must bind their fingers with rags as a protection against the oil compound. When they sit at all, they sit on hogsheads or on parts of the machine. Boards and floor, as well as girls, are oil-spattered.

Sometimes for three months out of the year, at regular intervals, overtime is worked until nine or ten o'clock at night. This depends on the way in which orders come in. The same piece rate is paid after hours as during the regular day work.

MISCELLANEOUS TRADES

TINWARE FACTORY

Under this general heading are grouped five factories, each representing a different industry. One is a tinware factory where nine girls are employed on salt cellars and small novelties, assembling them for the men to polish. They are young girls from the neighborhood who have had no previous trade experience, but are ready to do simple work of this sort for $3.50 a week. This factory has never required overtime.

CABLE COMPANY

Some blocks away is a cable company with a force of 160 men and 40 girls. The men, most of them unskilled, operate the larger and heavier machines, such as the pairing machines for twisting strands of telephone wire together. Girls are employed at the wrapping and braiding machines. A whirr of wheels greets you upon entering the wrapping room—a confused vision of varicolored tapes, twisting themselves into strands, of wires and bobbins, of rows and frames, six or eight together, tended by one girl. At these machines telephone wires are wrapped with strands of paper of different colors, the wires to be finally fastened together into cables. The girl places the bobbin covered with thick tapering paper in the machine, draws the paper around the pegs and through a small hole in the centre to fasten it to the wire. It is her business to see that the machine does not run down, and if the paper breaks, to fasten a fresh piece around the wire; also to put in bobbins filled with paper whenever the bobbins run out. There is a chair for each girl, so that she may sit down when the machines do not keep her busy; this may be for fifteen minutes at a time, and then again, as one bobbin after another runs out and the papers break with a malignant persistence, she may have to stand for two hours.

At the wrapping machines, the girls begin at $ .50 a day and are advanced first to $ .75, and finally to $1.00, which is their maximum wage. The ten girls at the braiding machines on the second floor are advanced to $1.10. This work, like the other deafening with its whirr of wheels, requires much the same attention from the girls. Cords from eight spools are twisted together about another kind of telephone wire, and in this case the machine stops automatically if the thread breaks. The girls have only to keep the bobbins full, and when the thread breaks, to retie it. In this department, and in a lesser proportion in the wrapping department, the girls are Americans, but not young; most of them have worked here for years, from the time when the neighborhood was Irish and German instead of Polish, as it is now, and when the cable company was the nearest place for them to secure employment. They have not shifted and today there seems no other place for them to work. Some have married, and after a few years returned to their old places. They have a ten-hour day, and overtime only rarely in the spring and fall. During the slack season in winter, the girls are kept on part time or half pay until orders begin to come in again. The only time within recent years that they have had to work at night was on a special government order in 1905, when for ten days they worked on twelve-hour shifts in order to keep the contract.

HINGE FACTORY

At the hinge factory on the North Side, even in slack seasons there are 175 girls, and a force of 600 employes altogether. Here are made all manner of hinges, from long flat hinges for cellar doors, to little "butt hinges" of a size just large enough to hold four holes for screws. Girls, half of them Polish and half American, are the hinge makers. A boy cuts long strips of steel into the proper lengths; the rest of the work is done by power-driven machines into which the girls feed the hinges in turn. The first machine punches four holes in the hinge, and the next "countersinks," or rounds out the holes at one end; a third machine splits the hinge into halves, called the "one-er" and the "two-er," because the "one-er" fits between the two projecting parts of the other half. The next process is bending and the fifth is bending again, or nipping the ends of the two halves more tightly; then the "one-er" is pressed and a pin driven through, to hold the two halves together. The rounded ends of the pins are "burred" by machine or worked smooth, and last of all, the hinges are inspected and packed.

On floor after floor these processes are repeated, with rows of machines, a network of belts, girls sitting or standing with attention fixed not to miss a turn of the machine, and ever the roar of wheels, the rapid motion, output multiplied again and again by duplication of machinery, by pace quickening, and by sub-division of labor into processes of lesser and lesser individual significance. Formerly only American girls were employed here. They still come in large numbers from nearby narrow streets that waver forlornly toward the river's edge, but Slavic girls are making their way into the packing room, into the driving and burring departments, and to a lesser extent to work at the machines. They are kept sedulously apart from the Americans; they are paid at different times, and work in different parts of the room. Whether they are making less than the American girls or not they do not know, and the barrier of a different language effectively prevents their knowing. They, like their people, are not far on the way, as they shift from machine shop to hinge making and out again to yet another trade, toward assimilation with the current of American life.

Some girls—but they are in the minority—work by the day, for $1.00 or at most $1.10. This is a surer income than that of the piece workers, whose output may be lessened by a run of bad work, or by the breaking down of their machines, which is their loss always, not the loss of the firm. The girls say that they have never known a piece worker to make more than $7.50 a week, and one steady little worker told me that the most she had ever made was $13 in a two weeks' pay, and that she considered $12 for two weeks' work fine money. Girls are always docked for their bad work, as, for instance, if three holes are punched in a hinge instead of four, or if one end of the pin is burred and the other smooth, although both these things may happen through the fault of the machine. Sometimes $1.00 will be taken from a girl's pay for scrap, as a disciplinary measure.

The bending machines, to take one kind only as an example, are set so that 500 hinges may be fed into one in ten minutes, or 3,000 in an hour. For small hinges, $ .03½ a 1000 is paid, and for large hinges, $ .04 and $ .04½ a 1000; this means that if no motion is lost, the rate of pay will be about $ .10 an hour, and with a working day of ten and a quarter hours, the pay will be about $1.00 a day. The pay of piece workers often falls to $ .70 or $ .80 because of a run of bad work.

Except for the monotony of it, the work is not hard, although one or two of the machines are somewhat dangerous. Accidents are most likely to occur on the punching machine and the splitter, even on the bender sometimes, because the hand has to be withdrawn quickly at each revolution of the machine. In one family, the oldest girl has the record of having had one finger hurt eight times, and another had two fingers cut off, but a third was lucky enough to have her hand only strained in the belting. There are two men, machinists, on each floor, to take charge of and to clean the machines, but the hurry of a girl who is unwontedly ambitious, or the weariness toward the end of five hours' continuous work, is sufficient to account for inattention that sometimes results in serious injury. A punching press is difficult to guard, but the risk of working at it is increased by the very familiarity of the operator with the danger and by the goad of a piece rate.

The factory works ten and a quarter hours a day for five days in the week and shuts down half a day Saturday. Although these are the regular hours, overtime until half past eight is worked one or two nights a week almost throughout the year. There seems to be no regular alternation of busy and slack seasons, but change according to orders, although as a rule the busiest time comes in winter.

I asked one girl, four years an inspector, at $6.00 a week, why she had worked there so long, and her answer threw some light on the motives that lead girls of her type to enter various occupations. She said: "Well, I never supposed there was any other place I could work. The factory's only across the street, and the only other thing nearby is the laundries, and they are very hot, and one has to work at night and isn't paid extra, and for your work you don't get any more than you do at the hinge factory, while when you work overtime here, you get twenty-five cents and fifteen cents for your supper."

The hinge makers as a group seem to have drifted into this factory for the simple reason that they "never supposed they could work anywhere else." Competing industries in the immediate neighborhood are few. The square brick building with its continual roar of wheels and belting and metal-cutting machines offers at least steady employment both to Slavic women and to

American girls from families that by their inefficiency have been left behind in the streets and alleys now largely filled with immigrant peoples.

ENAMELING AND STAMPING COMPANY

Between railroad track and creek, beyond that part of the city where the streets have names, are the long, low buildings of an enameling and stamping company. Here men and girls to the number of 200 each are employed at making japanned and enameled ware,—lunch boxes and drinking cups, coffee pots, saucepans and different sorts of tins. On each finished piece, the wrapper pastes the label of the star. Except for the men who tend the enameling ovens, and possibly for the soldering girls, the work in this factory is done by unskilled hands. On the upper floor is the tinware department. Here fifteen soldering girls put wooden handles on the lids of saucepans. They push the nail through holes in the wood and in the lid, and touch the point of it with the solder, at the rate of $ .10 a gross. The output of the quickest girl is fourteen to fifteen gross a day. Other girls solder the rings of the trays in dinner pails and fasten parts of the pails together. Twelve japanning girls on this same floor stand at benches near the japanning ovens, brushing the liquid on pails and tins. No forced ventilation is provided to carry off the heavy fumes.

The enameling department is on the first floor. The Slavic girls employed here dip enameled ware, taking each piece separately and dipping it by hand in the tub of enamel. This unskilled work is learned quickly and paid for at the rate of $ .75 a day. The dipping girls and some others are paid directly by the firm, but a few are paid instead by the foreman, who in turn receives so much per gross for the output. It is expected that the girls will earn in general from $1.00 to $1.25 and the men not less than $2.00. The men work on double shifts in some departments, but the girls have only day hours, ten and a quarter a day. Overtime rarely occurs.

SORTERS IN A SHEET AND TINPLATE MILL

SHEET AND TIN PLATE MILLS

Conspicuous among metal trades employing women are the sheet and tin plate mills, a chain which runs from the Monongahela plant on the South Side to the works at McKeesport and farther, to Monessen. In the half light and black dust, in the midst of the mill where men stand turning white-hot sheets of steel in the furnaces, women work by the glowing and partly cooled piles of steel. An "opening" job is given indifferently to women or to boys; of the twenty-two openers at McKeesport*, eight are women. The sheet of steel comes from the furnaces with five to eight plates welded together, and these must be torn apart while still flexible from the heat, before they can be put through the pickling process. The "openers" wear gloves with a heavy lead piece in the palm, and, taking the sheet of welded plates beat it on the ground to separate the parts; then with the lead piece in the glove, they make an opening. They forcibly tear apart the plates, holding part of the sheet down with one knee, while tearing the metal with the other. The violence of this work takes all the strength of even the earth-toughened peasant women who have followed their husbands from Poland to the mill country in America. Each plate of steel weighs six to eight pounds. The women carry the separated plates in piles to the general pile of stock some distance away, which is later taken to be pickled. Ten hours a day in the mills and pay by the ton is the reward for this strenuous exertion. At the noon pause, the women sit down on their rough benches, on which all morning they have been breaking steel, and eat in the glare of the furnaces and amid the black dust from the metal piles.

In another room there are 22 girls sorting finished plate. They have a clean place to work in, and an occupation less violent, but somewhat exacting still. The polished and finished plates of steel are separated into two grades of good plate and a waste grade. Each girl wears a felt glove on her right hand, with which to polish the two better grades of steel. There is lifting to

* Figures are given for McKeesport, because the Monongahela plant was not running at the time this investigation was made. The Monongahela plant has eight mills, whereas the McKeesport plant has eleven; the estimated number of women employed at the South Side (Monongahela) plant is twenty.

do, but little moving about. The girls have an eight-hour day and are paid by the box, each box containing 56 plates. The pay is $1.10 per 100 boxes. From 50 to 60 boxes a day is the average output, and each box of 27 x 48 inch sheets weighs 191 pounds. Yet even among American girls, applicants are readily found for these positions, as there are comparatively few opportunities for women to find employment in McKeesport.

SUMMARY

This review of the metal trades as occupations for women has brought out that metal novelties, tinware, hinges, screws and bolts, cables and mica, are products on which the women employes exert no physical strength in the making. They require either light hand work or the tending of a machine. They attract a grade of labor which is on the whole unintelligent, but capable of repeating a simple process at regular intervals. They occupied 1123, or nearly 60 per cent, of the 1954 women metal workers in 1907. Coil winding, which is also a simple process, requires some muscular strength and a high degree of nervous strength when it is done by a power machine. Muscular strength, too, is required for the lifting of trays of sand cores, but most of all for the opening and cleaning of plates done by women in the sheet and tin plate mills. At these processes which require strength of different de-grees and kinds,—processes, too, which are simple and easily learned,—831, or over 40 per cent, of the women in the metal trades were employed. The quality of simplicity runs through all processes alike. The subsidiary relation which they bear to the finished product is alike true of all these processes.

The simplicity of the work and the frequent strain of it—a strain which often is not essential, as in the work on sand cores, but which the management in most cases makes no effort to over-come—have been determining factors in selecting the prevailing nationalities in the trade. Two-thirds of the women in the metal trades are Slavic,—Hungarian, Polish and Croatian. They are women of recent immigration, raw from their peasant earth, unacquainted with the language and ignorant of the ways of this country. They live in colonies of their own people. They accept the work and conditions that go with it which more often than not are unnecessarily degrading. Except where the nervous speed of American girls is in demand, these foreign women who ask neither for comfort nor for cleanliness nor higher wages, form the group characteristic of the trade.

They are in large measure a group of day laborers. They are without skill or training and they can turn to one occupation as easily as to another. The men hired by the day to fetch and carry in these same plants where women are employed, earn $1.50 to $1.80 a day. The women whose work is of about the same importance and of the same unskilled nature as the work of the men, are piece workers at from $ .75 to $1.00 a day. When they earn more, they are paid for the speed which comes from experience. The following table shows their wage groups by trades:

TABLE 26.—NUMBER OF WOMEN IN EACH WEEKLY WAGE GROUP IN THE METAL TRADES

Trade	Number of Women in Each Weekly Wage Group		
	$3.00–$6.00	$7.00	$8.00–$10.00
Electrical appliances . .	202	150	300
Foundries . .	80	27	208
Miscellaneous .	344	100	..
Screws and bolts	318	225	..
Total . .	944	502	508

The coil winders with their nervous speed, and the experienced core makers who are beginning in a measure to compete with men, have worked up to $8.00 and $9.00 payments on a system of piece work. They have a dexterity specialized by their occupation, but they are in the minority. At the pay for which they work, they, like their unskilled co-workers, are earning half to a third of what men are paid for the same work. They, too, through the pressure of increasing numbers of immigrant women, accept working conditions based on a standard of living in many cases lower than their own.

CHAPTER XIV

LAMP MANUFACTURE

A LAMP is a challenge to the inventive faculty. Possibilities of lustre, form, glow, suggestions of warmth and security, are all bound up in this bit of colored glass, that brass mounting, or the line of blue flame along an asbestos log. There must be adaptation for the mock grate-fire in the den, for the bright transparent lanterns of a café, for shades that throw a mellow gold over a hall carpeted in velvet, and for the gay brilliance that sets off a musical play on a theatre roof. There must be cheap lamps, too, of ruby glass and lacquered holders, such as share with the full-sized crayon family portraits the burden of giving an air of prosperity to the more ambitious tenement homes. Then, for the sake of sheer utility in this city of ambitious youth and night work, there must be incandescent lights and gas mantles—the omnipresent expression of practical Americans who forego the poetry of indefinite color and wavering shadows, but insist even in the night-time on a bright, hard light that will make labor without sunshine possible.

For possibilities of various charm in its results, the prosaic making of lamps and burners seems to have no end. Moreover, Pittsburgh is in the belt of natural gas; rich and poor burn it for warmth and light. The trades that spring from their various uses of gas are so diverse that it is difficult to gather them together for consideration as a single industry. The occupations offered to both men and women are perplexing in their variety. Men shape brass and iron, women rivet and punch holes in brass, girls and boys prepare tanks of lacquer and color logs. There are women who in their kitchens at home take odd moments to sew gas mantles at so much a dozen. Polish girls in factories shape, burn and cap the mantles, labeling and boxing them preparatory to sale. In other factories girls fuse platinum wire in a white-hot flame, scrape porcelains and assemble the parts of the round globes that light great halls. In still other factories asbestos drifts like snow about the shoulders of women who work on grates.

In 1907, 471 women and about as many men were engaged in lamp manufacture. Of the women,* 30 operated punching presses, 21 fibred asbestos, 98 worked on gas mantles, 247 wound platinum wire and blew balises, 26 assembled lamps, and 49 were engaged at miscellaneous occupations, such as riveting, soldering, tapping, inspecting, log decorating and scraping of porcelains.

ASBESTOS FIBRING

A tour through a few of the eleven factories employing this force will visualize the actual processes of lamp making. In one, a long, low frame building in the East End, burners are manufactured on a small scale. Men are employed for all the iron work. Up and down the lane of machines, on the rough earth floor, they are at work in groups, shaping and assembling the parts of iron. Three women work near the entry, fibring asbestos. Sometimes at the height of the season, eight or nine girls are employed, but in the winter one girl is sufficient to handle all the work. She is given a grate with the design for the asbestos marked in pencil; sometimes the design is scalloped, but for the most part, it is in plain, straight strips. The girl gums a strip with a mucilage brush, then taking a handful of asbestos, she lays it on the gummed strip, flattening it down with two small stone points and a fork. Each strip is gone over separately in this way. The process needs care and deliberation as well as some dexterity. New hands seldom learn to do it well in less than three or four months, and to do it quickly would take from six months to a year. Except in one factory, wages are paid by the piece. For a 15 x 22 inch burner with twenty asbestos strips, the pay is $ .13, and with high speed the burner can be made in thirty minutes, but more often it requires three-quarters of an hour to an hour. The pay varies according to the size of the burner and the design;

* See Appendix B, pp. 402–403, Table 66, for division of work among women in each factory.

the highest is $ .45 for a 22 x 22 inch scalloped burner. The girls say that they cannot earn any more at this than at the cheaper work, because they have to work so much more slowly. There is on record the case of a girl who made $18 in one week by working overtime five nights, but her work was carelessly done and would not pass inspection. Usually not over $6.00 to $9.00 is earned in this department.

The girls sit at their work, and except for the irregular seasons and hours, have advantages over some other factory workers. Girls of the better type, from families of prosperous mechanics, do the fibring in some factories. Again, on the North Side, are Polish girls of inferior capacity and training. There is a tendency, however, for the hands in the fibring room to be largely American, leaving the Polish and German girls to drift into the more unpleasant and less cleanly branches of the trade.

Fibring is a seasonal trade. The busy season lasts from September to December, and usually through March and April. In four factories out of six, overtime is customary two nights a week or more, and the total working hours overpass the legal limit of sixty per week, often reaching seventy-two when the season is at its height. After that, there is very little to do. The girls are laid off or kept on short time and, when discharged, seem to fit into other trades with difficulty. They sometimes get another job, but the dull season in summer is a bad time in which to be out of work.

RIVETING AND FOOT-PRESS WORK

On the North Side is a plant where burners, fenders, lamps and brass goods are manufactured. Eighteen men and twelve girls—most of them Polish—are employed, the men at iron work and on machines, the girls on foot presses, riveting and fibring. The shop refuses to be classified. Half of it is like a machine shop with its lathes and bores, its earth floor, and dim, dust-grimed windows, and half like the rear of a tinshop with odd metal shapes and nameless machines for all manner of undefined purposes. Men are the mechanics and laborers, but upstairs the girls do fibring and downstairs they have three different sorts of work. Some of them operate presses which put three holes in the brass rim of a lamp. The girl holds the brass with her two hands and presses heavily on the treadle with her foot. She makes the three holes in a little less than a minute, repeating this operation ninety times an hour as a minimum. The girl is paid by the week instead of by the piece, so she is not obliged to hurry and the danger of accident is minimized. Yet though the machine is made safer, I saw one operator who was in danger because of the machinery near her. From a flywheel about four feet from the floor, a three-inch belt ran diagonally to another flywheel at the ceiling, and the lower wheel almost touched the head of the girl as she bent over to place the brass bowl in her press.

Other girls rivet cross sections of a 12 x 12 fender for the front of a gas grate. This is done by hand, one rivet being put in at a time. Some hammer into shape the long burners, whose seams have been bent but not welded. The burner is placed over an iron form and the seam hammered tightly until only a line between the two parts is visible.

The manager of this plant says that all his women employes support themselves and must be paid enough to live on; a flat rate for all departments is best in his opinion. At the start, new hands are paid $5.00 and later advanced to $6.00, although most of the work is extremely simple and easily learned. Overtime, he thinks, does not pay; when orders are heavy it is necessary to take on more hands, for the girls cannot work to advantage for more than nine hours.

In another factory nearby, where articles of the same sort are made, the employes are sometimes forced to work twelve and fourteen hours, and accidents are so frequent that the place has been characterized as a butcher shop. Forty girls are employed, most of them under sixteen years of age. Some are American girls, slight and pretty, with curling hair and thin faces; some are stocky German youngsters, whose work period has been too brief to have lessened their irresponsibility. Others are Polish,—girls with round, white faces and tightly-combed, fair hair,—girls without skill, without training, without a trade ambition, who have drifted in from the neighboring alleys "to get a job." These girls, as soon as they have their working papers, are put to work on foot presses. Even while they are learning, they are paid by the piece. They do not understand the machines, the danger is not explained to them; when an accident occurs they do not know how it happens or whose fault it is. One girl, only sixteen now, who had worked at a foot press for a year, said that she thought when her finger was cut the press came down of itself through a jar on the floor. She could make about $5.00 a week, sometimes $7.00, she said, but was afraid to make more because the rate would be cut. Among neighbors of the factory, there is a suppressed current of bitterness because of the children who are paying by minor injuries for their inexperience. One woman told me of ten girls hurt at the foot presses from August to October, 1907. At another time in the fall of 1907, five girls out of the twenty in this department were away because parts of their fingers had been amputated.

Some of these girls, young as they are, are yet old enough to have trade histories. I talked with one such girl, after a search one November night through alleys and among rear tenements. The home of this lamp maker was on a street so void of light, so grim and forbidding, that I could not see pavements or fences. She was a young willowy German girl, with long brown hair falling loosely about her as she talked. At the age of thirteen, she had started to clean mirrors in the mirror factory and during the three months that she was there she was cut by glass five times. A four-inch scar on her right arm, a two-inch scar on her wrist, and three minor scars on her hands were the record of her first work-experience. She went to a pickle factory for a while, and then to the hinge factory, which was much nearer her home. There she was employed for over a year and had her finger cut open at a press. She left and went to the lamp and brass company, and worked for a time by hand on the fourth floor; but later she was brought down to fill a vacancy in the foot-press department, and set to work without explanation and without previous experience of this sort of machinery. How the accident happened she does not know. It was her first day there, and "I was working quick," she said, "and the thing came down and cut me." The bone had to be taken out above the first joint and the top of the finger amputated. A nine weeks' absence from work is the smallest part of the penalty, and Nettie is now only fifteen years of age. She told of such accidents as a matter of common experience among girls of her acquaintance. One sister twice had her fingers cut in the same factory, and another sister had two fingers crushed while working at hinges. "Almost all the girls get cut on the foot presses," she said, "but the lacquer kills you." In less pithy speech, but none the less soberly, physicians tell you of the serious effect of the lacquer work on a girl's health.

Four girls work in the lacquer room of this factory. The brass dust sifts through the air and in winter the windows have to be closed because the room is not heated. Piece rates are paid, —$ .10 a 100 for the bases of lamps, $ .06 a 100 for the screws around the bases. Crowns are $ .15, and ore-pots $ .12 a 100. One girl, an American, after working there a year, and earning from $1.00 to $1.50 a day, has broken down nervously from speeding, and two of the girls have tuberculosis. Sometimes the girls work on antiques, putting the black lacquer on; that is the most dangerous to health. There were two boys putting on the white lacquer before the girls overlaid it with brass, the day of my visit, and one of the two boys had tuberculosis.

For one factory, especially for a factory that levies upon the children of the streets nearby, this is an ugly bit of history. Even the partial safeguard of good ventilation is denied to workers in the lacquer room, and in winter the cold makes relief through open windows impossible. A visitor was refused access to the foot-press room on the ground of danger, yet this room is not considered too dangerous for girls of fourteen and fifteen, with no training and no knowledge of the machines.

GAS MANTLES

Foot-press work is found in factories where metal lamps are made, but the making of gas mantles involves work of a very different sort, in asbestos. Ninety-eight girls are employed in gas mantle factories, but it is impossible to estimate the number who, like the Russian Jewish women on the Hill, sew bits of asbestos in the intervals of their housework. The largest factory in this line now has all its work done inside for the sake of more careful supervision and of cleanliness. This change in policy has materially reduced the extent of the sweated work. The factory work on gas mantles includes both sewing the asbestos together and capping, or fastening to the mantle support, burning the mantles, and sometimes shaping and dipping them. In one case a girl is employed to tend the drying oven and two girls are used as wringers.

INCANDESCENT LIGHTS

The making of incandescent lights, by still other processes than those which have been described, occupies 300 of the 471 women in the lamp industry. In one large factory, electric bulbs are prepared and instruments made for different kinds of electric lighting. There are girls winding coils, tapping and punching, inspecting and assembling lamps, scraping porcelain and winding platinum wire. In every department the work atmosphere is intense. Haste dominates the quick fingers, the stooping shoulders, the unwavering intentness of eye and hand and thought.

On the fifth floor, plain coil winding, punching and tapping are done,—machine operations all of them, of the simplest sort. Of the 12 girls, five work at coils. The piece rate is $ .12 for the largest coils, of which the girls can usually make 12 a day, but they can make 22 of the $ .07 coils and 10 of the $ .15 coils. Their speed has been brought to a point where each girl has the same output, and the greatest variation is only two coils more or less. The base rate for punching is $ .14 an hour if 600 pieces are turned out, and for every extra 100 pieces the girl is paid $ .01. But if $ .14 an hour is paid for 600 pieces, this would be at the rate of $ .02⅓ a 100, so the apparent premium for the additional hundreds is less than half the regular rate. Tappers are paid at the same rate as punchers, but by the piece, and the policy of the firm seems to be to cut the rate whenever total earnings of a girl exceed $ .14 an hour. For instance, in January, 1907, water glass coils were paid at the rate of $ .02 a piece, and three girls in the department were able to make $1.90 a day. The rate was at once cut to $ .01½ a coil, so that no one was able to make more than $1.50.

On the floor below are the inspection rooms, where lamps are assembled, and where the work on porcelains is done. The girls who put together the parts of lamps are paid $ .04, $ .05 and $ .06, according to the intricacy of the article, and during three or four months of the year they make $2.00 a day; but in no other department is work paid so well. On work of medium grade, for which $ .05 is paid, they are given a tray holding twenty lamps and expected to finish it in five hours, but if they do not succeed in doing this, they are paid at the time rate of $ .10 an hour. More training is necessary for accuracy here than in the other departments and the girls have a higher standing. Some girls on this floor put on the globe ends and clean the globes. Others are inspectors of all the coils, lamps and so forth, that are turned out by the factory; they are paid $ .10, $ .12, and in some cases, $ .14 an hour, according to length of service. The work on porcelains consists merely of scraping off with a knife the rough edges of the small porcelain parts of the lamp.

On the third floor the girls are in greatest number, 247 of them, winding platinum wire and blowing balises. You see rooms full of stooping women whose eyes look intently through colored glass at a white-hot flame, and who hold the end of the wire in the flame until it fuses. Intense jets of light reflected from one part of the room to another strain the eyes of even the casual passer-through, and it is small wonder that girls who work there nine and three-quarters hours a day find their muscles failing after a time. Many wear glasses, but except for the colored glass on the table in front of the white flame, the company offers no protection for the eyesight of its employes. Here, as upstairs, the rate of pay is $ .10 to $ .14 an hour.

On the second floor are girls assembling holder bases and lamps that are to be repaired. A tray of holder bases contains 100, and thirteen hours are allowed the girls for the completion of certain kinds of work. The base rate is $ .10 an hour, but if the work is finished in twelve hours instead of thirteen, the rate is raised to $ .14. In another case, ten hours are allowed, and the same premium is paid if the work is finished in nine hours. The girls say, however, that it is almost impossible to finish in less than the time allowed and that sometimes they cannot make even their regular time wages.

Except for the pace in this factory and for the eyestrain involved in the platinum wire department, the conditions of work are good. Four-fifths of the girls earn from $7.00 to $9.00 a week. The workrooms are well kept; there are comfortable cloak rooms and lunch rooms. Here, as in the coil-winding room at East Pittsburgh, American girls are preferred, because they have nervous strength that can be lifted to a high pitch of speed, although they have not the physical strength to continue for a term of years.

The manufacture of lamps is unlike the other metal trades in that only a very small percentage of the work requires trained workers. The men are for the most part unskilled laborers. Save for a few electricians and metal smiths, they work at riveting, punching and allied processes which differ from the women's work only in the degree of strength required. Similarly the women have not as a rule a high degree of proficiency. Punching, riveting, asbestos sewing, capping, and porcelain scraping, are quickly learned by inexperienced employes. These women, in effect day laborers, turn indifferently to any other equally unskilled occupation. Paid by the piece, they earn from $ .75 to $1.00 a day. A third of them, in fact, earn less than $6.00 a week. Another third who have worked long enough at their occupations to have acquired greater dexterity are earning $7.00; a third more earn $7.00 to $9.00. These latter are the girls whose occupation has to be learned, although the time given to learning is short. They fibre asbestos, wind platinum wire and assemble lamps. They do not shift readily to other occupations because their dexterity is specialized. The fibring girls usually continue at this occupation during their working life.

The shifting group of day laborers, among whom the majority of the women lamp makers is to be found, is made up of Hungarians, Poles, and the mixed races of southern Germany. The girls whose dexterity is greater, upon whom the nervous strain is more intense, are for the most part· Americans. Not so quickly as in the electrical works at East Pittsburgh, but surely, nevertheless, the girls who have the highest proficiency in the lamp industry are worn out and set aside. Those who stay on are white and tired and drawn of face.

GLASSWARE IS WASHED AND CLEANED PREPARATORY TO PACKING

CHAPTER XV

GLASS FACTORIES

FROM the making of lamps to the making of lamp shades and chimneys and glassware, is an easy transition. Glasswork is a man's industry. Men do the mixing, the blowing, the molding of the glass. Boys hold the secondary jobs about the furnaces, "carrying-in," "breaking-off," "holding molds." But from the square room where men and boys are working in the fierce heat and uncertain shadow, it is only a step to the bricked floor and walls of the packing room where women are employed finishing and boxing glass.

The work of women in glass factories falls into three distinct groups of occupations. Women may be used for totally unskilled work, such as cleaning molds, washing, or packing; they may be used for light finishing processes, such as cutting off rough edges of glassware, or grinding and shaping edges by machine; or they may be used in decorating processes, preparing glassware for etching, stamping designs on glass, or laying on the design by hand. Of the 353 women in the Pittsburgh glass industry in 1907-08, the following table gives the number at each of these occupations, the arrangement being from the least numerous to the most numerous group:

TABLE 27.—OCCUPATIONS OF WOMEN IN THE GLASS INDUSTRY

Occupation	No. of Women
Cleaning molds	5
Cutting off	14
Washing	27
Decorating by stamping designs on glass	27
Grinding and finishing	36
Preparing glass for etching	40
Gold enameling, etc., on glass	55
Packing	149
Total	353

239

If this table be rearranged so as to show the number and percentage of women not in each separate occupation, but in the three distinct groups of occupations, the order will be as follows:

TABLE 28.—OCCUPATIONAL GROUPS OF WOMEN IN THE GLASS INDUSTRY

Occupational Group	No. of Women	Percentage of Women
Unskilled work (cleaning, washing, packing) .	181	51.2
Finishing processes (cutting-off, grinding, finishing)	50	14.1
Decorating (stamping, preparing for etching, gold enameling)	122	34.5

Although the degrees of proficiency vary considerably within these occupational groups, this order indicates roughly the advance from least to most dexterity.

Most of the glass-houses are on the South Side. Where the union is strong, all the employes, even in the packing rooms, are men, but in nine non-union factories women are employed. Some American girls work in the glass factories, especially in the decorating departments, but the greater number of the women employes are Slavic, drawn from the colonies of Polish and Croatian families which have grown up around the glass-houses where the men are day laborers.

WASHING AND CLEANING

The bottle factories have their packing done by men, but women packers are employed for the most part on glass chimneys and tableware of different sorts. As the glassware is finished near the furnaces, it is placed by the "carry-in" boys in the lehrs—the annealing furnaces through which it is slowly carried by means of moving trays out to the packing room. The packing girls stand near the lehrs, surrounded by crates and barrels and tables heaped with fine tissue and excelsior. Toward the day's end, they are covered with excelsior and dust. They wrap each piece separately and crate the glass, in some factories taking charge of the order blanks and making out the shipments. When they do this additional work they are usually women of more intelligence than the characteristic glass-house packer, for in order to make out the shipments properly they must know the stock numbers of all the articles manufactured in the factory, and be able to select the pattern by the stock number without hesitation or mistake.

In factories where the surface of the glass has to be cleaned and polished for decorating, the glass must be washed. In such cases, the washroom, and not the packing room, is placed at the far end of the lehrs. Although the work is entirely unskilled, in a sense it serves as an apprenticeship for the decorating department proper, since when vacancies occur in the decorating room they are usually filled from among the washing girls.

The mold cleaners, as their name implies, clean and scrape out the molds which have been used at the furnaces in shaping the glass. The work is hard and is likely to injure the hands, since the cleaning liquid is a mixture of acid, emery and oil.

Mold cleaners are paid $5.00 a week, which is more than many of the packers earn. All of the women in this occupational group are time workers, the usual rates of pay being $3.00 to $3.50 a week. A few are paid $4.00 a week, and some of the packers who make up shipments are paid $5.00 a week.

GRINDING AND CUTTING-OFF

The work of the finishers is more closely allied to the actual processes of glass making. Some of these finishers do work in the outer room similar to what the boys are doing near the furnaces. They take the annealed chimneys from the lehrs and carry them to a second annealing oven. Others cut off on a machine the spun edges of rough glass left by the blowers on chimneys and unfinished tumblers. The carrying girls are paid by time, $4.00 to $5.00 a week, but the cutters-off are paid in some places by time and in others by piece. They are paid $4.00 to $6.00 a week in tumbler factories. For work on chimneys they earn considerably more by piece. The rate is $ .15 a 100, and their day's pay is usually from $1.25 to $1.40. With a run of good work they sometimes make $1.75.

Grinding and finishing glass edges is done by girls in Pittsburgh in tumbler factories only. The girls first grind the edges of the tumblers on a wheel fastened to a table and operated by power, a small three-inch belting running from table to ceiling. The action of the wheel on the glass produces a fine dust for which no exhaust is provided and which in consequence is inhaled by the operators. Grinding requires some training before it can be done well. It is paid for by the piece at the rate of $ .75 a 1000, and the girls grind 1000 to 1500 tumblers a day.

The edges are finished at another machine after they have been ground. The finishing girls set the tumblers in metal holding-cups on a disc which revolves horizontally, passing the upper edges of the tumblers under a white-hot flame, which slightly melts and smoothes the surface of the glass. The heat from the flame of the machines and from the nearby annealing ovens makes this work especially trying. A foreman told me that he loses time frequently because the girls faint at their work. Finishing edges, like grinding, is paid by the piece, but at a lower rate because the machine finishes several tumblers at one time. The rate is $ .35 a 1000, the output of the girls being from 3000 to 5000 a day.

GLASS DECORATING

This brings us to the occupations grouped under the general head of decorating, and here again I shall take them up in the order of least to most skilled. Decorating of some sort is done in four of the nine factories, the work in two cases being largely mechanical, and in the other two requiring some experience and skill. Stamping designs on glass and preparing glass for etching rank as mechanical, but gold enameling is work of much higher grade. By the first process, drinking glasses are stamped to order. The design is cut in a rubber stamp shaped to the glass. The girls brush ink over the design, place the inky surface next the glass, and rub the dry, outer surface until the design shows clear on the glass. The ware is then annealed. This stamping is paid for by time, at $4.50 to $7.00 a week.

Designs are etched on wine glasses and on different kinds of fine ware by an acid process. The girls ink the design, which is printed on tissue paper, and wrap it around the glass; when they remove the paper, the pattern is outlined in heavy ink on the glass, the untouched surface of which must be protected from the acid. Others of the girls then wax over the broader parts of this exposed surface, and still others paint with heavy red ink the parts of the surface that the wax is too stiff to reach. The inside of the glass is then filled with paraffin. A boy is employed to carry this ware to the bath of hydrofluoric acid in which it remains for half an hour while the acid eats out the design. Paraffin and ink are then scraped off, and the glass is cleaned and packed. The women employes at this work as at the rubber stamping are paid by time, the wages of most of them ranging from $4.00 to $4.50 a week, and in a few cases from $5.00 to $7.00.

The hand-decorating department offers the highest grade of work done by women in the glass industry. A new girl is given small articles to edge with gold first, and later to touch daintily with gold on edge and sides; then she is taught the use of ruby paint, and finally a combination of ruby and gold. From small articles, such as individual cream pitchers, she is advanced to larger articles, six or eight inches wide, and to more complicated designs. The chief materials used are a liquid gold, ruby paint which looks like amber when first put on, white enamel, and sometimes a dull silver, which, when finished, has the appearance of nickel plate. A new girl is not given enamel and silver work until she has thoroughly learned the other materials. All this decorating is done by hand, the color being put on with an artist's brush after a model copied by the forewoman from some design sent in by the management. The work is more or less mechanical. The main difficulty is to put on the color smoothly and to avoid wasting the gold. In the larger factory, no account is kept of the amount of color used by individuals, but finished articles are inspected for their appearance, which deviates from the standard if the right quantity of color is not used. Glass painted a ruby color is polished on a small hand wheel, so that it will look like ruby glass.

Hand decorators are paid by the piece, and never within the memory of those now employed has the rate per piece been cut because some employes were able to earn more than the usual amount. After six weeks' training, a girl is expected to make $1.00 a day, and a good worker can increase her speed until she earns

$8.00 a week.   In one factory, twenty out of the thirty earn $8.00, but a few make as much as $12.   A decorator strikes her pace after a while, and although she does not lose speed, she does not increase her output.

The regular working day in all the glass-houses is ten hours. Sometimes an hour is allowed at noon, and sometimes, especially in the decorating works, the girls prefer to take only half an hour and close earlier at night.   The work in the packing rooms is fairly even throughout the year, with overtime occurring only rarely under special pressure.   The busy time for the decorators comes at the end of every month.   The girls often have to work two nights a week to get out a shipment in time, although in the entire year this night work does not amount to more than a month of overtime.   Summer is the time of underemployment. For six weeks as a rule the furnaces are shut down, and women and men employes alike are out of work.

The heat of the work is one of its chief disadvantages. Although the glass-house proper where the men work is wide open, the packing rooms are usually enclosed, dusty, and hot from the lehrs and cooling glass.   The same is true of the decorating rooms. The radiation from the ovens even on cool days makes the work-rooms overheated, and decorators, unlike packers, cannot well open their windows, since a draft dries the fresh color on the glass too quickly and tends to make the surface rough.   Some scheme of forced ventilation which should carry the excess heat away from the workrooms and cool the air would do much to make the work more desirable.

A bit of industrial biography may serve to show the bounds which may confine the talent of an exceptionally able girl.   Louise Smead learned decorating at Tarentum, and for several years was employed on lamp shades, plates and other fine ware, with pay by the piece, and earnings of from $10 to $14 a week.   Then for a year she worked on the backgrounds of plates, blowing on the color.   The girls were told to put cheesecloth over nose and mouth, but they were often careless and neglected to do this, especially when they were hurried.   When Louise's throat became affected she was frightened and went back to plain decorating. Soon a German foreman took charge of the department,—a man

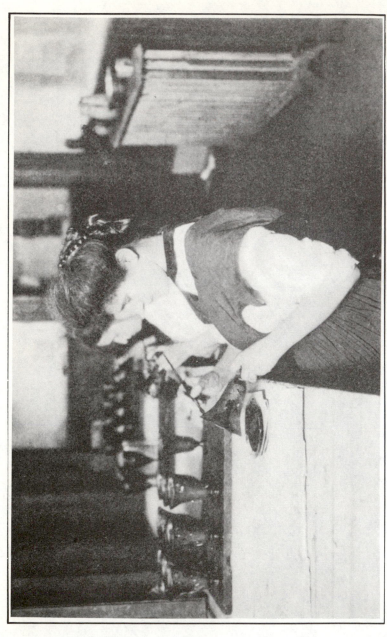

GLASS DECORATORS AT WORK

with fixed opinions as to the pay suitable for women. He said that no girl ought to earn more than $1.00 a day, and cut down the wages, paying by the day instead of by the piece. Many of the decorators left, but a few kept on, Louise among them. After a few months, she saw that she could not hope to better herself there, so she left and came to Pittsburgh to take a position in a glass factory, boarding at a Home for Girls. There she paid $3.00 a week and as she had some clothes when she came, she was able to keep on for a while, although her pay amounted to only $5.00 or $6.00 a week. The ware was small and cheap, different from that to which she had been accustomed, and she could not get the knack of putting on the color rapidly. She did the work well, but she took too much time over it. A quick dash for effect was outside her experience. She was on the point of leaving and trying something else when the firm promised to advance her; just then it was that she contracted typhoid fever. The fever so exhausted her nervously that she did not regain strength of arm to work by the piece, but her former ability secured her a permanent position at $10 per week. This is the trade history of an idealist, a girl who spends the weeks when the factory is shut down at work in crayon, watercolor and oils, whose mind is full of images of the color in trees and fields, but whose hand spends ten hours a day putting gold edges on glassware, after a pattern which must never vary.

Her story carries us a-field into another range of questions, the need for developing means more effective than any yet attempted in this great technical center, to find out and develop those artists and genuine craftsmen among the children of the people, who, stunted or undiscovered, are lost to the city and the race. It is a field too big with questions to go into here other than to suggest that it lies just outside, or even within, the trades, as shown in the life of one girl.

MIRROR MAKING

This subsidiary branch of the glass industry is represented by one firm on the North Side. One hundred and fifty employes, 40 of them girls, make up the working force, whose occupations are various as the kinds of mirrors that the market demands. Large mirrors and small, cheap mirrors that sell for a few cents and fine bits of plate glass for the dressing table,—all these are made, buffed, silvered, riveted, and framed in this busy three-story brick building a few squares from the river.

On the first floor, you see a line of girls buffing plate glass. Their calico dresses, their hands and their faces are stained with the oxide of iron in which they work, from the red of the tables and the dull edges of the mirrors, which are only by degrees acquiring the fine polish that is to make them saleable. Each girl stands, holding the glass against the buffing wheel.

There are some others at the same work upstairs, but on the upper floor the occupations are more various, polishing and cleaning, and silvering the backs of the mirrors. There are three girls riveting parts of frames, and one lacquering. Five girls earn over $7.00 a week, three earn exactly $7.00, and the rest sums from $4.00 to $6.00.

On the third floor, packing is done. Here there are 18 girls, some of them framing mirrors, some of them fastening the corners of boxes by a machine, some of them wrapping and preparing the goods for shipment.

The regular day is ten hours, and this is seldom exceeded, as the management believes that overtime does not pay.

MISCELLANEOUS TRADES

CHAPTER XVI

BROOM, BRUSH AND PAPER BOX MAKING

PRECEDING chapters have dealt with large groups of industries, industries that by adaptations of a single machine or by use of a common material or by similarity of product, have naturally been thought of together in a summary of women's work. Such are the needle trades, the industries for the production of food, the metal trades. We come now to a group of industries which have no such basis of similarity. They are alike neither in product, material nor machines. Some of them, such as broom and brush factories, because of their product are of necessity local. Others, like the paper box factories, owe their importance to major local industries. A few are apparently sporadic; the success of their local plants is not clearly traceable to any of these influences.

Just as the industries are distinct from each other, so the processes at which the women work are distinct. Arranged from least to most importance numerically, the trades are as follows:

TABLE 29.—NUMBER OF WOMEN IN MISCELLANEOUS TRADES

Trade	No. of Women
Broom making	12
Trunks and suit-cases	14
Brushes	20
Paint	50
Caskets	74
Soap	128
Paper boxes	238
Cork	600
Total	1196

More than half of these women are employed as machine-tenders, a third are employed filling cans and boxes, sorting and

249

packing, and the rest are employed at some form of hand work. This hand work, however, varies from the comparatively unskilled process of sorting corn in broom factories, to the difficult and expert work of raying silk for caskets. Some form of hand work, as some form of machine work, is found in almost every industry, and it is impossible to group the industries in toto according to the kind of work that they require. But it may be said of these miscellaneous trades as a whole, that the percentage of women employed at expert work is small, while those employed at routine hand work or at routine tending of a machine are greatly in the majority.

BROOM MAKING

Scarcely a city of importance is without its broom makers to meet the needs of the vigilant housewife. The reason lies in the fact, odd as it may seem, that a broom is after all a perishable commodity, unsaleable if made in quantities and stacked away for long periods of time. Like other perishable goods that are in constant local demand it can be more readily handled by small shops, which make only such articles as they have orders for, than by dealers on a larger scale, who must be prepared at times either to make up quantities of their product for stock, to run their plant at a loss, or to lie idle. Pittsburgh housewives have their source of supply near at hand, in several workshops and in one factory that is among the largest in the trade in this country.

Another factor enters in, especially in Pennsylvania, in determining the character of the trade. Broom making is one of the prison trades. Efforts of the trade unionists to prohibit convict labor by statute in Pennsylvania have so far been ineffectual, and in the Western Penitentiary today, convicts are making by hand brooms which are afterward bought cheaply and sold at a large profit by jobbers and wholesalers in Pittsburgh. So long as any part of the broom making is done outside the penitentiary, this affords a loop hole by which to evade the statute* passed with the intent of prohibiting further competition.

The small shops in Pittsburgh do not concern us, as they employ practically no women. Two are family shops where

* Act April 28th, 1899. Sec. 1 and 2, P. L. No. 100.

fathers and sons work together and no outsiders are employed. Others are conducted in small two-story buildings, in lofts, or parts of houses; they recall the era of the small business man who hired a few hands and earned a fair income, but never developed his interests along large lines. In these small shops boys are preferred to women because some of them may be depended upon to learn the trade.

The one factory employs 32 people, 12 of whom are girls. The girls tend to stay in the one branch of the trade to which they have been admitted.

The various processes at which women are not ordinarily engaged illustrate the limitations met with in women's work as a whole. First is the preparation of the corn. The stalks are washed and then immersed in green aniline dye, which gives the bright attractive color that we look for in a new broom. Herein lies the reason why brooms cannot be made for stock. The brightness given by the dye scarcely outlasts the sale of the broom; if the finished goods are retained for a short time in the warehouse it entirely disappears. A dull looking broom, the dealers say, will not sell.

Women and boys sort the corn after it has been stacked and dried, but all the actual broom making is done by the men. They choose the different kinds of corn that go to make up a broom, bind them to the handle in the desired shape, and then send them to another department to be sewed. The sewing is done sometimes by hand, but usually by machine. To make the double rows of sewing that bind the corn, two needles flash back and forth, threading and unthreading, making stitch after stitch with a rapidity that the eye can scarcely follow. Bleaching, dyeing, and cleaning the corn are among the occupations included in the sorting department, but the girls lack the ambition to learn these other processes, or to become forewomen in charge of a department. They are of the shifting group, who drift indifferently from one to another unskilled occupation.

In sorting, the one requisite is a good eye for color. It takes only a day to learn. The stalks of corn are spread out on a table and separated into piles of different grades and colors— a task which at first glance seems intricate. To the untrained eye yellow and green, or coarse and fine corn look so nearly alike that it would be puzzling to make even two absolute categories, and hopelessly confusing to attempt to distinguish the seven or eight different yellows and greens which sorters are expected to know. Sorters are paid $5.00 a week.

The sizing, which is simply another sorting process, is also done by women or boys. The corn is separated according to its lengths, either by hand work or by a sizing machine. Both methods are used in the Pittsburgh broom factory, but the finer grade of corn is sized by one girl who works by hand. A small wooden box nailed to the side of the table serves her as a holder for the corn. A notched stick which is fastened to the side of the box, with eight notches each corresponding to a standard length, is used for measuring. Taking a handful of corn, the girl measures it against the stick, and puts the different lengths in different piles, with remarkable rapidity. Unlike her co-workers, she has behind her the experience of fourteen years in a broom factory, and has reached a high machine-like precision in the execution of her task. She is a week worker, earning $7.50, the largest amount paid to any girl in this factory. The work of the machine operators is exceedingly simple, but as they could do it either fast or slowly, the incentive of a piece rate is resorted to by the management. Narrow belts run lengthwise along the upper surface of the machine, and as the corn is laid on these belts, the different lengths are carried to different points; thus the sizing is done automatically. The operator merely places the corn on the machine. I am told that these girls often cannot make more than $2.50 a week, and that their maximum is from $4.00 to $5.00.

One girl employed in a small shop has work more varied than that of other women in the trade. She not only does sorting and sizing, but cleans the brooms after they have been made, and sometimes when there is special need, she sews. She is paid $7.00 a week.

The hours of work in the factory are ten hours a day. To gain speed the girls stand at their work tables, although the work itself could be done as well if they were seated. The air is full of dust from the corn, especially in the sorting department where sorters and sizers throw the yellow handfuls from one pile to another, but except through the windows which are usually closed to keep out the smoke, there is no means of ventilating the workroom. The trade agreements of the broom-makers' union, since May, 1907, have contained the clause "All shops shall be provided with proper heat, light and ventilation," and the men say that the conditions are better. Yet the union is too weak to thoroughly enforce a point so open to differences of interpretation.

Only dyers and sewers are organized. Sorters are not excluded, but no group large enough to form a separate local has ever joined the national body, and in Pittsburgh they are not affiliated at all. Their work is considered so unimportant that no effort has been made to organize them. The men do not care whether the women are in the union or not. Yet the fact that the women are not organized leads to evasion of the convict labor law. Since the women in the factory sort and size the corn used by the penitentiary, the penitentiary cannot be held to be a broom factory in a technical sense. The factory arranges with the penitentiary for the sale of the brooms. This means that enough women must be employed to supply two factories, for the work of prisoners goes on irrespective of seasons, panics or depressions. This also means that although the women have been considered too unimportant to be organized, yet by keeping the prisoners supplied they are really acting in very concrete fashion against union interests and against the interests of their co-workers in the same shop, who were laid off in the winter of 1908, while the men in the penitentiary were kept busy.

BRUSH MAKING

This trade is grouped with broom making, not because of similarity in process, but because of joint association of brooms and brushes with cleaning day. There is only one brush factory in Pittsburgh; a large four-story building, it stands near the river on the South Side. It is one of the largest in the country, and makes brushes of every imaginable kind, from the soft camel's hair that artists use, to the great rough street brushes that clean trolley tracks and cobble-stones. It imports fine hair from

Russia, and sea grass from the tropics, and exports far more of its product than it sells locally.

The trade of brush making is still largely a handicraft. Within the last twenty years, the only change in method has been the substitution of steam power for foot power in drilling holes. A mixing machine is sometimes used in combining the different kinds of hair, but aside from this, combing, nailing, drawing, and all the various intricate processes, are carried on by hand. In cities farther east most branches of the trade are connected with the union, but here they are not. The men brush makers shift about a great deal. In the winter, they drift into the city and work until July; then with the coming of the slack season, they take to the road, and turn up the following winter, perhaps here, perhaps in some other city, for the next half-year's work.

The Pittsburgh factory employs 110 people, 20 of them girls. In other cities women are sometimes used for setting bristles in street brushes with pitch, but here that work is done by men. The girls work only at brush drawing. They sit at tables close to the windows in a long room with windows on three sides. The light is good, and there is little dust from the seagrass. Most of them work on scrubbing brushes,—prosaic articles of household use made from bristles of tampico gathered in the South Seas. The bristles are bleached and dyed before they reach the factory. On the first floor, men drill the holes, semiconical in shape, in the wooden backs of the brushes, the number of holes being gauged according to the standard shape of the brush. The backs are then sent to the girls, who clamp them, one at a time, to the table, so that the openings of the holes are exposed on each side. To "draw" a brush, the girl starts at the center. She fastens the wire to one hole, and pushes the wire through the wood from back to front. Next she takes a small bunch of bristles, doubles it into a U-shape, and pulls the wire through the loop of the U. Then she inserts the wire in the same hole again, drawing the bristles down with it. As the further end of the hole is smaller, the bristles cannot be drawn all the way through, but are held tightly in place. With the same wire, the girl goes on filling hole after hole until the row is complete. In the body of a brush there are usually five rows, and at each end is a V-shaped row of holes called "the wings." After the brush is completed, the body is trimmed by a gauge, so that the bristles of the wings stand out higher than the rest by a quarter of an inch. Sometimes for cleaning-brushes with long four-inch bristles, the loop is not made of even length on each side, but has one long side, and one small butt through which the wire is drawn. These variations and others, together with the routine work of the trade, the new girl has to learn, although the returns at the end of her trial period are not high. Pay is so much a hundred holes. The number of holes in a particular kind of brush is the basis for rates of pay in that line of work. The pay for common scrubbing brushes, for example, is $ .40 a dozen. The most skilful girl of the twenty in the factory earns $10 a week, but there are others who do not make more than $5.00, while the majority earn $6.50 to $7.00 the year round. The work cannot be learned in less than four or five months, and to acquire expertness takes at least a year. Time wages are paid for the first four weeks, although this is really a loss to the firm, because so much work is spoiled. After the four weeks are over, the newcomer must strike out for herself and do the best she can.

The regular working day is ten hours, except for the four months from April through July, when there is usually two hours overtime every night, making a total working week of 72 hours for this period of the year. The possible earnings of piece workers during this busy time are counterbalanced by slack weeks in August and in the fall, when the manufacture of stock for the winter demand is not sufficient to keep the entire factory force employed. Allowing for this seasonal difference, the trade is steady, and the girl employes generally remain year after year.

The demand for machine-drawn brushes is limited by their appearance, for the bristles are never so smooth nor so thick, and the brush consequently does not look well finished. In the Pittsburgh factory there are four machines for drawing scrubbing brushes, each built for a different style of brush. Since the demand is so light that only one machine needs to be run at a time, one girl operates all four machines. The holes for machine work are drilled only part way through the wood. The bristles are carried under the wire, which forms a staple, loops itself around the hole and is forced into the wood like a nail. For each loop the operator presses the treadle. This work takes several months longer to learn than the hand drawing, but it is too new a thing and the demand for it is too irregular, to admit of a definite statement as to the differences in wages earned by the two methods, and as to the differences in physical strain.

PAPER BOX MAKING

Cigar boxes, gay striped in yellow and red, demure wedding-cake boxes in white satin finish, large gray hat boxes and plain pasteboard shapes with strong corners guaranteed to wear,—the demand for these has created a trade important among the minor occupations in which Pittsburgh women are engaged.

The maker of round pasteboard stogy boxes knows how his Russian compatriot shrinks from entering unfamiliar places to purchase supplies, so he sets his factory in the midst of a nest of Hill shops where stogies may be made in one tenement attic, and the boxes for them in the loft across the street. Within a few blocks is built up a colony of small interdependent industries.

Of the nine box factories in Pittsburgh where women are employed, four make stogy boxes. For the rest, candy factories, department stores, and commercial stationers are the chief customers. Candy boxes lead, perhaps, in the bulk of the output, but close behind come shelving and file boxes, millinery bandboxes, and a host of nameless contrivances whose virtue lies in their adaptability.

The largest of the factories, one where wooden boxes also are made, employs 70 people, of whom 30 are women. In the others, the proportion of men to women is reversed. From the small factory on the Hill, where the proprietor himself does all the scoring and cutting, and employs seven women for paste work, to the large factory in the business district with a force of 45 women and five men, one finds women in the majority by more than two to one. Out of the total 337 employes,* 238 (70.9 per cent). are women.

* See Appendix B, p. 406, Table 71, for number of women and division of work in each paper box factory.

256

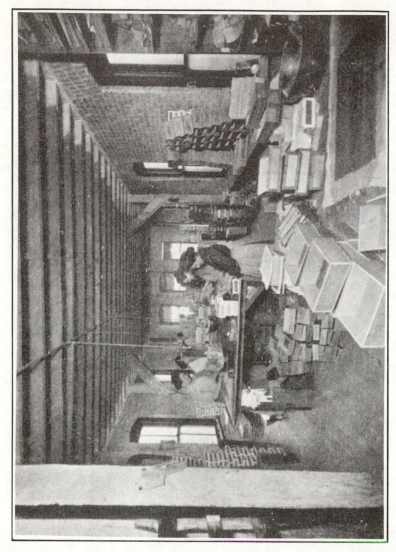

PASTING CIGAR BOXES BY THE THOUSAND

The character of the work varies with the kinds of goods made. For instance, in one department of the large factory mentioned, the girls clamp the edges of pasteboard boxes for cheroots, and cover the edges with paper; while on the next floor there are girls making the large round boxes in which a hundred stogies stand on end. In another factory, almost all the girls are used for fine paste work on small goods of the better sort, or yet again, on rapid work at machines.

The nationality of the employes is not distinctive, but varies with the neighborhood. Some girls are Jewish; a fifth are German. Here and there one finds an ambitious girl of Slavic origin, but more frequently an unambitious American, usually quite young and a little stupid. Indeed American girls are in the majority, but they are of the stock which has dropped behind in physique and in occupation.

PROCESSES

In the larger factories, men and women work on different floors. The men have sole charge of scoring, printing, and also of paper cutting, which is done by a heavy machine that has a record for minor accidents. Only one woman in the trade is used for cutting, and she does it not regularly, but at odd times. On the upper floors, girls do the actual box making. A new hand is put on as helper at the covering machine. The glue pot at one end of the machine is kept warm by steam, and the moving ribbon of paper is dipped in glue and passed through the machine to the operator who slips it into place about the box that whirls on a pivot at the other end. For high output, the machine is run by power, but I have seen it turned by hand, when the girls were doing especially careful work. When all the machines are in use, one sees a roomful of rapidly moving paper ribbons, slipped into place, caught and finished by the helpers alongside. As the boxes come from the machine, their edges are turned in by hand; they are then piled high, and carried away. Two girls to a machine can keep it running full capacity. After the new girl has been a helper for some time, she is taught stripping; that is, covering corners of boxes with small muslin pieces and strengthening ends and bottoms by pasting muslin strips along the edges.

The last step in promotion, if the girl is a machine hand, is the actual operating of the covering machine. She stands * at the end and holds the moving paper ribbon, adjusting it around the turning box. If the girl is a hand worker, she is considered expert when she knows how to cover boxes, but this takes six months to a year to learn, and even then a new girl will not have gained speed.

The hand workers stand at tables in a long room, each girl with her glue or paste pot, her brush, cloths and strips of colored paper, and the pasteboard forms. The skirts and waists of the girls are spattered with the glue and the air is full of the strong smell of it. At times one finds a foreman with a passion for an immaculate workroom, following after his employes with warm water and cloths, but often the accumulated glue of weeks has dried and hardened on the sides of the work tables, the accumulated smell of glue has found no determined breeze to carry it away. For the machines, the glue is made after a formula by workmen on another floor, but the hand workers are expected to know how to thin their own glue to the proper consistency. They have the knack of brushing on neither too much nor too little, of placing the strips of paper, each with one deft movement, so that they lie flat, without wrinkles. All this means a kind of expertness, a degree of familiarity with the materials and the way of handling them, that cannot be acquired except with time. At present, only one factory has a covering machine for small boxes, and all this fine work is done by hand; but for the large boxes, two or three factories have covering machines.

Some firms have machines for incidental work, such as tacking and wire-stitching, or for printing even, when the boxes are to be letter-stamped. The Knowlton-Beach staying machine, used in six out of the nine factories, is, like the covering machine, characteristic of the industry. This machine carries a muslin or manila stay, dipped in glue, and clamps it on the corners of box covers and other small work. The operator holds the box in the machine as she presses the treadle, and in order to have firm hold, her hands are often dangerously near the knife that comes down to clip the stay. There are guards on either side of the

* This work can be done equally well whether the operator stands or sits.

knife, but the girls seem to think that the guards interfere with their work, and fasten them back rather than lower the rate of output. In a factory where two of these machines are used, I saw one with both guards fastened back, while in the other, one guard was entirely removed and the other fastened back. Sometimes I was told that the girls kept the guards down, but wherever it was possible to see the machines in operation, the guards were found fastened out of the way of the operator. Two factories are trying the experiment of guarding the girl instead of the machine. The operator is given steel thimbles, which cover her forefingers to the first joint, and which should serve to check the downward progress of the knife if the fingers chanced to get in its way.

HOURS AND WAGES

The regular working day is nine hours in some cases, ten in others. A third of the factories open at eight in the morning instead of at the classic hour of seven, and others start work at seven thirty in concession to employes in whom the habit of tardiness seems to have been born.

Overtime, while possibly less general in the Pittsburgh paper box factories than in those in the east, is yet characteristic of the trade. The box maker depends on the candy maker and on the stogy maker for his orders. He can make up only a small part of his goods for stock. The candy maker and the stogy maker, however, cannot order their boxes until they in turn receive orders from the wholesale dealers. As these orders from retailers and from wholesalers are delayed until the latest possible moment before the Christmas season actually begins, the congestion of work and consequent overtime in the fall in candy and stogy factories affects related industries such as box making, and causes similar congestion of work and overtime in box factories. The best equipped and best organized factories consciously attempt to limit the amount of night work and to have their order work distributed over a longer period of time. They realize that long hours are wasteful of their employes' strength, yet without change in the arrangement of work in other industries, they are powerless to avoid night work in the fall. Two factories, through special conditions in their trade, are in general able to do without more than a few nights' overtime. Another firm keeps its employes only six nights in the season. In the five remaining factories, however, the working hours during November and December range from 63 to 78 per week, an excess both by day and by week of the limit set by the factory law.

Beginners are paid from $2.50 to $3.00 a week,* in one case $3.50, and are expected in six weeks at least to be able to make their time. After that they work by the piece. In one factory, the girls who clamp and cover edges of cheroot boxes, are paid at the rate of $ .30 a 100. In one day, a girl can clamp 400 boxes, and the next day cover the edges, so that the pay for the two days is $1.20, or $ .60 a day. Others paste strips of paper above the edges of cigar boxes. The rate is $ .50 for 50 boxes of one grade, with a maximum output of 100 boxes a day. Another box, a little larger, pays $ .60 for 50 boxes, for work of the same sort, and the girls can make 90 to 100 a day of these. Shelf and file boxes, which are made entirely by hand and covered with either cloth or paper, pay from $ .50 to $ .60 a dozen; the quicker girls can make two dozen in a day, but the majority in these factories do not make more than $5.00 or $6.00 a week, and the number who are earning less is surprisingly large. For instance, one manufacturer says that after a girl has learned the trade, he does not expect her to make less than $4.00 a week, but that even in a year she can scarcely gain speed enough to make $1.00 a day. One firm made a contract to finish a certain number of candy boxes within a specified time and the manager asked the girls how many they could turn out. They said 200, but upon much urging thought that they could turn out 250. Finally, he induced them to try to make 400, and when they succeeded in this, he promised a box of candy to the first girl who finished 500 boxes in a day. In a little while all the girls in the department had reached a daily output of 500 boxes and were earning $1.25. Yet as soon as the order was finished, the speed of the girls dropped with the change in their work, and as before, they earned from $ .75 to $ .80 daily.

* See Appendix B, pp. 406–407, Tables 72 and 73, for details of wages in paper box factories

THE DANGEROUS STAYING MACHINE AT WORK

Some managers complain that the girls lack ambition; that they are unwilling to work hard in order to get work out. Others call them irresponsible. Yet even in the foregoing instance of speeding, the wages earned by the quickest could scarcely be called high. For those whose speed fell below the highest point, and for all the girls during the greater part of the year, the wages were unquestionably low. One manufacturer states that he employs only girls who live at home, because the trade does not offer a living wage. Altogether 79.8 per cent (190 girls) are in the ranks of the less efficient, earning less than $6.00 a week. There are 32 girls in the $7.00 wage group, and 16 who earn over $7.00.

The percentage in the lowest wage group is seen to be remarkably high. Behind the secondary reason for this, based on the lack of ambition among box-factory employes, there is a primary reason. The number of women in the trade, the number of positions open, and the number of possible employers is relatively small; the chances of employment are constantly becoming less. Twenty years ago, one of the factories employed 110 people and the output was not so large as it is today. By the introduction of small covering machines, the number of employes was reduced first to 75, and later to 50, when staying machines were put in and some improvements made in the cutting room. If the covering machines for the small candy boxes should be introduced now, the force could be reduced to 35 and there would be less difficulty in getting hands, because less training is necessary for successful operation of the machines than for accurate hand work.

This fact, that to a great extent machine work is surely, if slowly, taking the place of hand work, and that machine operators can be taught more quickly and paid less than expert hand workers, means that within the trade potential machine production is a factor in keeping wages down. Lack of ambition among the employes, in part due to the poor physique and the lower grade of the American girls employed, is both an effect and a cause of low wages. The occupation at present offers a temporary expedient to the many without efficiency who are shifting and uncertain in tenure of position.

CHAPTER XVII

CASKETS, CORK, PAINT, SOAP, TRUNKS

CASKETS

THE two casket factories of Pittsburgh employ 74 women, 60 of them being in the larger plant on the North Side.

Glue work is done on one floor. At an oblong table sit the girls, each with her glue-pot, her strips of black silk and the plain wooden bars. With one stroke of the brush, the reverse side of the silk is covered with glue and by a turn of the hand it is folded around the bar. Another girl is busied assembling the long metal bars for caskets, adjusting the different parts by a measuring rod and hammering them together. All the work on this floor is simple and easily learned.

On the floor above, other girls are at miscellaneous work. Ebony, silver and composite, lead, brass, copper, and all the conventional shapes into which habit has worn our ceremonial for the dead,—bars and handles and decorations,—are piled high the length of the room. Of the 15 girl workers, all but two are assembling or packing. Some put together the ears, arms and tips for short bar handles, and others hammer the arms and tips together. All of them stand at their work.

One girl sits at the table in another room, laying ebony paint on a silver base, for parts of metal bars. Judgment is needed to avoid waste of material, but otherwise this is the simplest of all decorating.

Nearby is the lacquering room. Through the open door I could see one girl moving about, dipping trays of metal pieces in the lacquer bath, lifting them out, drying and placing them in the oven for final finish. Ordinarily the doors are shut, and the fumes are so strong that the manager said as we watched the work, "We won't stay in here more than a minute, if you don't mind

I can't stand the air." The girl, who is now well over twenty, entered the factory when she was fourteen; she says that she can stand the lacquer very well, although the fumes are apt to make one's head ache. The main difficulty about the work is to keep the lacquer clean. Windows have to be closed most of the time, as dust blows in from the nearby mills, and the least speck in the lacquer will disfigure some metal pieces, such as handles of solid brass. Fresh lacquer is used for brass work. When it becomes muddy and unfit for articles of this grade, it is strained and used for dull gray handles on which imperfections are not so noticeable. After a second straining, it can still be used for iron and other cheap materials. This means that there are always three baths of lacquer to be tended, one that is constantly being renewed with the freshly mixed liquid, and two that are strained between each two sets of handles dipped. When lacquer is being either mixed or strained, the fumes are heaviest. Sometimes in a busy season an assistant is needed, besides the girl regularly employed. The volume of lacquer work varies according to business prosperity, since the amount of ready money helps to determine choice of funeral accessories. For instance, during the business depression of 1907–08, the bulk of the orders were for plain silver handles rather than for the more expensive finish of composite lead, a choice which made considerable difference in the quantity of lacquering done.

The lacquer girl is paid $9.00 a week, but in the other metal work departments few are earning more than $7.50, and at least half are not earning more than $6.00. Work is steady the year round, except for the first week in July, when the factory shuts down to take stock and all the girls are laid off. The ten-hour day is the rule, and in the departments first described, there is little overtime. In the sewing room, however, the night hours are the girls' chief grievance.

In the sewing rooms the robes are made. The lining of caskets is done here; also the tufting and raying, which only two or three in the department understand. New hands are started at $5.00, and are put on piece work after three or four weeks, making pillows or parts of linings or sections for the casket. They earn $7.00 or $8.00, never over $9.00, for, "If you earn ten,"

263

said one of the girls, "they cut the rate and you have to wear
out your life and soul trying to make anything at all." Some
who are employed here have been dressmakers; most of them
are a few years older than the majority of factory girls. Only
those women whose hope of more normal occupation is gone
continue in the sewing rooms. They are women who have lost
a little of their strength; women who have the patience, the
acquiescence that is born of failure.

Nominally, they work from seven until six. Actually,
each girl is on call two nights a week and every third Sunday.
She must hold herself ready to work on her night whenever a
special order comes in. If, for instance, an undertaker orders
a casket lined with pearl white, and the manufacturer has none
in stock, the girls are expected to work at night to execute the
order. If the order is for a casket a little larger or a little smaller
than the usual size, the girls on night duty will be called out.
Indeed, they almost invariably have to work at the time when they
are subject to call.

After six o'clock, they are paid at the rate of a time and a
quarter, but some of the machinery is shut down and the night
orders always drag. The girls are not obliged to come the next
morning, nor do they need to come at seven o'clock if they have
worked until twelve the night before, but they nearly always do
because they are on piece work, and they can make more in the
morning than during the night.

One woman in the department worked twenty-four hours
at a stretch in July, 1907, and another has been called out at
three in the morning and expected to work on through the next
day. A third has sometimes sewed from seven at night until
two the following morning, and often has worked until one
o'clock.

The very late night hours are less frequent than formerly,
because the firm is carrying a larger stock; but even so, for small
differences in the orders, the employes are still on call. One
cannot challenge the length of the working week, for the total
might not be over sixty hours. But the length of the working
day? Not twelve but sometimes fifteen hours; sixteen or eighteen
when orders are heavy; in one case twenty-four. If the law

represents a possible maximum under which health can be conserved, what shall be said by the community vitally concerned, when this standard which it has set is thus violated?

CORK

The largest cork factory in the United States occupies two seven-story brick buildings near the river-front in Pittsburgh. The employes number 600 girls and from 800 to 900 men. From floor to floor, the river breeze sweeps up wide staircases and through open windows into high-ceilinged rooms. You can see lanes of power-driven machines, cutting, shaping, polishing corks, cutting cork-paper, shaping cork soles. You can see men punching cork-bark or shaping the large heavy sizes of corks, and you can see girls at work on the ordinary commercial sizes, tending machines, sorting, shaping, or finishing.

The first process of cork making is blocking or punching; that is, cutting the oblong piece of bark to the desired size. Following this, the corks are tapered, the ends are polished, and then the sides, and finally they are washed and sorted.

The blocking or punching is done by machine, some of it by men and some by girls. The machine cuts the elongated piece of cork into squares which can be readily shaped; the operative simply feeds the cork into the machine.

Tapering is the most dangerous of the finishing processes. By the old method,—and half the work is still done in this way,— the cork is fed into a groove, and carried by the machine to the edge of the knife, which shaves off one end on a slightly curved line. The hand of the operator is between the cork and the knife, which, though guarded by a steel rung, yet is responsible for the frequent clipped fingers that have given the tapering room an unenviable reputation. Recently the number of accidents has been lessened by the introduction of machines built like the polishing machines with a large funnel at the top, from which the corks are carried to the knife, and tapered automatically. Four machines of the new type are operated by one girl. The records of the company show that from January 1, 1908, to October 1, 1908, only 6 per cent of the employes in this department were injured, the small percentage being undoubtedly due to the method now in use.

The sides and ends of corks are polished by machines, four of which can be tended by one girl. She has simply to feed the corks into a great funnel at the top, whence they are carried, one at a time, past a buffing wheel that polishes the sides or the end. The operator inhales the fine cork dust from the wheel which has no exhaust to cover it.

The cork-paper cutting department illustrates a further development of the industry. By an adjustment of the machine, the blocks are cut into thin sheets which are recut into strips for the cork tips of cigarettes. This work requires some judgment; the operator watches the machine carefully, so as to stop it whenever there is a flaw in the cork, and to adjust a fresh block. Men were employed for this work in 1906, but they have been discharged, and although one or two are still needed to look after the machines, the firm saves appreciably by employing 21 girls at half the wages formerly earned by the same number of men.

In other departments, girls are engaged at hand cutting, sewing cork soles, and making life preservers. Imperfect corks which did not pass inspection are sent to the docking department to be recut by machine and pared down to a smaller size. Accidents rarely occur in this department, as the girl's hand does not necessarily approach the knife.

Sorting is perhaps the most difficult work of all. The sorters sit at long tables on which compartments are marked off for the different sizes and kinds of corks. According to the quality of the bark and according to the grade of workmanship, corks apparently exactly alike are inspected and separated into different grades.

Wages in the cork factory range from $3.00 or $4.00 a week to $9.50. Usually a new girl is started at $ .70 a day, and put on piece work as soon as she begins to "make her time," although if her work is changed, as often happens, she sometimes falls below her original time rate. Often it is three months before a new hand can "make out well" by piece payments. Some of the sorters do not make more than $ .80 or $ .90 a day, but others make from $1.25 to $1.35. The hand cutters seldom make over

$1.25.   The docking girls are paid $1.10 and the girls at the funnel machines $ .80 a day.   Cork sewers earn usually $1.00 a day, and the cork-paper cutters from $8.00 to $9.50 a week.

In general, $1.25 may be regarded as the standard pay of the best girls.   When piece workers have exceeded this, especially when the piece rate was experimental because of some change in method or the introduction of new machinery, there is evidence that rates have been cut.   For instance, in 1905 a new kind of work ("fine ends") was given out in the hand cutting room, at $1.10 a barrel.   After three months at this, the girls were able to make two barrels a day ($2.20), and the rate was promptly cut to $ .90 a barrel.   But in a year's time, the girls had again increased their speed, and again the rate was cut, this time to $ .60 a barrel.

All departments have a ten-hour day, five days in the week, with a half day Saturday, but in one department there are frequent calls for overtime.   The busy season lasts from February to November.   The machinery is stopped at night, but the sorters, who need no machinery, are often required to work later in order to finish the day's output of the other departments.   For probably 150 days out of the year, during a normal year, the sorting department works from six in the evening to nine, though as a rule not more than two nights in one week.   This keeps the weekly hours within the limit of the state factory law, but exceeds the law in the length of the working day, which is thirteen hours instead of twelve.   In the smaller sorting room, there were only six nights overtime during the season of 1907, but in the other building, the girls at times worked every night except Wednesday.

During the slack season from November until February, there is no very general dismissal of employes, but a whole department will sometimes be laid off for one day each week.

On the whole, the girls' work in the cork factory is either routine machine tending or routine hand work which is quickly learned.   The location of the factory near the Lawrenceville section has brought in a large number of Irish-American employes, but it has also brought many a fair-haired Polish girl from the streets of low houses near the river.   The working force is not notable for its stability.   Without sense of appreciable change, the girls drift from one kind of machine tending to another kind of machine tending at which they have about the same hours, and after they have caught the knack of the thing, about the same limit to advancement.

PAINT MANUFACTURE

Although there are several paint factories here, only two are employers of women, and the women in these two are in the minority, 50 in all. Paint making is done by men. Women are used, however, in four capacities: (1) In the filling and sealing department, where the small cans are filled with paint and then closed by light, easily running machines; (2) in the labeling department, where the girls apply labels to the packages; (3) in the color department, where the girls paste on sheets of paper small strips of sample cards showing the shades in which the paint is made; (4) in the printing department, where the sample cards are prepared.

One paint factory employs five girls, one to fill and four to label cans; the other factory employs 45 girls. In this larger plant, 10 are at the printing presses, turning out the bright sample cards. Labeling, at which the greater number of girls are employed, is paid by the week instead of by the piece, wages ranging from $4.00 to $9.00, with three-fourths of the girls earning not more than $6.00 a week. The higher pay is determined in part by length of service, in part by speed.

Labeling is on the lower levels of unskilled employment, and this fact, together with the irregular seasons, tends to create a shifting group of employes in the trade. From February to May, and again in September and October, are the busiest seasons, although in January, 1908, the girls worked two nights a week to get out some orders. When the rush is over, when the spring and fall painting and refurnishing of houses is at an end and the pressure of business subsides, half the force is discharged.

SOAP FACTORIES

A stranger to the industry in Pittsburgh might suppose that the term "soap factories" implies a certain unity of product.

This impression could not outlast one walk through the long low buildings where, in the main, the soap manufacture of the district is carried on. It would be displaced by successive impressions of confusion, of incoherence, almost of repulsion. The stench from the stockyards and the odor from the soap combine to daunt any but the most hardy seekers for employment. Unventilated and sometimes dirty rooms, a heterogeneous series of industrial processes, an atmosphere of nervous haste, low piece rates, high pressure,—such facts as these characterize a plant unique among Pittsburgh factories.

In a single group of buildings there are made baking powder, laundry soap, perfumes, preserves, patent medicines, and various miscellaneous food products, such as chocolate and jelly powders. When so many unrelated processes are conducted under one roof, the growth of each process is necessarily somewhat restricted by every other, and it is not possible to effect that economy of production which is gained by the manufacture of large quantities of a single article. Economy must then be secured either in quality of material, in lack of care for the buildings, or in high speeding and low payment of employes,—possibly in all these ways.

As elsewhere, men are employed here in the actual making and girls in packing and bottling the different articles. In the basement of one building, common laundry soaps are packed. Eight girls sit at a table; the room is almost totally dark, its low ceiling not over ten feet high, and most of the air space taken up by crates of finished stock. These girls are the most expert employes and at times they work so fast that one can scarcely follow the motions of their fingers. The standard box holds 100 cakes, other boxes hold 150 cakes of soap. Each cake is wrapped with a single square of paper. One of the packers has the record of having wrapped 12,100 cakes of soap in a day, and another for the last twelve years has averaged nearly 11,000. Occasionally a girl earns $12 a week. The most poorly paid in this department get $6.00, but for the majority, even at this rate of speed, $8.00 to $9.00 per week is a maximum. On the same floor, 15 girls work at machines, removing and packing away in crates the cakes of soap that pass on a traveling chain.

Soap powder is packed on the first floor of the second building. Windows are gray with dust, fine gray dust sifts through the air, and at long gray tables, gray women pack with rough hands and swift fingers in a swirl of fine soap particles. At the side of the room are great wooden tubs full of the powder. Pasteboard packages and heaps of powder are on each section of the tables. The need for haste, like an electric touch to a nerveless limb, stirs the women to quick motion, lifting and forcing their arms into place swiftly, irregularly, with painful but continuous effort. The faces of the women are partly covered with cloths, but although this keeps some of the dust away, it cannot give them air where there is no air to be had. Every window is closed tight and the room is stifling. No one in this room earns more than $4.50 a week.

On the upper floors, girls are employed to pack silica and baking powder, toilet soaps and extracts. Some fill bottles with perfumes; twelve others bottle pickles. The packers of silica and baking powder, like the packers of soap powder on the first floor, work in an atmosphere which it is impossible to breathe; there are 31 women in these two departments.

In the two soap factories of Pittsburgh, 128 girls are employed. Three of them, in a small factory on the South Side, are paid the wages of unskilled labor, $3.50 to $5.00 a week, and are shifted from one occupation to another, from wrapping soap to salting soap, or removing it from the machine. The other factory employs the remaining 125, many of them low-grade Germans from the unsightly shacks on the hills along the river, many of them Polish from the lower North Side. "They don't know there is any other place than ———'s where they could work," said the manager. "They never think of working anywhere else, and we don't have any trouble to keep them."

Except for a cannery near by, there are no neighboring employers to compete, and it is possible to keep a hundred unskilled girls at $5.00 or $6.00 or often $4.00 a week. The few in the bottling department and packing laundry soap earn from $6.00 to $10.00. A new hand is paid $3.00 during her first three weeks, and if at the end of that time, she is not able to earn more than her week wages, she is not retained. She cannot become an expert packer in less than three months. The management has been successful in inducing the girls in all departments to work at high speed. The laundry soap was at one time put up in two wrappers and the girl used to slap one wrapper down, slap the soap on it, then take the other wrapper and wind it around. Now only one wrapper is used, but the girls who worked the former way think they must go through the same motions as if there were still two wrappers in order to keep their muscular and nervous speed.

High speeding is often characteristic less of a trade than of individual systems of management, but in this case, the individual system is the trade. The demand for lavish expenditure of muscular and nervous force, the neglect of the workrooms, the fine flying particles in the powder packing rooms, the buildings actually dirty and in the direct path of the wind that blows through the stockyards,—all these conditions put soap factory work in the lower levels of occupations for women in the Pittsburgh district.

TRUNKS AND SUIT-CASES

This industry is represented by one factory in which 56 men and 14 women are employed. Small leather goods are not made in Pittsburgh but are shipped from cities farther east; but trunks and suit-cases in wide variety of style and shape are turned out with the help of an up-to-date machine equipment.

Most of the work on trunks is done by men, women being employed chiefly to paste in the paper or cloth linings. There are five women in the trunk department.

On suit-cases, the work is divided more evenly. Girls have to be trained by this firm, because there are no other places in the district where they can learn; it takes about a year and a half for a new hand to become proficient. A man does not learn his part of the trade in less than three years, for he does more of the hand work and is kept at the better materials and on the better grade of suit-cases. Girls make the cheaper goods and do more of their work by machine. Men do all the leather cutting, but women glue the leather about cardboard frames, and make the handles, which are set in wooden frames and nailed into place until they assume the desired shape. They put on the handles, stamp the corners into shape on a cornering machine, rivet the corners and rivet handles and straps into place. Much of this is stiff, heavy work.

This factory works a nine and a half hour day. Expert trunk makers among the men earn up to $35 a week. The women earn from $4.00 to $7.00, ten out of the fourteen earning from $5.00 to $7.00.

THE COMMERCIAL TRADES

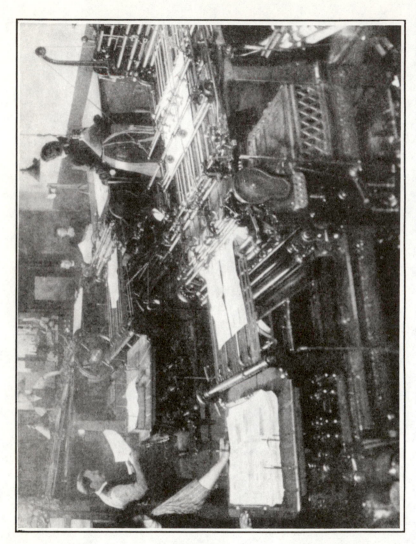

GIRL PRESS FEEDERS AT THE PRESSES

CHAPTER XVIII

THE PRINTING TRADES

NOT only as a manufacturing district, but as a commercial center and as a market, Pittsburgh makes use of numbers of women working at allied occupations under one management.

Printing offices and binderies might well be considered factories because of the nature of their machinery and of much of their product, and yet in another sense they are more nearly allied to the offices to which their product goes. Women in binderies are numbering and indexing and arranging more frequently perhaps than they are working at machines. Conditions in the trade are dependent upon conditions in offices.

The telephone exchange and the telegraph office are striking examples also of the collective work of women. They are clearly commercial in that they manufacture no product but make the transaction of business possible.

In the mercantile house, we come finally to the marketing of the articles which factories have produced, and which by means of commercial activity have been brought to their destination.

It has been beyond the limits of this inquiry to consider stenographers and accountants and other office workers. In the bindery, the telephone exchange, the telegraph office, and the mercantile house, however, workers are gathered into organized groups which have much in common with the true factory system, and must be taken into consideration in surveying the women-employing trades in Pittsburgh.

The printing trade has assumed an aspect like that of the district, intensely practical. We need not look in the small job offices or on the third or fourth floors overlooking dingy alleys for fine edition work, for gold-sticking in graceful designs, for backing in vellum on tooled leather, or even for the printing of the ordinary utilitarian novel. Save for the newspaper offices, an almanac, local society weeklies and a telephone directory, edition work is negligible. The demand which printing offices and binderies have risen to supply is the demand of office buildings for blank books and ledgers, office sheets and legal documents.

Between printing work and bindery work in Pittsburgh, no sharp line can be drawn. Binding is done in printing establishments; it is subsidiary to the printing and is done very largely by the same force of employes.

The establishments in general are small. The largest employs 240 people. Few others employ more than 60 and many have only four or five names on their payroll. Twenty establishments, including all the large and many of the small shops, employ 397 women, and with the possible exception of a few women engaged at odd jobs, this is the total number employed in Pittsburgh printing establishments.

THE PRESSROOM

The work of women in pressrooms and binderies differs, as the trade itself differs, from that in other cities. The smallness of the establishments and the development of the industry to meet local needs, has interfered with specialization. Few of the employes are kept continuously at one occupation. Two-thirds of them are "miscellaneous workers," which includes occasional press work, hand folding, wire stitching, sewing, gathering, collating, feeding the ruling machines, punching, perforating, round cornering and sometimes indexing. A small number have regular work at one occupation such as compositing or steady press feeding. So far as could be learned, Pittsburgh had eight women compositors in 1907. Three of them are old hands who "set up" side by side with the men, and whose employment dates from the days when the shop, now one of the largest in the city, was small. Others work at linotypes, which are operated like typewriters and at the press of a key drop the die which gives character to the warm type metal. The hand work in this latter shop is done by men, but the manager prefers women for the machines on the ground that they are more dependable.

Press feeding is a field of work contested by men and women. Some firms employ men or women indifferently at both job and cylinder presses. In smaller establishments, where no girls are employed, it is claimed that boys are more useful, because they can "set up," and help in other ways. Boys are apprenticed to learn the trade, but girls never go beyond press work and are apt to leave in a few years, so the managers feel that it is not worth while to teach them. On the other hand, boy press feeders are paid $1.00 to $3.00 a week more, and the employment of girls means a saving to the larger shops. When a girl becomes a press feeder she tends to stay in the industry as long as she works rather than to change to some other where the way of the machine would have to be learned anew.

BINDERY WORK

In the bindery proper you see men finishing, backing, working with heavy canvas, or holding gold leaf with their delicate tools. No women are employed in Pittsburgh at this part of the trade. Their work in the binderies is various; more are employed steadily at folding than at any other occupation, but a girl is expected to be able to do a dozen different things.

Machines have not yet invaded the Pittsburgh binderies to any extent, and the work at them has not become in any sense a well-defined occupation. A folding machine into which the sheets are fed as into a press is sometimes used in place of hand folding, but by some managers is considered unsatisfactory for register work. Similarly, some hold that machines cannot run a thread strong enough for books and ledgers, therefore many of the girls sew by hand. A sewing machine does the work of eight girls, and sews each section of a book separately, whereas if the threads of a single section of a hand-sewn book are cut the book is likely to fall apart. While in the big publishing centers machine sewing is displacing large numbers of hand sewers, here the hand sewers as yet scarcely seem to be threatened. They have not begun to know the strain of trying to keep up with the ever-increasing output of machines while behind every motion lurks the fear that in six months another machine will do all that they have learned and their whole department be swept aside. Wire-stitching machines are used for small folders. Treadle pressure forces the wire through the leaves and presses it flat. This work, like the operation of punching machines and perforating presses for pads and for loose-leaf ledgers, is usually done by girls.

Gathering and collating are of so little importance, because of the small amount of edition work, that they are in the nature of odd jobs to be done by any one in spare moments. Indexing and numbering also are done by hand in all but the largest establishments, the volume of work not being large enough to necessitate the use of machines. Twenty thousand numbers can be stamped by hand in a day, but where ledger pages are numbered by machine, the output is 50,000. The indexing machine does even better, for it cuts the edges of the ledger at a rate which could be equalled only by the output of five girls. Hand work then, in these processes, gives employment to girls at present, but cannot be considered permanent.

THE RULING DEPARTMENT

In contrast, the ruling machines, with their bowls of colored inks, their cords and wooden frames, are in Pittsburgh a department in themselves. Men prepare the inks and superintend the ruling. The girls, perched high on stools, sit feeding sheet after sheet of the ledger pages with a perfect machine-like precision by the help of a left-hand gauge. On a slow-moving machine they feed in 500 sheets every fifteen minutes, or 18,000 in a nine-hour day, but on a machine that moves quickly, this rate may be doubled. "Faint line ruling" is for the horizontal lines of the ledger and "down line ruling" for the vertical lines. This latter process, complicated by a double set of gauges, is the more difficult. The constant unvarying motion of the machines makes the feeders dizzy, and they forget to think as they gauge the speed to which the machine is set and make each sheet follow exactly upon the last, with only a second's interval between. Some of them say that they cannot learn in less than three months.

Yet even in this department the Pittsburgh trade is in a transitional stage. One establishment has a ruling machine with

Folders at Work in a Job Printing Office

automatic feeding attachment,—two metal lifters with hollow rubber ends which take up the sheets by suction. In the larger publishing centers, hand feeding has been entirely superseded in all but the small shops.

WAGES

Beginners in printing and bookbinding establishments are paid $3.00 or $4.00 a week.* In time, as they become familiar with the several different kinds of work, they are advanced a few dollars, but as a rule they are not highly paid. With a few exceptions they are "job hands," not specialists. They work in most places at an easy pace, for piece work in this industry is almost unknown in Pittsburgh. Under times of stress there have, of course, been exceptions. At one time, for instance, an establishment was trying to get out a rush order in small edition work, when the rate of the register folders was only 300 per hour. The girls said that they could not increase their speed, but they were put on piece work and in two days the rate went up to 500 per hour. Time payments were resumed, but the girls were expected, as in other cases quoted, to continue at the same pace. The forewoman said that those who learn under a time-payment system, can never work so fast as those who learn under a piece-payment system, but that by the latter plan they are soon exhausted nervously.

Feeders at the ruling machines are usually paid $6.00. The press feeders earn slightly more, from $5.00 to $7.00 at job presses and from $6.00 to $8.00 at cylinder presses. A very few of the hand indexers and operators of numbering machines who have acquired high speed earn $8.00 to $9.00. The most highly paid girls in the trade are the linotype operators. They are paid by time from $12 to $18 a week.

Taking the trade as a whole, the percentage earning over $7.00 is small; 31 per cent of the girls have just reached $7.00 a week, and 45.59 per cent are earning $4.00 to $6.00 a week. One reason for this probably is that the work attracts the better type of American factory operative by the fact that it is clean

* See Appendix B, p. 407, Table 74, for table of wages.

and comparatively pleasant, and it can in consequence secure desirable hands without offering great financial inducements.

Hours in printing establishments are in most cases nine or nine and a half. Five shops, however, have an eight-hour day, and even among the "open shops" the tendency toward a shorter work day is apparent. Nevertheless, the busy months bring overtime. Sometimes in July and sometimes in January, the season of heavy work sets in. One firm with orders to fill for the glass journals, follows its overtime during January and February by almost complete cessation of work in May. "We are not Rockefellers," the manager said, "and we can't keep the girls just for the good of the cause." The five girls employed by this company are on call when orders come in. Another firm requires night work regularly once a week in the cylinder press and folding departments. Once and a half the day rate of wages is paid. Twenty minutes are allowed for supper and work continues until twenty minutes past nine. Sometimes, when there is special business, such as getting out the telephone books, or a section of one of the weekly papers, the girls are on duty three nights a week. One girl, paid at the rate of $ .16⅔ an hour, worked 87 hours in one week, earning $14.50 for a week which averaged 14½ hours' work each day. She was the feeder at a cylinder press. Her firm pays its job feeders $ .12 an hour and workers in the bindery department $ .07 and $ .08. In another establishment, a premium is paid for overtime, the $8.00 girls earning $1.00 extra, and the others $ .75 extra, for every three hours of night work. Some firms, although they keep the presses running all night, employ a double shift of men, and expect only occasional overtime from the girls. Some, on the contrary, regularly require four days' overtime a week in winter. Others keep all their employes 12 to 14 hours a day.

SEASONAL WORK

Since the busy time usually comes in the winter months, it is seldom that a girl can keep her time filled in the slack months of summer by changing employers. If she chooses this occupation, she is certain to be without employment for several weeks during the year. The seriousness of the situation is intensified in that a third of the girls in the printing trades have come from neighboring towns and are boarding in the city. Few girls are without homes to go to during a long season of unemployment, but when slack periods are scattered through the year, when at any moment the call to resume work may come, the expense of railroad fare looms large, and the advantage of going seems slight. Pay during the busy season is only occasionally sufficient to tide over a period of idleness. Sometimes, it is true, the girl in the printing trades is a casual worker, who wants work only occasionally. Yet, if she is not, if she has set herself to learn her work and to stay at it, three or four years' experience at one occupation does not prevent her from being thrown face to face with the city by periodic unemployment.

A word should be said about the several unions in the printing trades, and their attitude toward women. The two or three women members of the typographical union are no longer in active employment, and the demand for women compositors has been so slight in Pittsburgh that the union has apparently not considered them in relation to the trade at all. The bookbinders have some remnants of a union, but they do not now control any of the shops. They excluded all women from membership who were not finishers, forwarders, or rulers, which was equivalent to excluding women from the union entirely, for women do not hold these positions.

Among the press feeders, women are admitted to membership on the same terms as men, and make a third of the total membership of the Pittsburgh local. At the time that this study was made, the union was struggling to win its strike* based on the eight-hour-day issue, but complicated by considerations of the wage-scale. The union scale has been $9.00 for cylinder press feeders and $8.00 for job press feeders. Possibly of equal if not of greater importance than the scale, is the present frequency of long hours, the periodic unemployment, and the danger of work at ill-guarded machines.

* Eleven women were on the strike rolls during 1907, and in December, 1908, three were still on strike.

CHAPTER XIX

TELEPHONE AND TELEGRAPH OPERATORS

TELEPHONE OPERATORS

WHEN you enter a telephone exchange, you see a half-circle of girls seated at the switchboard, thousands of "jacks," or holes for inserting the plugs in which wires terminate, the intermittent glowing of small lights, quick movements of operators covering the board with connections and clearing it again; you hear a constant low buzz of questions and replies. There may be seven girls, as at the smallest exchanges, or there may be a hundred. All of them are young. Seldom is a telephone girl over twenty; most of them are seventeen or eighteen years of age, nervously flexible, adaptable and able to work at high speed. In some exchanges, the calls are few and easily handled, but in business districts, and even in the more populous residence sections, traffic is heavy and apt to be difficult to deal with, unless the management provides for a greater number of operators when the number of calls increases, and sees to it that the one increase keeps pace with the other.

The switchboard in many ways is the most complicated tool which women use in industry; apparatus and operating methods can well be described at sufficient length to give a working conception of what a day's calls mean to a switchboard girl. To quote S. J. Larned, general superintendent of the Chicago Telephone Exchange:*

"The machinery must be capable of making on an instant's notice any one of nearly seventeen billion possible combinations. The end of the conversation must be accurately noted and the

* Originally published in the "Telephone Exchange." Quoted in "The World To-day," July, 1907, p. 686.

line promptly disconnected. Before connection is made, it must be ascertained that the line asked for is not already carrying another message or temporarily disabled or unavailable for any other reason, ... yet the time consumed in each step of the process of connection must be measured as seconds or even fractions of a second. . . . .

"The answering jack is the point on the switchboard at which contact is made with subscriber's line by an operator, in response to his call. Connection is established between two lines by means of a set of flexible wires or conductors, generally of tinsel, incorporated in a braided linen cord. At each end, the cord terminates in a metal plug, which, when pushed into an answering jack, makes a contact between the subscriber's line and the tinsel conductor of the cord. When, therefore, the two plugs, or the pair of cords, are inserted in the spring jacks of two different lines, those lines are connected together, and in a condition for conversation. Just over every answering jack, in the face of the switchboard, is mounted a small electric lamp, known as the line lamp, which is lighted whenever the telephone receiver at the corresponding subscriber's station is picked up. These answering jacks are placed in the lower part of the switchboard, a certain number before each operator, that number depending upon the use of the telephone, as each operator must answer all of the calls made by the subscribers whose answering jacks are placed directly in front of her. Some lines are used so frequently that but five or ten can be placed in a single operator's position, while other lines may be used so infrequently that more than one hundred can be placed in each position.

"When any line lamp begins to glow, the operator promptly picks up a plug connected with any pair of cords and inserts it in the answering jack corresponding to the lighted lamp. The flexible wires leading from the plug to its mate are also connected to a small switch, called the ringing and listening key. By moving the handle of this ringing and listening key, the operator is able to bring the wires leading from her own telephone set into contact with the wires leading from the plug and consequently into contact with the line wire of the subscriber making the call. The operator is then able to converse with the subscriber and ascertain his

283

wishes. Having received an order to connect his line with any other subscriber's line, the operator inserts the second plug of the pair into a spring jack connected with the called subscriber's line, and by another movement of the handle of the ringing and listening key, brings the line wire of the called subscriber into contact with the wires leading from the ringing generator, the effect being to ring the bell associated with the latter's telephone set and summon him to the telephone. The connection of the second plug with a spring jack of the called subscriber cannot be made with the answering jack of that second subscriber because that answering jack may be in a position a hundred feet away from the position in which the call is made. It is to meet this condition that the inward or multiple branch of the subscriber's line is designed. This branch is connected to spring jacks, exactly like the answering jacks, except that they are arranged to occupy as little space as possible. They are all marked with the call number of the subscribers that they represent, and are arranged in numerical order, and are piled row above row in the vertical face of the board.

"It is possible to bring multiple jacks representing about ten thousand lines within the reach of an operator, and such a portion of the switchboard as contains one jack for each line connected with the office is called a section. Not more than three operators can work at a section of a switchboard and it is necessary to repeat the sections as often as the number of operators employed demands. Each section is the duplicate of every other, each subscriber's line being extended from the multiple jacks in one section to the corresponding multiple jack in the next section and so on throughout the entire length of the switchboard."

For the human bearings of this complicated mechanism and its operation, we have equally authoritative testimony. The recent report of the Royal Commission* on the Bell Telephone Company at Toronto, has so fully covered the conditions of work as they affect the girls employed, that I can perhaps best indicate the Pittsburgh situation by making comparison point by point be-

* Report of the Royal Commission on a dispute respecting hours of employment between the Bell Telephone Company of Canada, Ltd., and Operators at Toronto, Ont. Ottawa, 1907.

tween the two cities, and finally by summarizing the findings of the Commission in so far as these findings are applicable in the same or in greater degree to Pittsburgh.

RATES OF PAY

The main points to be noted are the rates of pay, the intensity of work, the hours of work, the system of reliefs, and the duration of service. In Toronto, under the former five-hour schedule,* the beginning wage of operators was $18 a month, being gradually advanced after three years' service to $25 dollars, and by overtime work mounting at times to $35. In Pittsburgh, after the learner has worked three weeks on probation, the lowest wage paid by one company is $15 a month; overtime is regarded as so regular a requirement that nothing extra is paid for it. The other company pays $ .85 a day to beginners, and a few cents extra for overtime. In time, but by no absolute schedule of advancement, wages are raised to $30, with a possible maximum of $35 to local operators, and $45 to chief supervisors. At the long distance exchange, a newcomer is paid $20 at the start, and is advanced every six months until if her work is good, she is earning $35 at the end of a year and a half. Assistants are paid $45 and the chief supervisor $70. These wages are lower than the wages of girls in the employ of the same company in Chicago or New York, but in spite of the wages, employes are always to be had. The fact that a telephone girl ranks higher socially than a factory operative, together with the fact that the actual work may be learned in three weeks (although speed efficiency is slower to develop), tends to keep the exchanges supplied with applicants, many of whom are unstable and entirely untrained.

INTENSITY OF WORK

From the description of the workings of an exchange, some idea may be gained of the character of the occupation upon which young and untrained applicants enter. To quote from the report of the Royal Commission (p. 48.):

* Some changes were made after the report submitted by the Commission, August 27, 1907.

"The intensity of work, the amount accomplished within a given space of time, or in other words, the speed of operating, will depend first, upon the number of lines which an operator has running into her board and for which she is responsible; secondly, upon the number of phones connecting with the exchange, which of course determines the number of possible connections that can be made; and thirdly, upon the extent to which the different phones are used by subscribers."

This work does not become automatic even after a girl has been long in the service, for each time a call is made, the rows upon rows of multiple jacks must be noted and the count made carefully and quickly, to avoid the unnecessary ringing of bells; when not in action, the operator is yet intent and alert to note the glowing of a lamp in any part of the board. The speed of operating is measured by the time consumed in making a plug connection, that is, connecting one subscriber with another, which should be done in three seconds. This never means that an operator carries a load of 1200 calls per hour. A period of intense application must always be succeeded by a period less intense, although not without nervous strain. It does mean, however, that at intervals the three-second rate must be maintained, the duration of these intervals being dependent on the number of lines per operator, as specified before.

"The average number of calls per operator during the busy hour for the first four months of the year (1906) were 287.6 for Toronto . . . . The operators in Toronto carry a heavier load, answer more calls than operators in cities of the same size elsewhere."* In Pittsburgh, the rate during the busy hour is 250 to 350 calls.

The element of strain is increased sometimes by the excessive height of the switchboard, which varies from eighteen inches to thirty, and occasionally to thirty-six inches where traffic is heavy and the maximum number of lines is admitted to the exchange. At the higher boards, a girl can only with difficulty reach the upper rows of jacks, unless she stands or stretches in her chair, a motion which involves physical strain and causes

* Report of the Royal Commission, pp 47, 52

A Telephone Exchange

delay. Stretching to either side of the three-part section of the switchboard is simplified by the system of team work. A less efficient operator will be placed between two older and more rapid hands whose duty it is to watch the board of the middle girl as well as their own, to help her out with her calls if they come in too fast, and to carry her plugs over on their own boards when they can reach more easily than she. But it must not be supposed that the three-part sections are separate and isolated from each other. The outside girl of one section is the middle girl in the next section. With the group working together and each girl the length of the switchboard having watch of her neighbor's work as well as of her own, the operating force becomes a series of teams, in which weaker girls are supplemented by stronger ones and in which stronger ones are given supplemental work in order to effect speed and economy of service.

The operating force is made up not only of girls at the switchboard, but of supervisors, who continually walk back and forth behind the board to note any carelessness or inefficiency, and of chiefs, who have general supervision of the exchanges. A relief operator has no regular position at the board, but takes the place of one operator after another who is granted her few minutes' rest twice a day. The relief operators are the only extras; therefore, when one of the girls is absent, the force is rearranged either by giving one of the reliefs a regular place temporarily, or by asking some of the day operators to stay overtime. The work of monitors and teachers, separate in some other cities, is here merged with that of the supervisors. For Pittsburgh, the division of work is as follows:

TABLE 30.   DIVISION OF WORK IN PITTSBURGH TELEPHONE
EXCHANGE

Division	No. of Operators
Day operators	505
Night operators	46
Relief operators	69
Supervisors	28
Assistants	10
Chiefs	29
Total	687

The presence of the supervisors, while necessary for the efficiency of the service, often tends to increase the nervous strain upon the girls at the switchboard.

In addition to the rate of speed, the height of the switchboard, the development of team work, the system of surveillance, a few minor points affecting health must be discussed before we pass to the hours of work and the collective effect of all these things on health. One minor point is with regard to the mouthpiece worn by each operator, although changing owners from time to time. In some cases this mouthpiece is sterilized daily, but in others the matter is left to the discretion of the chief operator. In one company, headgear is for the exclusive use of the individual, but in the other, it is an object of common ownership. The seats of the girls are comfortably constructed, but ventilation of the rooms is provided for only in haphazard fashion. The occasional presence of electric fans in some exchanges is an insufficient guarantee that the air in all of them is kept fresh and fit to breathe.

HOURS OF WORK

The effect of intense work with its various elements of strain is heightened if working hours are prolonged. When the company in Toronto proposed the change from a five-hour schedule without reliefs at high pressure, to an eight-hour schedule with discretionary relief, the trade dispute between operators and company followed. The problem of the management is to maintain the telephone service without break during the twenty-four hours. The "traffic curve," or increase of business, mounts to "the peak of the load" at eleven in the morning, and at two-thirty to three-thirty in the afternoon. The business is handled successfully only when the "operating curve" follows both accurately and adequately the "traffic curve" to the time when traffic is heaviest and the rate of calls mounts to the highest point.

The situation is met in all city exchanges by employing relays of operators to come on duty at different hours of the day. For example, from seven to eight-thirty in the morning, each half hour brings on an additional group of girls. At nine, a few girls come and stay until one, returning at five to stay until ten in the evening. This "split trick" as it is called, is a favorite method of dealing with the heavy traffic in mid-morning and mid-afternoon. Other girls come at noon and still others at one o'clock; at ten in the evening the night force comes on to stay until seven a. m. In general, a girl neither changes from one set of hours to another, nor is assigned in rotation to different turns, although after a year's service she may be granted leave to change from a split trick or "skip turn" to hours running straight through the day. Managers find that some girls prefer the lighter work of night hours, and that new girls can without difficulty be assigned to the night force or to the split turn for a period of a year. Sunday work devolves upon the girls as extra service,—a seven-day week once in three weeks for all who serve an unbroken turn of hours, and for split turn operators a seven-day week once in two and a half weeks.

FINDINGS OF THE TORONTO COMMISSION

When called upon to testify at the hearings in Toronto, the twenty-six physicians* (including those who were called on behalf of the telephone company) were practically unanimous, even as to minor details of their evidence. Dr. Robert Dwyer's† testimony was as follows: "Four or five hours would be the maximum of work I would consider for telephone girls on account of the extraordinary tension of most of the faculties that the operator is under; would divide the five hours into two equal periods with an hour and a half at least between. Operators would deteriorate with the five hours' continuous work. Eight hour service divided into two with an interval of one hour would render the work more injurious; twenty minutes' relief in each of the

* "Twenty-six medical practitioners gave evidence before the Commission. Of this number six appeared at the request of the parties, the remainder were subpœnæd at the instance of the Commission from among physicians of the city who it was believed could speak with authority and from a wide range of experience. The physicians subpœnæd were nearly all selected from the medical faculty of the University of Toronto, and were without exception among the leading members of the profession in the city." Report of the Royal Commission, op. cit. p. 65.

† Practicing in Toronto since 1891, for seven years Superintendent of St. Michael's Hospital, now visiting physician; Associate Professor of Clinical Medicine in Toronto University.

four-hour periods would be no material relief, not long enough for the operators to recuperate from exhaustion. Five hours' continuous work would be preferable to either and easier on the operator. I find the service intense all the time. Five hours' continuous service for two or three years would somewhat injure the nervous system of the average operator, the more so, if say, seventeen, eighteen, or nineteen years of age. If load were made so that operator could be working continuously within her ability, it would be better for her than if she was at times waiting, expecting calls—this thing has very far-reaching effects—the Telephone Company nor the doctors who see the operators do not see the final result; after these girls have gone on for four or five years and served the company, and they get married or for other purposes leave, then they turn out badly in their future domestic relations. They break down nervously and have nervous children and it is a loss to the community." This testimony is typical of that given by the other Toronto physicians.

In the face of accumulated evidence of this sort, the Toronto Telephone Company modified its position with regard to the schedule, and adopted a seven-hour day with this arrangement of hours: two hours, then an intermission of half an hour, then an hour and a half, then an intermission of half an hour, and then an hour and a half. In conference, the counsel for the operators, J. Walter Curry, stated with reference to this arrangement: "The opinion of the Committee is that this schedule is more in the interest of their health, but they say further that the seven hours' work is still too heavy a load for them, and it is not such hours of service when it is spread over nine hours that they ought to be asked to work, that the strain is too great upon them for that period."*

In Pittsburgh, where the traffic is no less heavy than in Toronto, and where in some cases there are 180 subscribers to a position, the employes of one company have an eight-hour working day, as against seven in Toronto at present; the employes of the other company have a nine-hour working day, as against seven hours in Toronto. The first company has two twenty-minute reliefs for its operators, one in the morning and one in the afternoon.

* Report of the Royal Commission, p. 92.

The other company has two fifteen-minute reliefs as against half an hour in Toronto.*

DURATION OF SERVICE

We have seen that the intensity of work, as measured by the number of calls per busy hour of the day, is greater in Pittsburgh than formerly in Toronto. The hours of work are longer than either the earlier or later schedule of the Toronto operators. The system of reliefs in Pittsburgh is the system declared by the medical experts before quoted to be totally inadequate. The duration of service in the two cities may serve as a further indication that the degree of strain on Pittsburgh operators is even greater than formerly on operators in Toronto.

The "life of an operator" in Toronto† is two and one-quarter to three years. In Pittsburgh the "life of an operator" was stated to me by the managers to be from eighteen to twenty months in one company, fifteen months in the other. In other words, the duration of service in Pittsburgh is from 44 per cent to 50 per cent less than in Toronto, where the work was declared by a local manager to be done at "the pace which kills." Although some of the girls doubtless leave in order to marry, and although others leave through mere desire for change, the presumption is strong that the difference in duration of service between the two cities is the measure of the difference in intensity of work, hours of work and systems of reliefs; and that this indicates more ill-health and nervous exhaustion among Pittsburgh operators than among the operators in Toronto where the conditions of work called forth the censure of the medical commissioners.

It would seem that the experience of the Bell Telephone Company in one city should not need to be repeated by its own branches or by other companies in other cities. Where the social loss caused by this business policy has been so clearly demon-

---

* A little girl who had wrapped chewing gum and split mica before going into a telephone exchange, said to me in reference to her new experience: "Fifteen minutes' relief isn't enough to rest you. You no sooner lie down than you hear the bell, and you nearly go crazy with the number of calls, and the supervisor at your back and the subscribers often so mean."

† Report of the Royal Commission, p. 34 ff.

strated, public opinion in a local community should demand a change, so far at least in accordance with the laws of health as has been found practicable in Toronto. The human cost to a city is too great if before adopting a change in policy the need and the practicability of which have already been proved elsewhere, it must repeat the same laboratory experiment with the nerve-cells of its young girls.

TELEGRAPH OPERATORS

The main office of a telegraph company impresses the uninitiated observer but does not enlighten him. All that electricity implies of the miraculous seems expressed in the keys of the Morse instruments and in the wizardry of control that connects the operator at the board with his co-worker a thousand miles away. You see men and women, row back of row, receiving, sending, writing messages. You hear the intermittent click of the telegraph keys, the banging of typewriters, and you are conscious of a steady undercurrent of haste, concentration, quick efficiency.

The main and branch offices of the two telegraph companies in Pittsburgh employ 90 women and 198 men. Men and women do the same kind of work, which they learn for the most part through apprenticeship as floor messengers and gradual promotion to manipulation of the keys. If there is a difference in the grade of work assigned, it is that the women are employed more generally at branch offices and at the lighter wires.

Yet although the work done by men and by women in telegraph offices is apparently the same, conditions growing out of the employment of women proved to be the pivot about which swung the strike of the summer of 1907 against one of the Pittsburgh companies. A statement of the claims made by the strikers and the attitude of the company will serve to illustrate some of the more important points with reference to the industry.

In Pittsburgh 38 women and about 150 men were in the union, together making up 75 per cent of the operating force. When the strike was ordered, the union asked that typewriters be furnished by the company, that the sliding scale of wages be abolished, and that a shorter working day be arranged.

The typewriter is part of the operator's equipment. When it was first introduced, a special bonus was offered to employes who would learn to use it, and as its use became general, it proved as valuable to the employes as to the company. Many whose handwriting was poor, and who on this account had been classed below first-class, were able to draw higher pay. Operators, however, are required to buy and to keep in repair their own machines, which is a heavy initial expense.

The demand for a shorter working day grew out of the fact that the telegraph service is continuous through the twenty-four hours. Shifts and relays have to be arranged for among the operating force. The schedule provided for a nine-hour day with overtime service to fill the places of absentees or in cases of emergency, and different turns were assigned to the operators in rotation. The night work schedule was shorter, seven hours and a half; and the "split trick," planned to accommodate the period of heaviest traffic, was eight hours,—ten to two, and five to nine. Once at the key-board, relief was granted for no cause, without specific permission from the traffic chief; and operators complained that at times they would have to stay at their posts all day without being relieved, and when relieved would frequently be allowed only twenty minutes at noon. Sunday work was assigned to different members of the force as extra work with pay based on seven hours as a full day.

But important as these points were, abolition of the sliding scale was the cardinal demand. The grievance referred to as the "sliding scale" was the outcome of alleged differences in the work done by men and by women, and of resultant unfair discrimination. Managers and operators as a rule agree that the lesser physical strength of women tells against them after several years of light wrist and finger motions; that because of this lesser strength, women have neither the speed nor the accuracy of men; and that they get "glass arm," a nervous inability to work, more frequently. On the other hand, both managers and operators agree that although women work for the most part on light wires, the quantity of work done by given operators is fairly well equalized, and that the difference between a light and a heavy wire is less than would be supposed. Whereas an operator on a heavy wire does sending only, or receiving only, the operator on a light wire does both sending and receiving, or else works by a system of "floats" whereby three wires are handled by two operators. Yet the potential ability of men operators to do heavier work than women is reflected in the differences in wages. One company paid $30, $35, and $44 a month to women in branch offices, and $62 to women in the main office. The other company paid two-thirds of its women employes $30 to $55 a month, and one-third of its women employes from $55 to $75 a month. It was charged that the former company paid its salaries on the basis of individual bargaining, and not on the basis of kind or quantity of work done; that a man who had earned $82.50 on a heavy wire would be superseded by a woman at $75; and that a man who had been receiving $75 would be superseded by a woman at $62. By this system, the rates of payment for given wires were being lowered. Although the work might tell on women sooner than on men, and although they might in some cases be less efficient than men, they were yet sufficiently capable to supersede men at a lower rate of pay. They were lending themselves to a scheme for cutting wages.

The strike was broken in the fall, in part through the agency of unorganized women. Most of the women went out when the men went out, but a few of them stayed in, and others who had formerly been in the employ of the company were impressed for the occasion. In one point, however, the strike was not without effect. Conditions in the company against which the strike was chiefly directed remained unchanged, but the other company granted a 10 per cent increase in wages by which some of the women operators are now earning as much as the men can earn at the heavy wires. Two-thirds of the women employes of this company now earn from $33 to $60.50 a month, and one-third of the women earn from $60.50 to $82.50 a month. This scale would seem to show that this company does not discriminate against women nor force competition between women and men, but pays equally for equal work.

CHAPTER XX

MERCANTILE HOUSES

SEVEN thousand five hundred women were employed in twenty-four Pittsburgh stores in 1907. No other one occupation in which women work in groups has so large a following in the city. No other has within four thousand as many women. As many as 1900 were employed in one store, wrapping, checking, selling goods, or, on the upper floors, engaged at subsidiary occupations, such as making draperies, trimming hats, or altering cloaks to the wearer's size. Occasionally, even a laundry is part of a department store, or again a kitchen with a group of red-cheeked Polish maids preparing vegetables. Or again, the whole force may number no more than nine, and the girls may step from one counter to the next.

No attempt has been made to cover the small stores in which five women or less are employed. What is said of the large stores will be in the main applicable to them, although to a degree they are a problem in themselves. It is the large stores primarily,— the knot in the business centre of the city and the scattered ones in the East End, and on the main streets of the North and South Side,—with reference to which statistics of employes and of conditions have been obtained.

In discussing these mercantile houses, I shall not speak of obvious sanitary needs in many of them, common also to many different industries, and within the jurisdiction of the health officers. Another chapter will treat of welfare work as such. Here, discussion may be confined to conditions which grow out of "clerking" as distinct from other women's occupations.

A store must aim not merely to supply needs, but to create them; to meet the idea in the customer's mind, to profit by the indolence of other people's thought-processes, and to stimulate fancies by adroit suggestion. All these fall within the merchant's province, along with his heavy commercial and administrative responsibilities. They are his problem of sales psychology in dealing with the public. He faces a different problem in dealing with the women who make up the sales staff,—from the cash girl who has just entered the store, to the experienced saleswoman. A review of store conditions in Pittsburgh will not show that the merchants as a whole have addressed themselves to this second problem with any such imagination and measure of success as characterizes their approach to the first.

The cash girl may be advanced to the position of wrapper or stock girl. If she is a wrapper, she will begin to feel her responsibility for maintaining a standard of work. An exclusive store in part maintains its exclusiveness by distinctive paper and seal, and even a more plebeian store gains many a customer by the care and attractiveness with which its parcels are wrapped. I was told by a manager that his wrapper girl was one of the most important employes in the drapery salesroom and worth at least $5.00 a week.

How quickly a bright cash girl is allowed to sell goods will depend somewhat on her size. Other things being equal, we are apt to fancy a tall person more efficient than a short one, and the burden of proof is on a short person who is young as well. This holds true of salesgirls as of mightier people. A short young person of timid appearance will scarcely convince us of her familiarity with her stock, and if we too are timid, and need to be encouraged to buy, we are likely to turn aside and go the other way. For speedy advancement, the cash girl needs to be well built and usually tall for her age, as well as quick to learn.

She may show aptitude for clerical work and be turned aside into one of the offices, without ever working on the floor at all. The office work is like any office work. The other special departments, however, that are not in touch with customers, draw their recruits not from among the cash girls, who indeed know little of their existence, but from women in factory trades outside.

SPECIAL DEPARTMENTS

The special departments which are not in touch with the customers are sometimes laundries and kitchens; in other cases, drapery or awning workrooms. Numerically, these by-employments are usually not important. Work in the alteration room, however, is sufficiently distinct to warrant pausing long enough to describe it. In 1907, 971 alteration hands on cloaks and suits, or trimmers of "Parisian" millinery, were employed in Pittsburgh department stores. They produce by wholesale, but after a fashion different from that in a manufacturing house. A characteristic room of this type is one on a twelfth floor, which I visited in the midst of the spring season. Bare and whitewashed, with windows on two sides, the hugeness of the room, which was a block wide and long, made artificial light necessary throughout. Of the 115 people employed, only five or six were men. From the first of February until June, and from the middle of August to December, the power-driven needles whirr back and forth for more than ten hours a day. At eight o'clock the hands come in and work, with an interval for lunch, until half-past five. Then they go down to the lunch room and come up again at six, with a stretch of two and a half hours in the evening. They work hard while they can, for in the dull season they lose at least two months by periodic unemployment. Some have been dressmakers before, hand workers whose business it was to know how to cut and fit a garment. They put all that behind them when they enter an alteration room. If a girl has done only individual work before, the trade has to be learned again. The needles are power-driven. Changes are chalked on the goods, and suits are turned out wholesale for unknown customers. Rarely is an apprentice employed. Busier than in a wholesale house, the managers of the workroom have no place except for those with experience, to whom they pay $10 a week during the season. "What's the use of paying more?" said one. "You can get a fine worker for $10, who knows how to do anything you want."

Similarly, the girls in the millinery workrooms, like those in wholesale millinery houses, have their seasons of work. Except that some hats are altered and some are trimmed to order, the work is much the same as elsewhere in the trade, and the larger part of the time is given to trimming hats ready-made and ready-to-wear. The trimmers, like the alteration hands on suits, have a trade which for years they may have followed under other circumstances, until chance brought them into the group of department store employes. The drapery and awning makers, too, are not apprenticed in the stores. Without factory experience in the use of material and tools, they could not obtain their positions. All these trained and taught hands in the department stores, however, are in the minority, numbering 14 per cent of the women employes.

The salesgirls, untrained and untaught, are in the overwhelming majority. Of them, there were 6,534 in 1907. It is perhaps stretching a point to say that the material upon which they have to work is the pliant and receptive customer, or at other times, the irritable and impatient customer. It remains true that the tools at their hand are the cases of stock behind the counter, the counter displays, and the books or cases of samples. Equally true is it, that aisles and counters and departments make up the workrooms of these girls. As in the case of the factory industries, our first concern may well be the prime facts of the physical work-plant, hours and wages.

STORE CONSTRUCTION

Economy of floor space, ventilation and other elements in store construction have a direct bearing on health. To an unusual degree these Pittsburgh stores are in parts of the city where land is expensive, and available ground space limited. Pittsburgh's business centre is wedged by hills into a fan-shaped piece of land at the intersecting point of the Allegheny and Monongahela rivers. Here office buildings, stores and railroad terminals are crowded together. Like the other business enterprises, the stores have followed the slope of the hills. Some have succeeded in getting a flat site, only to have basements and cellars threatened by the spring floods. Others have built farther from the river, following an ascending street which opens impartially on first floor front and second floor rear of the store. The rear of the first floor is, therefore, below the street level and would be dark except for electric lights. Yet this rear of the store, far from being unused, is usually in these stores an active centre of business. Clearly, if this half-underground area is to be a healthful place either for customers who stay there a short time, or for sales people who stay until the release bell rings at night, provision for ventilation is essential. A fan or two in summer is an inefficient remedy. The dead air that tires the casual shopper weighs unrelieved on brain and nerves of the salesgirl who must breathe it the day through.

The unwisdom of using a tunnel-like salesroom is surpassed only by the use of a cellar workplace, in which not even one end is open toward the light. Some stores use their basements for stockrooms only; others use them as the workplaces of their cashiers. Five stores, however, use their basements as salesrooms. In these underground compartments which are without any openings to the outside air, 75 girls were employed in 1907 to sell goods in Pittsburgh. An electric fan in such a case is wholly ineffectual, either to drive out impure air or let fresh air in.

This economy of space entails a serious physical drain. That the effects of it are not spectacular should render us no less quick to recognize them and to apply our American inventiveness toward developing a better method of shop arrangement and ventilation. Upper floors, too, although in lesser degree, are many of them in need of more thorough ventilating systems. To an unwarranted extent, reliance is placed by Pittsburgh store managers on the chance opening of a window and occasional openings on shafts to the roof, yet obviously the rooms are too wide for such a system to be effectual, and most of the salespeople are at too great a distance from the vent¹ :tors for them to profit by this method. Since adequate ventilation is as yet only half insisted upon in churches and courts and schools, we can perhaps be tolerant of the backwardness hitherto of stores in this respect. Yet we can scarcely continue to be so indefinitely. The stores have a direct economic advantage to be gained by fresh air. We expect of commercial enterprises an alert adaptation of what is new and serviceable.

A word should be said about two stores which have been built up by throwing several smaller stores together. When all the component parts are on the same level, it is not easy to do this successfully, but when they are on different levels of a hill, difficulties are increased. The network of small stairways at right angles, the series of elevators, the arrangement of counters, and the crowding of much merchandise into small space in these stores, make effective ventilation even more difficult.

SEATS

Health and efficiency in a measure go hand in hand. The kind of efficiency that results from a clear brain and physical buoyancy, the kind that even an untrained salesgirl may have, is sapped constantly by the breathing of vitiated air. It is sapped, too, by needless physical weariness, whether this results from counters built so close that the girls have not room to pass each other, and even when standing are cramped and uncomfortable, from the firm's neglect to provide seats, or from the tacit understanding, of all too frequent occurrence, that seats when provided are not for use. This tacit understanding at times finds expression in definite rules with penalties for non-observance.

Insistence by managers that the girls shall be found standing at their posts, seems a primitive way to recognize the psychological value of a welcoming smile. Horses that are checked up to appear spirited, hardly counterfeit the free lift of a well-bred horse's head. Girls untrained in the ways of their trade, at work often under conditions distinctly unhealthful, are expected to counterfeit attentiveness by constantly standing. At times during the day they are not waiting on customers. At times, they have no stock to arrange and are obliged only to be at their places. That any should have always to stand seems obviously unnecessary, and has become a point of specific legal attack in states that have built up a factory law. The law of Pennsylvania* requires that "every person, firm or corporation employing girls or adult women, in any establishment, shall provide suitable seats for their use, and shall permit such use when the employes are not necessarily engaged in active duties."

The ratio which the number of seats bears to the number of girls in the stores is sufficient answer as to how the law is observed. In three of the best known Pittsburgh stores, the situation in 1907 was as follows:

* Act May 2, 1905, Sec. 7, P. L. No. 226.

TABLE 31.—NUMBER OF SEATS SUPPLIED FOR SALESWOMEN

Store A:	1st floor	.	.	.	.	.	500 girls;	19 seats.
	2d floor	.	.	.	.	.	300 girls;	12 seats.
	3d floor	.	.	.	.	.	75 girls;	4 seats.
	4th, 5th and 6th floors	.	.	.	.	.	Alteration, millinery, and other workrooms.	
Store B:	1st floor	.	.	.	.	.	400 girls;	16 seats.
	2d floor	.	.	.	.	.	175 girls;	10 seats.
Store C:	1st floor	.	.	.	.	.	600 girls;	32 seats.
	2d floor	.	.	.	.	.	10 girls;	no seats.
	3d floor	.	.	.	.	.	400 girls;	3 seats.
	4th floor	.	.	.	.	.	10 girls;	no seats.
	5th floor	.	.	.	.	.	15 girls;	1 seat.

With reference to a smaller store, I find the following note: "Two floors used for salesrooms. Second floor, 6 girls, 3 seats. Girls allowed to use seats on this floor, but not on the first floor, where there are 39 girls, 11 seats." Ten stores have no seats at all, and in two stores there is one seat each.

In contrast to all these, two stores observe not only the letter but the spirit of the law, providing in one case no less than four seats behind each counter, and in the other, two seats for each counter. Among the other stores, on the contrary, whole sections of the floor are without a seat accessible to the salesgirls, or at counters fitted out with one seat there are perhaps a dozen girls to share it. When 19 seats are allotted to 500 girls, or 12 seats to 300 girls, there is no need to ask whether in the eyes of the law this is a provision of "suitable seats" for the female employes.

The policy of the management as to the use of seats, when provided, often differs on first and second floors. Because the girls on the first floor are seen by the customer first, it is felt that they especially need, by always standing, to create an impression of attentiveness. In consequence, first floor girls are expected not to sit; while, if there comes a spare moment on the second floor, the girls may be seated without danger of reprimand. The head of stock in one department told me that if a girl were seen sitting, she would be discharged at once. Acknowledged rules against the use of seats are few, but in their place is the tacit understanding in seventeen of the stores that a girl has to stand if she is to retain her position.

HOURS OF WORK

The daily working hours in fourteen stores are from eight to five-thirty, and in eight stores from eight to six. Two stores are open not only Saturday evenings, but evenings during the week as well, until nine and ten o'clock. In the first of these all the girls are obliged to stay every night, but in the other the schedule is so worked out that each girl is on duty but two nights a week beside Saturday. When she works at night, she does not come until ten the next day. A typical schedule would be:

TABLE 32.—HOURS SCHEDULE OF SALESWOMEN IN A SMALL
MERCANTILE HOUSE

Monday	8 a. m.– 6 p. m.
Tuesday	8 a. m.– 9 p. m.
Wednesday	10 a. m.– 6 p. m.
Thursday	8 a. m.– 9 p. m.
Friday	10 a. m.– 6 p. m.
Saturday	8 a. m.–10 p. m.

Total, 57 working hours a week.

The time of year when long hours are felt most is before Christmas or during stock-taking time in January. It seems unbusinesslike that these night hours should be counted in as part of the week's work; that the girls should not have the option either of staying or of going; or if they do stay, the opportunity to earn extra pay in proportion to their time.

Whether as a matter of health they should be allowed to work for the hours that the Christmas trade sometimes demands is another consideration.* One store has no Christmas overtime. Its trade apparently has not lessened because of its refusal to depart from its standard working day, but the others have ten

---

* The Pennsylvania Statute, Act May 2nd, 1905, Sec. 3, p. 8, No. 226, which was in effect when this investigation was made, reads in part as follows: "And provided further, That retail mercantile establishments shall be exempt from the provisions of this Section (i. e., a 60-hour working week) and a 12-hour working day permitted on Saturdays of each week, and during a period of 20 days, beginning with the 5th day of December and ending with the 24th day of the same month: Provided, That during the said 20 days preceding the 24th day of December, the working hours shall not exceed ten hours per day, or sixty hours per week."

As might be inferred, this confused and unmeaning clause has proved ineffectual as a barrier to overtime.

The law which goes into effect January 1, 1910, provides for a 58-hour days or two weeks of night work. Six of them have a double shift, an arrangement whereby the girls are on duty alternate evenings, coming later on the days following nights at work. Seventeen stores had no double shift the Christmas season of 1907, but required a working week of from 72 to 84 hours; seven gave extra pay in some form. In one case, "We go down and get what we like from the fountain," the girls said; in others, $ .25 or $ .35 was paid for "supper money." This bears no proportion to the girl's weekly wages or to the estimated worth of her time, but simply enables the management to avoid appearing to require work without pay. One of the stores, a five and ten cent store, by the way, gives a bonus of $5.00 to each girl at Christmas time, after a year's service. This bonus is increased in amount yearly until the maximum sum of $25 is reached, after five years, service. The other small stores of this name not only give their employes no bonus, but do not even give supper money for the nights at work.

It is in part the youth of the employes, in part their inability to bargain, and their lack of cohesion, that have helped to make an arrangement of this sort customary. Petty exactions in individual instances, that are manifestly unjust, could not exist any more than overtime without pay, were the girls to understand their bargaining power as a compact group. In one store, for instance, belated employes are docked a cent a minute, and the girl who is late half an hour is docked half a day's pay. In this same store, only two girls are paid as much as $5.00 a week. The rest are earning $3.50 and $4.00. Christmas week, all the girls were given $6.00; but the next week, when trade was slack, the girls state they were all paid only $2.75. Two of the girls complained and the manager said, "Give them their regular wages and let them go." They were discharged.

It is not at all necessary to go outside of Pittsburgh to find a higher standard, both as to the physical conditions of the sales-

---

week and for a 10-hour day for girls under eighteen. It excludes them from all night work (after 9 p. m.), making no exception for mercantile houses at Christmas time.

Ten hours is the legal day for all boys and girls under eighteen, by the new law, and boys under sixteen may not work after 9 p. m. except in glass-houses. These provisions should in effect close all stores at 9 p. m. at any time.

rooms and as to the justness of work relations.   Points of excellence
are to be found in several stores, and in one, that marginal all-
around excellence which sets it in a class by itself, ahead of its
competitors.   It exemplifies this higher standard at each point
under discussion; in the comprehensiveness of its ventilating
system; in its observance of the spirit of the law in providing an
average of four seats to a counter for its employes; in the fact
that it has no Christmas overtime and is consequently free from
the imputation that it asks unpaid-for work; and finally, in its
wage standard.   The manager says that salesgirls are paid on
the basis approximately of 5 per cent of their total sales.   Work
at counters where goods are cheapest, such as the notion counter,
is paid at the lowest rates; an employe of little experience can be
used, as sales are quickly and easily made.   A girl who shows
ability is advanced to a counter where she can earn more, and
theoretically there is no limit to the increase in wages of a capable
girl.   In practice, it works out that approximately 100 cash
girls and wrapper girls are paid from $4.00 to $6.00, and that
700 saleswomen are paid $7.00.   No saleswoman who is worth
less will be retained.   At the lace counter, in the cloak and suit
department, and here and there where the selling of goods requires
experience, 100 girls are paid from $8.00 to $10, and sometimes
$15, in the case of a head of stock.

WAGES

How far this system of payments exceeds the rates which
are paid in the general trade in Pittsburgh is shown by the fact
that in the twenty-four stores as a whole the number of women
and girls in the lowest wage group is overwhelmingly large.
Five thousand five hundred and ten of the women employes, 73
per cent of those in the trade, were earning from $3.00 to $6.00 in
1907; 1555 women were earning $7.00; 475 were earning from $7.00
or $8.00 to $10 or $12.   These wages do not go so far as the same
wages in a factory, for the period of unemployment in summer is
likely to be longer.   Saleswomen are laid off for from two to six
weeks, and often for much longer in the cloak and suit departments.   The total yearly income is therefore lower than the in-

come estimated from what is paid by the week. Then, too, the shop girl must dress better than the factory girl. A clean shirt-waist and a trim skirt are part of her stock in trade, and her expenses for clothing and laundry are correspondingly high.

Shop girls without friends or family ties are few. Shop girls to whom the family tie means an additional burden, are many; and there are many more who, with family ties and friends, are yet dependent upon themselves for support. Among girls in these circumstances, the temptation is ever present to lay hold of the opportunities which employment in a mercantile house offers to increase their income in unsocial ways. Low wages and the desire for pleasure incite the factory girl, but the shop girl is spurred in addition by her association with people of a higher standard of living than hers. Moreover, the stores are avenues through which any who will may come. The larger stores are in the busiest part of town, and the girls are free at noon to meet men on the streets. Without attracting attention, men can come into the stores and talk with the girls, and these conditions may exist not only without the encouragement of the management but even without its cognizance. Where the store is particular as to the mode of life of its employes and makes a point of dismissing those who offend against its standards, the percentage of girls who lead irregular lives is unquestionably lower than in stores where such conduct is tolerated or, as sometimes happens, is encouraged. Yet from among the girls themselves, from those who deal with them, and from police sources, my information was both explicit and general enough to indicate that in the moral jeopardy of shop girls lies one of the most widespread and serious social problems of the women-employing trades. This problem was beyond the scope of this investigation, but a few of the cases that came to my knowledge may serve to illustrate the as yet unanswered call to the best forces in the community to address themselves to it with courage and understanding.

Rose ——— was employed at the ribbon counter. She had a mother and two sisters dependent upon her, and her mother was always urging her for more money. She began while still in the store to "make money on the side." The management discovered this and dismissed her. She left for a city in Ohio; went into a house of prostitution there from which she sends her mother money. Her wages at the ribbon counter were $6.00 a week.

Vera ———— is twenty years old. Four years ago she was employed as a salesgirl at $3.50 a week. After a year she left for another store where she was employed as a cashier at a salary of $10 a week, for making concessions to her employer. After two years she left the store for a house of prostitution.

Jennie ———— came to Pittsburgh from Akron, Ohio. She had no friends in the city and was obliged to be self-supporting. She obtained a position at $6.00 a week as a saleswoman. After five months in the store, she consented to be kept in an apartment in the East End. She still keeps her position in the store.

Emma ———— was employed in a waist department at $5.00 a week. She had no friends in the city, but sent money home to her people and paid board. At the end of six months, she became an occasional prostitute; after a year was discharged by the firm.

These girls are at the start not different from other girls. Their cases indicate simply that the pressure of low wages combined with the opportunities of a department store result in a social problem that cannot be ignored. Further investigation would be needed to disclose the extent of it. Some employers are generally reputed among salesgirls to assume that their women employes secure financial backing from outside relationships, and knowingly pay wages that are supplementary rather than wages large enough to cover the cost of a girl's support. Questions asked of girls seeking employment cannot be otherwise interpreted. In other cases, probably in the majority, the rate of wages is fixed not by any reckoning on the part of the employer with unsocial conduct, but by the tradition of the occupation. It is assumed that shop girls are only partly self-supporting and need only work for pin-money. The social position of the shop girl is in consequence higher than that of the factory girl, and the shop girl loses financially through her desire for social esteem. The very popularity of work in a store is another reason why the rate of wages remains low. Girls who come to Pittsburgh from small towns nearby would lose caste if they worked in a factory, but they can work in a store and keep the respect of their friends. Likewise many a workingman's daughter who wants more money than her parents can give her, and the social standing held by well-dressed employes in the stores, looks for a position as a saleswoman. Some stores have a waiting list of applicants, and the girls, when they get positions, are loath to give them up. As one girl said, "The fact is, it 's so hard to get a job anywhere that when you do get one, you hang on to it for fear you might be months getting another." Competition for positions in the stores is indeed often so keen as to create a shortage of workers in the factory districts, much more in domestic help. It is all part of the natural craving of American girls to get ahead; a part of the psychology of some of the most creative and progressive tendencies in our national life, which in other spheres we applaud. Yet the fact remains that, for the vast bulk of salesgirls, the wages paid are not sufficient for self-support; and where girls do not have families to fall back on, some go under-nourished, some sell themselves. And the store-employment which offers them this two-horned dilemma is replete with opportunities which in gradual, easy, attractive ways beckon to the second choice; a situation which a few employers not only seem to tolerate, but to encourage.

TRADE TRAINING

Yet, while the factors entering into the wage situation in the department stores are thus complicated along custom-hardened lines, it seems not impossible to hope for the gradual working out of a system of payments on a sounder economic basis. Recognition of the commercial value of trade training is undoubtedly a first step. The exceptional girls are quick to pick up knowledge, or to profit by the hints of older employes. They become self-made saleswomen. Their hard-won proficiency sets a standard, which shows the business advantage of bringing out in the girls who come to take places beside them, with least loss of time, such capacity as will sell goods well, and earn fair wages for doing it.

Floorwalkers and inspectors ordinarily do not supply their

saleswomen with a knowledge of the tools, an understanding of the goods. Their business is to oversee the daily events in the store, and for the previous training of the girls they can assume no responsibility. Neither do they teach a new girl, except by a few general directions, in what way her stock is distinctive and how she is to offer it. She is not often a person sufficiently experienced in buying to be herself a judge of quality. She repeats what she has been told, but she cannot follow the goods to the customer's home where fabric has the actual test of wear.

It is beginning to be felt that salesmanship, like many other occupations, is not an instinctive art, but an art that can be taught and understood. One Pittsburgh store, the same in which we found the physical conditions of work best, has started a course in salesmanship for those of its employes who have the ambition to study out of hours. Ninety people are in the morning class, and 36 in the evening class; all of them have home-work and text-book lessons. The women who go through that course will give more valuable service and know something of their industrial value; they cannot fail to have a conception of their responsibility to the enterprise as a whole and of justice in industrial relations. Should this movement grow among Pittsburgh stores, inevitably we should see developed an esprit de corps which would go far to remedy small tyrannies, and to secure fair conditions of hours and wages. This women's work, as a whole, in Pittsburgh would be on a new plane, more profitable to the management, and more practicable to young women as a means of livelihood.

With salesmanship training should go some system by which a girl's earnings increase with her interest and efficiency in her work.

THE SOCIAL LIFE OF WORKING WOMEN

Lunch Room for Workers in a Stogy Factory

CHAPTER XXI

IN THE FACTORIES

THE very grouping of 600 women in a single building under one management for ten hours a day, suggests possibilities for congregate recreative activity. Here is a centre of association about which could be built such healthful occupation and interest as would renew the strength and freshen the mind that days of monotonous toil have dulled.

THE NOON HOUR

For such social activity the noon hour might well be a point of departure. Effective rest, as well as recreation, demands such an interval in the middle of the day. But in the Pittsburgh factories the noon "hour" is in most cases only half an hour long. The law* permits the time at noon to be shortened "for good cause" by the chief factory inspector if the closing hour is correspondingly earlier, and usage has interpreted this "good cause" as the wish of a majority of the employes. Judging by appearances, employes have very generally wanted an earlier closing hour. Factories with the full time at noon are so few as to be noticeable in the industrial group. One girl who told me about the change in her own workingtime, was asked why she did not care to take the full hour. "Well," she said, "we have no place to eat but just at our benches, and we get sick of the odor and the look of the room, and want to get away from it as soon as we can. Of course, if we had any place to go to at noon, or if we didn't always stay in the same room, it might be different. We don't think of it as noon to rest in. We just know that it doesn't take us an hour to eat lunch, and we want to get to work again and get through as soon as we can." Such are the motives

* Act May 2, 1905, Sec. 9, P. L. No. 226.

that lead the majority of the employes, when consulted, to vote for shortening the rest time.

But the law of the body is not modifiable at the wish of a majority of the employes, nor in the service of industrial convenience. The framers of factory legislation in Pennsylvania in declaring for an hour's rest at noon, had in mind the need of the body to reënforce its strength after five hours of work. For proper assimilation of food, too, there must be an interval of rest before resuming work. In other words, the period necessary for eating a cold lunch at the work bench is by no means sufficient to enable the worker, with nervous loss restored, to go back when the whistle sounds in the afternoon as good a worker as when the whistle sounded in the morning. The time of rest may be reduced, but it will be reduced at the expense of the employes' strength and efficiency.

LUNCH ROOMS

Yet, even with the hour cut short, were lunch rooms more general, there might be spontaneous development of recreation groups. Rest is undoubtedly more complete with a change of surroundings, especially a change from an atmosphere of work. From the viewpoint of health it may almost be said that no large plant is fully equipped unless lunch rooms for men and women are provided apart from the general workroom. This need has won only a limited recognition. It is a gain, perhaps, when a space is set apart for a lunch room, even if that space is inadequate. Yet we should scarcely be willing to stop at that, or to think that the need is filled if a dark, ill-ventilated corner is set with tables and turned over to the girls at noon. That is a lunch room reduced to its lowest terms. It is a relief from the workroom atmosphere, but not a place for healthful recreation. I know one such place which is wholly useless in summer because it is so near the ovens that the most elaborate system of ventilation would be insufficient to dispel the heat, and not even the rudiments of ventilation have been installed. In contrast, a North Side laundry has set aside a bright, sunny section of the building; there are attractive dishes, tables covered with white cloths, comfortable chairs. The noon interval is an hour and a half.

The management considers it worth while to give the girls this time so that they may return to their work with energy. Two of the stogy factories and the cork factory have good lunch rooms.

Of the mercantile houses, it is not possible to speak in general terms. Thirteen out of the 27 mercantile houses which employ over five saleswomen, have a space set apart for a lunch room, and seven of these serve light lunch at cheap rates. But the conditions in these rooms vary as greatly as the stores themselves. In one store, whose employes number 2000, the lunch room is in a totally unventilated basement. A space near the cashier's desk is boarded off and lighted by one glaring electric globe, while the long table with a few benches is expected to serve for 1300 women. This room has acted not as a socializing but as a disintegrating force. In another case, some twenty bare and unscrubbed tables have been placed on an upper floor. At either side of the tables are greasy benches without backs. The dark monotony of the room is unbroken, and the row of windows at one side is obscured by packing cases. The lunch room in a neighboring store has all the desirable features that this one lacks. The furnishings are attractive; there are small tables of weathered oak and comfortable chairs. An inexpensive lunch is served at nominal rates, and light and fresh air are abundant.

Although there is only this limited recognition of the social possibilities of factory grouping, other outgrowths from the congregate employment of men and women have won a certain popularity. These spring chiefly from a kindly feeling on the part of the management toward the working force, or from recognition of the value of the advertisement gained by welfare work. In one case they show a far-sighted business policy.

A rest room for employes who are ill is provided in one or two of the larger factories, and four of the mercantile houses have such a room, in two cases arranging for a physician to be in attendance at certain times of the day. A more popular philanthropy, irrespective of lunch or rest rooms, is the furnishing of coffee for the force at noon. Coffee, with its spur to nervous energy, is unquestionably what most of the girls wish. Few of them understand the difference between stimulant and nourishment.

WELFARE WORK

I can only mention these minor provisions looking toward the health or comfort of the employes. In two establishments, however, the system of welfare work is extensive. One of these, a factory, has a force of 600 girls. They are given excellent workrooms, clean, well-ventilated, well-constructed. The stairways are marble, and on the walls are engravings of action and battle and plunging horses. The stained-glass windows in the halls display mottoes about work and industry. In the auditorium is a large painting, rich in color, of Christ before Pilate. The girls are often summoned to the auditorium at noon to hear an address by some visitor or to sing; in this case they have an hour's recess, instead of half an hour. This does not involve financial loss to the day girls, because they are paid their day rates in any case, but the piece workers lose just so much in possible earnings. A roof garden for summer use has been erected above one of the buildings. There is a natatorium, with schedule so arranged that most of the girls may have a chance to swim once or twice a week after hours. The dressing rooms in the general factory building are beautifully kept, and the rest room is well equipped with necessities for those who are ill. The large lunch room, filled with long tables, can seat all the 600 girls at once, and for one cent a day, each girl is furnished with coffee, milk and sugar. In one corner stands a piano, and the walls are bright with pictures. Throughout the building everything is bright and trim and clean. The girls wear fresh blue and white aprons and trim white caps. They are as well-kept in appearance as the place in which they work.

Excellent building construction, thorough cleanliness, dressing rooms, rest rooms, natatoria, are the tools of welfare work. Wherever they are at the service of the employes, we have reason to be glad. Yet in our enthusiasm for these tools, we must not forget that their value is to a great extent dependent on the conditions of work and wage which accompany them. Good in and of themselves, their service is of little effect if it serves merely to obscure facts of low wages and a high speed rate. Pleasant surroundings compensate neither for excessive work, nor for

314

RECREATION ROOM IN THE MCCREARY STORE

LUNCH ROOM OF THE KEYSTONE LAUNDRY

a fundamental deficit in the financial basis of self respect. When higher wages are paid, even if fewer gifts are given, women employes have the precious opportunity to work out their own lives, with their margin above a living wage. Speed pressure and a low rate of pay destroy nervous vitality, and keep the standard of life near the margin of degradation. It is true that a girl untrained to habits of systematic attention, needs to be taught a standard pace for commercial efficiency. There is a point, however, beyond which the pace becomes excessive. A girl who works at so high speed that she cannot change her position, or turn her head, is unable to appreciate an engraving on the wall. The girl who cuts onions at $ .75 a day, cares very little for the polished upright piano in the lunch room, or for the roof garden which is reached only after a hard climb. Some necessities we need in order to appreciate luxuries. The pace of the machine is the primary nervous stimulus to a working girl, and if that pushes her too hard, especially if her returns are low, she is likely to be ungrateful for cleanliness and fresh air, incapable of enjoying recreation.

Less elaborate, and developed after a somewhat different policy, is the work of one department store. First of all, you note that the quality of the air is different there from that in the streets outside, or even in other places indoors. For first floor and basement all the air is passed through a solid sheet of water, its grime and smokiness washed out before it is sent through shafts for the people on these two floors to breathe. Then too, you note the surprising cleanliness of everything, not only in the parts of the store where customers go, but in places that they do not ordinarily see. Behind each counter are seats, seats which the employes are expected to use. On the upper floors are ample dressing rooms, and a lunch room with mission chairs and tables, dignified and harmonious in its furnishings, but bright with sunlight. Here the girls are free to bring their own lunch, or to buy at cost the same things that are served in the customers' dining room. There is a hospital room, with a trained nurse in charge. The recreation room, with its smooth floor, its quiet furnishings, its piano and books, gives opportunity for making the noon hour really a rest hour. The social secretary visits employes who are ill, and is always in her place upstairs at noon to talk with and help the girls who may need her.

Employes in a mercantile house, if themselves content, convey an atmosphere of satisfaction to customers. In adopting a policy, not of "doing good," but of "making the employes happy, to the end that they may give efficient service," the management repudiates the idea that it is philanthropic. It recognizes that many acts called philanthropic are agencies, if one sees far enough, for upbuilding a successful business. Fundamental to the art of selling goods, are the poise, the courtesy, the spontaneous readiness and pleasure with which the seller meets the possible customer. Little by little they arouse in the buyer a similar readiness and pleasure. A far-sighted business management realizes that this poise and readiness must be built from within. There must be a sufficient number of employes to handle the trade. The working force must have faith in the firm's sincerity and genuine goodwill; it must be paid wages high enough to live on; and must have rest time, and a place in which to rest. The tools of welfare work in this case are much the same although less elaborate than in the other. But the informing spirit is different. While it is true that store work calls for a more intelligent grade of girl, the basic fact is that this store has set a standard for the wages of saleswomen in the district. The force is kept to its work, not by a system of speeding which taxes nervous energy to its utmost, but through the influence of the firm's kindly criticism, unfailing courtesy and goodwill.

THE EXTENSION WORK OF THE Y. W. C. A.

In concluding this discussion of the social possibilities in factories and shops, a word should be said about the extension work of the Young Women's Christian Association. In eight factories, a fifteen-minute noon meeting is held once a week, from October until the last of May. Before the opening of these meetings in the fall, and for several weeks after their close, personal visits are made by the secretaries in the attempt to develop a friendly acquaintance in the neighborhood. Character building, rather than social betterment, is the point emphasized by the extension workers. Sometimes they have a reading, and sometimes calisthenic exercises; in five factories there is a piano and an organized chorus of the girls. Very often, this extension work has been a means for the immediate improvement of conditions, as, for instance, in four factories which have established lunch rooms so that there might be a place where the secretaries could hold their meetings. The time allowed for singing and calisthenics, and for reading, is inordinately short, but it is at any rate a good beginning toward making the noon rest constructive.

To sum up. Opportunities for wholesome social life among working women are few. In factories or stores the gathering together of men and women affords a chance for valuable constructive work along lines of social intercourse. Recreation rooms, with time in which to use them, are a medium for spontaneous betterment. With wise direction, they may become centres for manual, cultural, and, more especially, industrial training. Physical exercise, so chosen as to overcome the fatigue caused by routine work, calling forth a social effort, may occupy certain intervals of the day. The community loses, if the relationship of co-workers in a factory is only a work relationship. The workers lose if their ten hours is a steady stretch of expenditure, without chance to regain physical and mental vigor. The social possibilities of factory grouping are recognized only partially in Pittsburgh; they are utilized to a less degree. Lunch rooms are not general, and many of those in use are inadequate. Hot coffee at noon, hospital provision for illness, have appealed to the philanthropic instincts of some employers. In two cases, there is a developed system of welfare work, a system that in one plant, however, co-exists with high speeding, a thing which does harm that no half hour in a rest room can undo. In the other case, so far the flower of social effort in Pittsburgh's industrial establishments, the welfare work which is not called welfare work seems a natural part of the industry itself, a feature that is worth while to the management, in that it keeps the employes efficient.

CHAPTER XXII

OUTSIDE THE FACTORIES

A SIGHT of the factory does not enable us fully to understand the life of working women. We must know the homes and lodging places; we must know to what extent social life is made possible by the factory management, and in what way outside agencies, like settlements and clubs, supply the social privileges that home conditions deny. Important also are the districts in which these agencies are found and the opportunities which they offer, as showing how far the living place in itself is a source of social life and recreation.

The occupational map* of Pittsburgh working women is in a sense an interpretation of their home life. The workshops along the upper parts of the river, in Allegheny and in the East End, draw their workers from nearby streets. The tendency is strong for neighborhood women to go into the factories whose smokestacks have stared them in the face since babyhood, and in addition to lower their weekly budget by saving carfare to and from work. The nearby factory sometimes means a saving in clothing, too, as well as in carfare, as in the case of the two young girls who went to the neighboring factory "because then they didn't have to wear hats as they would if they rode in the car." The grouping of industrial establishments on the Point, however, and in Allegheny near the Point, represents a working population which is a car-ride away from home. This group includes the large stores and some of the larger factories.

THE NEIGHBORHOODS

At the eastern end of town, a few girl workers live in the narrow streets that curve away from the larger avenues. Some

* See map p. 23.

of them are coil winders, or makers of gas mantles, or laundry workers, but the occupations and the business streets are alike heterogeneous. This end of town is young. The years behind it are too few to have given it distinctive character in population, housing, or industrial development.

On the Hill, the bluff not far above the meeting of the two rivers, the greater part of the immigrant Jewish population lives; this too, is a district where the number of working girls is relatively small. Along the unevenly paved streets, with their row after row of small brick houses, their dark courts with yet other houses thrust back and between, their little ill-smelling kosher shops, the life of the Jewish immigrant shows itself stripped of the picturesqueness, the gay colors and the ritual that blend not unfitly with the ways of an older city. A tenement here does not proclaim itself for what it is by lifting story above story out of all just relation to the width of the street, but crowds its three or four families into two small floors. For example, here is a family of seven living in two rooms of a house on Davis Street. The five children are from five to nineteen years of age, and the sleeping arrangements are on the principle of even division. The two younger children sleep in the room with their parents. The three older ones have the other room, which is also kitchen, dining room and parlor. The oldest girl in this family is a stogy maker and another daughter works in the paper box factory. Custom prevents the girls of a Jewish family from seeking recreation out of doors, and such social life as they have is largely in the crowded rooms of their home.

The Lawrenceville section is heterogeneous. Poles, Greeks and Assyrians are among the residents, but the characteristic nationality is Irish. From their homes along the uneven streets that dip toward the river, the girls go into the cork factory or the cracker factory, or they enter one of the two or three stogy factories nearby. Some of the houses are frame shacks, weathered and unsightly; others are dull red brick, two stories high. They may accommodate one or three families, according to circumstance. Frequently from the hall you are ushered directly into the parlor, impressive with its cheap draperies and crocheted coverings for the chairs, wax flowers, and large photographs of the family.

You realize that whatever may be the crowding in the sleeping accommodations, this one room is sacred to the daughters of the family for their use in the evening's leisure. The family is poor indeed among the English-speaking group when the first floor front is a sleeping room obvious and unashamed. It is chiefly among the foreign residents of the section that the girls are forced to take to street corners for the opportunity to see their friends.

On the South Side are numbers of Polish families; but across the river, at the north of Pittsburgh, the working districts are harder to characterize. Large sections of the town are filling up with Slavic people. Foreign districts are thus gradually set off chaotically, with streets of Americans straggling along the edge of them. These English-speaking families are often those who by reason of poor physique, or lack of ambition, or the cumulative effect of bad environment, have been left behind when their neighbors have climbed away from what was not then a slum. Among these Americans distinctive characteristics are effaced as in their neighborhood. Some live in brick-paved, unlighted alleys, in the shadow of the mills where they work. Others, a little removed, live toward the districts that have been claimed for the uses of vice. The majority are of low grade, physically, mentally, industrially; the home environment has clamped within narrow limits the developing faculties of the child.

The neighborhood to which the working girl goes home is less a matter of choice than an accident of birth or convenience. She is born into a family group that has drifted through race affiliations, for cheap rent, or for convenient nearness to the mills, to one or another section of the city; she stays with the group, and from it builds out her own life.

The girl who boards away from home is likewise limited in choice. She is not a figment of the imagination, this girl. She numbers in the garment trades 38 per cent* of their total force; in the printing trades, 33⅓ per cent; in the confectionery trade, 33⅓ per cent; in the wholesale millinery trade, 10 per cent; in

* These percentages are based on factory-to-factory investigations, the number in each case being given by the forewoman personally acquainted with the girls.

Lodging Houses Flanked by Disreputable Resorts

mercantile houses, 20 per cent. On the lowest estimate, there are 2,300 of her kind in Pittsburgh, 10.5 per cent of the total working women studied. Poverty sends the seeker for room and board into districts of grade as low, and sometimes lower, than the usual slum. One unsightly shack on a mud-paved alley offers board for $3.00 a week. In others, by sleeping in the kitchen and helping with the housework, a girl can get board for the same sum. She will hardly find a room to rent in the thickly settled parts of the city for less than $10 a month. Even at this price, she cannot be sure that the character of the house is above reproach. It gave me fresh appreciation of the problem faced by homeless girls to hear a conversation between two would-be lodgers and a slim Jewess whose house, twice raided within the few months past, again had a "To-let" sign on the door. "Where do you work?" was her first question, and one girl answered that she was in a cigar factory, the other that "she worked downtown." They stood hesitating, shrinking back, like prisoners before the bar rather than wage-earning women in search of rooms. The Jewess eyed them shrewdly, noting details of untidy dress, stocky figure, curly hair. Working girls of their type, she thought, were not sufficiently promising customers. Finally she said, "Well, my rooms are $2.50 a week, and I might as well tell you that I don't allow no companies, no gentlemen friends and no lady friends; I can't be having no noise and talking in my house. Now, if youse want to see the rooms, youse can see them."

The barren outlook afforded by dingy rooms in which there can be "no companies," is further darkened by the character of many of the neighborhoods where the "To-let" signs hang. The narrow cross-streets shelter houses of assignation and other resorts of vice; they are slums touched by more than the primary effects of poverty, more than low wages and the confusion attendant on life in a new land; they contain poverty in its secondary, its hereditary effects, the taint acquired by years of unwholesome stimuli and unnatural responses.

For the stray wage-earner who prefers lodging with a group of co-workers to lodging alone, boarding homes* have been es-

---

* For the census and capacity of each home, see Appendix B, p. 408, Table 76.

tablished in Pittsburgh to the number of seven. In June, 1908, the capacity of these homes was 396, the census, 275, the difference being due in large part to the general trade depression, which made even the low rates charged too heavy for some girls to pay. There is wide variety in occupation among the residents; but 143, or a little more than half, are among the occupational groups considered in this study. The rest are stenographers, teachers, clerks, or workers in miscellaneous occupations.

Criticisms commonly directed against boarding homes in general, are applicable to a majority of those in Pittsburgh. Five of them are large old residences made over into institutions, and characterized by monotony of dormitory arrangement, meagreness of furnishing, lack of attractiveness, and by the denial of that right so precious to the adult of either sex, the individual latchkey.

One home, which may serve as an example of the rest, is in the business district. Smoke from the railroad clouds the windows, and the noise of trains interrupts sleep. Altogether, there are three single rooms, one double room, two rooms with four beds each, and 16 rooms with three beds each. All sleeping rooms are large and seem well-aired, but everything about them is dingy and barren. The wall paper is old, faded, of set design. The furnishings are void of interest. They have an ugliness that leaves the observer apathetic instead of arousing her to wholesome wrath. Closet room is meagre. Often three girls are obliged to manage with two bureaus, and no wardrobe or closet.

Rates are from $4.75 to $5.25 a week for board and room. On the first floor is the parlor, a long hairclothed place, with an atmosphere which would resent the intrusion of levity. I asked the matron how the girls managed with their guests, and she said that the one parlor was quite sufficient, for it rarely happens that girls have callers on the same night. At ten-thirty lights are extinguished. Any one who remains out after that hour must give notice, and if it does not happen too often, some one will be waiting for her when she comes in.

In this home the girls have no complaint to make, as they have in some of the homes, about the quality of their food, sometimes the positive unhealthfulness of it. Their complaint, so far as they can justly make one, is that personal expression is checked, and the leisure hours of the day stript of their value. A girl may stay in the house three years, and in the course of that time contribute nothing to the atmosphere of the room in which she lives. Scarcely a picture on the walls distinguishes the characteristics of the girls in one room from those in another. Lack of privacy, emphasis of the dormitory idea, represses the individual.

A new departure is the remodeling of a tenement for a non-sectarian home, under the direction of the Catholic church. The bedrooms suffer a little for lack of light, because of adjacent buildings, but the furnishings, even though cheap, are attractive, making the rooms seem bright and cheerful. Here there is one dormitory with five and another with six beds for transients, but most of the rooms are double, renting for $3.00 and $4.00 a week. Residents are entitled to three meals, laundry privileges, the use of the parlor and sitting room. It is a relief from some of the funereal rooms which go by the name of parlors, to turn to this bright place furnished with piano, writing table, and comfortable couches, its very air an invitation to social intercourse. Some class work has also been undertaken as one of the regular functions of the home.

Mention should be made, too, of the recently opened Athalia Daly Home, endowed for the express purpose of furnishing comfortable accommodations to self-supporting women who are not earning over $12 a week. The ground plan of the building is so arranged that each room is an outside room, well lighted. The walls are rough plaster over tile, and cherry woodwork and furniture add to the artistic effect. For each room there is a white enameled bed with excellent mattress, white enameled washstand, a cherry bureau, table and chairs, and a closet. Bathing facilities are ample. A sewing room is provided, and in the basement a laundry with washing machine, ironing boards, tubs, drying-closet, and other up-to-date appliances. The large parlor on the first floor is, like the rest of the building, fitted out in rough plaster and cherry, with artistic furnishings, rugs, chairs, and some fine etchings on the wall. There are small parlors for the use of girls and their guests. This home has 39 single and 16 double rooms, but a flat rate of $4.00 is charged each resident. One thing that has tended to keep down the number of residents is the distance of the home from the business centre, which makes it necessary for the girls to spend carfare each way.

To the girl at home, the stimulus of her surroundings is slight, and evenings pass with an unbroken sameness. The homes, whether they be with family or friends, cannot of themselves supply recreation. If in no other way, they are limited by mere lack of space. There is no opportunity for social intercourse, for conversation, except in connection with the family group that includes young and old. One is impressed by the lack of coherence in different neighborhoods, by the lack of heart to make use of leisure, and the absence of more than sporadic efforts to enjoy the free hours. "We just stay at home," one girl said, "we haven't anything else to do." She could not read at night because her eyes became so tired during the day from the fumes of lacquer; she sat in the window looking out at the uninviting street. Lack of vitality more often than the absence of desire for recreation, keeps the girls within doors in the evening without occupation. "What do you do with your evenings?" I asked so many girls, and grew used to hearing the answer, "Nothing." This simply expresses the attitude of the individual who disdains, or lacks animal energy for, the more violent diversions. For those who have both the vitality and the desire for pleasure, there are few opportunities for recreation except roller-skating rinks, picture shows and dance halls.

In recognition of this need of working women, outside agencies have been developed with the idea of supplementing the imperfect opportunities of the home, and supplying a means for social intercourse. There are settlements and semi-religious associations; there is the field house of the Playground Association. How far their influence goes, it would be difficult to estimate. Their impalpable share in the life and thought of the community cannot be gauged by roll-books or class records; yet the record of attendances on clubs and classes is a measure, at least, of their closer relationships. The total attendances by working women from the industrial groups under consideration are 720.

Kingsley House, and the Columbian School and Settlement, in the Hill district, have a relatively small contingent of working

MRS. MATTHEW'S WORKING GIRLS CLUB AT KINGSLEY HOUSE

women. Neighborhood needs have led, in the main, to class work with men and small boys, and to some extent with mothers, although both settlements have some industrial classes for girls, and some social clubs. The industrial classes in cooking and sewing are an attempt, not to give trade training, but to overcome the pitiful inadequacy of an experience that includes only factory work, and leaves no time for a girl to learn the trade of housekeeping before she undertakes it. In these settlements, the weekly dances are a means of reaching many who have no other connection with class work.

Perhaps the strongest work of the Wood's Run Industrial House is its girls' clubs. The Slovak population of the district seems to be untouched, but of Irish and German and scattered Jewish families, there are many who use the house, its gymnasium and reading rooms, as their own. Girls come from the stogy factory on the next street, and from the pickle factory with its low sheds near the river, from the broom factory and from restaurants nearby. Classes are held in cooking, shirtwaist making and gymnasium work. The play and study clubs have an organization often fluid enough to admit any neighborhood girl, whether in regular attendance or not, without the payment of dues. Except for this settlement house, all this section of the North Side, and the sections farther toward the river have been untouched by socializing influences. Near the Ohio River, in the mill region, where the hinge factory and the metal works are, a Congregational church is planning to carry on some social work, but as yet its plans are somewhat indefinite. As a whole, the North Side is marked by a lack of wholesome meeting places.

At the Soho Baths Settlement, where a stand is being made against the desolation of the steel-shadowed slope near the Monongahela, one of the most successful clubs has been an evening social club, attended by 16 factory girls. A few are from paper box factories, and others are from the little stogy sweatshops on neighboring streets. Some evenings have been given up to dancing, and some to an address by a visitor, but not to industrial work, for the girls have wanted relaxation rather than class routine. This settlement's other activities are in part relief work, in part elementary teaching of household economics as a means of uplift. It is handicapped by lack of a gymnasium and of a reading room for adults, which might serve to make the house more of a social centre than it can possibly be with its present limitations. Soho has no other social centre.

The Young Women's Christian Association is strong in the business section of the city, on the South Side, and in Lawrenceville, where an extensive work is done among factory girls. In each case the work is varied by the needs and the racial differences of the people. Only three or four factory girls are reached on the South Side, perhaps because the population is so largely Polish. When membership in a semi-religious association is required for admission, the neighborhood influence of the club is inevitably limited in a district where religious sects vary with nationality. The chief success of this branch of the association has been with mothers and with children's clubs, although industrial classes are offered in millinery, cooking and sewing. To some, the tuition must be prohibitive, but there has been a fair attendance of girls—at least ten department store girls and one from a glass-house—in the millinery and sewing classes.

One of the most valuable parts of the South Side Young Women's Christian Association work, from the point of view of the working girl, is the lunch service daily and night lunch Saturdays. The department store just opposite, open late on Saturday nights, has a force of 60 girls, and no lunch room, but the cozy dining room of the Young Women's Christian Association offers a choice of dishes for either a whole lunch, or a supplement to the girl's own. Emphasis seems to be laid on the latter, because so many of the shop girls bring a part of their lunch from home with them.

In Lawrenceville there is no lunch service, but a gathering in of girls from factories and stores to the number of 125 in various classes and clubs. An outdoor club has a membership of 32, all of them from factories, workers at cork and crackers and stogies. The dues are $1.00, paid all at once or in instalments, as the members please, for the use of the recreation grounds with tennis courts and different games, and for the trips which the club promises during the summer. At the Philodora club, built on the broadest democratic lines, kindergarten teachers, school teachers, servants, four factory girls, five clerks, and several stenographers, meet on common ground once a week, for a social evening varied with talks and discussions and sometimes visits to places of interest. The millinery and sewing classes are conducted more for the personal use of the girls, to meet their own home problems, than with the idea of trade training. In the Bible class, the social value of meeting together is not forgotten, and once a month the class gives a supper and spends most of the evening time in games.

The central Young Women's Christian Association has a large attendance of business women,—clerks and stenographers,—but it has yet to reach factory and shop girls in numbers that are at all comparable. Some are in the millinery class, and one social club, made up of wrapper girls from two nearby stores, meets on the same evening with a club of factory girls. These two clubs have light gymnasium drill together. Eight girls from factories and shops are being sent to Silver Bay by the association, although this means, as a rule, that the girl has to lose her time in her place of employment. The lunch and dinner service of the association is largely useful to working women, but there are no statistics to show exactly what groups make most use of it.

Mention should be made here of the work carried on in noon and evening classes by the First Presbyterian Church in the midst of the business district down town. The shop girls come in during their hour at noon to the number of 50 or 75, for class work in sewing and basketry, and at night 200 girls take gymnasium drill and class work in basketry, cooking and sewing. The church has a strategic position near the shopping district; its cool basement, filled with quiet light through stained-glass windows, offers a restful interval between worktimes for those who are tired out with the hurry and confusion of the department store.

The Business Woman's Club, an outgrowth of the Helping Hand Society, was started on the North Side some twenty-two years ago. It first leased and now owns the fine old house which it occupies, just one block from the main business street. The cool, dark hangings of the reception room are restful in themselves, and upstairs there is a real rest room for any one who may have

a moment to spare.   Lunch is served in the room back of the parlor, about one hundred lunches a day, to non-members as well as
to members.   The food is varied, well-cooked, and all dishes are
either five or ten cents.   The shop girls from the neighborhood
are among the regular customers, and from offices comes many a
girl welcoming this opportunity to lunch in a quiet place.

Club membership has nothing to do with club lunches; it
entitles a girl to join the evening classes at reduced rates and to
share the social evenings that occur at intervals.   The number
on the roll runs from 170 to 200, and if a year comes when a girl
cannot pay her membership fee, she is dropped until the time when
she wishes to join again; she does not have to pay back membership dues.   Of the 170 to 200 girls in the club, 31 are from the
groups of working women studied.   Their work is as follows:

TABLE 33.—OCCUPATIONS OF THIRTY-ONE MEMBERS OF BUSINESS
WOMAN'S CLUB

Occupation	No. of Women
Laundry work	1
Milliners	1
Telephone operators	2
Printing office	2
Stogy rollers	2
Sales clerks	23
Total	31

The classes in millinery, fancy work, sewing and cooking,
are not for industrial training; they are attempts to give the girl
an equipment that will make her personal life more worth while.
In the millinery class, the girls are taught to sew braid, to make
bows, to put on trimming and to combine colors.   They are not
taught to make wire frames, or to do such other things as would
be essential to a milliner by trade.   They make hats for themselves and for their families; sometimes they come into the same
class year after year in order to learn the season's styles from the
teacher.   Tuition is $1.00 a term, with three yearly terms.

In the fancy work class, the girls are taught to make practical
and attractive gifts, such as centre pieces, table covers and embroidered neckwear.   Color values are explained to them and the

CRAFT-WORK OF GIRLS' CLUB AT KINGSLEY HOUSE

place of decoration in home furnishing. The sewing class confines itself to shirtwaist making. The girls make shirtwaists for themselves. If they become extraordinarily proficient in making both plain and fancy waists, they may go on to learn skirt making and the principles of more difficult sewing. They are not transformed into finished dressmakers, but are shown how to buy to the best advantage, and to put together garments that they or their families can wear.

The tuition for the cooking class is a little more than for the others, $1.50 a term, but materials are furnished. The principles of cooking simple food are explained, and the class is taught combinations of foods, something of food values and how to use left over materials. The idea is to give the girls such practice as will be useful to them in their homes.

Millinery and shirtwaist making have been the most popular classes, but in all its activities the club has won a place for itself as a thing of immediate usefulness. The monthly social evenings from October to June have usually some special form of entertainment besides dancing. Since this is preëminently a woman's club, the policy of its leaders is not to invite men to the social evenings, for difficulties are anticipated should the character of the club be changed.

The last of the outside agencies for social occupation is the Lawrence Field House, maintained by the Pittsburgh Playground Association. This is not a settlement, nor wholly a play place, but something between the two. In this, its first year (1907–08), it has succeeded in becoming a vital part of the neighborhood life. On a little hill, barren as yet, after the wont of Pittsburgh hills, stands the small red brick building, with its sloping roof and leaded windows, altogether inviting and attractive in the midst of the dreary sordidness of the Lawrenceville slums. The gymnasium, two stories high, is the all-important room; it is used not only for gymnasium work, but for dances, for basket ball, and as an auditorium. There are smaller rooms upstairs and down, and a basement finished in concrete.

The house, opened in November, 1907, is emphatically a neighborhood house. Afternoon classes are held for the children, and evening classes for working girls. Every first and third

Saturday night a concert or lecture is given for the parents of the children, and some parents who have come during the day to see what the children are doing, have asked if they might not have similar classes for themselves. They are families of mill workers, some of them German, but in most cases Irish and American.

In this connection, the evening work with the girls is of especial interest, although the classes have changed in membership several times since the house opened in the fall. In the beginning there was an evening attendance of 150,* 25 stenographers, 15 factory girls, and 110 sales clerks. Some of the factory girls were stogy rollers and others were employes in the cork factory; two were from the Westinghouse plant, one was from a cracker factory, one from a telegraph office, and one from a laundry. Ten or twelve laundry girls applied, but found that they could not come because they had to work every Monday and Friday night. On these nights, although they live near the laundry, they do not even go home to supper, but have barely time for a cold lunch in the midst of their work. With the Christmas recess, the working girls began to drop out, and as the spring wore on there were more high school girls, more from offices, fewer from factories and stores. The teachers at the Field House think that these latter classes are harder to interest than the girls who came in the beginning of the year, because they are less in earnest, less serious.

The wand and dumb bell work of the gymnasium pupils, the running, dance steps, and games, are all light movements that serve in a measure to counteract the effects of long sitting or standing in one position.

Besides the gymnasium, two other classes are offered without charge for tuition. Each class has two one-hour sessions a week and any girl may take two courses out of the three. The classes make no attempt to teach a trade, but rather to suggest a way by which the girls may enrich their own lives.

The sewing class might more accurately be called a class in embroidering, for here different kinds of stitches are taught, buttonhole work, cross-stitch on scrim, Hardanger embroidery,

* These figures are based on estimates made by the teachers.

and such simple line work as would be applicable to home decoration. In the art class, a similar principle is followed. The aim is to stimulate the imagination and the sense of beauty, not to turn out indifferent artists. Designs that suggest the possibility of making a living room or a garment beautiful, color combinations that develop the perception of harmony—these are the points toward which the class work is directed. In the beginning of the year, the room was bare. There were no decorations, no draperies; but the girls themselves stenciled draperies for the wall, and curtains for the windows. The best of their compositions in charcoal and water color, done always from life, are the pictures on the wall. The one or two prints set inconspicuously in a corner are frequently changed so that no girl has a chance to become indifferent to them before she has begun to love them.

One cannot question the value of art teaching of this sort. Here, as in the other classes, the work of the Field House suggests not so much an adding to the interests of the girls, as a leading out to conscious perception the faculties, physical and spiritual, that had been stifled in the dark. The girls who came to the classes before the Christmas recess, the working girls, had begun to feel that the house was their own, to be used as a significant part of their lives. They themselves thought out the idea of engaging the gymnasium for a Christmas dance on a Saturday night. They invited their friends, planned and gave the dance without suggestion from the leaders. In this and other ways the house is building its influence as a vital outgrowth of neighborhood needs.

This discussion of the different agencies that attempt to meet the social needs of working women has of necessity been scattered. Diversity of aim and of method makes it impossible to treat the agencies as one group. Varying as they do, they have by no means districted the city among them. The wide-spread system of home libraries and book stations of the Carnegie Library is a beginning in this direction; and there are five or six branch libraries, enough to make one eager to see many more such buildings, with cheery open rooms, with shelves of books and magazines, where the people of a neighborhood may meet for quiet study, if not for gayer relaxation. The homes of working women serve only the most prosaic uses, and as a rule, the social possibilities of factories and shops are not utilized. For the present, these outside agencies, exotic as they sometimes are, are the only forces that aim to give social definiteness to leisure hours. It may perhaps explain them more clearly, if they are classified according to the means they use:

TABLE 34.—RECREATION FACILITIES OFFERED BY TEN OUTSIDE AGENCIES

Recreation work	No. of agencies
Classes in manual training	3
Classes in manual training and social clubs, with membership in semi-religious association obligatory	3
Social clubs, but no meeting room for non-members . . .	1
Social clubs, gymnasium and reading room for the use of non-members	3
	10

Of these ten agencies, only the last four meet a social need. Classes in trade training* and manual work further the efficiency of their students, but they have constantly to battle against weariness at the end of a working day, and they cannot be really recreative.

In the four social clubs, social meeting is, of course, the point of emphasis. One of these agencies, a settlement, is hampered by lack of any room for the use of neighbors who are non-members. The last three have gone far toward meeting the girls' need. They have taken strategic positions at Wood's Run, in the Lawrenceville district and on the Hill. They have friendship with 258 working girls† recorded on roll-books. They can scarcely reach beyond that, however, to the great numbers among whom, except for profit, there is no social leaven working.

There were then in Pittsburgh in 1907, 22,185 working women in factories and stores, besides many more in occupations uncounted in this census; yet of this number only 258, less than 2 per cent, were in touch with a centre for social development and recreation, either in the play or re-creating sense. Even a little leisure is a by-product of life too valuable to waste, and the community is the loser if the free hour is spent only in weariness or

* See Appendix C, pp. 410–411. The Margaret Morison Carnegie School for Women.

† In the industrial groups studied.

This Narrow, Ill-lighted Alley Houses Many a Working Girl

some undesirable form of entertainment. Nickelodeons and dance halls and skating rinks are in no sense inherently bad, but so long as those maintained for profit are the only relief for nervous weariness and the desire for stimulation, we may well reckon leisure a thing spent, not used. These amusements take a toll from the people's income, disproportionate to the pleasure gained. They divert, and to the work-weary girl, diversion is essential. Yet there should be possibility for constructive diversion. A diversion is needed which shall be a form of social expression, and with slighter toll from strength and income, be of lasting value to the body and spirit.

I shall not soon forget a Saturday evening when I stood among the crowd of pleasure-seekers on Fifth Avenue, and watched the men and women packed thick at the entrance of every picture-show. My companion and I bought tickets for one of the five cent shows. Our way was barred by a sign, "Performance now going on." As we stood near the door, the crowd of people waiting to enter filled the long vestibule and even part of the sidewalk. They were determined to be amused, and this was one of the things labeled, "Amusement." They were hot and tired and irritable, but willing to wait until long after our enthusiasm was dampened, and we had left them standing in line for their chance to go in.

It was an incident not without significance, this eagerness with which they turned toward leisure after a working week of unmeaning hours. Are we very sure that this eagerness is not as well worth conserving as any river fall that makes electricity or drives a mill?

In large measure today, the working women of Pittsburgh are spending their leisure, not using it. The beginning whereby they may use it is already made. How rapidly this 1.16 per cent now influenced shall increase, depends in part on the choice of the working women and the character of their industrial life, and in part on the social foresight of the community.

SUMMARY OF INDUSTRIAL CONDITIONS

CHAPTER XXIII

WAGES

IN earlier chapters I have described the different factory industries in Pittsburgh. It remains to summarize and in part
to interpret the facts that have been presented. For clear
understanding, let me gather compactly four separate strands
that have been followed through trade after trade: (1) wages,
(2) hours, (3) health, and (4) the economic foothold which women
have gained in the Pittsburgh industries.

The table (page 338) summarizes what has been learned
about wages. It shows that of the 22,185 women workers in
Pittsburgh, varying in age from fourteen years to fifty, something
over three-fifths earn less than $7.00 a week; one-fifth are earning
$7.00 to $8.00, and the rest $8.00 or over.

At the upper level are women who have familiarity with
their tasks, a certain dexterity, or an inborn knack for the thing
they do. They are copyists of model hats in wholesale millinery
houses, or expert dippers of fine grade chocolates in candy factories, or experienced and tactful saleswomen in a mercantile
house. Others are to be found, not in these "white-handed"
occupations, but where metals are molded for use, or in workrooms gray-brown with the fine dust of heat-dried tobacco leaves.
They have learned to speed in making sand cores for brass found-
ers or winding coils for an electric motor, or with quick fingers
to roll into shape more than a thousand strong-smelling stogies
in a day. Some of them are expert bottlers of pickles and candied
fruits; others are section hands in a garment factory, who every
year have pushed pace and output a notch ahead. Speed, and
capacity to gain more speed, is the talisman which has opened
the way to a higher wage rating for this more fortunate 17 per
cent of the working women.

337

TABLE 35.—NUMBER OF WOMEN IN EACH WAGE GROUP IN EACH TRADE

Trade	Unpaid Apprentices	$3.00 to $6.99	$7.00 to $7.99	$8.00 or over	Total
Crackers . . .	..	900	28	...	928
Confectionery . .	..	697	203	66	966
Molasses . . .	..	30	6	4	40
Canneries . . .	..	458	167	157	782
Stogy	..	1,182	441	988	2,611
Garments . . .	..	103	285	480	868
Awnings . . .	..	21	5	15	41
Mattress . . .	..	11	12	48	71
Gloves	..	90	10	8	108
Millinery . . .	14	214	70	108	406
Laundries . . .	203	1,637	131	214	2,185
Dyeing and cleaning .	..	110	300	100	510
Metal trades . .	..	944	502	508	1,954
Lamps	..	172	152	147	471
Glass	..	241	33	79	353
Mirrors	..	32	3	5	40
Brooms and brushes .	..	15	16	2	33
Paper boxes . .	..	190	32	16	238
Caskets	..	44	25	5	74
Cork	..	255	295	50	600
Paint	..	35	10	5	50
Soap	..	103	15	10	128
Trunks and suit-cases .	..	8	6	...	14
Printing and bookbinding	..	181	123	93	397
Telegraph . . .	..	...	...	90	90
Telephone . . .	..	312	201	174	687
Mercantile . . .	..	5,510	1,555	475	7,540
Total	217	13,495	4,626	3,847	22,185
Percentage of total .	.97	60.83	20.85	17.35	100

This threefold division of wages is largely arbitrary, but is based in part on the estimated cost of living in the Pittsburgh district, and in part on the groupings into which degrees of intelligence and of dexterity have naturally separated the earnings of the women employes in the different trades. No attempt was made to reduce to tabular form the wages of every working woman; but rather to learn the percentage which fell within each wage group in each mercantile and manufacturing establishment.

For the workers in the middle group, who for the most part are in the same range of occupations, less speed has meant less pay.

At the lowest level are found the majority of the women, some of them "casual laborers," some "temporarily permanent" at least, many under-nourished, unambitious, inefficient; many more in occupations which, for trade reasons already described, can secure workers at their own terms. They pack crackers to the pace of a traveling conveyor, or stogies, or metal pieces, or mirrors, or lamps, or glass. They make telephone connections in the central exchanges, sell goods without interest or proficiency, operate machines in stogy factories, laundries, and canneries. For the few who in time work their way to one of the upper groups, there are hundreds more who enter these industries yearly to take their places at a beginning wage. We may safely assume that percentages remain constant, for the personnel of the women workers is continually in process of change.

This lowest wage group challenges further explanation. Why is it that 60 per cent of the working women earn no more than $ .50 to $1.00 a day? For example: The girls who pack crackers are paid $ .50 a day. Should we take as a basis of comparison the wages of workingmen in the same district, we should find unskilled laborers, employed to fetch and carry in the mills, earning $ .13 to $ .16½ an hour, or $1.30 to $1.65 for the ten-hour day.*

But many women, when entering upon their industrial life, are not adults but girls of fourteen and fifteen, just out of school. We can compare the beginning wage of such a girl only with the beginning wage of a boy of fourteen, working a 10-hour day. A boy is paid, as a rule, $ .10 an hour. Although some firms vary slightly from what might be called the market rates, the beginning wage of a working girl is generally $ .50, or exactly one-half the beginning wage of a working boy, $1.00 a day. Maturity does not always mean possibility of advance-

---

* According to the law of the state, women cannot be employed more than 60 hours a week; they cannot, therefore, be employed 12 hours a day every day in the week. In making our comparison, therefore, we can justly compare women's wages only with those of laborers working on a 10-hour basis. As a matter of fact, many laborers work 12 hours, and earn $1.80 to $1.98.

ment to working girls. There are firms which never pay their adult women more than $4.00 a week, although their men earn $1.60 a day; but usually the wage bears a certain correspondence to the term of service; and as the years pass the general ratio between the wages of men and of women undergoes no material change. Unskilled workmen who have not yet acquired a certain dexterity and familiarity with their tasks are paid $2.00 a day, or $12 a week. Unskilled workingwomen, who have made themselves valuable by length of service and by familiarity with a certain operation, are paid $1.00 a day, $6.00 a week. That is, the ratio between the wages of unskilled workmen and of unskilled workingwomen, is two to one.

This ratio, which represents the wages generally accorded to men and women who are unskilled but have the dexterity gained by practice, is also the ratio between their wages when skill is gained by preliminary study or by trade apprenticeship. I have had fewer opportunities to make this latter comparison, for I have perforce dealt scarcely at all with skilled trades, and have even fewer examples of men and women whose skill is comparable working at the same occupation. In the millinery trade, there is a two-season apprenticeship, but men are not employed. In telegraphy, although the apprenticeship, or period of preliminary study, is shared by men and women operators, it does not leave them in entirely comparable positions. A man's wage is double that paid to a woman, for less strength keeps women at the lighter wires. A clearer instance is the situation in laundry checkrooms, where the standard wage of women checkers is $8.00 a week, as against a standard wage for men checkers of $17 a week. Another comparison is that between women and non-union core makers. A majority of the women receive $1.20 to $1.30 a day, but for similar work men receive $2.50. The ratio in a few of these instances confirms what has been said, that where skill and occupation are comparable, alike in skilled trade and in unskilled occupation, the man's wage is double the woman's.

Here, then, lies the crude, economic force which has conquered sex traditions and the resistance of domestic institutions, in reaching out and gathering women into the Pittsburgh industries, as into modern industries everywhere. Why they have come is another matter. They have been wanted because women's work can be had cheap. The employer in the steel district seeks labor at the lowest price; if the Slav is cheaper than the German, he employs the Slav; if the Slavic woman is cheaper than the man, and can do the work or some part of it, he employs the Slavic woman. Because women are the cheapest laborers available, a large number of occupations have been given over to them. Men will not compete with them at all at these levels for work and wages. Here the competition between men and women may be vaguely potential; but it is no longer active, nor of practical consequence. Every year, the field of women's employment has been extended laterally into corresponding occupations in more and more trades, and with the development of machinery such occupations have increased. At the same time, the women have worked up in these industries to higher grade occupations which have brought them apparently, and in some cases actually, into competition with men as co-laborers on the same footing and in the same trades. Sixteen of the occupations studied are on this border line. A brief inquiry into the character and extent of competition between men and women in these occupations may throw light not only on why women are paid less than men, but on why they continue to accept what they do.

Various reasons have been advanced by economic writers for the inequality of wages between men and women. Gonnard* holds that the wages of working women are less because their needs are less than those of the workingman. As further reasons he mentions the weakness of women's unions, the large number of unemployed, unskilled women, the limited demand for women workers, and finally, their alleged lower productivity. Dr. Alice Salomon† speaks of the temporary character of women's wage-earning life; of the unwillingness of young girls to undertake a long apprenticeship. Because of this unwillingness, in large part based on the presumption that the working life will be short, young girls tend to undertake unskilled work which brings them an immediate return, but gives no opportunity for advance-

* Gonnard, Réné: La Femme dans l'Industrie, pp. 108 ff.
† Salomon, Dr. Alice: Ursachen der ungleichen Entlohnung der Männer- und Frauen-Arbeit.

ment. She also holds that men and women do not actually compete; that the apparent difference in wages is based on an actual difference in proficiency. This latter point represents the stand taken by Sidney Webb.* He states that men and women do not really compete; that even when they tend similar machines, the cleaning and repairing of the machines must be done by men. J. Ramsay MacDonald† holds that the wages of women are lower, because women (1) have less technical skill and are less useful all round; (2) have more broken time owing to bad health, and have less strength at work; (3) change positions frequently, and leave work entirely after a short term of employment.

Such an inductive study of women's trades as I have made offers a practical test of this reasoning. In many instances the active competition between men and women is seen to be apparent but not real. In stogy factories, for example, it is not at skilled handwork that women are displacing men, but a machine-made product turned out by women is contesting with a hand-made product turned out by men, at a rate of pay to machine operators only a third as much as to skilled handworkers whom they are displacing. Similarly, in trunk and suit-case factories, women are apprenticed for a period half as long as men, and the product made by them is cheaper in quality. Women pressers in garment factories or in dyeing and cleaning works either have lighter irons than men, or work on garments of inferior quality. In mercantile houses, the most difficult articles (those which require experience in fabric) are usually given to men to sell. Women core makers are limited in their displacement of men to work that is simple, light and easily learned. In a broom factory, women compete with boys, but only for the simple and mechanical part of the work.

Even where the occupations may in themselves be identical, men and women are often actually in different categories because of the capacity of men and boys to do subsidiary work, or to advance to a position requiring greater strength. Boys are often preferred to girls as press feeders, for instance, because they can

* Webb, Sidney: Alleged Differences Between Wages of Men and of Women. Economic Journal, 11 : 173.

† MacDonald, J. Ramsay: Women in the Printing Trades: pp. 50, 51.

be relied on to learn the trade, and women cannot; they can be asked to lift and carry and to clean the presses, but women cannot. In consequence, a boy's service, both in pressroom and in lamp and burner factories, is often worth to an employer the additional cost of his wages.

Sometimes men and women do work of the same quality and kind, but competition between them is still apparent, not real, because of what might be called the recruiting necessities of the position. The majority of women telegraph operators earn half what men do in the same offices, even when both are employed on light wires. The reason for this is that men are needed for heavy wires, but must be trained on light wires and kept there for the heavier service when needed. They must pass up through women's positions, but they are paid partly for what they do and partly as a reserve force. The competition here again is apparent not real.

In other industries it is clear that active competition is temporary, not permanent. In the stogy sweatshops, men and women, paid at the same rate, make bunches or roll stogies side by side. This industrial process, however, is being superseded by machine-made stogy rolling, and this group of workers by the trust factory. These men and women are temporarily competing for work of the same kind, but the work itself is in course of transition. In laundry checkrooms, too, men and women are still competing for work of the same kind, but the co-labor will not last. The women at their cheaper wage rate will displace the men entirely, eliminating all but potential competition. In these cases the active competition is transitional. The coil-winding room of an electric manufacturing company affords another illuminative example. Ordinarily women wind light coils and men wind heavy coils, the men's rate of pay being double that of the women. During a rush order, men on the night shift were given some of the women's work to finish, and for some days women by day and men by night worked at the same thing for different pay. With approximately the same output, the men were paid double what the women received. At half the wages, women have easily displaced men in the cork-paper cutting department of the cork factory; and in the tin-cutting room of a cannery they have displaced boys for the time being, because of their greater reliability. In these cases, the experimental competition was fought to an end, and resulted in the employment of women.

Analysis shows that in only a few cases are women permanent active competitors with men for identical work, within the limits of their working life. I found this true in Pittsburgh among press feeders and compositors in printing offices, and among "openers" in sheet steel mills.

It seems, then, that women and men tend to separate into non-competing groups, the wages of women being approximately half those of men. They rarely work together on the same wage level, or at identical work. Such work as women can do they largely have a monopoly of, because they work for half pay. With a few exceptions, even in those trades where men and women are found in the same occupation, the latter are paid generally at this same ratio. As an explanation, we have noted that at times the superior strength of men makes their output greater, as among garment pressers, and their capacity for undertaking work makes them more valuable employes, as in lamp and burner factories; yet neither women's lower productivity, nor their incapacity to care for their own machines, is sufficient to account for the fundamental difference between the wages paid to them and the wages paid to men. Alike in cases where the quality of women's work is inferior, as in suit-case factories, and in cases where men and women do the same work, as in laundry checkrooms, the difference in wage rating is the same. The women come into each of these occupations not on its customary wage level, but at a level analogous to that paid women generally in other occupations.

These facts seem to suggest an explanation of why women work for low wages, in the special conditions attending the incidence of sex in the labor field.

A first reason for the $3.00 or $4.00 wage, not universal, but characteristic of cities of Pittsburgh's industrial type, is the limited circle of industries in which women workers are used. In a city of mills and metal work, where arduous employments make a demand for men, and where dust from the mills checks the growth of textile factories, it is inevitable that the lines of employment open to women should be relatively few. "Why don't you advertise in the papers when you want a girl?" I asked the forewoman of a candy factory. "It wouldn't be worth our while," she answered. "All we have to do when we want anybody is to put a sign out, and we have all the applicants we can possibly use." Advertisements for hands are so rare as to be noteworthy. This limitation to demand may be obscured by an era of unwonted prosperity, or by the untrained choices of women workers in the matter of trades; it is, however, a factor in keeping the wages of Pittsburgh women low.

A second reason is that within this limited circle of industries women remain in the lower grade occupations and still further glut them. Women are sometimes prevented by inferior strength from competing for superior occupations in the industries in which they are engaged, but more generally they are prevented by inferior training and experience. They will not compete for the more exacting, better paid work if their ambition is lessened by the knowledge that they will probably be wage-earners for only five or six years. Hence their unwillingness to spend time in trade training, and their tendency to be apathetic as to trade associations and other forms of unionism. These points will be developed further in the final chapter. Of more direct economic as well as social bearing is the fact that they will neither compete for superior positions involving training, nor for higher wages at inferior positions, if their necessary living wage is less than men's, or if their cost of living is in part met by men. Although the lower wages of women may represent a lower standard of responsibilities to be met by earnings, $3.00 or $4.00 a week does not cover the individual cost of living, however extreme the degree of restraint and limitation. The difference between her wage and the cost of living, however met, represents the extent to which she is subsidized from some quarter.

That women workers are thus usually subsidized tends to keep their wages low, not only in Pittsburgh, but wherever they enter the industrial field. Only here and there a powerful women's union, or the personality of an exceptional woman, has counteracted this tendency. Being in fact a recognition that wages must approximate cost of living, it affects the determination of rates paid by nearly every firm employing women. If the cost of living* is met in part by the woman's father or husband, or if she takes the way that is always open to her for self-support, her employer needs to pay only a supplementary wage fixed in part by custom, and in part by the purchasing power in the district of the wages paid to men. "We try to employ girls who are members of families," a box manufacturer said to me, "for we don't pay the girls a living wage in this trade." The social fact of woman's customary position in the household, the position of a dependent who receives no wages for her work, thus lies behind the economic fact of her insufficient wage in the industrial field. It is expected that she has men to support her.

This discussion of what is the cost of living for women carries us beyond mere nominal wages, the amount they receive in dollars, to what is more significant, a consideration of wages estimated according to their purchasing power in the Pittsburgh district. To get approximately at what is a living wage for a working woman in Pittsburgh, I made inquiries among working girls themselves, forewomen in factories who had had long experience with working girls, settlement workers, and club leaders who knew at first hand what rent, food and the other necessaries of life cost in different sections of the city. Among the opinions of these women, there was no majority. Some declared for $7.00 a week, others for $8.00 and others for $10. Not one was willing to consider $6.00 a living wage.

They agreed that the minimum below which a working girl cannot live decently and be self-supporting in Pittsburgh is $7.00 a week. If the girl is not one of a family group, she is in all probability obliged to share a furnished room with another girl. Eight dollars to $10 a month is the rate usually charged. By dividing expenses, the weekly outgo for food and lodging would be from $4.50 to $5.00 a week. If $2.00 a week were spent for clothing, there would at most be less than $ .50 a week left for washing and ironing; for sundries, which make so formidable an item in the budgets of most of us; for illness, for medicine and for medical care, or for recreation.

*Gonnard, Réné: La Femme dans l'Industrie, p. 108.

346

Yet $2.00 a week is the lowest estimate for clothing made to me by girls who have themselves grappled with the problem at first hand in Pittsburgh, either by buying the material and making their own clothes, or buying the clothes ready-made. Such a girl meets almost insuperable obstacles in keeping to the standards set by her shopmates. In every sort of position, the clothing of the applicant is of increasing importance. I have seen poorly dressed girls "turned down," and well-dressed girls taken for subordinate work in a thread mill, a position where, if anywhere, one's appearance would seem to be a secondary matter. In choosing employes for positions which necessitate the use of working clothes, employers tend to give preference to girls whose street clothes are trim and well-made. Both in securing and keeping a position, the street clothes of the working girl are part of her stock in trade. Not only cleanliness, but neatness and quality of material all count toward the sum of impressions. The girl who has neither the experience nor the time necessary to evolve "creations" out of odds and ends, and yet estimates truly the social and economic value of appearances, must spend money for clothes, although $2.00 per week allows for only a very moderate standard and crowds from her budget many sundries which seem essential.

These are the possibilities for the girls who have what may be termed a living wage. From the introductory table (page 338), it will be seen that they are 20 per cent of the whole number. Seventeen per cent more are earning slightly larger pay. The wages paid 60 per cent of the working women of Pittsburgh do not afford them even this meagre subsistence. It may be said that if, as has been stated, a girl's wages are supplemented by her family, her condition is really far from desperate. She is personally comfortable, and living according to the standard of her associates. In many cases, this is true. How far it is true, we have no means of knowing until a more extended investigation is made of the individual cases, their budgets, and contribution to their families. Clearly, however, the tradition that a girl's father and brothers always help toward her support has become, in the Pittsburgh district at least, in many cases illusory.

That a girl is one of a family group is quite as likely to indi-

347

cate that she is chief breadwinner, as that her family is her chief bulwark against the world. One quick, pale-faced American girl is a decorator in a glass factory. She gets $8.00 a week. Her little brother is a messenger at $4.00. For five months in the winter of 1907–08, they were the only ones in the family of seven who were earning anything. One plump little German girl whose soft brown hair and pink cheeks contrast pleasantly with the less attractive types about her, is a salesgirl in a mercantile house. With a wage of $6.00 a week, she is responsible for the support of a mother and two younger sisters. Accidents to workmen in the mills have often thrown such heavy responsibilities on the young daughters. A girl whose father was killed by an electric crane was the only one of the family old enough to work. Forced by financial needs to accept a wage fixed by custom at a point below her own cost of subsistence, much more below the cost of helping to maintain a family of dependents, she drifted into occasional prostitution. Another Pittsburgh girl was induced by the bitter need of her younger brothers and sisters to raise her wages from $6.00 a week to $10 by concessions to her employer, and finally to choose prostitution as a means of support. A comrade of hers came long ago from a country town to work in a cigar factory, but after an unsuccessful struggle with the city, drifted into this same way of life. Without a home to supplement her wages, she caught at what seemed to her the only way of making them meet her needs. In such cases, scarcely typical, but far from uncommon, cause and effect are glaring in their directness.

Were women totally without means of supplementing their pay-envelopes, wages would of necessity be forced above a subsistence level in order to keep a sufficient labor supply in the local market. Otherwise the women would have to move away or slowly starve. That wages are not so forced up, indicates the widespread, though sometimes unconscious, reliance of merchants and manufacturers on the ability of women employes to find a source of support in their families or friends. The family may at times cease to give assistance; but the latter avenue for money making is never ·closed. It is a way of escape, both to the solitary working woman who earns less than it costs her to live, and to the woman who is leading a barren existence on wages that just meet expenses.

Few will hesitate to condemn the degradation that attends the woman who chooses unsocial means of self ·support. Yet one form of subsidizing a wage-worker leads to another form of subsidizing, and so long as custom or fact renders the payment of a full living wage non-essential, economic needs impel many a girl toward a personally degrading life.

It is not within our province to speculate as to what might be the social consequences of a general increase in women's wages in Pittsburgh. That would involve questions as to whether or not more girls would be induced to enter factory work, more men would be thrown out of work, or men would be given more work because women's work cost as much. The problem of women's work and wages cannot be adequately solved without reckoning with the family and the home. We may be sure, however, that the practice of industries, whether in Pittsburgh or elsewhere, of not paying women employes enough to live on, is economically unsound. Every manufactured article in such case is paid for only in part by the consumer and in part by someone else who partially supports the women. And we may be sure that where women, thrown on their own resources, are paid less than subsistence wages, ill social consequences result. Beyond that, we may further question whether a community does well to have any of its workers, however supported, paid less than subsistence wages.

For social strength, it would seem that the question ought to be: What wage must a girl have in order to live decently, maintain sound health, and have reasonable recreation? For decency's sake, a community cannot afford to permit five girls from an iron mill to diminish expenses by sharing one room with five men from the same workplace; neither can it afford to permit a girl to hire board and a couch in the kitchen of a crowded tenement flat for $3.00 a week. I question whether it can even afford the dimming of bright thoughts, the effacing of individuality, that tend to follow occupancy of one bed in the dormitory row of a working girls' home.

For health's sake, the community cannot afford to permit

its girl members to receive a wage too low for nutrition, or for the refreshment of exhausted strength. It reacts ultimately to the harm of society when a garment worker has weak coffee for breakfast, goes without lunch altogether, and eats two or three sandwiches for dinner, as her habitual diet. She may keep up through her working life, but in her domestic relations she leaves a heritage of weakness and inefficiency. We all are the sufferers when a shop girl continues at her work after vitality has ebbed, because her wages are too low to permit treatment or rest.

Moreover, the community cannot afford to deny any of its members reasonable recreation. Industrial success is of small value, if the contributors to that success lead lives void of spiritual meaning or spiritual impression. Among those girls who have sufficient imagination to grasp what is denied them, there is sure to be reaction, perhaps in ill-health, perhaps in indecency, to the cost in either case of the whole community. Recreation, richness of life in leisure hours, is equally a source of decency and of health.

As things stand in an industrial district like Pittsburgh today there is scarcely a minimum to which women's wages may not be depressed. The situation is one which demands close study and close thinking. That it is possible to influence it in some degree is shown by the success of women's unions in some trades, by the work of Consumers' Leagues in some cities in demanding certain standards in women's wages, by the proposals for minimum wage legislation brought forward in certain countries, and by the action of progressive employers here and there in establishing rates that can be sanctioned from the standpoint of the public good. And can we reasonably be content if the standard of wages be raised merely to the level that makes existence possible? Shall we call sufficient a sum less than enough to make possible a life decent, healthy, colored and individualized by recreative leisure?

CHAPTER XXIV

HOURS

THE customary working day for women in Pittsburgh factories is ten hours. This may be shortened in some industries to five hours on Saturday, but in general, the working week is 60 hours long. In part, this customary limit to hours of work is due to the Pennsylvania law, which has for 12 years limited the working week to 60 hours; in part it is due to the general tendency, both in Europe and in the United States, to regard 10 hours a day as a reasonable maximum for women's work. This tendency seems to be gathering strength, notwithstanding the attempts made by groups of manufacturers to nullify or to render unenforceable the laws of the more progressive states. Recent years have witnessed several of these judicial battles; most recently of all, the state of Oregon* has been sustained in its defence of the constitutionality of its law.

Overtime work is held in check more or less effectively by the laws of 22 states. Where overtime is permitted "for the preservation of perishable goods" or "to make a shorter workday on one day of the week," or where the sum of the legal working days exceeds the maximum of the legal working week, it is almost impossible to prove a violation and the law is in consequence difficult to enforce. Pennsylvania is in the latter class. Twelve hours a day is permissible and no closing hour is fixed, although the total working hours must not exceed 60 per week. Overtime is possible; within these limits it is legal.

Some of the difficulties in enforcing the Pennsylvania law against illegal overtime will be removed when the new law goes into effect January 1, 1910, which for all girls under eighteen provides a ten-hour day† and prohibits night work after 9 p. m. The

---

* Supreme Court of the United States, October term, 1907. Curt Muller, Plaintiff in Error, v. State of Oregon.

† The ten-hour day and the 58-hour week affect certain specified employments. The law for adult women is unchanged. See Appendix D, pp. 412–417.

working week for them is reduced from 60 to 58 hours. Yet the greatest difficulty in enforcing the law still remains, the proviso that the working day may be extended "for the sole purpose of making a shorter workday one day in the week," without any limit being set to the number of working hours in any given day. It would seem probable that violations of the law, frequent at the time of the investigation, would still be frequent in many industries, sometimes by extension of the legal working day, sometimes by extension of the legal working week, sometimes by both.

Overtime may be irregular, as the volume of business changes, or it may be seasonal. Cracker factories, laundries, dyeing and cleaning establishments, metal works, casket factories, cork factories, trunk and suit-case factories, printing and bookbinding establishments, telephone and telegraph offices, are Pittsburgh industries liable to irregular overtime. Overtime in steam laundries is characterized less by a lengthy working week than by a lengthy working day. On Mondays, though the regular work begins late in the morning, the employes are usually kept busy with such duties as cleaning the machines, cleaning the traveling conveyor or scrubbing the floors; and it is customary for laundries to keep their employes until nine o'clock on Mondays, so that goods which are taken on short time may be returned the same day. Although they come at nine in the morning, instead of seven as they do on the other days of the week, their working day (when three-quarters of an hour or less is allowed for lunch and for supper) is therefore ten and a half hours long. On Fridays, the day begins at seven, but lasts late into the night; ten or eleven or twelve at night, as the case may be, whenever the week's work is finished, is the closing hour. Friday is a fifteen-hour day, and cases have been found where the working hours lasted through the whole of the night. These extreme hours are found, too, as we have seen, in the sewing departments of the casket factories when an order comes in for a casket lined with some color or with some material that is not kept in stock, or for a size not usually carried. Employes in this department who are on call may be sent for at one o'clock in the morning to work on an order that has just come in. Cork factory operatives nominally work ten hours a day five days in a week, and half a day Saturday. Machinery is stopped at night; but during the busy season, from February until November, the sorters, who need no machinery, are often required to work after hours. This department keeps the weekly hours within the limit of the state factory law, but exceeds the legal limit to the length of the working day. "Customers must be satisfied," is the rule in too many of the trades, although an unexpected rush of orders may keep the employes at work for hours into the night. Yet "the tendency to put off giving orders to the last moment is easily checked when the customer can be met with a universal legal prohibition,"* and were there such a prohibition, overtime would in few instances prove unavoidable. The hurry of customers, habit, and the elasticity of the law, are in large measure responsible for the continuance of occasional long hours.

Seasonal overtime presents a more difficult problem. Confectionery, stogy and paper box factories, as well as mercantile houses, are affected by the Christmas trade. In summer, on the other hand, summer fruits and berries keep the canneries busy through the warm months, and chewing-gum packers must work at night to supply the frequenters of circuses and picnic parks. Incoming orders from drummers on the road keep the garment workers busy at night during the fall, and the first warm days of spring bring congestion of work again, not only to them but to the awning makers who must work often 72 hours a week to enable tradesmen to put their shops promptly in summer trim. The wholesale millinery houses have overtime through almost the whole of their spring and fall seasons (January 15 until the middle of May, and August 1 until December 1). The interdependence of many of these industries, the perishable nature of the goods, the financial importance of the season of heavy trade, thus present obstacles to the observance of a ten-hour working day throughout the year.

Manufacturers complain that overtime is a loss to them. They say that their employes do poorer work at night, and that the cost in wasted material, in light and heating, is more than

* Report of the British Association for the Advancement of Science, 1903, p. 7.

the profit gained by a lengthened day, but that they are forced to work overtime by customers who will not send in orders ahead. Night work, they say, is a means of holding their trade rather than of increasing their profits. Perhaps a universal legal prohibition would prove effective in overcoming the dilatoriness of customers in these seasonal trades, as well as in the trades where work pressure is irregular. Unquestionably much overtime has been eliminated in states that have stringent laws; much has been voluntarily avoided by manufacturers who have come to realize that night hours are in the long run a financial loss.

It seems probable, too, that overtime means in the long run an economic loss to women employes as well as to their employers. Opponents of legal prohibition of excessive working hours for women have argued that as women work by the piece and need the extra money, they are glad to work overtime. Yet there is reason to think that because of women's weaker physique, long hours have led to more lost time and have more seriously reduced industrial productivity than in the case of men, and that reduction of hours might lead to increased productivity and consequent rapid recovery of wages.

In reality the economic bearings of overtime work are bound up with the question of health. The specific evils attendant upon standing or sitting in a cramped position, operating heavy machinery, or continuously repeating a light but undiversified motion, are intensified with extension of the number of hours during which the operation is continued. As soon as these evils begin to manifest themselves in concrete physical results, the "point of diminishing returns" has been reached. Further work means greatly decreased productivity.

It is by some physical standard that we must judge as to when hours are "long," and when extra hours, from the viewpoint of health, are overtime. At present, ten hours as the limit of the working day is far from universal; yet clearly in the occupations at which we have seen large numbers of Pittsburgh workingwomen engaged, anything over ten hours may well be considered "long." Should ten hours, however, be set as a permissive standard? Or should we seek rather to work out, on the basis of health, a lower maximum beyond which no employe may go, and below this maximum set others corresponding to the degree of strain in different industries?

The fight of the unions has been for an eight-hour day, as the only fair maximum of working time. We may concede temporarily that ten hours may be tolerable at some occupations, but we cannot fail to recognize that ten hours at others is not tolerable. Considerations of social welfare, which adjudge hours "long" or the reverse, according to their effect on health, should prevent us from measuring all industries by the same standard. It has been pointed out that a factory law in which the provisions are general, applicable to all industries alike, fails to deal with the more serious evils which can be reached only by specific provisions. That any employer in any sort of establishment may legally keep his women employes at work for ten hours each day—such a law altogether ignores the difference in strain produced by different occupations. Speeding and pace making in most factories are an initial cause of strain. If, however, we assume that a girl can, without undue harm, work for ten hours in a candy factory where the pace required is high but where external conditions are good, have we, therefore, a right to assume that a girl can still, without undue harm, work ten hours at coil winding, where nerves are strained not only by the high pace but by excessive noise? If the former is all that a girl can well endure, and if ten hours be the legal maximum for work under the better conditions, is it reasonable to assume that under more trying conditions, she can stand the strain of work equally well? And how is it in the ironing room of a laundry, where there is often both noise and excessive heat? Can we justly permit ten hours to be the maximum for all industries, even for those in which strain-producing conditions are heaped one above another?

Suppose a ten-hour day to be permissible for a chocolate dipper; suppose an eight-hour day to be permissible for a saleswoman; can we therefore consider either a ten- or an eight-hour day permissible for a telephone operator, whose work is carried on under conditions of severe strain? Toronto physicians * concurred in the recent dispute respecting hours of employment between the Bell Telephone Company and operators, in the opinion

* Report of the Royal Commission, op. cit., pp. 65-78.

that more than a five-hour day (and a five-hour day broken by rest periods) would be injurious to the telephone operators. Yet legally, telephone operators in Pennsylvania may be employed ten and occasionally twelve hours a day. They are regularly employed eight hours a day, with occasional overtime, in Pittsburgh, and their rest periods, according to these same physicians, are too brief to be at all effectual.

Hours are "long," whether the day is eight hours or ten, if the work is continued so long that it causes ill-health or interferes with the employes' capacity for recreation. From the standpoint of social welfare, the maximum working day must be limited to a number of hours in which in most industries no more energy is expended than may be regained by a night's rest. From the standpoint of social welfare again, occupations involving special strain must be provided for specifically.

The relation between hours of work and capacity for healthful enjoyment is a vital phase of the question. Not only strength but mental alertness must be renewed by the evening's leisure. In so far as hours of work tend to dull and stupefy the worker, they are longer than the community can afford. Dulled senses demand powerful stimuli; exhaustion of the vital forces leads to a desire for crude, for violent excitation. Little time is left for pleasure after a ten-hour day. In such circumstances, culture of hand or brain seems unattainable, and the sharing of our general heritage a remote dream. A consideration of even more immediate importance is that such circumstances impel undisciplined girls toward unsocial action, toward vicious or criminal behavior. Craving for excitement is the last symptom of a starved imagination. At this point, discrimination has become too great an effort; foresight and social judgment have become impossible. Any excitation, destructive or not, is acceptable, if only it be strong; the effect of it is to create a desire for stronger stimulation. Roller skating rinks, dance halls, questionable cafés, may figure only temporarily in the worker's life, or by increasing the demand for excitement, may lead to sexual license.

A life enriched by a reasonable amount of leisure among all its members is no less important to the community than moderate health and moderate morality. Constructive enjoyment is a social force. Destructive excitement is an unsocial force. Hours are "long" if they tend to sway the workers toward wasteful or unsocial employment of leisure, and this, jointly with our standard of health, must be taken into consideration in arriving at a reasonable standard for the length of the working day.

CHAPTER XXV

HEALTH

THE health of the workers is a social as well as an industrial asset. It is affected by social conditions and industrial environment, wages paid, hours of work required, and the nature of the occupation itself. The Pittsburgh public has something at stake in the conditions under which 22,000 Pittsburgh women spend 10 hours or more out of every 24. Foregoing chapters have indicated that low wages are likely to mean incomplete nutrition, and long hours a dulling of the sensibilities, a lowering of the nervous tone. It remains to speak of specific conditions in certain groups of industries, and of types of workroom construction hardened into custom by demands of commercial convenience, which make for ill health among employes. How much, it is not easy to say; for inimical trade conditions are complicated by insufficient food, by improper cooking at home, by ignorance of fundamental hygiene, and by bad housing conditions. The majority of industries have yet to be studied exhaustively from the aspect of health. Yet there are many very simple and obvious elements in factory work which bear directly upon the physical well being of the people employed, and which lend themselves to ready adjustment.*

The trades of Pittsburgh women may be grouped with reference to disease according as they involve standing for prolonged periods of time, working in dust, in a steamy or gaseous atmosphere, carrying heavy weights, or operating machinery by treadle pressure. Employes are expected to stand continuously in most departments of cracker factories, laundries, dyeing and cleaning establishments, metal works, lamp and glass factories, mirror, broom, cork, paper box, soap and trunk factories, in some

*The subject of industrial accidents and protective machinery is considered in a companion volume in this series.

358

pressrooms, and in mercantile houses.   Two factories, one laundry, and two mercantile houses provide seats for their women employes, but with these exceptions, the state law in this matter is very generally ignored.   Its recurrence on the statute books of different states implies almost universal recognition of its need.   A woman may become mentally accustomed to constant standing, but she does not become physically accustomed to it.   It involves injury, though the woman herself may not understand or relate cause and effect.   "Long hours, and being obliged to stand all day, are very generally advanced as the principal reasons for any lack or loss of health occasioned by the work of the girls";* the majority of workingwomen who stand, have always at least a deficit in strength.   The law of Pennsylvania places on the factory inspector the obligation to see that seats are provided for women employes in factories and stores.†

Among dust-producing occupations examined in Pittsburgh are stogy making, garment and mattress making, mirror polishing, broom, cork and soap making.   Most of these occupations are productive of vegetable dust.   The high percentage of tuberculosis among tobacco workers, second only to that among stone cutters, has led to the supposition that there is something inherently dangerous in the trade itself.   The amount of dust varies greatly, however, according as the tobacco is dried by air or by heat. In the latter case, the leaf is brittle, breaking readily into dust, and in the former, it becomes smooth and mellow.   Where the air-drying process is used, there is reason to suppose that careful separation of workroom and drying room,‡ and provision for adequate ventilation, would go far toward eliminating danger. With reference to present conditions, Dr. Kober§ states that "Workers in tobacco suffer more or less from nasal, conjunctival, and bronchial catarrh, and digestive and nervous derangements, and although the mucous membranes gradually become accustomed to the irritation of the dust and fumes, the occupation appears to be dangerous."

*Report of the Massachusetts Bureau of Labor Statistics, 1884, p. 5.
† Act May 2, 1905, Sec. 7, P. L. No. 226.
‡ See below, p. 363.
§ Kober, Dr. George M.: Industrial and Personal Hygiene, p. 23.

The prevalence of dust and lint in garment factories, particularly where cheap jeans are made, emphasizes the need for special ventilation. Women in mattress factories work for the most part in sewing rooms shut off from departments where the ticks are filled, but a few "close" or sew the ends of ticks amid drifting dust of cotton and felt. Cork factory girls wear caps to protect their hair, but neither they nor packers of soap powder have respirators to protect the lungs. In spite of the wet process used in buffing mirrors, dust is always present in the mirror factory just as it is in the foundry where mica splitters scatter fine metal particles all day.

Dr. Kober comments on dust-producing occupations as a whole: "It has long been known that dust-inhaling occupations predispose to diseases of the respiratory passages, which may result in consumption. The particles of mineral dust produce an irritation of the mucous membrane of the throat, nose, respiratory organs, and eyes; . . . causing catarrhal conditions of the respiratory organs, so common among persons engaged in dusty occupations. The chronic inflammatory conditions thus produced favor infection with the tubercle bacillus. At all events, Hirt's statistics show that men employed in dust-producing occupations suffer much more frequently from pneumonia and consumption than those not exposed to dust, and that there is practically no difference in frequency of disease of the digestive system."

The steamy or gaseous atmosphere in laundries, and in dyeing and cleaning establishments, is likewise productive of ill health. "The cleaners of woolen goods, etc., with naphtha, not infrequently suffer from dizziness, nausea, vomiting, headache, sleeplessness, hysteria, and symptoms resembling alcoholic intoxication."* In casket, lamp, and japanning works, the lacquer girls are subject to headache from the irritating fumes. Laundry workers are stated† to be especially liable to rheumatism and to diseases of the respiratory organs, because of their long hours in an overheated, steamy atmosphere, and the abrupt exit at night to the outside air.

*Kober, Dr. George M.: Industrial and Personal Hygiene, p. 46.
†Oliver, Thomas, Medical Expert on Dangerous Trades, Committee of the Home Office. London, 1902. Dangerous Trades. Chapter LVII, p. 668.

Most of the machinery operated by violent treadle pressure is found in three industries. The button-stamping machine in garment factories, the perforating press in binderies, and the laundry cuff press, are the most conspicuous examples. Although the effect of these machines has yet to be closely studied, the testimony of physicians tends to confirm the lay observer's opinion, that operators are liable to pelvic disorders. Similar dangers beset women who push trucks from room to room in the larger canneries, and women who in machine shops carry the heavy trays of cores from benches to ovens.

We have yet to learn, in many cases, how to eliminate or modify the share of industry in responsibility for disease. The substitution of a wet for a dry process, the use of respirators, or the attachment of exhaust machinery to grinding wheels, undoubtedly reduces the danger from vegetable or mineral dust-making processes. The Pennsylvania law provides for exhaust machinery in connection with wheels where mineral dust is produced, but in the Pittsburgh district this law is enforced only spasmodically and such protective devices are very generally absent. The law takes no cognizance of occupations in which the dust is due not to the kind of machinery but to the kind of material, and in which the amount of dust might be lessened by a change in process, or the operative might be protected by the use of a respirator.

It is of importance to recognize that the whole plant in which an industry is lodged is a force for or against health. Planning a building with reference to the needs of a particular industry is, if possible, more important than safeguarding the individual in the interest of health. Laundries offer a conspicuous example of undesirable building construction. Most of the ills from which laundry workers suffer are due either to gas-heated apparatus or to a steamy atmosphere. The British law* has met the problem of gas-heated apparatus by prohibiting the use of gas-heated ironing machines unless properly protected by exhaust pipes and vents so that the gas and excess heat shall be carried away from the operator. One source of illness is thereby minimized. More serious, however, than the ills caused by gas-heated ironing

*Factory and Workshop Act: August 17, 1901, Ch. 22, sec. 103 (1. Edw. VII).

machines, are the ills caused by ten or twelve hours of work in a hot, moist atmosphere, and a walk through the cold night air afterward. These ills can only in small part be met by the protection of an individual machine. The hot, moist atmosphere is caused by clouds of rising steam; yet save in two cases, the washroom, the source of the steam, is on the lowest floor. Greatly increased comfort might be gained by extensive systems of forced ventilation, but so long as the washroom is below instead of above the other departments, the origin of the trouble is untouched. A primary move toward health for laundry workers would be the establishment of a standard for complete forced ventilation in laundries, and for the arrangement of laundry departments with reference to each other. If the washroom is properly built of concrete, separate from and placed above the other departments, comfort and health are possible on the lower floors; if it is placed below or with the other departments, all of the employes must suffer both discomfort and injury to health.

The situation in the cracker industry is somewhat similar. Here the difficulty is not with steam, but with the intense heat of the cracker ovens. The heat rises; yet only one of the five cracker factories of Pittsburgh has its ovens on the upper floor. The result is that the hot dry air, together with the pace of the work, tends to drag down the strength of the workers and to lay the foundation for positive ill-health. Ventilation in a cracker factory must needs be of a different sort from ventilation in a laundry; but here, as in laundries, the arrangement of departments with reference to each other is as important as ventilation, from the standpoint of health. A well constructed cracker oven on the upper floor of a well ventilated factory can do the workers little harm. On a lower floor, a cracker oven, whether well constructed or not, is certain to be a menace to health.

Core rooms and stogy factories are instances of the need in some industries for a separation of departments. One Pittsburgh core room is placed directly above a brass foundry in which there are no devices for carrying off brass dust and fumes. Although the girl core makers work not in brass but in sand, and have no necessary connection with unhealthful or dangerous foundry work, they are in much the same danger from dust and

A Workshop on "The Hill"

The unswept floor, half-filled boxes of stock, closed windows, and shelves of drying tobacco are characteristic

A Cellar Stripping Room

WORKROOMS WHERE HEALTH CONDITIONS ARE BAD

fumes as the men on the floor below. In other core rooms, the benches are ranged on either side of the ovens, and work is carried on at all times in an atmosphere of intolerable heat and much dust. Since cores are made without machinery at benches covered with moist sand, the drifting dust found in all the Pittsburgh core rooms save one plainly does not result from the work itself. One core room, clean, well ventilated, separate from the rest of the building, proves that there is no need inherent in the occupation for the dangers and discomforts to which core makers are exposed.

Much of the danger from working in tobacco results from a combination of drying room and workroom. Tobacco is placed on racks or spread out on the floor in little heaps to dry. As the leaves grow mellow and workable, the gathered dust of the fields and brittle bits of the tobacco itself are blown or scattered about the room. Fumes of nicotine from the drying tobacco are heavy. Sometimes the benches of the stogy makers are placed directly beneath the high heaps of leaves on brown canvas racks, and sometimes wooden racks are built against the walls of the room. Sometimes there is just a little hill of tobacco in a dark corner. Although the danger from tobacco dust is greatest when the racks are overhead, it is always present when the drying process is carried on in the workroom. By complete separation of workrooms and drying rooms in stogy factories, one grave source of danger to the workers would be removed.*

Garment factories and mercantile houses illustrate the need for a standard floor plan in certain groups of industrial plants. The ease with which ten to twenty machines, set up in an ill lighted, ill ventilated loft, can be made to produce profits for their owner, has resulted in Pittsburgh in an unhealthful type of garment factory. A long, narrow room, with windows at either end, insufficient light, many machines, and no forced ventilation, is the dominant type. It has been suggested that the bad air, the cramped position in which the girls sit at their machines, and lint from cheap goods made in quantity tend to induce diseases

---

*The International Cigar Makers' Union has also emphasized the need to lessen the danger of infection, by placing work benches with one row behind the other, rather than facing each other.

of the respiratory organs. In the garment industry as definite a standard as in school codes should be set, for seats and windows, distance of machines from windows, and for circulation of air.

Mercantile houses need a standard floor plan in connection with the provision of seats for saleswomen behind the counters. Adequate space should be required between counter and case of stock. The economy which results in forcing more counters into the available floor space than the floor can comfortably hold, gives the merchants ground for saying that they have no room for seats and that girls do not use seats when provided. Of course, girls who must crowd by each other to reach down boxes of goods, cannot but turn back the seats at a busy counter. A wider minimum space between counter and case of goods would, by allowing room for seats, make it easier to enforce this regulation.

The provisions of the factory law are general. Because they are applicable to all industries alike, of necessity they fail to cope with the trade danger which is not general, but characteristic of a particular occupation. For all industries alike, there must be a legal minimum in sanitation, ventilation, fire protection. Yet, as a prerequisite to health, each industry in this group has need of an especial standard of ventilation, based upon its particular conditions. For example, the general factory law in requiring adequate ventilation, in general terms, must base its requirements on the conditions in the majority of manufacturing plants, where dust-producing elements are in no way excessive. "It has been found that the average adult requires 3,000 cubic feet of fresh air per hour, and this amount should be supplied without discomfort to the occupants. Experience has shown that the air of a room cannot be changed oftener than three times in one hour in winter, without causing a disagreeable draft; hence every occupant should have a cubic air space of 1,000 feet. . . . . . Such a standard, however, is not always attainable in workshops, and it is believed that for practical purposes an air space of from 400 to 500 feet per capita will suffice."* Suppose this to be taken as the standard in the general factory law. This law extends and is adapted to the vast number of industrial plants

* Kober, Dr. George M.: Industrial and Personal Hygiene, pp. 74, 75.

where the work is not dust-producing. Is it reasonable, however, from considerations of health, to accept the same standard of ventilation for plants in which excessive dust is produced? Industrial plants of the latter type should plainly come under a special and separate standard.

Equally it would seem that the standard building plan should be worked out in dust-producing or otherwise dangerous industries, according to the particular conditions of the industry. Not only ventilation adapted to the disposal of dust or steam, but a rearrangement of departments with reference to each other, as in cracker factories and laundries; a separation of departments, as in core rooms and stogy factories; a change in floor plan, as in garment factories and mercantile houses, would seem to be fundamental in a concerted effort against trade disease.

A third factor affecting health, besides essential trade disease and unhealthful building construction, enters into the industrial environment. This is speeding.

In the different industries, we have seen how the pace of many workers is kept high by the speed of machinery. A traveling chain carries cans of beans past a row of cannery operatives. They must slip a bit of pork into each can as it passes, and the chain is set at a pace which keeps each girl rigid in her place, with every nerve at a tension, fixed on the one motion required of her. In a cracker factory girls lift hot crackers from a traveling conveyor, packing them in oblong boxes with one quick motion, as the conveyor passes; each girl is responsible for all the crackers on a certain section of the conveyor, which is set at a pace requiring her utmost physical and nervous effort.

Among hand workers, and workers who control their machines, systems of pace setting are combined, as we have seen, with piece-rate payments to keep up the speed. Four stogy factories, for example, stimulate their girl rollers by a sliding scale which provides $ .13½ a 100 when 400 stogies are rolled from a pound, but only $ .10 when 300 are rolled. To earn the pay customary in the district ($ .12 a 100) girls must cut close, and at the same time work at an almost impossible rate of speed. In another factory, rollers receive only $ .09 a 100 if they make less than 6000 stogies a week, and $ .11 a 100 (the market rate in one district) if they make 6000 or over. The foreman of a printing establishment paid his girls $7.00 a week for an average output (in register folding) of 300 an hour. A system of piece payments was introduced, and in two days the rate went up to 500 an hour; week work was then resumed at the old price, and the girls were required to keep the new pace. A lamp factory pays $ .14 an hour for punching 600 pieces, and $ .01 'for every 100 pieces finished within the same time. This list of examples could be extended indefinitely.

Thus the speed of machinery, when pay is by the week, or a piece-payment system, impels the worker to increase the quantity of her output, and repeated rate-cutting in some industries seems not only to keep weekly earnings down to a customary level, but to spur the workers to a fiercer pace. The nervous strain inevitable under these conditions has no inconsiderable share in causing the positive breakdown which so frequently follows a girl into her home after she has left the factory. It is the final exaction that the trade makes of her.

Industrial work and environment must induce health and not disease if the future shall justify us in employing women in factories. Processes can be made harmless if we work at the problem long enough; workrooms can be made wholesome, speed cut short before the point of depletion. In such an industrial city as Pittsburgh, either the medical profession or the department of factory inspectors might take the initial steps toward overcoming the tendency to trade disease by giving employers and legislators more facts about industrial hygiene, exact knowledge of what and how a trade contributes to ill health. The progressive manufacturer who rearranges his old building or builds his new on the basis of what we already know of safeguarding against trade dangers, sets a standard for his industry and for allied industries, which should be incorporated in the law of the state. A manufacturer who keeps a health record of his employes and seeks to eradicate the causes of disease which it may indicate, is a signal contributor to industrial science.

The opportunity of the employer goes farther. Positive good health, which must ultimately be our national physical standard, can perhaps be shadowed forth in factory conditions first of all.   More hours are spent at work than are spent sleeping, and a well ventilated, well built factory may in large measure offset the deteriorating effect of an ill ventilated, ill built home. Employes may grow discontented with confused, overcrowded living rooms if their workplace is roomy and harmonious.   Factory planning, both of the building and of the system of work, may make one of the most valuable present day contributions, not only to the mere avoidance of pathological conditions, but to the development of effective health and high vitality among the working people of America.

CHAPTER XXVI

ECONOMIC FOOTHOLD

WAGES, hours, and factory conditions which affect health concern the public well-being too closely to be utterly neglected by a community whose women go out at labor. This much our survey of employments in Pittsburgh makes clear. Bound up in these considerations is the question of workmanship—the processes assigned to women, their skill, and the economic foothold which they have gained.

In interpreting these employments, I have discussed them as parts of the different industries. Yet while I have called them for convenience by the name of their products, as candy making and lamp making, these are not really the women's occupations. A closer analysis shows that very nearly identical processes run through many of these employments. Women are pasting labels not only in canneries, but in paper box, cigar and paint factories. They are tending machines no less in cracker making and cork cutting than in the metal works. Here we have a basis for recapitulating our employments in a way that will afford a fairer index of how far women have actually come into the industrial life of the district as factors in production. They may be grouped according to the nature of their occupations as skilled workers, workers at a handicraft, hand workers at a process which requires speed or dexterity, machine operators, machine tenders, wrappers and labelers, and hand workers at a process which requires no intelligence.

The following table gives the number of workers in each of these groups:*

* The 6534 saleswomen in mercantile houses are not included in this enumeration.

368

TABLE 36.—NUMBER OF WOMEN WORKERS IN VARIOUS OCCUPATION GROUPS

Kind of Work	No. of Women	Percentage
Skilled work	139	.8
Handicraft	305	1.9
Hand work requiring dexterity . .	3641	23.2
Machine operating	4885	31.1
Machine tending	2188	13.9
Wrapping and labeling . . .	2118	13.3
Hand work requiring no dexterity .	2475	15.8
	15,651	100.0

The only women in the trades considered who can be called skilled in any true sense are the millinery trimmers and telegraph operators. Both these must serve an apprenticeship until they have learned the routine work of their occupation; and having learned the work they must serve a still longer time to gain a mastery of its details. They must have intelligence and an aptitude for what they do; beyond that they must have training.

The group of women who possess a handicraft is also conspicuously small. Makers of hand stogies, expert makers in millinery houses, and fine ironers in laundries, have occupations for which they must spend time in training. They do the whole of the thing. Although speed in execution counts in these occupations as in all others, quality of product is emphasized. The workers must think of the workmanship first, and of the quantity second.

Added together, however, the women of these two groups make less than 3 per cent of the 22,185 under consideration in Pittsburgh; and from their work we can scarcely judge of the nature of women's work as a whole. That work is, as a rule, of a nature to require neither strength, endurance, intelligence nor training.

As we take up hand work which in contrast requires speed or dexterity and only that, we find that the percentage of women has jumped to nearly one-fourth of the total. The women in this group are bottling pickles, dipping chocolates, icing cakes, rolling stogies, making bandeaux for hats, shaping sand cores, winding wire, pasting paper boxes, sorting corks. They learn what they have to do sometimes in a week, sometimes in two or three months. In six months they work rapidly; in a year they have often reached their maximum output. They work by hand, it is true, but at the kind of hand work in which they repeat continuously a simple, undiversified motion.

The machine operators are the largest group of all. Many of them run sewing machines by power; they press the treadle and hold the cloth in place. Others cut tin, or bunch stogies, or run ironing machinery or wind coils. As more and more machines have been equipped with power, thus making muscular strength unnecessary, the increasing employment of women has become possible. Even when an additional man is employed to keep the machines in repair, the total outlay for wages and power is less than the total outlay for the wages of hand workers and the material which they use.

To increase the automatic efficiency of the machine so that not an operator but merely a machine tender is necessary, is the next step. Labor cost to the manufacturer is saved not only by the employment of fewer people, but by the payment of lower wages to those who remain. One Pittsburgh paper box factory has reduced its force one-half by the introduction of new covering machines, and by the introduction of still other machines it might reduce its force a third more; yet the output of the factory has steadily increased. The marking machine has dispensed with from one-half to three-fourths of the checkers in four laundries. In the cork factory, new tapering machines are being put in. For each of the old machines, one operator was necessary, but four of the new machines can be tended by one girl. Instances without number from Pittsburgh's industrial experience could be cited affirming how machinery is labor-saving both of human strength and of the numbers of employes. By thus cheapening the cost of the product, it stimulates demand and ultimately results in an actual increase both of machines and employes. But it should also be borne in mind that machinery is wage-saving. Not only fewer people relative to output are employed, but those few are paid the wages, not of skilled, but of unskilled labor.

One woman puts fifty hinges a minute through a machine. Each second a hinge is lifted out and slipped into place, the hand drawn back as the machine moves, another hinge lifted and slipped into place—this for ten hours each working day.

Other women spread out a tobacco leaf on the suction plate, put the half made bunch in the leaf, press the treadle and push the rolled stogy aside; spread out another leaf, cut, put the bunch in place, press the treadle and push aside. Still others steady the paper in a box-covering machine, guide it according to the gauge, replace it when the strip runs out, guide it according to the gauge, and so on. Such work not only requires no thought; it is stupefying. The operative who has become in truth an adjunct of the machine, works with a machine-like precision, and with machine-like absence of thought. Work which demands nothing of the intelligence, costs the intelligence more than work which demands too much.

There are 2000 machine tenders in Pittsburgh. Closely akin to them, and of equal numbers, are the women who wrap and label. They pack crackers, candy, glass, lamps, with quick, machine-taught, unvarying motions, lifting, wrapping, putting in place, for ten hours a day.

Lowest of all, perhaps, in grade of intelligence are the hand workers of whom neither training nor dexterity is required. They are the preparation hands in canneries, the strippers in stogy factories, the hand-washers and starchers in laundries, the miscellaneous hands in printing establishments, and the women day laborers in the metal works. These women can be set at their jobs without preliminary explanation and can do these jobs adequately, for the occupations are of a sort, whether slicing pickles, stemming tobacco, or screwing nuts on bolts, at which they soon gain their maximum speed.

With the development of machinery, then, which has disintegrated many of the skilled men's trades, and along with that subdivision of labor which, in districts like this about Pittsburgh, has put ten immigrants at the machines for every all-around mechanic set to work, women are called into factories in large numbers, but they are called to simple, unskilled, and unstimulating labor. In discussing wages paid in the Pittsburgh district it was clear that women had displaced men altogether in many of these occupations; that they had been hired because they would work for less; that they could work for less when their living expenses were met by family or by outsiders; and that they were often forced to work for less, because, through lack of strength or training, they were limited in their chance for work to a small group of industries, and to certain restricted levels in most of those industries, where the labor market has naturally become glutted.

It remains to discuss here more in detail the reasons which have kept women in this limited range of occupations. Some of these occupations require greater dexterity than others, and some emphasize speed, but the overwhelmingly large proportion require in their women employes neither training, nor stability, nor intelligence.

Skill, judgment, the way of a machine, and the relation of one machine to another cannot be learned in three to six months. The understanding of these things belongs to men who have years of working time before them. But to a woman who hopes to be out and away from her employment in factory or shop before the end of six or eight years, knowledge of several different processes in the same shop and training in the organization of a department, have no apparent utility.

Women are a shifting body of workers, first, because they give up their industrial work at marriage, and second, because of their consequent lack of ambition. Together these facts produce among them an unprofessional attitude, a conscious instability. For these reasons, women are undesirable apprentices, and since it does not pay to take them for the greater part of a year step by step through the intricacies of a trade, they can be employed profitably only at such occupations as are quickly learned. They may be allowed from three to six months in which to gain the requisite speed, but in most cases the actual operation is learned in a few weeks.

Their opportunities for employment are still further circumscribed by the opposition of men's unions.* Telegraph operators and press feeders admit women on the same terms as men, but neither union has succeeded in enforcing the closed shop, or in gaining a large following among Pittsburgh women workers.

---

*An exception to this is the United Garment Workers of America, which has many women members, and in Pittsburgh has been notably successful.

The National Stogy Makers have barred women from their union. The broom makers do not include in their union the subsidiary employment at which women are engaged. The core makers have not only kept women out of their union, but are attempting to close all shops against them. The bookbinders' union admits only men. All these are unions of skilled workmen. Either they include only such parts of the trade as are really skilled (as among the bookbinders who admit finishers, forwarders and rulers), or they include all the workmen at a single process (as among stogy makers and core makers), but specifically prohibit the admission of women to their union.

Three conditions then—the more obvious lack of physical strength which interferes to some extent with a woman's operation of heavy machinery, opposition from men's unions, and, most important of all, industrial instability—have combined to leave to women the subsidiary processes, and the mechanical operations which demand little of the intelligence.

Cause and effect in their case work in a circle. Expectation of marriage, as a customary means of support, stunts professional ambition among women. This lack of ambition can have no other effect than to limit efficiency, and restricts them to subsidiary, uninteresting, and monotonous occupations. The very character of their work in turn lessens their interest in it. Without interest, they least of all feel themselves integral parts of the industry and in consequence assume no responsibility, affect no loyalty. They do not care to learn; opportunity to learn is not given them; both are causes and both are effects. Women see only a fight for place, and very uncertain advantage if they gain it; wages are low, again both cause and effect of their dependence in part on others for their support. They shift about on lower levels of industry from packing room to metal work, from metal work to laundry work; a very few through unwonted good fortune, unwonted determination, break through the circle and rise.

The physical effect of long hours under high speed pressure is comparable to the mental effect of continuous unstimulating work. We cannot afford that the work which women do should leave them with a deficit in health; nor can we afford that it should leave them with a deficit in mental alertness. Suggestions have been made for possible checks and safeguards against trade dangers in order to standardize the health of the workers. To standardize intelligence is a far more subtle problem, but one which there is reason to hope will be met in part by the newer educational ideals.

The experiments which have been made in trade training, for women as well as for men, suggest one fairly defined way of advance and improvement. By trade training is not meant the sort of training often most in demand, class work in amateur cooking, dressmaking, and millinery. The training meant is class work comparable to that of trade-trained men, which reacts to the benefit both of industry and of customer, by improving the quality of the product. This should develop in women industrial intelligence by teaching them the practice and the significance of allied industrial processes. To be concrete: Pittsburgh women are largely employed in printing and bookbinding establishments, but as feeders, not as rulers. Why not teach them to mix inks, to fill pens, to manage the ruling machines, as well as to slip into place one piece of ledger paper after another in rhythmic succession? Women are employed for sorting and sizing in broom factories. Why should they not be taught to dye and wash and stack the corn, so that they could rise, if they had opportunity, to positions of responsibility in the sorting department? Women are employed in machine shops and foundries. Why are they not taught the principles on which sand cores are made, the combinations of sand, the kinds of sand for different sorts of work, the necessary allowance for shrinkage, and the combinations of simple into complex cores? Women are employed in garment factories. Why should they not be taught to cut out garments as well as to run the machines; to plan and direct as well as to execute? Women are employed to sell goods. Why should they not be taught the plan of store organization, differences in fabric, the psychology of meeting a customer's needs? Such an educational program implies building on the present occupations of women to increase the efficiency of women at present employed. It would not mean merely manual training; nor would it mean a feminizing of trade courses. It would mean co-operation between trade schools and manufacturers, which should result, through the success of a few women, in wider opportunity for the many.

Were such trade training general, the depressive mental effect of much factory work might in part be overcome. The worker would understand the relation of her occupation to others and the relation of her industry to others; she would cease to be an altogether unintelligent cog in the wheel. An occupation that calls for a little knowledge as well as for dexterity becomes immediately a stimulus to the intelligence.

It is not my purpose to suggest that all women would profit by trade training. Many, no doubt, under any circumstances, would tend to move from unskilled work to unskilled work, and out to uncared-for homes. Nor would I, in looking for economic as well as psychological effects, claim that were all workers trained in their trades, wages would magically rise. The wages of trained workers are relatively high today because the trained are few; were they many, their payment might be on a different basis. My belief is simply that, were trade training general, one reason for the present low wages of working women would be removed. The advocates of equal pay for equal work would have more instances of equal work to show, and could with justice demand for skilled workers what for unskilled workers they cannot. These skilled workers would be equipped to demand with justice more for themselves, and with larger show of success.

A girl's well grounded self-reliance, even in a semi-skilled trade, such as garment making, is enough to extend her six possible working years to ten, and to lead her ambition far. The tendency toward lengthening the term of woman's working life seems likely to be strengthened among trained and skilful workers. The resulting conflict between trade opportunities and domestic responsibilities must be met by further adjustment. Yet pending such adjustment, we shall do well to remember that inferior and monotonous work processes are no preparation for intelligent home making. Higher earnings and increased industrial efficiency go far toward developing in working women a sense of responsibility, personal and social, toward whichever group they choose to become a part.

APPENDICES

APPENDIX A

PLAN AND METHODS OF STUDY

W E chose for this study from among the groups of industries fostered by the city. In marking out a field for investigation, it was not practicable to draw a circle wide enough to include all the wage-earning women of every class. Some industries, such as domestic service, are so scattered, with each woman in a separate workplace, that limits of time alone were sufficient to forbid a sally into this field. Agricultural pursuits are not, it would seem, extensive within the city limits, and professional service presents problems of a different sort from those faced by uneducated and untrained workers.

In the year which was given to the investigation, an attempt was made to study in the cities of Pittsburgh and Allegheny all the women-employing industries in which the units are organized on factory lines. Within this definition are included all industrial plants wherein the women workers are, in general, grouped under one management in one building for work which is subdivided and specialized, so that each operation or fraction of an operation is a contributing part to a single whole. Clerical service was logically excluded from consideration, on the ground that the typical clerk or stenographer is employed either alone or with one or two others in an office; that the employment of a large office force under a single management, while possibly the type of the future, is not the dominant type of to-day. On the other hand, the work of telephone and telegraph operators is included because the characteristic forms of these industries are the telephone exchange and the main office, rather than the private branch wire or the private exchange. Steam laundries are to all intents and purposes factories, but the solitary laundress is of a different genus. Saleswomen in mercantile houses come within the definition of workers under a factory organization; but although an attempt was made to include all cases where more than five women were working, limitation of time made it impossible to include the innumerable small stores with their quota of one or two saleswomen each. It was felt that these latter presented a different problem, were affected by a different set of circumstances, and might logically be excluded. Yet the single stogy maker in a sweatshop was studied together with the factory worker, because the industry is so knit together that one phase of it would be incomprehensible without the other.

The waitress in a restaurant is on debatable ground. From one point of view, it would seem necessary to include service of this sort, because the girls work usually in groups under one management. In Pittsburgh, however, there are few dining rooms of any size where the serving is done by women; the type is either the large dining room with waiters in attendance, or the small restaurant with one or two women behind the counter. The conditions of the work in Pittsburgh seemed so closely akin to those of domestic service that logically both should be excluded from consideration here.

Where less than ten women were employed at a trade, as for instance the manufacture of caps and hats, which engages only five women, that trade has been excluded. With these limitations, the field of manufacturing and mechanical pursuits has been covered, and in addition to this, the work of laundry employes, saleswomen, press feeders, bookbinders and telephone and telegraph operators.

In considering each trade, an attempt was made to show primarily what the conditions of work were at the time of the investigation, what wages and hours are characteristic, and what the relation of the women is to the several trade processes and to the trade as a whole. The summary of conditions in all the trades in a measure should indicate the economic and social significance of the work of women in Pittsburgh today.

A word should be said about the method of investigation. Each of the 448 shops and factories under consideration was visited, and with the exception of twenty where special circumstances made it impossible, all were inspected. In each case a statement was obtained from the management of the number of men and women employed, of the hours, and of the wages paid. In several cases the payrolls were opened to the visitor. Each statement made by the management was tested by interviews with employes and by interviews with people familiar with the trade, who stood on neutral ground. Conversely, statements made by employes were tested by interviews with employers. In consequence, the discussion of each trade may justly be regarded not as a reflection of either the employer's or the employe's point of view, but as description resulting from consideration of the several viewpoints and the neutral truths concerned.

Little prominence has been given to individual cases of exploitation and injustice, unless these cases were characteristic of a trade group rather than of individual method. Meanness is a personal trait. Night work may be the result of meanness in a single firm, or it may be the result of a commercial maladjustment. In the former case it deserves passing mention, but in the latter case it must be commented upon as, temporarily at least, characteristic of the industry. My effort has been to study the conditions growing out of the trade itself, not out of the foibles or the unkindness of any individual, and to present a sketch of the trade process in terms of the life of the workers and of its place in present day industrial methods.

The study of each firm in the trades under consideration and of the workers in each trade, was supplemented by talks with union men, with settlement and club leaders, and with many social workers and manufacturers whose work lies on the fringe of that undertaken here. It is through the courtesy and kindness of men in each industry that I have been able to understand something of the work and of the problems, racial and educational, that they have to meet in dealing with the workers. It is through the kindness of many a factory girl that I have been able to understand something of her problem, and through the splendid courage of a handful of women workers that I caught a glimpse of the industrial power they are to be in the day that lies ahead.

381

APPENDIX B

TABLES ILLUSTRATIVE OF WAGES, HOURS AND CONDITIONS IN THE INDUSTRIES

THE figures here given, both of the number of employes in each factory and in each trade, and of the range of wages of these employes, were obtained by a factory-to-factory investigation during the winter of 1907–08. The actual number of persons on the payrolls at the time of the investigation is given. In no trade does this number coincide with the number of extras taken on casually and irregularly during some sudden press of business, as in the canneries in summer, or in wholesale millinery houses in August. Neither does this number coincide with the shrunken payroll of a season when trade is at lowest ebb, as in January in the stogy factories.

While investigation of all the trades was more or less continuous during the year, visits to the factories were so timed as to cover a normal busy season, avoiding both periods of excessive dullness, and of excessive pressure of work. For instance, the investigation of the stogy factories was made during the months of September and October, when the factories were running steadily, but were not yet at the height of their Christmas trade. Mercantile houses were investigated, in part during the month of September, in part during the month of May. Laundries were visited during February, when trade was at the normal mid-year point, and only regular hands were in employment. Candy factories were visited in March, when business was steady, but before any extra hands had been taken on for the Easter trade.

The industrial depression following the panic in October, 1907, interfered with the accuracy of this census less than might at first be imagined. Factories and shops very generally laid off their hands for half the time each week, or dismissed a part of the force for a week at a time. The relation of the number actually working at the time the factory was visited, to the total number on the payrolls, was thus not a matter of guess-work, but sufficiently definite to be stated in exact figures. If half the force in a factory had temporarily been laid off at the time the visit was made, this fact was ascertained, and the total number of employes noted in the census, notwithstanding the extraordinary circumstance which prevented some of them at that time from working. In this way it was possible to note both the number of persons in regular employment, and the extent to which the depression had affected a given trade. The number of regular employes in all these industries is fairly constant, in spite of reductions in an off season, or accretions in a season of heavy work. It is this normal level, generally coinciding directly with the time of the investigation, which is given in the tables that follow.

Wages.—The method pursued in obtaining figures with reference to wages was to question the forewoman, or other person in close contact with the girls, and to compare her statements with the testimony of the employes themselves. Direct inspection of the payrolls was in some cases possible. It was found, however, that women workers who have acquired a certain dexterity in their occupation tend, in their earnings, to approximate a certain fixed level, determined by the local market, and by various social cross currents. When the investigator has ascertained this fixed level, it becomes possible in each factory to discover what percentage of the total employes have reached this level, how many are still below it, how many have passed beyond it, and how far. The sum of these figures, which are not based on a statistical study of the wages of each individual, does not pretend to represent actual wages. Yet both totals and percentages, built up as they are for each factory upon testimony based on intimate knowledge of the employes involved, may fairly be considered representative of the wage groups, indicating the limits within which the wages of an occupation may range.

No trade employing less than ten women has been included in this study.

TABLE 37.—CANNERIES. NUMBER OF EMPLOYES IN EACH PITTS-
BURGH CANNERY

No. of Plant	Men	Women	Total
1	2	2	4
2	50	100	150
3	400	600	1000
4	6	4	10
5	151	54	205
6	4	2	6
7	5	20	25
Total	618	782	1400

TABLE 38.—CONFECTIONERY. RANGE OF WEEKLY WAGES PAID
TO WRAPPERS, LABELERS, CHOCOLATE AND CREAM DIPPERS,
IN EACH FACTORY

No. of Plant	Packing (Including Labeling and Miscellaneous Work)			Dipping (Including both Chocolate and Cream)		
	Minimum	Maximum	Majority($\frac{3}{4}$)	Minimum	Maximum	Majority($\frac{3}{4}$)
1		$6.00	(flat rate)	..	..	..
2	$2.50	8.00*	$5.00	..	..	..
3	4.00	5.00	4.00	..	$7.00	$6.00
4	1.98	6.00	4.00	..	..	..
5	..	5.00	(flat rate)	..	7.00	..
6	3.00	5.00	5.00	$3.00	6.50	5.00
7	4.00	7.00(?)	5.00	..	..	..
8	..	7.00	..	..	8.00	..
9	4.00	7.00	5.50	4.00	9.00	5.50
10	3.50	7.00	5.00	4.00	9.00	9.00
11	4.00	6.00	5.00	6.00	7.00	..
12	4.20	8.00*	5.00	..	..	..
13	4.00	7.00	6.00	4.00	7.00	6.00
14	3.00	7.00	6.00	3.50	9.00	7.00
15	4.00	7.00	6.00	4.00	8.00	7.00
16	..	7.00†	..	..	..	..
17	5.00	7.00	6.00	6.00	9.00	7.00

* Forewoman.
† Only one girl employed.

384

TABLE 39.—CRACKER FACTORIES. NUMBER OF MEN AND OF WOMEN IN EACH FACTORY

No. of Plant	Men	Women	Total
1	13	25	38
2	44	53	97
3	75	100	175
4	650	450	1100
5	100	300	400
Total	882	928	1810

TABLE 40.—CRACKER FACTORIES. RANGE OF WEEKLY WAGES PAID WOMEN IN EACH FACTORY

No. of Plant	Minimum	Maximum	Majority		Time or Piece Work
1	$3.00	$7.00	$5.50,	$6.00	Time
2	4.00	7.00	5.50		Time
3	3.00	7.00*	5.00,	6.00	Time
4	3.00	6.60*	4.00,	5.00	Piece
5	3.50	5.50	5.00,	5.50	Time

* Head girl only.

TABLE 41.—THE STOGY INDUSTRY. LOCATION OF FACTORIES AND SWEATSHOPS AND DISTRIBUTION OF WORKERS

A. Factories

District	Number of Shops	Number of Workers	
		Men	Women
Hill District . .	9	162	264
South Side . .	1	12	4
Downtown . .	9	147	1027
East End . .	4	29	71
North Side . .	9	113	845
Total . . .	32	463	2211

B. SWEATSHOPS

District	Number of Shops	NUMBER OF WORKERS	
		Men	Women
Hill District . .	124	297	323
South Side . .	23	56	22
Downtown . .	3	4	3
East End . .	23	45	19
North Side . .	30	51	33
Total . . .	203	453	400

TABLE 42.—THE STOGY INDUSTRY. PHYSICAL CHARACTERISTICS OF HILL SWEATSHOPS

Grade	VENTILATION	
A	Good	5
B	Fair	5
C	Gas jets exhausting air	5
D	None	109

SANITATION

A	Sanitary	28
C	Unsanitary; damp; dark	5
D	Unsanitary	91

CROWDING

C	Crowded	29
D	Very much crowded (7 ft. ceiling)	4

CLEANLINESS

B	Fairly clean	39
C	Dirty (tobacco heaped on floor)	77
D	Very dirty	8

It should be said that shops are not arbitrarily grouped in these categories, but are arranged according to a definite standard. There is, for instance, no means of ventilation in any of these tenement shops, except through windows or doors. When windows and doors are habitually closed, so that the air is difficult to breathe, the heading under "ventilation" is "none."   If the air is further vitiated by gas burning, the heading is "very bad." If windows are open, even if air is not good, heading is "fair."

Shops are judged to be unsanitary if there is no other toilet provision than a privy vault in the yard, or if the inside plumbing is not properly connected with the sewer. A room is judged to be crowded when there is less than 200 cubic feet of air space per person. When tobacco waste and refuse, the accumulation of weeks, is heaped under benches, a room is considered "dirty." If the whole floor space is so covered, it is considered "very dirty." When there are evidences that the room is swept, it is adjudged "clean."

TABLE 43.—THE STOGY INDUSTRY. PHYSICAL CHARACTERISTICS OF SWEATSHOPS OUTSIDE THE HILL DISTRICT

	East End	South Side	Downtown	North Side
CROWDING				
Overcrowded	1	1	..	4
SANITATION				
Sanitary	17	16	..	16
Unsanitary	6	7	3	14
VENTILATION				
Good	1	6	..	2
Very bad; gas burning . .	..	2	..	4
None	22	15	3	24
CLEANLINESS				
Clean	13	14	1	22
Dirty	10	9	2	8
LOCATION OF WORKROOM				
Rear of store	11	15	1	16
Shed	3	1	1	2
Cellar	..	1	..	2
All others	9	6	1	10
DRYING OF TOBACCO				
Racks in room { Side . .	3	2	..	6
{ Overhead .	3	3	..	1
Floor of workroom . . .	6	7	1	7
Cellar	3	4	..	10
Attic	1	..	1	3
All others	8	7	1	3

TABLE 44.—THE STOGY INDUSTRY. LOCATION OF WORKROOM AND OF DRYING ROOM IN HILL SWEATSHOPS

Location of workroom:

Rear of cigar store	9
Second floor	41
Cellar	17
Attic	27
Small shed	6
All others	24

Location of drying room:

Racks in workroom { Side	34
{ Overhead	10
Floor of workroom	9
Cellar	28
Attic	14
All others	29

TABLE 45.—THE STOGY INDUSTRY. DISTRIBUTION OF WORK AMONG MEN AND WOMEN IN SWEATSHOPS AND FACTORIES.— BY DISTRICT

District	Hand Stogies		Rollers		Bunchers (Hand)		Bunchers (Machine)		Drying Room		Teachers		Stripping		Packing		Total	
	Men	Women	Men	Women	Men	Women	Men	Women	Men	Women	Men	Women	Men	Women	Men	Women	Men	Women
Sweatshops — Hill	112	26	71	131	98	54	5	..	3	..	..	..	8	109	..	3	297	323
Down-town	3	1	..	..	..	..	..	..	..	..	..	..	1	2	..	..	56	22
South Side	49	9	3	..	3	..	..	..	..	..	..	..	1	13	..	..	4	3
East End	31	1	4	7	9	1	..	..	1	..	..	..	..	10	..	..	45	19
North Side	29	7	10	9	8	1	..	1	1	..	..	..	3	14	..	1	51	33
Factories	168	12	77	1185	190	289	4	161	18	2	..	..	5	357	1	205	463	2211
Total	392	56	165	1332	308	345	9	162	23	2	..	..	18	505	1	209	916	2611

Total number of workers, 3527.

TABLE 46.—GARMENT TRADES. NUMBER OF WOMEN EMPLOYED AND NUMBER IN EACH WEEKLY WAGE GROUP IN EACH FACTORY

No. of Plant	No. of Women Employed	WAGE GROUPS		
		$3.00–$6.99	$7.00–$7.99	$8.00–$10.00
1	18	4	8	6
2	160	15	45	100
3	2	..	..	2
4	4	..	..	4
5	19	3	4	12
6	30	4	6	20
7	55	7	8	40
8	65	12	12	41
9	38	9	22	7
10	9	2	5	2
11	70	8	50	12
12	30	3	5	22
13	90	20	45	25
14	9	..	4	5
15	12	2	3	7
16	95	..	30	65
17	27	..	7	20
18	75	5	15	55
19	8	2	2	4
20	8	1	2	5
21	44	6	12	26
Total	868	103	285	480

TABLE 47.—AWNINGS. NUMBER OF MEN AND OF WOMEN IN EACH FACTORY

No. of Plant	No. of Men	No. of Women	Total
1	1	3	4
2	4	6	10
3	8	6	14
4	2	1	3
5	..	14	14
6	..	7	7
7	2	4	6
Total	17	41	58

TABLE 48.—AWNINGS. RANGE OF WEEKLY WAGES IN EACH FACTORY

No. of Plant	Minimum	Maximum	Majority
1	$6.00	$10.50	$7.50
2	6.00	10.00	7.00
3	5.00	?	6.00
4	6.00	6.00	6.00
5	5.00	9.00	6.00
6	6.00	10.00	9.00
7	6.00	6.00	6.00

TABLE 49.—AWNINGS. HOURS OF WORK, OVERTIME AND SLACK SEASONS IN EACH PLANT

No. of Plant	Regular No. of Hours Daily	Hours During Overtime Season	Duration of Overtime Season	Duration of Slack Season	No. Laid Off in Slack Season
1	9	14	May and June	Winter	2
2	8	8	..	Sept.–Mar.	4
3	?	12–14	Apr. through June	Sept.–Mar.	6
4	10	12–14	Apr. through June	Sept.–Mar.	..*
5	9	12–14	5 days	Sept.–Mar.	10
6	8½	12	Mar. through July	Sept.–Mar.	5
7	8	8	..	Sept.–Mar.	3

* Only 1 woman employed.

TABLE 50.—MATTRESSES AND BEDDING. NUMBER OF WOMEN AND DIVISION OF WORK

No. of Plant	No. of Women	Single-Needle	Springbed Making	Closing	Knotting Wire Springs
1	6	6	..	..	..
2	23	9	9	1	4
3	10	6*	3	1	..
4	32	13	16	2	1
Total	71	34	28	4	5

* Two of these single needle operators use binder attachment.

390

TABLE 51.—MATTRESSES AND BEDDING. RANGE OF WEEKLY
WAGES IN EACH FACTORY

No. of Plant	Minimum	Maximum	Majority
1	$7.00	$10.00	$8.00
2	4.20	12.00	9.00
3	6.00	18.00	8.00–$10.00
4	4.50	14.00	7.00– 9.00

TABLE 52.—MILLINERY. DIVISION OF WORK AMONG WOMEN

No. of Plant	Apprentices	Copyists	Trimmers	Sewers on Straw Foundations	Makers and Preparers	Total
1	3	6	3	40	24	76
2	3	..	3	..	19	25
3	3	..	37	..	60	100
4	8	5	3	..	84	100
5	..	30	3	30	42	105
Total	17	41	49	70	229	406

TABLE 53.—MILLINERY. RANGE OF WEEKLY WAGES BY DIVISIONS
OF WORK

Division of Work	Unpaid	$3.00–$6.99	$7.00–$7.99	$8.00–10.00	Total
Apprentices . .	14	3	..	..	17
Copyists . . .	..	..	8	33	41
Expert Makers .	..	..	50	18	68
Inexpert Makers and Preparers .	..	161	..	..	161
Straw Hat Makers .	..	50	12	8	70
Trimmers . .	..	..	..	49	49
	14	214	70	108	406

TABLE 54.—LAUNDRIES. NUMBER OF MEN AND OF WOMEN IN
EACH LAUNDRY

No. of Plant	Men	Women	Total
1	3	40	43
2	10	165	175
3	5	55	60
4	40	120	160
5	10	165	175
6	1	2	3
7	5	40	45
8	1	29	30
9	3	42	45
10	6	134	140
11	5	100	105
12	2	28	30
13	12	33	45
14	5	20	25
15	1	20	21
16	5	90	95
17	30	220	250
18	2	20	22
19	6	74	80
20	5	80	85
21	4	56	60
22	2	18	20
23	..	15	15
24	6	32	38
25	2	33	35
26	35	165	200
27	2	39	41
28	9	65	74
29	..	43	43
30	..	160	160
31	..	43	43
32	..	39	39
Total	217	2185	2402

TABLE 55.—LAUNDRIES. PHYSICAL CHARACTERISTICS OF CELLAR AND BASEMENT WASHROOMS *

Grade   DRAINAGE
A Gutters; drainage good; floor convex 1
B Gutters; drainage good. 3
C Gutters; drainage imperfect 7
D Floor 2

ESCAPE FOR STEAM
A Windows 4
B Windows, small and low (3 x 3) 6
C Shaft to roof 1
D No escape 2

FORCED VENTILATION
A Fan in wall 3
B Iron pipe admitting outside air 1
C Shaft to roof 1
D No forced ventilation 8

* See note to Table 21, p. 166.

TABLE 56.—LAUNDRIES. PHYSICAL CHARACTERISTICS OF MANGLE ROOMS *

LOCATION WITH REFERENCE TO WASHROOM
Third floor; wholly separated 1
Second floor; wholly separated 1
Second floor; directly above 1
Second floor; not separated 1
First floor; wholly separated 1
First floor; partly separated† 3
First floor; not separated 7
First floor; directly above 9
Cellar; not separated‡ 3

STEAM
Adequate provision for escape 3
Slight 5
Very noticeable 19

FORCED VENTILATION
Exhausts over mangle 2
Open skylights 1
Fans in wall 4
Shaft to roof and fan 1
Opening in floor above§ 1
None 18

GUARDS
Upright bar, 4 inch 3
Upright bar, 2 inch; wide space‖ 2
Small roll, 2½ inches in diameter 21
Large roll, 4 inches in diameter 1

* One laundry has no mangle, hence only twenty-seven are tabulated.
† "Partly separated"; wooden partition part way to ceiling, or other inadequate partitioning.
‡ Not separated from washroom.
§ No forced expulsion of steam; ventilation unsatisfactory.
‖ "Wide space" between base of bar and feeding apron; wider in this case than the thickness of the hand.

TABLE 57.—LAUNDRIES. RANGE OF WEEKLY WAGES IN EACH
MANGLE DEPARTMENT *

No. of Plant	No. of Girls	Wages Paid to Shakers-out, Feeders and Folders	Head Girl
1	10	$3.50–4.00	$6.50
2	15	3.00–3.50	4.00
3	6	4.00	6.00
4	12	4.00–5.00	12.00†
5	16	3.50–4.00	..
6‡	..	..	..
7	6	3.50–5.00	6.00
8	4	5.00	..
9	38	4.00–6.00	8.00
10	20	4.00–5.00	..
11	12	4.00–5.00	..
12	6	4.50–5.00	..
13	12	5.00	..
14	4	4.50–5.00	..
15	6	4.00–5.00	..
16	6	3.00–4.00	8.00
17	20	3.50–4.00	5.00
18	6	3.00–4.00	..
19	6	4.00–5.00	..
20	12	3.50–4.00	..
21	8	4.50–5.00	6.00
22	5	4.00–5.00	..
23	5	3.00–4.00	5.00
24	6	3.00–4.00	6.00
25	6	5.00–6.00	8.00
26	18	4.00–5.00	7.00
27	6	4.00–5.00	5.50
28	18	4.00–5.00	..

* The four institutional laundries are not tabulated with the twenty-eight
commercial laundries.   † Forewoman.   ‡ No mangle department.

TABLE 58.—LAUNDRIES. SUMMARY OF NUMBER IN WEEKLY WAGE
GROUPS IN MANGLE DEPARTMENTS

Wage Groups	Head Girl Employed		No Head Girl Employed	
	No. of Laundries	No. of Girls	No. of Laundries	No. of Girls
$3.00 to $3.99 . . .	7	68	3	34
$4.00 to $4.99 . . .	5	50	8	77
$5.00 to $5.99 . . .	1	6	2	16
$4.00 to $6.00 . . .	1	38	..	..

In one laundry where few of the mangle girls were over fourteen, the foreman explained that it was his policy to hire these small girls at $3.50 a week, rather than older girls at $4.50 because this meant a saving of $15 weekly in running expenses. The mangle girls were too young to be required to pad the mangles, but a man, a washer, was hired for $15 a week, and given this duty, in addition to his regular work. In this way the firm saved money. The mangle room, however, is not usually a kindergarten, and a $3.00 wage, when paid to girls sixteen or seventeen years old, is a serious matter.

The employment of a head girl noticeably affects the proportion of employes in the lower and higher wage groups. We may leave out of consideration the wage group of $4.00 to $6.00, for the one laundry* under this head is exceptional, both in wage rating, plan of organization and character of the work. In the other three wage groups, we find that where a head girl is employed, in only one case are the employes in the $5.00 to $6.00 group, but that in seven cases they are in the $3.00 to $4.00 group; whereas, when no head girl is employed, eight laundries pay their employes $4.00 to $5.00, and two laundries pay $5.00 to $6.00. We find twice as many girls earning only $3.00 to $4.00, and half as many earning $5.00 to $6.00, when a head girl is employed, as when a head girl is not employed. In the $4.00 to $5.00 wage group we find the number of employes half as great again in the absence of a head girl, as when a head girl is part of the force. This evidence seems to show a tendency to pay higher wages to all the mangle girls when responsibility is divided, and lower wages to the subordinates, when one girl assumes the whole responsibility. Lower wages paid to the group, enable the firm to pay relatively high wages for higher capacity in one; while on the other hand, when relatively good wages are paid to the group, this is in recognition of a higher standard of group capacity.

* Only wholesale mangle work is done in this laundry.

TABLE 59.—LAUNDRIES. RANGE OF WEEKLY WAGES OF STARCH-
ING ROOM EMPLOYES

No. of Plant	Wages Paid to Collar Feeders, Shirt Bosom and Band Starchers, and Wiping Girls*	No. of Plant	Wages Paid to Collar Feeders, Shirt Bosom and Band Starchers, and Wiping Girls
1	$3.00 to $4.00	15	$6.00
2	3.50– 4.00	16	3.00– 4.00
3	4.00– 5.00[1] (piece work)	17	4.50– 6.00
4	4.00– 6.00	18	3.00– 4.00
5	4.00– 5.00[1] (piece work)	19	6.00– 7.00
6	No starching room	20	3.50– 4.00
7	3.50– 5.00	21	5.00– 6.00
8	4.00– 5.00	22	4.00– 5.00
9	No starching room	23	4.00– 6.00[2]
10	5.00– 6.00	24	5.00– 7.00[2]
11	4.00– 5.00	25	6.00– 7.00
12	4.00– 4.50	26	6.00– 9 00[2]
13	7.00– 8.00[2]	27	4.00– 5.00
14	4.50– 5.00	28	5.00

* All wages are time wages, unless otherwise indicated.
[1] Rate for starching shirts, $.35 a 100.
[2] Wages of head girl.

The table shows the range of wages in each starching department from unskilled collar feeder to dexterous wiping girl. In laundries 5, 7, 17, and 28, collar starching is done by the newer machine process, which makes wiping girls unnecessary. Although by use of this machine, dexterity and judgment are no longer necessary in the starching room, the change is too recent to have affected wages, which are at about the same level in these four laundries as in the others.

TABLE 60.—LAUNDRIES. PHYSICAL CHARACTERISTICS OF CHECK-ROOMS

LOCATION

Second floor; wholly separated	2
Second floor; above washroom	4
First floor; above washroom	4
First floor; wholly separated	4
First floor; partly separated	3
First floor; in washroom	6
Cellar; partly separated	2
Cellar; in washroom	1

LIGHT

Good*	13
Fair†	2
Poor‡ electric lights used	11

VENTILATION

Good§	6
Poor‖ . . . . . . , ...	4
None**	16

* Large, clean windows; checking near windows.

† Large room, well lighted, but checking department not near windows.

‡ No daylight. Room dimly lighted with a few electric bulbs.

§ Large room; wholly shut off from steam elsewhere in laundry.

‖ Fans, but inadequate to carry off steam.

** No fans or other forced ventilation. Room is full of steam.

TABLE 61.—LAUNDRIES. DISPLACEMENT OF MEN BY WOMEN IN CHECKING AND SORTING DEPARTMENTS

No. of Plant	Head Checker	Head Sorter	Assistants	Reason for Employing Men	Reason for Employing Women	Number	
						Men	Women
1	Man	....	Men	More accurate	....	2	..
2	Man	Woman	Women	....	Cheaper	1	16
3	Woman	Woman	Women	Girls hard to get	Cheaper; more reliable	..	10
4	Man	....	Men. Women	....	Cheaper	8	2
5	Man	Man	Women	....	....	2	13
6*	....	....	....	....	....	..	..
7	Man	Man	Women	....	Cheaper; more reliable	2	4
8	Woman	....	Women	....	Cheaper	..	3
9*	....	....	....	....	....	..	..
10	Woman	Woman	Women	....	Cheaper	..	22
11	Woman	....	Women	....	Cheaper	..	5
12	Woman	....	Women	....	Cheaper; more reliable	..	5
13	Man	....	Men	More accurate	....	..	6
14	Man	....	Women	....	Cheaper	2	2
15	Woman	Woman	Women	....	Cheaper	1	3
16	Woman	....	Women	....	Cheaper	..	5
17	Man	Man	Men. Women	More accurate; good to oversee	Cheaper	5	10
18	Woman	....	Women	....	Cheaper	..	3
19	Woman	Woman	Women	....	Cheaper	..	12
20	Woman	Woman	Women	....	Cheaper	..	8
21	Woman	....	Women	....	Cheaper	..	4
22	Woman	....	Women	....	Cheaper	..	3
23	Woman	....	Women	....	Cheaper	..	2
24	Man	Man	Women	....	Cheaper	2	4
25	Woman	....	Women	....	Cheaper	..	4
26	Man	Man	Men	Men object to girls	....	10	..
27	Woman	Woman	Women	....	Cheaper; quicker; more reliable	..	11
28	Man	Man	1 Man. Women	....	Cheaper	3	2

| No. of Plant | CHECKING DEPARTMENT* | | | | SORTING DEPARTMENT | | | | CHECKING AND SORTING DEPARTMENT | | | |
| | Head Checker | | Assistants | | Head Sorter | | Assistants | | Head of Dept. | | Assistants | |
	Men	Women	Men	Women	Men	Women	Men	Women	Men	Women	Men	Women
1†	..	..	..	..	..	..	..	..	..	..	..	..
2	..	$8.00	..	$6.00–7.00	..	$12.00	..	$8.00	..	..	..	..
3	..	9.00	..	5.50	..	12.00	..	8.00	..	..	..	..
4	..	..	..	..	..	..	..	..	$20.00	..	$13.00–18.00	$9.00
5	..	..	..	..	..	..	..	..	18.00	..	17.00	$5.00
6‡	$15.00	..	..	..	..	..	..	..	..	..	..	..
7	..	..	$12.00	9.00	..	12.00	..	10.00	..	..	..	8.00
8	..	..	..	..	..	..	..	..	..	$12.00	..	10.00
9	..	..	..	..	..	..	..	..	..	..	..	..
10‡	..	12.00	..	7.00	..	..	..	..	..	..	..	..
11	..	12.00	..	..	..	10.00	..	8.00	..	12.00	..	5.00
12	..	..	..	..	..	..	..	..	20.00	..	15.00	8.00
13	..	..	..	..	..	..	..	..	..	13.00	..	5.00
14	..	10.00	..	..	..	..	..	10.00	..	9.00	..	8.00
15	..	..	..	..	..	..	..	..	..	..	..	16.00
16	..	..	..	..	..	..	..	..	..	9.00	..	8.00
17	..	..	..	..	..	..	..	..	21.00	..	17.00–18.00	10.00
18	..	10.00	..	..	..	..	..	..	..	8.00	..	7.00
19	..	10.00	..	5.50–6.00	..	10.00	..	5.00–6.00	..	..	..	..
20	..	..	..	5.50–6.00	..	10.00	..	4.50–6.00	..	..	..	..
21	..	..	..	..	..	..	..	..	..	10.00	..	7.00
22	..	..	..	..	..	..	..	..	..	10.00	..	10.00
23	..	..	..	..	$18.00	..	..	..	..	..	..	8.50
24	12.00	..	..	5.50–8.50	..	..	..	8.00	..	..	..	..
25	..	..	..	..	..	..	..	..	18.00	12.00	13.00–15.00	9.00
26	..	..	..	..	..	..	..	..	..	..	..	..
27	..	8.88	..	8.00	..	10.00	..	10.00	..	..	..	..
28	..	..	..	..	..	..	..	..	15.00	..	..	8.00

* Checkers are paid sometimes by the hour, and sometimes per hundred pounds of goods checked in. The gross sum per week only is noted in the table. ‡ No checking or sorting department.
† Foreman checks in.

TABLE 63.—LAUNDRIES. WEEKLY WAGES OF MACHINE IRONERS

| No. of Plant | Bosom Ironer | | All Other Machines |
	Type of Machine	Wages	Scale of Wages
1	Roll	$6.00	$4.50–$5.50
2	Roll	7.00	4.50– 6.50
3	Roll	7.00†	4.50– 6.50
4	Press	8.00	6.00
5	Press	7.50	4.00– 7.00
	Roll		
6*	..	..	..
7	Press	7.00	4.50– 6.00
8	Roll	7.00	6.00– 7.00
9*	..	..	..
10	Press	7.00	5.00– 6.00
11	Press	7.00	5.00– 6.00
12	Press	6.50	6.00– 6.50
13	Press	7.00	7.00– 8.00‡
14	Roll	8.00	7.00– 8.00
15	Press	7.00	5.00– 6.00
16	Press	7.00	5.00– 6.00
17	Press	7.00	5.00– 6.00
18	Roll	6.00	5.00– 6.00
19	Roll	6.00	..
	Press	7.00	3.50– 6.00
20	Press	6.00	3.50– 5.00
21	Press	8.00	6.00– 7.00
22	Roll	6.00	5.00– 6.00
23	Roll	8.00	6.00– 8.00
24	Roll	7.00	4.00– 6.00
25	Press	8.00	6.00– 7.00
26	Press	9.00	7.00– 8.00§
27	Press	6.00	5.00– 6.00
	Roll	6.00	..
28	Press	6.00	6.00

* No machine ironing.

† Piece work. The figure represents the amount generally earned by the experienced hands.

‡ Head girl.

§ Old employes; have been advanced for length of service.

This table shows that although the roll polisher is said to be a more difficult machine to handle than the bosom press, in five cases operators of the former machine are paid a $6.00 wage, while only three operators of the latter are paid a $6.00 wage. Indeed in No. 19, roll operators are paid $6.00 and press operators $7.00, which is the wage-rating most generally found.   Clearly the wage has reference to the importance of the fashionable finish rather than to the skill required for operation of the machine.   In other words, the higher skill of the roll operator is no longer sufficiently in demand to win her an increase in wages comparable to the increase given the less highly skilled press operator.   A few laundries recognize length of service by paying higher wages to old employes.

TABLE 64.—LAUNDRIES.   WEEKLY WAGES OF FINE IRONERS

No. of Plant	No. of Women†	Wages		
		Time	Piece	Max. (Summer)
1	4	$7.00, 8.00	..	$10.00
2	1	..	25%	12.00
3	1	..	25%	12.00
4	4	..	25%	13.00
5	5	..	25%	15.00
6*	..	..	..	..
7	3	$5.00	..	8.00
8	2	$9.00	..	10.00
9*	..	..	..	..
10	3	..	20%	9.00
11	5	$1.50 a day	..	8.00
12	1	.15 per hr.	..	7.50
13	2	$7.00	..	7.00
14	1	7.00	..	8.00
15	4	8.00	..	8.00
16	2	7.00	..	8.00
17	9	..	25%	14.00
18	2	7.00	..	8.00
19	8	7.00	..	8.00
20	3	6.50	..	8.00
21	4	7.00	..	8.00
22	1	7.00	..	7.00
23	2	8.00	..	8.00
24	9	8.00	..	9.00
25	2	8.50	..	8.50
26	15	..	25%	14.00
27	4	7.00	..	8.00
28	9	5.00	..	7.00

* No fine ironing.

† The number of women stated, refers to the number in employment in the spring and fall months, when there is still considerable demand for fine ironing; but not to the number in employment during the excessive slackness of midwinter, nor the excessive pressure of summer work.   The extra hands taken on in summer are casual laborers and are not reckoned at all in making up this table.

It will be noted that seven laundries pay $6.00 at the lowest wage in the ironing department (under the column "all other machines"), and that three laundries pay $7.00 as the lowest wages. One of the latter (No. 26) has advanced its employes for length of service. The other two and the seven which pay a $6.00 wage, require their operators to be proficient in the operation of several machines, instead of requiring mere dexterity at one process. This unusual proficiency commands the higher wages.

TABLE 65.—METAL TRADES. NUMBER OF WOMEN IN EACH WEEKLY WAGE GROUP

Trade	$3.00–$6.99	$7.00–$7.99	$8.00–$10.00	Total
Electrical appliances	202	150	300	652
Foundries	80	27	208	315
Misc.	344	100	..	444
Screws and bolts	318	225	..	543
Total	944	502	508	1954

TABLE 66.—LAMPS. DIVISION OF WORK AMONG WOMEN IN EACH FACTORY

No. of Plant	Punching	Riveting	Hammering	Fibring	Soldering	Lacquer	Log Decorating
1	7	1	1	3	..	..	..
2	..	..	..	..	..	..	..
3	..	..	..	..	..	..	..
4	..	..	..	..	..	..	..
5	..	..	..	3	..	..	..
6	..	..	..	5	..	..	..
7	3	..	..	..	..	..	..
8	..	..	..	2	..	..	..
9	20	..	..	..	10	4	..
10	..	..	..	3	.	..	3
11	..	..	..	5	..	..	..
..	30	1	1	21	10	4	3

TABLE 66.—LAMPS. DIVISION OF WORK AMONG WOMEN IN EACH FACTORY.—(*Continued.*)

No. of Plant	Sewing Asbestos	Capping	Burning	Shaping Dipping	Wringers	Labelling	Drying Oven
1	..	..	..	..	..	..	..
2	30	10	10	..	..	..	..
3	8	2	..	3	2	2	1
4	11	3	..	5	2	9	..
5	..	..	..	..	..	..	..
6	..	..	..	..	..	..	..
7	..	..	..	..	..	..	..
8	..	..	..	..	..	..	..
9	..	..	..	..	..	6	..
10	..	..	..	..	..	..	..
11	..	..	..	..	..	..	..
..	49	15	10	8	4	17	1

No. of Plant	Tapping	Coil Winding	Inspecting	Scraping Porcelains	Assembling	Winding Wire and Blowing Balises
1	..	..	..	..	..	..
2	..	..	..	..	..	..
3	..	..	..	..	..	..
4	..	..	..	..	..	..
5	..	..	..	..	..	..
6	..	..	..	..	..	..
7	4	5	10	5	26	247
8	..	..	..	..	..	..
9	..	..	..	..	..	..
10	..	..	..	..	..	..
11	..	..	..	..	..	..
..	4	5	10	5	26	247

TABLE 67.—LAMPS. NUMBER OF WOMEN IN EACH FACTORY, AND RANGE OF WEEKLY WAGES

No. of Plant	No. of Women	Range of Wages		
		Minimum	*Maximum*	*Majority*
1	12	$5.00	$6.00 (flat rate)	$6.00
2	50	4.00	8.00	7.00
3	18	4.00	8.00	5.00
4	30	4.20	6.00	5.40
5	3	6.00	9.00	8.00
6	5	6.00	8.40	7.00
7	300	6.00	9.00	8.00
8	2	6.00	10.00	..
9	40	6.00	9.00	7.80
10	6	4.00	7.00	5.00
11	5	6.00	9.00	7.00

No. of Women in Each Wage Group			Total
$3.00–$6.99	$7.00–$7.99	$8.00–$10.00	
176	162	147	471

TABLE 68.—GLASS MAKING. NUMBER OF WOMEN IN EACH FACTORY, AND DIVISION OF WORK

No. of Plant	No. of Women	Grinding and Finishing	Cutting Off	Packing	Decorating	Washing	Cleaning Molds
1	30	..	8	22	..	..	..
2	100	36	6	58	..	..	..
3	20	..	..	10	5	..	5
4	20	..	..	..	20	..	..
5	70	..	..	20	30	20	..
6	25	..	..	25	..	..	..
7	40	..	..	..	40	..	..
8	10	..	..	10	..	..	..
9	38	..	..	4	27	7	..
Total	353	36	14	149	122	27	5

TABLE 69.—GLASS MAKING. RANGE OF WEEKLY WAGES IN EACH FACTORY

No. of Plant	Minimum	Maximum	Majority
1	$3.50	$7.00	$5.00
2	4.00	9.00	6.00
3	4.00	9.00	6.00
4	5.00	14.00	7.00
5	3.50	12.00	6.00
6	3.00	3.50	..
7	4.00	7.00	6.00
8	3.00	3.50	..
9	3.00	8.00	5.00

TABLE 70.—GLASS MAKING. NUMBER OF WOMEN IN EACH WEEKLY WAGE GROUP IN EACH FACTORY

No. of Plant	$3.00 to $6.99	$7.00 to $7.99	$8.00 to $10.00 (or over)
1	30	..	..
2	64	..	36
3	17	..	3
4	5	5	10
5	40	..	30
6	25	..	..
7	30	10	..
8	10	..	..
9	28	10	..
Total	249	25	79

TABLE 71.—PAPER BOX FACTORIES. NUMBER OF MEN AND OF WOMEN IN EACH FACTORY, AND DISTRIBUTION OF WORK

No. of Plant	No. of Employes		Distribution of Work				
	Men	Women	Paste and Gluework	Knowlton-Beach Staying Machine	Wire Stitching Machine	Covering Machine	Misc.
1	10	40	38	1	1	..	..
2	5	45	36	3	..	6	..
3	10	30	21	2	2	5	..
4	9	11	9	..	..	..	2
5	10	30	27	1	2	..	..
6	5	15	13	..	1	..	1
7	..	7	7	..	..	..	..
8	10	30	22	2	1	5	..
9	40	30	26	2	2	..	..
Total	99	238	199	11	9	16	3

TABLE 72.—PAPER BOX FACTORIES. RANGE OF WEEKLY WAGES IN EACH FACTORY

No. of Plant	Minimum	Maximum	Majority
1	$2.50	$7.00	$5.00
2	3.00	9.00	5.00
3	3.00	8.00	6.00
4	3.00	10.00	6.00
5	3.50	15.00	6.00
6	2.50	7.00	6.00
7	3.00	7.00	6.00
8	3.00	8.00	5.00
9	3.00	9.00	4.00

TABLE 73.—PAPER BOX FACTORIES. NUMBER IN EACH WEEKLY WAGE GROUP IN EACH FACTORY

No. of Plant	$3.00–$6.99	$7.00–$7.99	$8.00–$10.00
1	35	5	..
2	40	5	..
3	20	5	5
4	9	..	2
5	25	4	1
6	13	2	..
7	6	1	..
8	20	4	6
9	22	6	2
Total	190 (79.8%)	32 (13.4%)	16 (6.7%)

TABLE 74.—PRINTING TRADES. NUMBER OF WOMEN IN EACH WEEKLY WAGE GROUP

No. of Plant	$3.00 to $6.99	$7.00 to $7.99	$8.00 to $11.99	$12.00 to $18.00	Total
1	..	..	20	..	20
2	..	..	5	..	5
3	..	1	..	..	1
4	1	1	..	..	2
5	15	4	2	..	21
6	3	1	6	..	10
7	..	2	1	..	3
8	80	50	20	..	150
9	25	10	8	..	43
10	..	2	3	..	5
11	5	1	..	..	6
12	3	2	2	5*	12
13	6	2	2	..	10
14	10	30	10	..	50
15	1	..	..	..	1
16	1	..	..	..	1
17	13	2	7	..	22
18	10	7	..	..	17
19	8	8	2	..	18
Total	181	123	88	5	397

* Compositors on linotype machine.

TABLE 75.—MERCANTILE HOUSES. NUMBER OF WOMEN IN EACH STORE AND DISTRIBUTION IN WEEKLY WAGE GROUPS

No. of Store	No. of Women	$3.00–$6.99	$7.00–$7.99	$8.00–$10.00
1	20	16	4	..
2	1300	1000	200	100
3	200	200	..	..
4	160	160	..	..
5	9	5	4	..
6	1000	700	200	100
7	1900	1600	200	100
8	45	45	..	..
9	40	40	..	..
10	60	60	..	..
11	25	25	..	..
12	900	100	700	100
13	250	200	50	..
14	40	40	..	..
15	400	300	75	25
16	200	200	..	..
17	600	480	70	50
18	100	100	..	..
19	15	15	..	..
20	6	4	2	..
21	150	100	50	..
22	35	35	..	..
23	75	75	..	..
24	10	10	..	..
Total	7540	5510	1555	475

TABLE 76.—BOARDING HOMES. CENSUS AND CAPACITY OF THE SEVERAL BOARDING HOMES, AND THE NUMBERS OF WOMEN FROM THE GROUPS UNDER CONSIDERATION, REACHED

No. of Home	Census	Capacity	Numbers Reached
1	49	71	2
2	17	26	5
3	60	125	50
4	65	70	52*
5	24	36	21
6	40	40	3
7	20	28	10
Total	275	396	143

* Forty-three of the girls in this home are employed in the convent laundry, being paid in board with a small additional weekly sum. They are included here, because in the chapter on laundry workers, they have been included in the general census of the industry. The other girls in this home, work outside, and pay board to the home.

TABLE 77.—WAGES. PERCENTAGES OF WOMEN IN EACH WEEKLY WAGE GROUP, IN EACH TRADE

Industry	Unpaid	$3.00–$6.99	$7.00–$7.99	$8.00–$10.00
	Per cent	Per cent	Per cent	Per cent
Crackers . . .	..	96.9	3	..
Confectionery . .	..	72	21	6.9
Molasses . . .	..	75	15	10
Canneries . . .	..	58.5	21.35	20.07
Stogy . . .	..	45	16.8	37.8
Garments . . .	..	11.8	32.8	55.3
Awnings . . .	..	51	12	36.6
Mattresses . .	..	15	16.9	67.6
Gloves . . .	..	83.3	9.26	7.4
Millinery . .	3.44	50.24	17.24	26.6
Laundries . .	9.28	75.56	5.99	9.79
Dyeing and cleaning	..	21.5	58.8	20
Metal trades . .	..	48	25.6	25.9
Lamps . . .	..	36.5	32.2	31.2
Glass	..	68.4	9	22
Mirrors . . .	..	80	7.5	12.5
Brooms and brushes	..	45.4	48.4	6
Paper boxes . .	..	79.8	13.4	6.7
Caskets . . .	..	59.4	33.7	6.75
Corks . . .	..	42.5	49.16	8.33
Paint . . .	..	70	20	10
Soap . . .	..	80.4	11.7	7.8
Trunk . . .	..	57	42.8	..
Printing and book-binding . . .	..	45.59	30.9	23.4
Telegraph . . .	..	..	..	100
Telephone . .	..	45.41	29.25	25.32
Mercantile . .	..	73.07	20.62	6.31

APPENDIX C

THE MARGARET MORISON CARNEGIE SCHOOL FOR WOMEN

NIGHT courses in the Margaret Morison Carnegie School (the woman's division of the Carnegie Technical Schools) are still in their beginnings, in a period of tentative reaching out for the best means of connecting with the local industries that need women employes. Certain obvious lines of instruction are sure to be in demand. The school has followed these first, starting classes in millinery, in sewing, in costume design, in stenography and book-keeping. Tuition is $5.00 per year, students being expected to buy their own textbooks and to furnish their own materials.

Of the 175 night school students enrolled in the winter of 1907-1908, only 19 come within the groups considered in this study. Some of the others were temporarily out of employment or busy at home during the day; some were employed in offices as stenographers and clerks. There were four factory girls, eight sales clerks, two milliners and five telephone girls. One of the milliners withdrew early in the year, because she was apprenticed in a wholesale house down town, and found that her night hours interfered with her class work.

The distance of the school from the business part of town has tended to attract girls who are living at home, and working girls of higher social grade, such as office clerks, rather than unskilled factory hands who live in the more congested districts and have neither carfare nor strength to go a journey at the close of the day. These facts possibly hinder the night classes from seriously attempting to teach their students a new trade, or to make them proficient in an old one. Of secretarial work, this is of course not true. The girls who study that can study it only with a trade purpose. But the millinery, the sewing and cooking? The need for a kind of dexterity in these enters so largely into the life of every girl whose income is small, that it is difficult in any trade school to keep the class free from the imputation of serving as an adjunct, a convenience apart from the working life which has been developed along other lines. It is especially difficult when the students of the night school, as in this case, are in large measure either unemployed or engaged in clerical work. How to make connections with the actual millinery and sewing trades in the city of Pittsburgh, and with other trades in which the possibilities of women workers have hitherto been limited, is one of the problems ahead, if the night trade school is to be a strong force among the working women of the city.

APPENDIX D

LEGAL RESTRICTION OF WORKING HOURS

TEXT OF THE PENNSYLVANIA LAW UP TO 1909

FIRST enacted in 1897 (No. 26), and re-enacted in Laws of 1905, No. 226, as follows:

Section 1. That the term "establishment", where used for the purpose of this act, shall mean any place within this Commonwealth other than where domestic, coal-mining, or farm labor is employed; where men, women, or children are engaged, and paid a salary or wages, by any person, firm, or corporation, and where such men, women, or children are employees, in the general acceptance of the term.

Section 3. . . . No minor under sixteen and no female shall be employed in any establishment for a longer period than sixty hours in any one week, nor for a longer period than twelve hours in any one day, and that retail mercantile establishments shall be exempt from the provisions of this section on Saturdays of each week and during a period of twenty days, beginning with the fifth day of December and ending with the twenty-fourth day of the same month: Provided that during the said twenty days preceding the twenty-fourth day of December, the working hours shall not exceed ten hours per day or sixty hours per week".

Act May 2d, 1905, P. L. No. 226.
Held constitutional in Comm. v. Beatty, 15 Pa. Superior Ct. 5.

A provision of the law limiting the hours of labor of adult females is within the police power of the State, and does not interfere with their constitutional rights, nor is it class legislation.

COMPARATIVE LEGISLATION IN THE UNITED STATES*

LEGAL MAXIMUM HOURS	KIND OF ESTABLISHMENT	STATE
8 hours per day	Manufactories, workshops and other places used for mechanical or manufacturing purposes.	Wisconsin

First enacted in 1867 (ch. 83, Sec. 1) and amended by stat. 1883, ch. 135, now embodied in Wisconsin Statutes, Code of 1898, sec. 1728.

10 hours per day *58 hours per week* †	Manufacturing and mechanical establishments.	Massachusetts

Exception: to make a shorter work-day one day in the week.

First enacted in 1874 (Chap. 221), now embodied in R. L. Ch. 106, sec. 24, as amended by Stat. 1902, ch. 435. Held constitutional, Comm. v. Hamilton Mfg. Co., 120 Mass. 383.

10 hours per day	Manufactories, workshops, and other places used for mechanical or manufacturing purposes.	N. Dakota

First enacted in 1877 (Penal Code, sec. 739), now embodied in Rev. Code, 1905, sec. 9440.

10 *hours per day*	Manufactories, workshops, and other places used for mechanical or manufacturing purposes.	S. Dakota

First enacted in 1877 (Penal Code, sec. 739), now embodied in Rev. Code, 1903 (Penal Code, sec. 764).

10 hours per day *58 hours per week*	Manufacturing and mechanical establishments.	Rhode Island

Exception: to make repairs, or for a shorter work-day one day of the week.

First enacted in 1885 (chap. 519, sec. 1), now embodied in Stat. 1896, chap. 198, sec. 22. As amended by Stat. 1902, ch. 994.

* This digest of legislation with reference to hours has been compiled in part from the Brief for the State of Oregon, prepared by Louis D. Brandeis and Josephine C. Goldmark, in the case of Curt Muller vs. State of Oregon, Supreme Court of the United States, October Term, 1907.

† The number of hours per day or per week italicized indicates that the law recognizes no exceptions to the prohibition of a working day or week exceeding this number of hours.

10 hours per day (average) 60 hours per week	Factories, warehouses, workshops, telephone and telegraph offices, clothing, dressmaking and millinery establishments and all places where the manufacture of goods is carried on, or where any goods are prepared for manufacture.	Louisiana

First enacted in 1886 (Act No. 43) and amended by Acts of 1902 (No. 49): now embodied in Rev. Laws (1904, p. 989, sec. 4.).

10 hours per day 60 *hours per week*	Manufacturing, mechanical, or mercantile establishments.	Connecticut

Exception: to make repairs, or to make a shorter work-day one day in the week.

First enacted in 1887 (ch. 62, sec. 1), now embodied in Gen. Stat., Rev. 1902, sec. 4691.

10 hours per day 60 *hours per week*	Manufacturing or mechanical establishments.	Maine

Exception: to make repairs, or to make a shorter work-day one day in the week.

First enacted in 1887 (ch. 139, sec. 1), now re-enacted in Rev. Stat., 1903, ch. 40, sec. 48.

9 hrs. 40 min. per day 58 *hours per week*	Manufacturing and mechanical establishments.	New Hampshire

Exception: to make up lost time, to make a shorter work-day, to make repairs.

First enacted in 1887 (ch. 25, sec. 1), now re-enacted by Stat. 1907, ch. 94.

10 *hours per day*	Manufactures of cotton and woolen yarns, fabrics and domestics of all kinds.	Maryland

First enacted in 1888 (ch. 455), now embodied in Pub. Gen. Laws, Code of 1903, Act 100, sec. 1.

10 *hours per day*	Manufactories, workshops, and other places used for mechanical or manufacturing purposes.	Oklahoma

First enacted in 1890 (Stat. 1890, ch. 25, article 58, sec. 101) now embodied in Rev. Stat. 1903 ch. 25, art. 58, sec. 729.

10 *hours per day*   Factories and manufacturing estab-   Virginia
                           lishments.

First enacted in 1890 (ch. 193, sec. 1), now embodied in
Virginia Code (1904), ch. 178 a, 3657 b.

10 hours per day   Factories.   New York
60 *hours per week*

Exception: to make a shorter work-day.

First enacted in 1899 (ch. 192, sec. 77), now embodied in
Stat. 1907, ch. 507, sec. 77.

10 *hours per day*   Manufacturing, mechanical and mer-   Nebraska
60 *hours per week*   cantile establishments, hotels, and
                           restaurants.

First enacted in 1899 (ch. 107), now embodied in Compiled
Statutes (1905, sec. 7955a).

(Held constitutional in Wenham v. State, 65 Neb. 400.)

10 *hours per day*   Mechanical and mercantile establish-   Washington
                           ments, laundries, hotels and res-
                           taurants.

Enacted in 1901, Stat. 1901, ch. 68, Sec. 1.

(Held constitutional in State v. Buchanan, 29 Wash. 603.)

8 *hours per day*   Mills, factories, manufacturing estab-   Colorado
                           lishments, shops and stores, where
                           the occupation by its nature re-
                           quires women to be upon their feet.

Enacted in 1903, Acts of 1903, ch. 138, sec. 3.

10 hours per day   Operatives and employes (except cler-   South Carolina
60 hours per week   ical force) in cotton and woolen
                           manufacturing establishments, en-
                           gaged in the manufacture of yarns,
                           cloth, hosiery, and other products
                           of merchandise.

Exception: to make up lost time caused by accident.

Approved Feb. 19, 1907 (Acts of 1907, No. 223).

10 *hours per day*   Manufacturing, mechanical, and mer-   Oregon
                           cantile establishments, laundries,
                           hotels, and restaurants.

Exception: The limit may be extended to 12 hours in any
one day for one week immediately preceding Xmas.

Acts of 1907, amended by ch. 200, p. 148.
(Held constitutional 85 Pac. Rep. 855, 25 Sup. Ct., Ref. 324.)

THE LEGISLATION OF 1909

In the legislatures of 1909, Oregon, Pennsylvania and Rhode Island have amended their existing laws; Illinois, Michigan and Missouri have enacted laws.

The law of Pennsylvania is as follows:

Section 5. That no male minor under the age of sixteen years, and no female under the age of eighteen years, shall be employed, permitted, or suffered to work, in or about or for any establishment, place of business, or industry, named in sections 3 and 4* of this act, for a longer period than ten hours in any one day, except when a different apportionment of the hours of labor is made for the sole purpose of making a shorter work day for one day in the week; nor shall a less period than forty-five minutes be allowed for the midday meal; and in no case shall the hours of labor exceed 58 in any one week. No male or female minor under the age of eighteen years, shall be employed or permitted to work between the hours of nine post meridian and six ante meridian.

It appears that the 1909 law does not annul the 1905 law because it applies only to females less than eighteen.

This Act to take effect Jan. 1, 1910.

29 April, 1909, Sec. 5, P. L. No. 182.

The Oregon statute has been extended (Acts of 1909, ch. 138, sec. 1, p. 204) to include employes engaged in transportation and communication.

The Rhode Island Statute has been amended (Acts of 1909, chap. 384, sec. 1) to make 56 hours the legal working week for all women employed in manufacturing and mechanical establishments.

*The manufacture or preparation of white-lead, red-lead, paints, phosphorus, phosphorus matches, poisonous acids, or the manufacture or stripping of tobacco or cigars; mercantile establishments, stores; telegraph, telephone, or other business offices; hotels, restaurants; or in any factory, workshop, rolling mills or other establishment having proper sanitation; or in any factory, workshop, rolling mills or other establishment having proper sanitation and proper ventilation, and in which power machinery is not used, or if used, that the same, and all dangerous appliances used, are kept securely and properly safeguarded; rules and regulations for the same to be prescribed and provided by the Chief Factory Inspector.

The Illinois statute (Acts of 1909, p. 212, sec. 1) makes it illegal for any woman to be employed more than 10 hours per day in any mechanical establishment, factory or laundry.

The Michigan statute (Acts of 1909, no. 285, sec. 9) makes it illegal for any woman to be employed in any place where the manufacture of any kind of goods is carried on, or in any laundry or mercantile establishment, for longer than an average of 9 hours in any day, nor for more than 54 hours per week.

The Missouri statute (Acts of 1909, p. 616) makes it illegal for any woman to be employed in any manufacturing or mercantile establishment, laundry or restaurant in any city of over 5000 inhabitants for more than 54 hours per week.

BIBLIOGRAPHY

BIBLIOGRAPHY

1. GENERAL

Taylor, R. Whateley Cooke: The Modern Factory System, Chap. 1, 2. London, Kegan Paul, French, Trübner and Company. 1891.

Devine, Edward T.: Economic Function of Women. Amer. Acad. of Polit. and Soc. Science, Publication No. 133.

Smart, Wm.: Studies in Economics. London, Macmillan Company, 1895.

Pearson, Karl: Chances of Death and other Studies in Evolution, Chap. VII, Woman and Labour; Chap. IX, Woman as Witch. London, E. Arnold, 1897.

2. IN DIFFERENT COUNTRIES

a. *England*

Abbott, Edith: Municipal Employment of Unemployed Women in London. Jour. Pol. Econ., 15: 513.

Women Workers: Papers read at the Manchester Conferences (Oct. 22–25, 1907) by Nat. Union of Women Workers of Gt. Brit. and Ire.

Booth, Charles: Life and Labour of the People of London, Vol. IV, pp. 256–326. Women's Work. London, Macmillan Company, 1902.

Cadbury, Matheson, Shann: Women's Work and Wages. Chicago, The University of Chicago Press, 1907.

Collet, Clara E.: Women's Work in Leeds. Economic Journal, 1 : 460.

b. *Belgium*

Julin, Armand: Le travail des femmes belges dans la grande et la petite industrie. La Réforme Sociale, 16 Septembre, 1901.

Julin, Armand: La production decentralisée en Belgique. La Réforme Sociale, 16 Mai, 1905.

c. *France*

Gonnard, Réné: La femme dans l'industrie. Paris, Armand Colin, 1906.

Julin, Armand: Les industries à domicile. La Réforme Sociale, 16 août, 1902.

Leroy-Beaulieu, Paul: Le travail des femmes au XIX siècle. Paris, Charpentier et Cie., 1873.

Négre, Mlle. A.: Le travail à domicile. Révue du Christianisme Social, 15 Avril, 1907.

Rochebillard, M. L.: Le travail de la femme à Lyon. La Réforme Sociale, 1er juillet, 1901.

Vovard, André: La sociétè pour l'assistance paternelle aux enfants employès dans les industries des fleurs et des plumes. La Réforme Sociale, 1er Avril, 1907.

d. *Germany*

Praktische Ratschlaege zur Berufswahl. Bearbeitet von Josephine Levy-Rathenau und Lisbeth Wilbrandt. W. Nider, Berlin, 1906.

Sombart, Werner: Der Moderne Kapitalismus. Siebenter Abschnitt: Handwerk und Handwerker in der Gegenwart.

e. *United States*

Abbott, Edith: Harriet Martineau and the Employment of Women in 1836. Jour. Pol. Econ., 14:614.

Abbott, Edith: Industrial Employment of Women in the United States. Jour. Pol. Econ., 14:461.

Abbott, Edith; Breckinridge, S. P. Employment of Women in Industries. Twelfth Census Statistics. Jour. Pol. Econ., 14:15.

Adams, Jessie B.: The Working Girl from the Elementary School in New York. Charities and The Commons, Feb. 22, 1908.

Lepelletier, F.: Le travail des femmes aux États Unis. La Réforme Sociale, 1er decembre, 1901.

Mies, Frank P.: Statutory Regulation of Women's Employment; Codification of Statutes. Jour. Pol. Econ., 14: 119.

Odencrantz, Louise C.: The Irregularity of Employment of Women Factory Workers. The Survey, May 1, 1909.

Report of the Committee on Female Labor. New York State Legislature, Albany, 1906.

Wisconsin Labor Bureau. Women employed in Factories. From the 10th biennial report of the Bureau of Labor and Industrial Statistics, pp. 641–759. Madison, 1902.

3. Wages

Webb, Sidney and Beatrice: Industrial Democracy, pp. 749–755. London and New York, Longmans, Green and Company, 1897.

Webb, Sidney: Alleged Differences in the Wages Paid to Men and to Women for Similar Work. Economic Journal, 1:635.

Salomon, Dr. Alice: Ursachen der ungleichen Entlohnung von Maenner und Frauen-arbeit. Leipzig, Duncker v. Humbold, 1906.

Hammond, M. B.: Women's Wages in Manual Work. Pol. Sci. Quar., Sept., 1900.

4. Hours

Bauer, Etienne: Le travail de nuit des femmes dans l'industrie. Publiés au nom de l'Association international pour la protecion ligale des travailleurs, et précédés d'une préface par Etienne Bauer. Jena, Gustave Fischer, 1903.

Van Kleeck, Mary: Working Hours of Women in Factories. Charities, Oct. 6th, 1906.

Webb, Mrs. Sidney: The Case for the Factory Acts. London, Richards, 1902.

Hours of Labor of Women and Girls in Factories. N. Y. Lab. Bul., Mar., 1907.

Supreme Court of the United States, October Term, 1907. Curt Muller, Plaintiff in Error, *vs.* State of Oregon.

5. HEALTH OF WOMEN WORKERS

Jacobi, A.: Physical Cost of Women's Work. Charities, Feb. 2, 1907.

Hamilton, Alice, M.D.: Industrial Diseases with especial reference to the trades in which women are employed. Charities and The Commons, Sept. 5, 1908.

Oliver, Thomas: Dangerous Trades. Chaps. VII, X, XLVII, XLIX, L, LIX. London, J. Murray, 1902.

Kober, George M., M.D.: Industrial and Personal Hygiene. President's Homes Commission, Washington, 1908.

6. LEGISLATION IN THE UNITED STATES

Goldmark, Josephine C.: The necessary sequel of child labor laws. Amer. Jour. of Soc., Nov., 1905.

Goldmark, Josephine C.: Working Women and the Laws; A Record of Neglect. Annals Amer. Acad., Sept., 1906.

Kelley, Florence: The Legal End of the Working Woman's Day. Charities, Dec. 29th, 1906.

Legislation regulating and prohibiting employment of women and children in the U. S. Mass. Lab. Bul., 1905, pp. 24–44.

Decisions of New York Courts. N. Y. Lab. Bul., Sept., 1906, and Dec., 1906.

Simplified Statement of Laws Affecting the Employment of Women and Children in Mass., 1906. (Issued by Industrial Committee, 264 Boylston St., Boston.)

Supreme Court of the United States, October Term, 1907. Curt Muller, Plaintiff in Error, *vs.* State of Oregon.

7. SPECIAL EMPLOYMENTS *

a. *Garment Trades*

Davis, Philip: Women in the Cloak Trade. Amer. Federationist, October, 1905.

---

* Only such books and articles are noted here as refer to the special employments touched on in the text.

Galton, F. W.: Workers on Their Industries. Chap. II. Dressmakers and Tailoresses. London, E. Sonnenschein and Company, Ltd., 1895.

Parton, Mabel: The Work of Women and Children in Cordage and Twine Factories. Federation Bulletin, Boston, May and June, 1905.

Willett, Mabel Hurd: The Employment of Women in the Clothing Trades. Columbia Univ. Studies, 16:234.

b. *Laundries*

Bosanquet, Creighton, Webb: Commercial Laundries. Nineteenth Century, 41:224.

Cavendish, Lucy C. F.: Laundries in Religious Houses. Nineteenth Century, 41:232.

Couper, James L.: Laundry Machinery. Cassiers, 20:507.

Greenwood, Madeleine: Small Laundries. Westminster Review, 147:698.

Tebbutt, Sidney: Steam Laundry Machinery. Cassiers, 15:291.

Over Steaming Washtubs. (Educational Work Toward Self-dependence carried on at the Laundry of the N. Y. C. O. S.) Charities, 10:562.

c. *Mercantile Houses*

Cranston, M. R.: The Girl Behind the Counter. The World To-day, Mar., 1906.

MacLean, Annie Marion: Two Weeks in a Department Store. Amer. Jour. Soc., May, 1899.

Price, Lucinda W.: Training for Saleswomen. Federation Bulletin, February, 1908.

Report of the Committee on Female Labor. New York State Legislature, Albany, 1896.

d. *Miscellaneous*

Barnum, Gertrude: Fall River Mill Girls in Domestic Service. Charities, Mar. 4th, 1905.

Occupations of Girl Graduates. Mass. Lab. Bul., May, 1906.

e. *Printing Trades*

    MacDonald, J. Ramsay: Women in the Printing Trades. London, P. S. King and Son, 1904.

f. *Sweatshops*

    Butler, Elizabeth B.: Sweated Trades in Hudson County. Charities, Dec. 18th, 1907.

    Sanville, Florence L.: Women in the Sweated Trades of Philadelphia. Railroad Trainmen's Journal, May, 1907.

    Report of the Committee on Female Labor. New York State Legislature, Albany, 1896.

g. *Stogies and Cigars*

    Abbott, Edith: Employment of Women in Industries. Cigar-making. Jour. Pol. Econ., 15: 1–25.

h. *Telephone Exchanges*

    Report of the Royal Commission on the Dispute Between the Bell Telephone Co. of Canada and the Telegraph Operators of Toronto. Ottawa, 1907.

INDEX

INDEX

439

DATE DUE
